STORAGE

Harp Music

Bibliography

Harp Music Bibliography

COMPOSITIONS FOR
SOLO HARP
AND HARP ENSEMBLE

Compiled by Mark Palkovic

Indiana

University

Press

BLOOMINGTON AND INDIANAPOLIS

The paper used in this publication meets the minimum require-
ments of American National Standard for Information Sciences—
Permanence of Paper for Printed Library Materials, ANSI Z39.48–1984.

Manufactured in the United States of America

Library of Congress Cataloging-in-Publication Data

Palkovic, Mark.
Harp music bibliography : compositions for solo harp and
harp ensemble / compiled by Mark Palkovic.
p.   cm.
Includes index.
ISBN 0-253-32887-X (alk. paper)
1. Harp music—Bibliography. I. Title.
ML 128.H3P35 1995
016.7879' 0263—DC20   94-44094

1   2   3   4   5   00   99   98   97   96   95
MN

Contents

INTRODUCTION

Bibliographies have been compiled of the music written for most major orchestral instruments. Unfortunately, however, harp music has not received the same degree of bibliographic attention. Most earlier listings of harp music have been modest in scope and, for the most part, use a brief citation style. Some have been issued by publishers or music dealers and do not represent a scholarly attempt at bibliographic method. Although many of them are classified, in general they have no indexes.

One of the earliest attempts at a bibliography for harp is incorporated in Johannes Snoer's *Die Harfe als Orchesterinstrument* (Leipzig: Merseburger, 1898). Of the book's 84 pages, 27 are devoted to "Harfen-Litteratur," listing a total of 1,449 titles. Helena Stone Torgerson's compilation *Harp Music: A Digest Classified Alphabetically and in Grades According to Degrees of Difficulty* (Chicago: Lyon & Healy, 1916) lists 1,115 titles in a classified arrangement. Another classified listing was Hans Joachim Zingel's *Verzeichnis der Harfenmusik* (Hofheim am Taunus: Hofmeister, 1965), with 1,252 titles. But none of these bibliographies gave the criteria for the selection of entries.

Roslyn Rensch's three books about the harp include selective and evaluative bibliographic information. *The Harp: From Tara's Halls to the American Schools* (New York: Philosophical Library, 1950) lists some 250 musical works. *The Harp: Its History, Technique and Repertoire* (New York: Praeger Publishers, 1969) includes a listing of more than 700 musicians who were concerned with the harp as composers, arrangers, or performers. References to the works themselves are to be found in other unnamed sources. In Rensch's most recent book, *Harps and Harpists* (Bloomington: Indiana University Press, 1989), the approach is that of a bibliographical essay, mentioning works premiered or commissioned, contest winners, and so forth.

The American Harp Society Repository was established in 1978 "as a destination for rare recordings and documents (scores, letters, instrument-building plans, photographs, etc.) that would provide an insight into the history of the harp in the United States." Project director Lucile Jennings oversaw this archive from 1980 to 1987 and issued *An Index to the Repository (Phase I) of the American Harp Society* (Athens, Ohio: American Harp Society, 1987). The index provides information regarding the archive's copies of specific music scores, audio and video recordings, letters, scrapbooks, and other ephemera. The materials themselves are housed at the Library of Congress in Washington, D.C., and do not circulate outside the Library.

Harpist Catherine Michel and musicologist François Lesure collaborated on a bibliography of early pedal harp music, *Répertoire de la musique publiée du XVIIe au début du XIXe siècle* (Paris: Aux Amateurs de Livres International, 1990). Its bibliography of 1,823 titles was drawn from the *Catalogue de la musique imprimée avant 1800 conservée dans les bibliothèques de Paris* and the *International Inventory of Musical Sources (RISM)*. As a result, the authors state, "the majority of the items in this list were published between 1770 and ca. 1820 in Paris and London, but most of the solo music is French." In addition, this excellent bibliography includes library sigla, showing libraries in 23 countries where these rare items may be found. However, there is no index.

The present *Harp Music Bibliography* uses a classified arrangement that separates original works from arrangements. It includes published works only, those specifically identified as having been written or arranged for harp. The listing was compiled from entries in the bibliographic utilities OCLC (Online Computer Library Center), RLIN (Research Libraries Information Network), the Pratt and Nebergall harp collections at Brigham Young University, and my personal inspection of the stock of the music dealers Lyon & Healy Harps, Vanderbilt Music Company, and Note-Ably Yours. Items mentioned in the "Recent Publications" section of the *American Harp Journal* are also included. Thus, both library and trade materials are represented.

Specifically excluded are manuscript scores, rental material, student theses and dissertations, publications before 1800, and reprints by the same publisher. I have not systematically included citations from the previously mentioned harp bibliographies; however, since many libraries own this earlier material, there is a certain amount of overlap. I have also collected data for chamber music featuring the harp and harp concerti, which may be presented in a future volume.

The bibliography was closed in January 1994, and publications entered into library catalogs or music dealers' stocks after that date are not included.

How to Use the Bibliography

Within each classification ("Method Books," "Orchestral Studies," etc.), citations are arranged alphabetically by composer, or by arranger or compiler for anthologies or anonymous works. (Terms such as "transcriber" or "adapter" are treated as synonymous with "arranger.") Each citation is assigned a number. When an entry appears in two or more classifications, citations after the first one are abbreviated and a cross-reference directs the reader to the complete citation.

Uniform titles (shown in square brackets) are used when necessary to properly identify the original title and/or instrumentation of a work. They are constructed according to the guidelines set forth in *Anglo-American Cataloguing Rules*, 2nd ed., 1988 revision (Chicago: American Library Association, 1988), with the following exception: uniform titles in Russian, Hungarian, Finnish, and Slovak are given in their more commonly known English-language equivalents. Uniform titles, when present, are used to sub-alphabetize works by the same composer. If a uniform title is not present, the title itself is used as the second level of alphabetizing. The third level is by date, in chronological order.

The symbol [NP] indicates that a work may be performed on non-pedal harp. It is used only for items specifically described by the publisher as playable on "troubadour," "folk," "Celtic," or "Irish" harps.

The index contains the titles of all the works cited. A piece included in an anthology or collection also appears in the index under the name of the composer or arranger, but the index does not duplicate the names of composers, compilers, and arrangers heading the entries in the main sections.

This bibliography is intended for use by music librarians and as an aid to practicing harpists in expanding their repertoires and research into the literature of the harp. As of the date of compilation, each item cited could be obtained from a library or music dealer. (For older scores, a visit to the holding library may be required because of circulation restrictions.) Titles are transcribed directly from the title page of each score, and imprint information is provided so that the score is properly identified.

Wherever possible, birth and death dates of the composers and arrangers are given, so as to provide some idea of the compositional style. The length of each item is indicated by the number of pages cited: front matter in lower-case roman numerals, body of text in arabic figures. Two or more sets of arabic numerals are given when the individual parts of a volume are numbered separately. The city of publication is cited in its English spelling.

ABBREVIATIONS

c	copyright
ca.	circa
n.d.	no date
S.l.	no place [of publication]
s.n.	no publisher
v.	volume(s)

Acknowledgments

Many people have been of great assistance in the preparation of this bibliography. The inspiration to undertake the project came from Lucile H.

Jennings, formerly Associate Professor of Harp at Ohio University and founder of the Repository of the American Harp Society. I owe a debt of gratitude to Jane B. Weidensaul, former editor of the *American Harp Journal,* for her encouragement and advice. Linda I. Wellbaum, retired harpist of the Cincinnati Symphony Orchestra and the University of Cincinnati College-Conservatory of Music was also very helpful to me. My thanks also go to the music dealers who graciously allowed me to dig through their stocks of music and generally get in their way for several days at a stretch. In particular, they are Janet Harrell (President), Natalie Bilik (National Sales Manager), and Bill Mohr (Accessories Department Manager), all of Lyon and Healy Harps in Chicago; Eleanor Fell and Lee Caulfield of Vanderbilt Music Company in Bloomington, Indiana; and Judy and Ed Ireton of Note-Ably Yours in New Carlisle, Ohio. This bibliography could not have been compiled without their cooperation and help.

Harp Music

Bibliography

Method Books

1. Attl, Kajetan A. *A method for the harp.* New York: Carl Fischer, Inc., c1924. xiv, 242 pp. "History and development of the harp," pp. viii–x. Pp. 195–242 consist of various harp cadenzas from the orchestral literature, and songs with harp acc. arranged.

2. ———. *A method for the harp: book 1.* Marina Del Rey, Calif.: Safari Publications, n.d. 86 pp.

3. Backofen, Johann Georg Heinrich, 1768–1839. *I.C. Backofens Harfen-Schule: mit Bermerkungen uber den Bau der Harfe und deren neuere Verbesserungen.* 3. umgearb. und verm. Ausgabe. Leipzig: Breitkopf & Härtel, [18—?]. 53 pp.

4. Balderston, Suzanne. *Step by step: a harp primer.* [California]: Balderston & Sons, c1986. 34 pp. [NP]

5. Bannerman, Marion, d. 1980. *The harp.* Fort Lauderdale, Fla.: Barger & Barclay, c1965. 32 pp.

6. ———. *The harp: an instruction book for beginners of all ages.* New York: Lyra Music Co., c1976. 32 pp.

7. Bochsa, Robert Nicolas Charles, 1789–1856. *Explanations of his new harp effects and passages: illustrated by numerous examples.* London: D'Almaine & Co., [between 1832 and 1899]. 95 pp.

8. ———. *The first six weeks; or, Daily precepts and examples for the harp, on a plan entirely new, and particularly adapted for beginners on that instrument. The whole illustrated by progressive and useful exercises, and attractive and improving lessons.* London: d'Almaine, [1835?]. 27 pp.

9. ———. *New and improved method of instruction for the harp.* Boston: O. Ditson, [18—]. 68 pp.

10. ———. *Nouvelle méthode de harpe en deux parties.* Paris: Mme. Duhan et Cie., [182–?]. 36, 255 pp.

11. ———. *Nouvelle méthode de harpe en deux parties, oeuvre 60. La. 1. contient [sic] tous les principes généraux du doigté et donne l'explication générale de la harpe. La 2. est composée de leçons progressives, préludes, sonates, fugues et divers morceaux dans tous les genres et dans tous les mouvemens, terminée par la maniere d'exécuter sur la harpe, des pas sages propres au piano et d'accompager.* Paris: Dufaut et Dubois, [ca. 1825]. 38, 255 pp.

12. ———. *Nouvelle méthode de harpe en deux parties, oeuvre 60.* Paris: Schonenberger, [183–?]. [iv], 38, 255 pp.

13. ———. [Nouvelle méthode de harpe. Selections] *Bochsa's Nouvelle méthode de harpe.* Translated, edited, with foreword and notes by Patricia John. Houston: Pantile Press, 1993. xvi, 83 pp. English translation of Bochsa's introduction and instructional commentary. Omits the scalewise repetitions of exercises, the teaching pieces in Part II (3 progressive sonatas, 8 preludes, etc.).

14. ———. *Petite méthode de harpe, op. 61.* Paris: Henry Lemoine & Cie., [18—?]. 55 pp.

15. ———. [Standard tutor for the harp] *Bochsa's standard tutor for the harp.* [London]: E. Ashdown, [19—?]. 23 pp.

16. Bochsa, Robert Nicolas Charles, 1789-1856, and Oberthür, Charles, 1819–1895. *Universal method for the harp.* New York: Fischer, c1912. 150 pp.

17. Boussagol, Émile. *Nouvelle méthode de harpe à double mouvement: théorique et pratique.* Ancienne méthode de Bochsa révisée et complètement transformée. Paris: Henry Lemoine & Co., c1904. 107 pp.

18. Calthorpe, Nancy. *Begin the harp with Nancy Calthorpe.* Dublin, Ireland: Waltons, c1987. 44 pp. "An elementary tutor for the folk or non-pedal harp written in easy style for the complete beginner." [NP]

19. Calvo-Manzano, María Rosa, 1943–. *Tratado analitico de la tecnica y estetica del arpa.* Madrid: Editorial Apuerto, 1987. 319 pp.

20. Campen, Ank van, 1932–. *Methode en etudes voor de keltische harp = Tutor for the Celtic harp.* Hilversum, The Netherlands: Harmonia, c1974. 56 pp. [NP]

21. Challoner, Neville Butler, b. 1784. [New preceptor] *A new preceptor for the harp, op. 16.* London: Skillern, [1813?]. 33 pp.

22. Clark, Melville, 1883–1953. *How to play the harp.* New York: G. Schirmer, c1932. 99 pp. "This course is the only which applies to both the concert and baby grand harps."

23. ———. *Instructions for playing the harp.* Syracuse, N.Y.: Clark Harp Mfg. Co., c1914.

24. ———. *Instructions for playing the harp.* With exercises and melodies arranged by Van Veachton Rogers and edited by J. Russell Paine. Third edition. Syracuse, N.Y.: Clark Harp Mfg. Co., c1916. [73?] pp.

25. ———. *Instructions for playing the harp.* With exercises and melodies arranged by Van Veachton Rogers. 4th ed. Syracuse, N.Y.: Clark Harp Mfg. Co., c1919. 78 pp. "These lessons apply equally well to the concert harp."

26. Coeur, Victor. *École du mécanisme: exercices pour la harpe.* Paris: Senart, c1930. 307 pp. Text in French and English.

27. Corbelin, François Vincent. *Méthode de harpe.* Geneva: Minkoff Reprint, [1972]. 84 pp. "Réimpression de l'édition de Paris, 1779."

28. Cousineau, Jacques-Georges, 1760–1836. *Méthode de harpe.* New York: Broude Brothers, [1968]. 48 pp. (Monuments of music and music literature in facsimile. Second series: Music literature, 86) "A facsimile of the [1786(?)] Paris edition." Sometimes attributed to his father, Pierre Joseph Cousineau.

29. ———. *Méthode de harpe.* 2nd ed. Geneva: Minkoff Reprint, [1972]. 64 pp. Sometimes attributed to Pierre Joseph Cousineau. "Réimpression de l'édition de Paris, c. 1790."

30. Cuthbert, Sheila Larchet. *The Irish harp book: a tutor and companion.* Including works by the harper-composers, 17th–19th century Irish composers, [and] contemporary Irish composers. Cork: Mercier Press, c1975. 245 pp. Includes Tutor for the Irish harp by A. Coffey. [NP]

31. Devos, Gérard, 1927–. *Methode de harpe.* Paris: Editions Rideau Rouge, c1967. 37 pp. French and English text.

32. Dobrodinský, Bedřich, 1896–. *Problemy harfove hry.* Prague: Panton, 1975. 5 pp.

33. Garnier, Frédérique, 1958–. *Les cahiers de la harpe = The harpist workbook.* Paris: Editions Musicales Transatlantiques, c1987. 193 pp. Text in French and English.

34. Gatayes, Guillaume Pierre Antoine, 1774–1846. *Nouvelle méthode de harpe: facile à concevoir et avec laquelle on peut se donner soi-même les premiers élémens de cet instrument, et acquérir un certain dégre de perfection, oeuvre 18.* Paris: Janet et Cotelle, [182–?]. 39 pp.

35. Genlis, Stéphanie Félicité, comtesse de, 1746–1830. *Nouvelle méthode pour apprendre à jouer de la harpe.* Geneva: Minkoff Reprint, 1974. 65 pp. "Réimpression de l'édition de Paris, 1811."

36. Grandjany, Marcel, 1891–1975, and Weidensaul, Jane B., 1935–. *First-grade pieces for harp: 18 solos for harp (or harp without pedals).* New York: Carl Fischer, Inc., c1965. 16 pp. [NP] CONTENTS: Drum and bugle; Patrol; Song; A little sad; The anvil; Just walking; Choral; Three o'clock; Treble

clef song; Step by step; Lullaby for Violet; Little waltz; Midnight stars; Passing by; Barn dance memory; Melissa; El número uno.

37. Griffiths, Ann, 1934–. *Saith gwers i ddechreuwyr: telyn = Seven lessons for beginners: harp.* [Wales]: Adlais, c1964. 13 pp.

38. ———. *Telyn dewi: a manual for medieval harp.* Tregaron, Dyfed, Wales: Telyn Dewi, 1980. 36 pp. [NP]

39. Grossi, Maria Vittoria, 1886–. *Metodo per arpa = Méthode pour harpe = Method for the harp = Harfenschule = Método para arpa.* Con l'aggiunta di 65 piccoli studi facili e progressivi di Ettore Pozzoli. Milan: Ricordi, c1946. 154 pp.

40. Hall, Locksley. *Locksley's harp method.* Phoenix: Bradley Graphics, 1976. 24 pp.

41. Hewett, Margaret. *The complete book of the small harp: for teachers, pupils and self-taught musicians.* [London: Margaret Hewett Publications], c1982. 184 pp. Includes numerous traditional songs, with texts, from the British Isles for harp. [NP]

42. ———. *The complete book of the small harp: for teachers, pupils and self-taught musicians.* 2nd ed. Carshalton, Surrey, England: H.E. Styles, 1985. 184 pp. [NP]

43. Heymann, Ann. *Secrets of the Gaelic harp: a method for clairseach based on remnants of the Gaelic oral tradition including the first tunes taught student harpers.* Minneapolis, Minn.: Clairseach Publications, c1988. 128 pp. [NP]

44. Holler, Berta. *Schule für die Volksharfe (Tiroler Harfe).* Munich: Josef Preissler, 1963. 41 pp.

45. Kathryns, Gael A, 1951–. *The wire strung primer: an introduction to playing the wire strung harp.* Edited by Mary-jean Z. Lucchetti. Edmonds, Wash.: Paradise Music, c1989. 34 pp. [NP]

46. Kinnaird, Alison. *The small harp: a step by step tutor.* Shillinghill, Temple, Midlothian, Scotland: Kinmor Music, 1989. 90 pp. Accompanied by audio cassette. [NP]

47. Krumpholz, Jan Křtitel, 1742–1790. *Principes pour la harpe: avec des exercices et des préludes d'une difficulté graduelle.* Recueillis et mis au jour, par J. M. Plane. Geneva: Minkoff Reprint, 1977. 65 pp. "Réimpression de l'edition de Paris, 1800."

48. Labarre, Théodore, 1805–1870. *Méthode complète pour la harpe: suivies de 20 exercices en forme d'etudes, op. 118.* Paris: Alphonse Leduc, [186–?]. 75 pp.

49. Lawrence, Lucile, 1907–. *The abc of harp playing, including The use of the harp in the orchestra: for harpists, orchestrators and arrangers.* New York: G. Schirmer, 1962. ix, 69 pp.

50. Lawrence, Lucile, 1907–, and Salzedo, Carlos, 1885–1961. *Method for the harp: fundamental exercises with illustrations and technical explanations = Méthode pour la harpe: exercises fondamentaux avec illustrations et explications techniques by Lucile Lawrence and Carlos Salzedo. Fifteen preludes for beginners = Quinze préludes pour commençants by Carlos Salzedo.* New York: G. Schirmer, c1929. 71 pp.

51. ———. *Pathfinder studies: for the troubadour or Irish-type harp.* New York: Southern Music Pub. Co., [1962]. 7 pp. "Supplement to Pathfinder to the harp." [NP]

52. Martenot, Raphael, 1875–. *Méthode de harpe.* Paris: G. Billaudot, n.d. 100 pp. (La harpe)

53. Mégevand, Denise, 1947–. *L'enseignement de la harpe irlandaise.* Préface de Lili Laskine; avant propos de Solange Corbin. Paris: Heugel, [1973]. 64 pp. [NP]

54. Mills, Verlye, d. 1983, and Castellucci, Stella. *Rhythm: for harp.* Hollywood, Calif.: Vignette Production Music, c1973. 40 pp. Includes 2 sound discs (33 1/3 rpm, stereo., 7 in.)

55. Mills, Verlye, d. 1983, and Zimmerman, Harry, 1906–. *New harmony for harp: chords, progressions, rhythms and how to use them in popular music.* North Hollywood, Calif.: Forrest Music Co., c1977. 55 pp.

56. Mimura, Tsutomu. *The basics of harp playing: necessary and sufficient hints.* Tokyo: Nippon Harp Ongakuin, 1986. 12 pp.

57. ———. *Harp kyohon = Harp method.* Second edition. Tokyo: Nippon Harp Ongakuin, 1973. 6 v. Japanese text with English title translations. Includes 1 vol. with English text for Books 1–5.

58. Moore, Kathy Bundock, 1952–. *Thumbs up!: beginning harp for the adult and college-level student.* San Mateo, Calif.: F.C. Publishing Co., c1988. vii, 70 pp.

59. Naderman, François Joseph, 1773 (ca.)–1835. *Methode raisonnée pour servir à l'étude de la harpe.* Refondue et modernisée par Denise Mégevand; rev. par Lily Laskine. Paris: Gérard Billaudot, c1973–1975. 2 v. (La harpe)

60. Ortiz, Alfredo Rolando, 1946–. *Latin American harp music and techniques: for pedal and non-pedal harpists.* Corona, Calif.: A.R. Ortiz, c1979. 80 pp. [NP]

61. ———. *Latin American harp music and techniques: for pedal and non-pedal harpists.* 2nd ed., rev. and enlarged. Corona, Calif.: A.R. Ortiz, c1984. vi, 69 pp.

62. Parfenov, N. G. (Nikolai Gavrilovich), 1893–1942. *School for harp.* Moscow: State Publishing House, 1960. 296 pp.

63. Pavelis, Harry. *Instant fun on the harp: a complete how to do it yourself manual:*

method for folk, Irish and student harps. Santa Rosa, Calif.: Harps Unlimited, c1975. 56 pp. [NP]

64. Pool, Ray, 1947–. *Blazing pedals: a guide to harmonic structure and lead sheet playing on the harp, volume 1.* [New York?]: Ray Pool, c1990. 43 pp.

65. Renié, Henriette, 1875–1956. *Méthode complète de harpe.* Paris: A. Leduc, 1946. 2 v. (224 pp.). CONTENTS: Vol.1. Technique; Vol.2. Syntaxe-Appendice.

66. ———. [Méthode complète de harpe. English] *Complete method for harp.* Translated into English by Geraldine Ruegg. Paris: A. Leduc, 1966, c1946. 2 v. Includes English translation (4 pp.). CONTENTS: v. 1. Technique; v. 2. Syntax-appendix.

67. Reyloff, Edmond. *Harp tutor.* London: J.R. Lafleur, [between 1856 and 1985]. 35 pp.

68. Roberts, Ellis. *Manual or method of instruction for playing the Welsh harp.* [London]: Clive Morley Harps, 1988. 54 pp. Originally pub. 1902. [NP]

69. Roberts, Mair. *Hwyl gyda'r delyn.* Talybont, Ceredigion: Y Lolfa, 1990. 128 pp.

70. Rollin, Monique, 1927–. *Méthode de harpe celtique.* Paris: Alphonse Leduc, c1983. 33 pp. [NP]

71. Rubin, Mark Abramovich. *Metodika obucheniia igre na arfe = [Method of instruction on playing the harp].* S.l.: s.n., 1973. 64 pp. Text in Russian.

72. Ruiz de Ribayaz, Lucas, 17th cent. *Luz y norte musical: para caminar por las cifras de la guitarra española, y arpa, tañer, y cantar a compás por canto de organo.* Geneva: Minkoff Reprint, 1976. xx, 151 pp. Reprint of the 1677 ed. published by M. Alvarez, Madrid.

73. ———. *Luz y norte musical.* Transcripción realizada con la colaboración de María-Rosa Calvo-Manzano. [Madrid: Alpuerto, 1982?]. 144, xl, 74 pp. (Opera omnia) Originally published: Madrid: M. Alvarez, 1677. Original work in tablature; transcription: pp. 1–74 (3rd set) in modern notation.

74. ———. *Luz y norte musical.* Transcripción realizada con la colaboración de Maria-Rosa Calvo-Manzano. Edición facsímil. Madrid: Roderigo de Zayas, c1982. [xvi], 144, xl, 74 pp. (Los guitarristas)

75. Saint Pierre de Newbourg, comte. *La nouvelle méthode françoise pour la harpe: composée d'après les principes des maitres les plus acreditées à Paris, Desargus, Cousineau, Les Naderman, &c., comparée au nouveau doigté.* London: Imprimée par Wilkinson, 18—. 56 pp.

76. Salzedo, Carlos, 1885–1961, and Lawrence, Lucile, 1907–. *Pathfinder to the harp = Guide pour la harp: and supplement, Pathfinder studies: for the troubadour or Irish-type harp.* New York: Southern Music Publishing Co., c1954. 33, 8 pp. [NP]

77. Schlomovitz, Phyllis, 1917–. *Beginner's harp book*. Sunnyvale, Calif.: Harpress of California, c1976. 116 pp.

78. ———. *Beginner's harp book*. 3rd ed., rev. 1980. [Palo Alto, Calif.]: Harpress of California, [1980?], c1976. 116 pp.

79. ———. *Beginner's harp book*. [London]: Salvi Publications, c1989. 2 v. Intended to accompany video-taped lessons.

80. ———. *Learning to improvise on the harp*. [Palo Alto, Calif.: Phyllis Schlomovitz], c1978. 3 v. CONTENTS: Book 1. For non- pedal or pedal harp; Book 2. Transposition and more about keys and chords; Book 3. For pedal harp.

81. Shaeffer, Arling. *Elite harp method*. Chicago: Arling Shaeffer, c1920. 64 pp.

82. Shaul, David, and Hughes, Virgil. *On playing the folk harp*. Denver: Hughes Dulcimer, 1974. 32 pp. [NP]

83. Smith, Wilfred, 1911–. *First tutor for the concert harp and clarsach*. S.l.: s.n., n.d. 34 pp.

84. Snoer, Johannes, 1868–1936. *Praktische Harfen-Schule: für Doppel-Pedal-Harfe*. Leipzig: Rob. Forberg, c1896. 51 pp.

85. Tassu-Spencer, Marie. *Méthode de harpe chromatique*. S.l.: s.n., 1899.

86. Thijsse, Wim. *Small pieces for small fingers on the small harp: Irish or troubadour harp*. Amsterdam: Broekmans en Van Poppel, c1970. 18 pp. [NP] CONTENTS: The first steps; Hand in hand; Quarreling?; A long walk; Repeat the note; A gay dance- tune; A drizzly day; In a few moments the count will arrive; Here he is; Little bird talking with big dog; Klopoefening; Climbing up the ladder carefully; French tune; Old march, played by modern band; Nursery song; Invent a title yourself; Strange bird; Quicker and quicker; In a gloomy mood; Eyes and hooks— Did I meet you before?; Zo klonk het Wilhelmus in 1574; Two hunting-horns; Be bright; Choral for 2 voices; Choral for 4 voices; Children's song; Little fugue; Sonatine; Extra.

87. Thomson, Lucien, 1913–, and Lovelace, William, 1960–. *Beginning at the harp: with or without pedals*. New York: O. Pagani & Bro., c1969–1987. 2 v. Vol. 2 co-authored with William Lovelace. [NP] CONTENTS: Vol. 1. Fun!; Great big bell; Ring and sing; The bells; Knocking; Swinging; Raindrops; Little bird; Sing!; Play; Hop and skip; Skip to my Lou; Sing and count; Go to bed; Sailing; Hymn tune; Time to get up!; Count out loud; Chorale theme by J. S. Bach; We dance; Into town; Winter's past; Melody.
   Vol. 2. Melody from Queen Elizabeth's Virginal Book; Buzzing bee; Air by D. Scarlatti; Winter; Chorale melody by J. Schop; Down in the valley; Floating by Lucien Thomson; The Vicar of Bray; Trio by W. A. Mozart; Irish melody; Air by Henry Purcell; Choral melody by César Franck; Red River valley; Little piece by Mendelssohn; Chinese lullaby by Lucien Thomson; The toy bugle by Lucien Thomson; Siciliana; Prelude by

Henry Purcell; Serenade by Josef Haydn; Longing by Feliks Rybicki; The alphabet; Il mio caro padre from the opera *Gianni Schicci* by Puccini; Bianco fiore by Cesare Negri.

88. Tombo, August. *Schule der Technik des Harfenspiels.* [Hrsg.] E. Schuëcker. Leipzig; New York: Breitkopf & Härtel, [190–?]. 3 v.

89. Trillon, André. *Solfège pratique: pour les instruments à clavier et pour la harpe.* Paris: Editions Choudens, c1975. 3 v.

90. Trotter, Louise, 1927–. *The creative folk harpist: arranging and performing.* Houston, Tex.: Louise Trotter, 1992. 50 pp. [NP]

91. ———. *Getting started in pop harp: helpful hints and shortcuts.* Houston, Tex.: Louise Trotter, c1984. 27 pp.

92. ———. *Let's play country harp.* Houston, Tex.: Louise Trotter, c1987. 14 pp.

93. Vera, Higino. *Metodo teorice e pratico para harpa paramusia.* S. Paulo: Permata do Brasil, c1961. 26 pp.

94. Waddington, Mary Kay, 1952–. *Suzuki harp school, volume 1.* Tokyo, Japan: Zen-On Music; Princeton, N.J.: Suzuki Method International, c1985. 1 v. CONTENTS: Twinkle, twinkle little star variations by Shinichi Suzuki; Lavender's blue; Lightly row; The honeybee; Mary had a little lamb; Crickets' song by M. K. Waddington; Lightly row; London Bridge; Go tell Aunt Rhody; Silent night by Franz Gruber; Long, long ago by Bayly; Little playmates by F. X. Chwatal; Chant arabe; Good-bye to winter; The good little king of Yvetot; Andante by M. K. Waddington; Christmas-day secrets by T. Dutton; Allegro by Shinichi Suzuki; Musette; Gigue by M. K. Waddington.

95. Watkins, David, 1938–. *Complete method for the harp.* London; New York: Boosey and Hawkes, 1972. 82 pp.

96. Weidensaul, Jane B., 1935–. *Lessons for the Renaissance harp: a beginner's book.* [S.l.]: Salvi Publications, c1979. 24 pp. Includes transcriptions of selections from *24 pieces for children*, op. 39, by Dimitri Kabalevsky.

97. Weigel, Karl. *Harfenschule.* S.l.: s.n., 1905.

98. Woods, Sylvia, 1951–. *Music theory and arranging techniques for folk harps.* Los Angeles, Calif.: Woods Music and Books Publishing, c1987. 112 pp. [NP]

99. ———. *Teach yourself to play the folk harp: first book in a series.* All pieces arranged by Sylvia Woods. Los Angeles, Calif.: Woods Books, 1979, c1978. 80 pp. [NP]

100. ———. *Teach yourself to play the folk harp: first book in a series.* All pieces arranged by Sylvia Woods. 4th ed. Los Angeles, Calif.: Woods Music and Books Publishing, 1984. 80 pp. [NP]

101. ———. *Teach yourself to play the folk harp.* All pieces arranged by Sylvia Woods. 5th ed. Los Angeles, Calif.: Woods Music and Books Publishing, 1985, c1978. 80 pp. [NP]

102. ———. *Teach yourself to play the folk harp.* All pieces arranged by Sylvia Woods. 6th ed. Los Angeles, Calif.: Woods Music and Books Publishing, 1987, c1978. 80 pp. [NP]

103. Zabel, Albert, 1834–1910. *Methode für Harfe = Méthode pour la harpe = Method for the harp.* Frankfurt/Main: W. Zimmermann, c1900. 3 v. (145 pp.). Text in German, English, and French.

104. Zingel, Hans Joachim, 1904–1978. *Neue Harfenlehre: Geschichte, Spielart, Musik = New harp instruction: History, Method of playing, Music.* Leipzig: F. Hofmeister, [1977]. 4 v. CONTENTS: Vol.1. Anweisung zum Harfenspiel (Schulwerk); Vol.2. Spiel- und Übungsstücke (Etüdensammlung); Vol.3. Einführung in das Orchesterspiel (Orchesterstudien); Vol.4. Die Entwicklung des Harfenspiels von den Anfängen bis zur Gegenwart.

Orchestral Studies

105. *Album of orchestra parts for harps.* New York: Edwin F. Kalmus, [n.d.]. 1 v. (various pagings). (Kalmus, 8651) CONTENTS: If I were king overture by Adam. Midsommarvaka, op. 19 by Alfvén. Invitation to the dance by Weber. Carmen fantasy by Sarasate.

106. *Album of orchestra parts for harps.* New York: Edwin F. Kalmus, n.d. 1 v. (various pagings). (Kalmus, 8654) CONTENTS: Carmen suites nos. 1, 2; Arlésienne suites nos. 1, 2 by Bizet. Dance of the hours by Ponchielli.

107. *Album of orchestra parts for harps.* New York: Edwin F. Kalmus, n.d. 1 v. (various pagings). (Kalmus, 8656) CONTENTS: Naenie by Brahms. Scottish fantasy; Kol nidrei by Bruch.

108. *Album of orchestra parts for harps.* New York: Edwin F. Kalmus, n.d. 1 v. (various pagings). (Kalmus, 8657) CONTENTS: Espana; Marche joyeuse; Suite pastorale by Chabrier. Concertino, op. 107 by Chaminade.

109. *Album of orchestra parts for harps.* New York: Kalmus, n.d. 1 v. (various pagings). (Kalmus, 8659) CONTENTS: Nocturnes; Afternoon of a faun by Debussy. Gymnopédies by Satie, arr. Debussy.

110. *Album of orchestra parts for harps.* New York: Kalmus, n.d. 1 v. (various pagings). (Kalmus, 8661) CONTENTS: Sorcerer's apprentice by Dukas. Scherzo capriccioso; Carnival overture by Dvořák.

111. *Album of orchestra parts for harps.* New York: Kalmus, n.d. 1 v. (various pagings). (Kalmus, 8662) CONTENTS: Roumanian rhapsodies nos. 1, 2 by Enesco. Symphony in B♭, op. 20 by Chausson.

112. *Album of orchestra parts for harps.* New York: Kalmus, n.d. 1 v. (various pagings). (Kalmus, 8663) CONTENTS: Symphony in D minor by Franck. Pelléas et Mélisande; Dolly suite by Fauré.

113. *Album of orchestra parts for harps.* New York: Edwin F. Kalmus, n.d. 1 v. (various pagings). (Kalmus, 8666) CONTENTS: Caucasian sketches by Ippolitov-Ivanov. Colas Breugnon overture by Kabalevsky. Symphony no. 1 by Kalinnikoff.

114. *Album of orchestra parts for harps.* New York: Edwin F. Kalmus, n.d. 1 v. (various pagings). (Kalmus, 8669) CONTENTS: Le cid ballet by Massenet. Prelude and siciliana by Mascagni. Ballet égyptien by Luigini.

115. *Album of orchestra parts for harps.* New York: Kalmus, n.d. 1 v. (various pagings). (Kalmus, 8678) CONTENTS: Symphony no. 1; Swan of Tuonela by Sibelius. Introduction to Khovanchina by Mussorgsky.

116. *Album of orchestra parts for harps.* New York: Kalmus, n.d. 1 v. (various pagings). (Kalmus, 8688) CONTENTS: Entry of the gods into Valhalla; Siegfried's Rhine journey by Wagner. Overture to Forza del destino by Verdi. Moldau by Smetana.

Attl, Kajetan A. *A method for the harp.* See 1.

117. Bartók, Béla, 1881–1945. *Album of orchestra parts for harps.* New York: Edwin F. Kalmus, [n.d.]. 1 v. (various pagings). (Kalmus, 8652) CONTENTS: 1st orchestra suite; Deux portraits, op. 5; 2 pictures, op. 10.

118. Berlioz, Hector, 1803–1869. *Album of orchestra parts for harps.* New York: Kalmus, [197–?]. 1 v. (various pagings). (Kalmus, 8653) CONTENTS: Harold in Italy, op. 16; Fantastic symphony, op. 14; Marche troyenne.

119. ———. *Album of orchestra parts for harps.* New York: Edwin F. Kalmus, [n.d.]. 1 v. (various pagings). (Kalmus, 8689) CONTENTS: Romeo and Juliet, op. 17; Les nuits d'été, op. 7.

120. Borodin, Aleksandr Porfirevich, 1833–1887. *Album of orchestra parts for harps.* New York: Edwin F. Kalmus, n.d. 1 v. (various pagings). (Kalmus, 8655) CONTENTS: Polovetsian dances; Symphony no. 2.

121. Cella, Theodore, 1897–. *Two cadenzas.* New York: International Music Pub. Co., c1923. 7 pp. Cadenzas for the Second Hungarian rhapsodie by Franz Liszt and Lucia di Lammermoor by Gaetano Donizetti.

122. Debussy, Claude, 1862–1918. *Album of orchestra parts for harps.* New York: Kalmus, [197–?]. 1 v. (various pagings). (Kalmus, 8658) CONTENTS: La mer; Danses sacrées et profane.

123. Delibes, Léo, 1836–1891. *Album of orchestra parts for harps.* New York: Kalmus, n.d. 1 v. (various pagings). (Kalmus, 8660) CONTENTS: Coppelia ballet suite no. 1; Sylvia ballet suite, Entr'acte and waltz.

124. Donizetti, Gaetano, 1797–1848. [Lucia di Lammermoor. Harp solo; arr.] *Harfensolo aus der oper "Lucia" von Donizetti.* [Ed. by] Albert Zabel. Moscow: W. Bessel, n.d. 9 pp.

125. ———. [Lucia di Lammermoor. Harp solo; arr.] *Lucia de Lammermoor:*

harp solo with cadenza. Revised and fingered by Carlos Salzedo. New York: Lyra Music Co., c1966. 4 pp.

126. ———. [Lucia di Lammermoor. Harp solo; arr.] *Harp cadenza from Lucia de Lammermoor.* Arr. Josef Molnar. [Calif.]: Harpress of California, 1991. 8 pp.

127. Dvořák, Antonín, 1841–1904. *Album of orchestra parts for harps.* New York: Edwin F. Kalmus, [n.d.]. 1 v. (various pagings). CONTENTS: Carnival overture; Cello concerto; Slavic rhapsodies, op. 45, nos. 1, 3; Legends, op. 59, nos. 1–5.

128. Gordzevich, L., comp. *Orkestrovye trudnosti dlia arfy: otryvki iz oper russkikh klassikov.* Moscow: Gosudarstvennoe Muzykal'noe Izdatel'stvo, 1961. 83 pp. Selections for harp from Russian orchestral works.

129. Grieg, Edvard, 1843–1907. *Album of orchestra parts for harps.* New York: Edwin F. Kalmus, n.d. 1 v. (various pagings). (Kalmus, 8664) CONTENTS: Peer Gynt suite no. 2; Symphonic dances, op. 64; Ein Schwan.

130. ———. *Album of orchestra parts for harps.* New York: Edwin F. Kalmus, n.d. 1 v. (various pagings). (Kalmus, 8665) CONTENTS: Norwegian dances, op. 35; Pieces from Sigurd Jorsalfar; Lyric suite.

131. Liszt, Franz, 1811–1886. *Album of orchestra parts for harps.* New York: Edwin F. Kalmus, n.d. 1 v. (various pagings). (Kalmus, 8667) CONTENTS: Faust symphony; Mephisto waltz; Les préludes.

132. Mahler, Gustav, 1860–1911. *Album of orchestra parts for harps.* New York: Edwin F. Kalmus, n.d. 1 v. (various pagings). (Kalmus, 8668) CONTENTS: Symphonies nos. 1, 4, 5.

133. ———. *Orchesterstudien: Harfe = harp.* Herausgegeben von Dagmar Busse-Lorberth. Frankfurt: Zimmermann, c1987. 76 pp. CONTENTS: Sinfonie Nr. 2 c-moll; Sinfonie Nr. 3 d-moll; Sinfonie Nr. 4 G-dur; Sinfonie Nr. 5 cis-moll; Sinfonie Nr. 6 a-moll; Sinfonie Nr. 7 e-moll; Sinfonie Nr. 8 Es-dur; Sinfonie Nr. 9 D-dur; Das Lied von der Erde; Das klagende Lied.

134. Mussorgsky, Modest Petrovich, 1839–1881. *Album of orchestra parts for harp.* New York: Kalmus, [197–?]. 1 v. (various pagings). (Kalmus, 8670) CONTENTS: Pictures at an exhibition; Night on Bald Mountain; Persian dance from Khovantshchina

135. Prokofiev, Sergey, 1891–1953. *Album of orchestra parts for harp.* New York: Kalmus, n.d. 1 v. (various pagings). (Kalmus, 8671) CONTENTS: Symphony no. 5; Symphony no. 7.

136. ———. *Album of orchestra parts for harp.* New York: Kalmus, n.d. 1 v. (various pagings). (Kalmus, 8672) CONTENTS: Romeo and Juliet suite no. 1; Romeo and Juliet suite no. 2.

137. ———. *Album of orchestra parts for harp.* New York: Kalmus, n.d. 1 v.

(various pagings). (Kalmus, 8673) CONTENTS: Romeo and Juliet suite no. 3; Lt. Kije suite.

138. ———. *Album of orchestra parts for harp.* New York: Kalmus, n.d. 1 v. (various pagings). (Kalmus, 8674) CONTENTS: Suite from The love of three oranges; Cinderella suite no. 3.

139. Puccini, Giacomo, 1858–1924. *Puccini operas: orchestral studies for the harp.* New York: Lyra Music Co., 1980? 54 pp. CONTENTS: La bohème; La fanciulla del West; Madama Butterfly; Manon Lescaut; Tosca.

140. ———. *Tosca: [complete opera: for harp].* New York: International, n.d. 32 pp.

141. Rimsky-Korsakov, Nikolay, 1844–1908. *Album of orchestra parts for harp.* New York: Kalmus, n.d. 1 v. (various pagings). (Kalmus, 8675) CONTENTS: Sheherezade; Overture on Russian themes; Introduction to Coq d'or.

142. ———. *Album of orchestra parts for harp.* New York: Kalmus, n.d. 1 v. (various pagings). (Kalmus, 8676) CONTENTS: Russian Easter overture; Capriccio espagnol; Coq d'or suite.

143. ———. *Orkestrovye trudnosti dlia arfy: otryuki iz prozvedenii N. Rimskogo-Korsakova = [Orchestral exercises for harp: excerpts from compositions of N. Rimsky-Korsakov].* Sostavila E. A. Sinitsyna. Moscow: Gosudarstvennoe Muzykal'noe Izdatel'stvo, 1958. 74 pp.

144. Saint-Saëns, Camille, 1835–1921. *Album of orchestra parts for harp.* New York: Kalmus, n.d. 1 v. (various pagings). (Kalmus, 8677) CONTENTS: Omphale's spinning wheel; Danse macabre; Bacchanale.

145. Salzedo, Carlos, 1885–1961, ed. *Famous harp cadenzas.* Edited and fingered by Carlos Salzedo. Philadelphia: Elkan-Vogel, c1934. 1 part (2 v. in 1). CONTENTS: Lucia di Lammermoor by Gaetano Donizetti. Mignon by Ambroise Thomas. Nutcracker suite by Peter Ilich Tchaikovsky.

146. Schirinzi, Alba Novella, 1941–, ed. *Passi difficili (studi d'orchestra) per arpa: tratti de opere liriche di Boito, Mascagni, Massenet, Puccini, Verdi [and] Wagner.* Milan: Carisch, c1961. 145 pp.

147. Schuëcker, Edmund, 1860–1911, ed. *Orchesterstudien: [für Harfe]: eine Sammlung der beteutendsten Stellen aus Opern, Symphonien und anderen Werken.* Ausgewählt und mit Fingersatz und Pedalbezeichnung versehen von Edmund Schuëcker. Berlin: Breitkopf & Härtel, [19—?]. 5 v. (Harfen-Musik mit und ohne Begleitung. Harfe solo)

148. Sebastiani, Augusto, ed. *Studio d'orchestra per arpa: su opere teatrali.* Milan: G. Ricordi, c1914. 100 pp. CONTENTS: Music of Boito, Catalani, Frachetti, Puccini, and Zandonai.

149. Snoer, Johannes, 1868–1936, ed. *Orchesterstudien [für Harfe]: Solobuch für*

die Harfe: eine Sammlung der wichstigsten Stellen und Soli der orchestralen Literatur dieses Instruments. Herausgegeben und bezeichnet von Johannes Snoer. Leipzig: Carl Merseburger, [190–?]. 3 v. CONTENTS: Der schwarze Domino by D.F.E. Auber. Des Heilands Kindheit; Die Trojaner; Fausts Verdammung; Harold in Italien; Romeo und Juliet; Symphonie fantastique by H. Berlioz. Lucia von Lammermoor by G. Donizetti. Jota aragonesa by M. Glinka. Das Heimchen am Herd by C. Goldmark. Die Jüden by J.F. Halévy. Die Königskinder by E. Humperdinck. Judith; Die Zerstörung Jerusalems by A. Klughardt. Die Afrikanerin; Die Hugenotten; Der Prophet by G. Meyerbeer. Boabdil by M. Moszkowsky. Die lustigen Weiber von Windsor by O. Nicolai. Sheherezade by N. Rimsky-Korsakov. Wilhelm Tell by G. Rossini. Szenen aus Goethes Faust by R. Schumann. Episodes chevalresques by Ch. R. Sinding. Symphonie by Sig. Stojowsky. Cassenoisette; La belle au bois dormant by P. Tschaikowsky.

150. Strauss, Johann, 1825–1899. *Album of orchestra parts for harp.* New York: Kalmus, n.d. 1 v. (various pagings). (Kalmus, 8679) CONTENTS: Acceleration waltz; Perpetual motion; Gypsy baron overture; Roses from the south.

151. ———. *Album of orchestra parts for harp.* New York: Kalmus, n.d. 1 v. (various pagings). (Kalmus, 8680) CONTENTS: Tales from the Vienna Woods; Voices of spring; Emperor waltz; Blue Danube; Wine, women, and song.

152. Strauss, Richard, 1864–1949. *Album of orchestra parts for harp.* New York: Kalmus, n.d. 1 v. (various pagings). (Kalmus, 8681) CONTENTS: Salome's dance; Don Juan; Death and transfiguration.

153. ———. *Album of orchestra parts for harp.* New York: Kalmus, n.d. 1 v. (various pagings). (Kalmus, 8682) CONTENTS: Ein Heldenleben; Don Quixote; Also sprach Zarathustra.

154. ———. *Orchesterstudien: Harfe.* [Ed. by] A. Kastner. Leipzig: Breitkopf & Härtel, [19—]. 2 v.

155. ———. *Orchesterstudien aus Richard Strauss' Bühnenwerken: Harfe.* Ausgewählt und bezeichnet von Franz Poenitz. London: Fürstner, c1912. 26 pp. 2nd harp part (15 pp.) in pocket. CONTENTS: Guntram; Feuersnot; Salome; Electra; Der Rosenkavalier.

156. ———. *Orchesterstudien aus Richard Strauss' Bühnenwerken: für Harfe.* Ausgewählt und bezeichnet von Franz Poenitz. Leipzig: Universal-Edition; Berlin: Adolf Fürstner, c1912. 26, 15 pp. CONTENTS: Guntram; Feuersnot; Salome; Der Rosenkavalier; Elektra.

157. ———. *Orchesterstudien aus Richard Strauss' Bühnenwerken: für Harfe.* New York: Lyra Music Co., 198–? 2 parts. CONTENTS: Guntram; Feuersnot; Salome; Elektra; Der Rosenkavalier.

158. ———. *Orchesterstudien aus den symphonischen Werken: für Harfe.* Ausgewählt und bezeichnet von Alfred Holy. Frankfurt: C.F. Peters, c1910. 2 v. CONTENTS: Vol.1. Aus Italien; Don Juan; Tod und Verklärung; Also sprach Zarathustra. Vol.2. Don Quixote; Ein Heldenleben; Symphonia domestica.

159. ———. *Orchesterstudien für Werken aus Richard Strauss' symphonischen Werken.* Ausgewählt und bezeichnet von Alfred Holý. Wien: Universal Edition, c1910. 2 v.

160. Stravinsky, Igor, 1882–1971. *Album of orchestra parts for harp.* New York: Kalmus, n.d. 1 v. (various pagings). (Kalmus, 8683) CONTENTS: Firebird suite (1919); Fireworks.

161. Tchaikovsky, Peter Ilich, 1840–1893. *Album of orchestra parts for harps.* New York: Kalmus, n.d. 1 v. (various pagings). (Kalmus, 8684) CONTENTS: Swan lake suite; Nutcracker suite; Suite no. 3.

162. ———. *Album of orchestra parts for harps.* New York: Kalmus, [197–?]. 1 v. (various pagings). (Kalmus, 8685) CONTENTS: Capriccio italien; Sleeping Beauty suite; Romeo and Juliet; Francesca da Rimini.

163. ———. *Orchestral studies.* New York, N.Y.: Lyra Music Co., [19—?]. 80 pp. CONTENTS: Swan lake; Sleeping beauty; Nutcracker suite.

164. Tournier, Marcel, 1879–1951, comp. *Traits difficiles: tirés d'oeuvres symphoniques et dramatiques: harpe.* Recueillis par Marcel Tournier. Paris: A. Leduc, 1943. 4 pp. "Répertoire du Conservatoire national de musique de Paris."

165. Wagner, Richard, 1813–1883. *Album of orchestra parts for harp.* New York: Kalmus, n.d. 1 v. (various pagings). (Kalmus, 8686) CONTENTS: Overture to The flying Dutchman; Parsifal prelude; Prelude to The Meistersinger; Prelude and Love death from Tristan und Isolde.

166. ———. *Album of orchestra parts for harp.* New York: Kalmus, n.d. 1 v. (various pagings). (Kalmus, 8687) CONTENTS: Der Venusberg; Wotan's farewell and Magic fire music; Siegfried's death and funeral music.

167. ———. [Operas. Selections] *Die bedeutendsten Stellen für Harfe aus Richard Wagner's Der Ring des Nibelungen, Die Meistersinger von Nürnberg und Parsifal.* Mit genauer Fingersatz- und Pedalbezeichnung hrsg. von Edmund Schuëcker. Mainz: Schott, n.d. 2 v. CONTENTS: Vol.1. Das Rheingold; Die Walküre; Siegfried.
Vol.2. Götterdammerung; Die Meistersinger von Nürnberg; Parsifal.

168. ———. *Orchester-Studien für Harfe: Heft 4–5: Richard Wagner.* [Überarbeitet von] Johanna Gerlach. Leipzig: F. Hofmeister, [1960–61]. 2 v. (Orchesterstudien für alle Instrumente).

169. ———. [Ring des Nibelungen. Walküre. Act 3. Selections; arr.] *Die*

Walküre: extrait du 3e acte. New York: Lyra Music, 1980. 5 pp. Arr. of the two harp parts of Act 3 for 1 harp.

170. Zingel, Hans Joachim, 1904–1978. *Einführung in das Orchesterspiel (Orchesterstudien): mit einer Einführung, zahlreichen Notenbeispielen, kritischen Anmerkungen sowie einer Tabelle (Orchesterstudies I) = Introduction in orchestra playing (Orchestral studies): with an introd., numerous music examples, critical notes, and a table (Orchestral studies I).* Leipzig: F. Hofmeister Musikverlag, [1967]. 153 pp. (Neue Harfenlehre, Vol.3) Text in German.

171. Zingel, Hans Joachim, 1904–1978, and Schmidt, Rudolf, 1894- 1980, eds. *Orchestra studies for the harp from twentieth-century orchestral music, book 1.* Edited by Hans Joachim Zingel with the assistance of Rudolf Schmidt. Cologne: Musikverlage Hans Gerig, [196–?]. 39 pp. CONTENTS: Kossuth; Bluebeard's castle; Dance suite; Music for strings, percussion and celesta; The wonderful mandarin by Béla Bartók. Musik für Saiteninstrumente by Rudi Stephan. Ein Tag tritt hervor, Pentaphonie by Michael Gielen. The young lord; Concerto for violin and orchestra; Night-pieces and airs by Hans Werner Henze. Le tombeau de Couperin; Ma mère l'oye; La valse; Rapsodie espagnole by Maurice Ravel. Variationen und Fuge über ein Thema von Mozart; Variationen und Fuge über ein Thema von Hiller by Max Reger. Variations for orchestra; Five pieces for orchestra by Arnold Schoenberg.

172. ———, eds. *Orchestra studies for the harp from twentieth-century orchestral music, book 2.* Edited by Hans Joachim Zingel with the assistance of Rudolf Schmidt. Cologne: Musikverlage Hans Gerig, n.d. 40 pp. CONTENTS: Symphonic pieces from the opera Lulu; Wozzeck by Alban Berg. Prélude à l'après-midi d'un faune; Nocturnes (III. Sirènes); La mer; Jeux; Iberia by Claude Debussy. Variations on a Caribbean theme by Werner Egk. Mouvements; Concerto for cello and orchestra by Wolfgang Fortner. Das Lied von der Erde by Gustav Mahler. Sigma by Ivo Malec. Symphonie no. 1 (Le printemps); L'homme et son désir by Darius Milhaud. Ouvertüre zu Kleist's Käthchen von Heilbronn; Das Christelflein, Ouvertüre; Palestrina by Hans Erich Pfitzner. Pini di Roma; Fontane di Roma by Ottorino Respighi. Symphonie en sol mineur by Albert Roussel. Firebird ballet suite; Symphony in three movements by Igor Stravinsky. Stabil-instabil by Günther Becker.

173. ———, eds. *Orchestra studies for the harp from twentieth-century orchestral music, book 3.* Edited by Hans Joachim Zingel with the assistance of Rudolf Schmidt. Cologne: Musikverlage Hans Gerig, n.d. 27 pp. CONTENTS: Ariadne auf Naxos; Capriccio; Arabella; Die Frau ohne Schatten by Richard Strauss.

Original Works for Solo Harp

174. Abbott, Alain, 1938–. *Cinq couleurs: pour harpe (sans pédales)*. Paris: Editions musicales Hortensia, c1979. 9 pp. [NP] CONTENTS: Induline; Chrysaniline; Smaragdine; Zinzoline; Alizarine.

175. Adams, G. *Scotch air with variations: as performed by Miss R. Brown on the harp, at the Boston Concerts*. Arranged for the harp or piano forte by G. Adams. Boston: James L. Hewitt & Co., [182–]. 3 pp.

176. Adler, Samuel, 1928–. *Introduction and capriccio: for harp*. New York: Southern Music Pub. Co., 1968. 14 pp.

177. Akimenko, Fedor Stepanovich, 1876–1945. *Consolation: pour harpe, op. 22*. Leipzig: Belaieff, 1903. 7 pp.

178. Alberstoetter, Carl. *Marsch, op. 5*. [Leipzig: J.H. Zimmermann], c1901. 7 pp.

179. ———. *Romanze, op. 4*. [Leipzig: J.H. Zimmermann], c1901. 7 pp.

180. ———. *Tokkata, op. 6*. [Leipzig: J.H. Zimmermann], c1901. 11 pp.

181. Alberti, Domenico. *The bohemian girl: fantasia*. New York: Carl Fischer, c1914. 7 pp.

182. ———. *Martha: fantasia*. New York: Carl Fischer, c1914. 9 pp.

183. Alberti, Freddy. *Études en forme d'exercices: pour petite harpe*. Paris: Éditions Musicales Hortensia, c1977. 13 pp. [NP]

184. ———. [Études progressives et techniques] *Dix études progressives et techniques: pour la petite harpe*. Paris: Éditions Musicales Hortensia, c1973. 21 pp. [NP]

185. ———. [Pièces, harp (1950)] *Six pièces: pour harpe*. Paris: Choudens, c1950. 16 pp. CONTENTS: 1. Echo d'Orient; 2. Menuet; 3. Mélancolie;

4. Chansons napolitaine; 5. Boîte à musique pour ma poupée; 6. Pour la señorita.

186. ———. [Pièces, harp (1982)] *Trois pièces: pour harpe*. Paris: Editions Choudens, c1982. 6 pp. CONTENTS: Prière: pour grande harpe; Souvenir: pour grande ou petite harpe; Virtuosité: pour grande ou petite harpe.

187. ———. [Pièces, harp (1983)] *Deux pièces: pour harpe*. Paris: Choudens, c1983. 16 pp. CONTENTS: Habanera: C'était un bel été; Éclat.

188. ———. *Voyage autour d'une harpe*. Paris: Editions Choudens; New York: C.F. Peters, c1967. 21 pp.

189. Albisetti Rotondi, Giuliana, ed. *Antologia di composizioni per arpa del Rinascimento spagnolo = Anthology of Spanish Renaissance compositions for the harp = Eine Sammlung von Kompositionen für Harfe aus der spanischen Renaissance*. Scelta, trascrizione dalle intavolature e revisione di Giuliana Albisetti Rotondi. Milan: Ricordi, c1977. 12, 27 pp. CONTENTS: Duo II; Duo III; Fabordones del primer tono; Diferencias sobre las vacas by A. de Cabezón. Tiento by A. Mudarra. Mira, nero de Tarpeya: romance by Palero. Cinco diferencias sobre las vacas by Anon.

190. *Album de piese pentru harpa*. Bucharest: Editura Muzicala a Uniunii Compozitorilor din R. P. R., 1964.

191. Alessandrini, Giuseppe. *Tre pezzi per arpa*. Ancona, Italy: Bèrben, c1985. 27 pp. CONTENTS: Piccola suite "Contrast" (1983); Solo (1974); Sequenza '77.

192. Alexander, Josef, 1910–. *Three ludes: for harp*. New York: General Music Publishing Co., c1971. 19 pp. CONTENTS: Pre; Inter; Post.

193. Alwyn, William, 1905–1985. *Crépuscule: for harp*. London: Alfred Lengnick & Co., Ltd., c1956. 6 pp.

194. Amada, Kohei. *Shokasoshinsho: for harp*. [China]: s.n., [1979]. 7 pp.

195. Ameller, André, 1912–. *Mozaïque: pour harpe*. Paris: Éditions M. Combre, c1976. 5 pp. CONTENTS: Turquoise; Lazuline; Opale; Emeraude; Grenat.

196. Amlin, Martin, 1953–. *L'intrigue des accords oubliés: for harp*. New York: Seesaw Music, c1977. 11 pp.

197. Amorosi, Michael, 1947–. *Berceuse and rondo: for harp with or without pedals*. [Santa Monica, Calif.]: Salvi Publications, c1977. 6 pp. [NP]

198. ———. *Galliard*. [Santa Monica, Calif.]: Salvi, 1977. 4 pp.

199. ———. [Jazz vignettes] *Three jazz vignettes*. [Santa Monica, Calif.]: Salvi, 1977. 9 pp.

200. ———. *Minuet*. [Santa Monica, Calif.]: Salvi, 1978. 4 pp.

201. ———. *Pavane.* [Santa Monica, Calif.]: Salvi, 1978. 4 pp.

202. ———. *Scherzo.* [Santa Monica, Calif.]: Salvi, 1977. 6 pp.

203. Andrès, Bernard, 1941–. *Absidioles: pour harpe.* Paris: Editions Rideau Rouge, c1974. 9 pp.

204. ———. *Acalèphes: pour harpe.* Paris: Éditions Musicales Hortensia, c1979. 3 pp.

205. ———. *Acrospores: trois pièces pour harpe.* Paris: Editions musicales Hortensia, c1984. 7 pp.

206. ———. *Alkermès: 3 pièces pour harpe à simple mouvement ou grande harpe.* Paris: Gérard Billaudot, c1989. 8 pp. (La harpe)

207. ———. *Amarantes: trois pièces pour petite ou grande harpe.* Paris: Editions musicales Hortensia, c1984. 7 pp.

208. ———. *Anamorphoses: pour harpe.* Paris: Éditions Musicales Hortensia, c1979. 11 pp.

209. ———. *Aquatintes: six pièces brèves pour harpe ou harpe celtique.* Paris: Editions Musicales Hortensia, c1974. 8 pp. [NP]

210. ———. *Asters: six petites pièces pour petite ou grande harpe.* Paris: Editions Musicales Hortensia, c1984. 4 pp. [NP]

211. ———. *Automates: pour harpe.* Paris: Editions Musicales Hortensia, c1977. 25 pp. CONTENTS: Menuet; Pavane; Bourrée; Sarabande; Gaillarde; Sicilienne; Gigue; Tambourin; Rigaudon; Gavotte; Passepied; Marche.

212. ———. *Charades: 15 exercices-etudes faciles et progessifs pour harpe (sans pédales) ou harpe celtique.* Paris: Editions Musicales Hortensia, c1977. 15 pp. [NP]

213. ———. *Contes vagues: pour harpe.* Paris: Hortensia, c1979. 2 pp.

214. ———. *Danses d'automne: six pièces pour petite (ou grande) harpe.* Paris: Editions Musicales Hortensia, c1990. 16 pp. [NP]

215. ———. *Duke: pour harpe.* Paris: Éditions Musicales Hortensia, c1985. 5 pp.

216. ———. *Elegie: pour la mort d'un berger: pour harpe.* Paris: Editions Musicales Hortensia, c1982. 8 pp.

217. ———. *Gimblette: variations sur un thème de style ancien: pour harpe celtique ou harpe (sans pédales).* Paris: Editions Musicales Hortensia, c1974. 6 pp. [NP]

218. ———. *Marelles: pour harpe (sans pédales) ou harpe celtique.* Paris: Éditions Musicales Hortensia, c1975. 2 v. (6 pp. each). [NP]

219. ———. *Parvis: cortège et danse.* [Harp solo]. Paris: Editions Musicales Hortensia, c1977. 14 pp.

220. ———. *Préludes: pour harpe.* Paris: Éditions Musicales Hortensia, c1974. 3 v. (11, 11, 12 pp.).

221. ———. *Ribambelle: pour harpe (sans pédales) ou harpe celtique.* Paris: Editions Musicales Hortensia, c1974. 10 pp. [NP]

222. ———. *Tanka: pour harpe.* Paris: Éditions Musicales Hortensia, c1985. 5 pp.

223. Andrews, Joel, 1928–. *Variations on Come, ye sons of art: for the harp.* New York: G. Schirmer, c1966. 9 pp. Theme from Henry Purcell's *Come ye sons of art.*

224. Andriessen, Jurriaan, 1925–. *Aubade: voor harp solo.* Amsterdam: Donemus, c1961. 2 pp.

225. ———. *Ballade: voor harpsolo.* Amsterdam: Donemus, c1961. 16 pp.

226. ———. *In memoriam Rosa Spier: voor harp-solo.* [Amsterdam: Donemus], c1967. 8 pp.

227. Angerer, Paul, 1927–. *Stadium veronicae: 6 Stücke: Harfe.* Vienna: Doblinger, c1979. 19 pp. CONTENTS: Harfenstück 71; Hommage à Nadermann; Harfenstück 72; Tristesse; Postalisches Interludium; Harfenstück 73.

228. Anglès, Higini, 1888–1969. *La música en la corte de Carlos V: con la transcripción del Libro de cifra nueva para tecla, harpa y vihuela de Luys Venegas de Henestrosa (Alcalá de Henares, 1557).* [Compilado por] Luys Venegas de Henestrosa. Barcelona: Consejo Superior de Investigaciones Científicas, Instituto Español de Musicoligía, 1944. 2 v. (Monumentos de la música española, 2) The Libro de cifra nueva contains works by various composers for keyboard, harp, and vihuela (unspecified). CONTENTS: Vol.1. Texto; Vol.2. Música.

229. Antoniou, Theodore, 1935–. *Musik: für Harfe, op. 18B.* [Munich]: Edition Modern, c1964. 8 pp.

230. Aparailly, Yves. *Pour s'amuser: harpe celtique.* Paris: Editions Choudens, c1979. 5 pp. [NP] CONTENTS: Dans le lointain; Cabrioles; Le chant du berger; Le petit patre; Boîte a musique!

231. Ardissone, Carlo. *Due poemetti: per arpa.* Naples: Edizione S. Simeoli, c1961. 6 pp.

232. Arnold, Malcolm, 1921–. *Fantasy: for harp, op. 117.* Edited by Osian Ellis. London: Faber Music; New York: G. Schirmer, c1978. 15 pp. CONTENTS: Lament; March; Nocturne; Scherzo; Finale.

233. Arteaga, Edward. *Solitaire: solo harp.* Toronto: Berandol, c1977. 12 leaves.

234. Asieh, Che-Chih, arr. *Amid flowers beside the river under a spring moon.* Trans. Asieh-Che-Chih; edited by Aristid Von Würtzler. Santa Monica, Calif.: Salvi Publications, c1983. 9 pp.

235. Avidom, Menahem, 1908–. *Adag'o: le-nevel = Adagio: for harp*. Tel Aviv: Israel Music Institute, c1966. 5 pp.

236. Avni, Tzvi, 1927–. *Chaconne: for harp = Shakonah: le-neve*. Tel Aviv: Israel Music Institute, c1965. 12 pp.

237. ———. *Vitrage: for harp*. Tel Aviv: Israel Music Institute, c1990. 15 pp.

238. Bach, Carl Philipp Emanuel, 1714–1788. *La battaglia di Bergen: per arpa*. Revisione di M. Vita. Milan: Edizioni Suvini Zerboni, c1970. 9 pp. Sonata for harp or piano.

239. ———. [Fantasien, keyboard instrument; arr.] *Zwei Fantasien: für Harfe*. Herausgegeben von Therese Reichling. S.l.: s.n., [198–?]. 17 pp. "Freien Fantasien, auf dem Klavier und der Harfe zu spielen." CONTENTS: Fantasie Es-dur (H. 277); Fantasie A-dur (H. 278).

240. ———. [Solos, harp, H. 563, G major] *Harfensonate G-dur: für Harfe (Klavier oder Cembalo)*. Erstmalig hrsg. von Hans Neemann. Leipzig: Breitkopf & Härtel, c1941. 13 pp.

241. ———. [Solos, harp, H. 563, G major] *Sonate: pour harpe*. [Edited by Marcel Grandjany]. Paris: Durand et Cie., c1963. 18 pp.

242. ———. [Solos, harp, H. 563, G major] *Sonata: for harp*. Edited by Lucile Lawrence. New York: C. Colin, c1963. 14 pp.

243. ———. [Solos, harp, H. 563, G major] *Sonata: for harp*. 2nd ed. Edited by Lucile Lawrence. New York: Lyra Music Co., c1965. 31 pp.

244. ———. [Solos, harp, H. 563, G major] *Sonate: für Harfe, G-dur [auch auf dem Cembalo und Klavier ausführbar]*. Hrsg. von Hans J. Zingel. Wiesbaden: Breitkopf & Härtel, [1968]. 15 pp.

245. ———. [Solos, harp, H. 563, G major] *Sonata in G major: (Solo für die Harfe)*. A scholarly performance edition with critical commentary by Jane B. Weidensaul. Teaneck, N.J.: Willow Hall Press, c1979. 16 pp., 3 pp.

246. ———. [Solos, harp, H. 563, G major] *Sonata in G major for the harp = Solo für die Harfe: Wq 139/H. 563*. Facsimile ed. of the copy in the Library of the Royal Conservatory, Brussels (13.287). With an introduction by Darrell M. Berg. Utrecht: STIMU, c1992. iv, 10 pp.

247. Bach, Johann Sebastian, 1685–1750. [Sonaten und Partiten, violin, BWV 1001–1006. Partita, no. 3. Preludio; arr.] *Preliudiia iz partity no. 3: obrabotka dlia dueta arf* [by] *I. S. Bakh. Tema s variatsiami: dlia arfy* [by] *F. Dizi*. Moscow: Muzyka, 1966. 2 parts (27 pp.). The first work is an arrangement for two harps; the second work is for harp solo.

248. Badings, Henk, 1907–1987. *Sonate: voor harp: 1944*. [Amsterdam: Donemus, c1965]. 10 pp.

249. Bagatti, Blanda. *Esercizi tecnici: per arpa*. 2nd ed. Florence: A. Forlivesi & C., c1928. 19 pp.

250. Bagirov, Z. (Zakir). *Cahrgah: arfa uchun fantaziia.* Baku: Azerbaijan dovlat musigi nashriiiay, 1955. 10 pp.

251. Baily, Jean, 1937–. *Impromptu: harpe.* Antwerp: Uitgave Metropolis, c1971. 4 pp.

252. ———. *Preludio: per arpa diatonica e cromatica.* Brussels: CeBeDeM, c1978. 8 pp. "Oeuvre imposée au Concours national de musique, Credit communal de Belgique."

253. Baker, Claude, 1948–. [Nachtszenen] *Vier Nachtszenen: for solo harp.* [St. Louis: MMB], 1991. 16 pp.

254. Balliana, Franco, 1954–. *Mosquitos: per arpa.* Milan: Rugginenti, c1984. 11 pp.

255. Ballif, Claude, 1924–. [Solfeggietti, op. 36, no. 9] *Solfeggietto no. 9: pour harpe.* Paris: Editions musicales transatlantiques, c1983. 9 pp. Additional title in caption: Hymnes sur le paradis. "Op. 36, no. 9."

256. Baltin, Aleksandr Aleksandrovich, 1931–. [Preludes, harp] *Preliudii: dlia arfy.* Moscow: Sovetskii kompozitor, 1976. 15 pp.

257. Bancquart, Alain, 1934–. *Ma manière de chat—: pour harpe seule.* Paris: Editions Jobert, c1980. 14 pp. Includes explanation of quarter-tone notation used.

258. Barati, George, 1913–. *Prisma: for harp.* New York: Peer International, c1953. 7 pp.

259. Barber, Gail, 1939–. *Improvisation on a familiar melody.* Lubbock, Tex.: Gail Barber, c1988. 4 pp. The melody is "Twinkle, twinkle, little star."

260. ———. *Windmill sketches: for troubadour or pedal harp.* [Lubbock, Tex.]: Barber, c1971. 17 pp. [NP] CONTENTS: Harp of the western wind; Landscape: Spanish mission; Tag around the windmill; Morning splendor; Indian rain dance; Crossing the prairie: dust devil.

261. ———. *Windmill sketches: for harp with or without pedals.* Lubbock, Tex.: Gail Barber, c1988. 13 pp. [NP] CONTENTS: Harp of the western wind; Landscape: Spanish mission; Tag around the windmill; Morning splendor; Indian rain dance; Crossing the prairie: dust devil.

262. Barbera, Giuseppe. *Lunaire: per arpa.* Milan: Curci, c1975. 5 pp.

263. Barclay, Robert, 1918–1980. *Alleluia: for harp.* Fort Lauderdale, Fla.: Barger & Barclay, c1962. 4 pp.

264. ———. *Arioso: for harp.* Great Neck, N.Y.: Barger & Barclay, c1964. 4 pp.

265. ———. *Pavan: for harp.* Great Neck, N.Y.: Barger & Barclay, c1957. 3 pp. For harp with string orchestra or harp solo.

266. ———. *Trenos: for harp.* Great Neck, N.Y.: Barger & Barclay, c1962. 4 pp.

267. Barkin, Elaine, 1932–. *Harp song: 1980, rev. 1983.* Ship Bottom, N.J.: Association for the Promotion of New Music, [1986], c1982. 7 pp.

268. Barrell, Joyce. *Prelude: harp solo.* [London]: Thames Publishing, c1978. 4 pp.

269. Bartholomée, Pierre, 1937–. *Fancy: pour harpe.* Paris: Jobert, c1980. 8 pp.

270. Bazelaire, Paul, 1886–1958. *Chanson grecque: pour harpe, op. 118.* Paris: Éditions Salabert, c1946. 2 pp.

271. Bédard, Jean Baptiste, ca. 1765–ca. 1815. *Variations sur l'airs des Tiroliens (Wann i in der Früh aufsteh ai ei ei a): pour la harpe.* Paris: Imbault, [ca. 1808]. 6 pp.

272. ———. *Variations sur l'air des Tiroliens: Wann i in der Früh aufsteh ai ei ei a: pour la harpe.* Leipzig: A. Kühnel, [1812?]. 5 pp.

273. Beethoven, Ludwig van, 1770–1827. *Variations on a Swiss air = Variationen über ein Schweizer Lied: for harp.* Edited by Nicanor Zabaleta. London, New York: Schott, c1954. 5 pp.

274. Bellisario, Angelo. *Jalibeau: per arpa.* Milan: Carisch, c1979. 11 pp.

275. Benda, Friedrich Wilhelm Heinrich, 1745–1814. *Sonata: for harp.* Edited by Samuel O. Pratt. New York: Charles Colin, c1965. 18 pp. (Pratt Music Library series of original masterworks for harp)

276. ———. *Sonata.* Revised and fingered by Vera Dulova. London: Salvi Publications, c1983. 18 pp.

277. Ben-Haim, Paul, 1897–1984. *Poème.* New York: Leeds Music Corp., c1959. 6 pp.

278. ———. *Poème: for harp solo.* [Tel Aviv, Israel]: Israeli Music Publications Ltd., c1959. 5 pp.

279. Berio, Luciano, 1925–. *Sequenza II: per arpa sola.* London: Universal Edition, 1965. 6 pp.

280. Berkeley, Lennox, 1903–1989. *Nocturne: for harp.* [Edited by David Watkins]. London: Stainer & Bell; New York: Galaxy Music Corp., c1972. 6 pp.

281. Bernier, René, 1905–. [Interludes, harp] *Trois interludes: pour harpe.* Brussels: A. Cranz, c1947. 15 pp.

282. ———. *Offrande à Érard: variations libres et coda: pour harpe.* Paris: Alphonse Leduc, c1962. 13 pp.

283. Berthomieu, Marc, 1906–. *Triptyque: pour harpe.* Paris: Editions H. Lemoine, c1984. 7 pp. CONTENTS: Valse lente; Atmosphère; Du soleil sur la rosée.

284. Bertouille, Gérard, 1898–1981. *Sérénade-impromptu: pour harpe.* [Brussels: CeBeDeM, c1956]. 3 pp.

285. Beveridge, Thomas, 1938–1981. *Eight preludes: for harp.* Edited by Richard Allen Kade. Falls Church, Va.: T. Beveridge, c1974. 19 pp.

286. Beynon, Jared. *Dialysis: pour harpe.* Paris: Joubert, c1977. 6 pp.

287. Bijvanck, Henk, 1909–. *Hymne, intermezzo en canzonetta: voor harp-solo.* Amsterdam: Donemus, c1951. 8 pp.

288. Bird, Chuck, 1925–. *The contempo harp.* [Composed by Chuck Bird.] Arranged by Chuck Bird and Susan Peters. Hollywood, Calif.: Katbird, c1988. 25 leaves. CONTENTS: Funky blues; Seventh heaven; Funky fool; Alligator shoes; Spunky funky pinky; Zig zag.

289. Bizet, Jean. *La mère lézarde danse aux étoiles; La valse du serpent soleil.* Paris: Editions Musicales Transatlantiques, 1985. 2 pp.

290. Blagrove, Richard Manning, 1827–1895. *The peasants joy: rondo for the harp or piano.* Philadelphia: Willig, n.d. 3 pp.

291. Blankenship, Shirley, 1938–. *Metaphysical waltz.* S.l.: Shirley Blankenship, 1988. 6 pp.

292. Blendinger, Herbert, 1936–. *Suite marseillaise, op. 48: Harfe.* Vienna: Doblinger, c1990. 15 pp.

293. Blyton, Carey, 1932–. *A shoal of fishes, op. 88: for pedal concert harp.* Ancona, Italy: Bèrben Edizioni Musicali, c1987. 45 pp. "A suite of nine miniatures for pedal concert harp after prints by Hiroshige (1797–1858) and anonymous poems of the period published in 1832–1833." CONTENTS: Tobiuwo = Flying fish; Suzuki = Sea-perch; Ebi = Shrimp; Shimahata = Grouper; Ai = Trout; Akodai/Kurodai = Red bream or golden tai/Black seabream or porgy; Bora = Gray mullet; Koi = Carp; Saba (Hirosaba or Marusaba) = Mackerel.

294. Bochsa, Robert Nicolas Charles, 1789–1856. *Les adieux: a military fantasia and variations for the harp on the favorite air of Vous me quittez pour aller à la gloire.* London: Birchall, [182–]. 11 pp.

295. ———. *The admired galopade: arranged for the harp or piano forte.* New York: Dubois & Stodart, [ca. 1830]. 4 pp.

296. ———. [Ah, perdona al primo affetto] *Mozart's favorite air of Ah, perdona al primo affetto: with variations and an introduction for the harp.* London: Printed & sold by Chappell & Co., [between 1819 and 1826]. 13 pp. The theme is from Mozart's *La Clemenza di Tito.*

297. ———. *L'aimable: rondino a la waltz: for the harp.* London: Goulding & D'Almaine, [183–?]. 5 pp.

298. ———. [Airs variés, harp, op. 66] *Trois airs connus: variés pour la harpe, oeuvre 66.* Paris: Bochsa père, [181–]. 25 pp.

299. ———. [Alpine march] *The celebrated Alpine march: arranged for the harp.* London: Goulding & D'Almaine, [183–?]. 7 pp.

300. ———. *Amusement: rondo facile et brillant: pour la harpe.* London: Mori & Lavenu, [1832?]. 5 pp.

301. ———. *Andante et rondeau à la Turcque: pour la harpe.* London: Goulding, D'Almaine, [183–?]. 7 pp.

302. ———. *Aurora che sorgerai: air favori de l'opera de la Dame du lac: musique de Rossini.* Paris: Richault, [1819?]. 15 pp. Variations for harp on the theme "Oh mattutini albori" from Rossini's *La donna del lago.*

303. ———. [Bagatelles, harp. Selections] *First set of bagatelles: for the harp.* London: Printed & sold by Chappell & Co., [between 1819 and 1826]. 13 pp. Contains 4 compositions for the harp.

304. ———. [Belle Bourbonnaise] *La belle Bourbonnaise: folie variée pour la harpe.* Paris: Bochsa père, n.d. 9 pp.

305. ———. *La biondina in gondoletta: barcarolle venitienne variée pour la harpe.* Paris: Carli, [181–?]. 12 pp.

306. ———. [Brilliant and short preludes, harp] *Fifteen brilliant and short preludes: for the harp in the principal major and minor keys, intended to be played before any piece of music.* London: Brewer & Co., n.d. 11 pp.

307. ———. *A brilliant fantasia: for the harp: on the favorite Scotch air, Kelvin Grove.* London: Chappell, [1825?]. 10 pp.

308. ———. *Les brilliants de la Pasta, no. 1: Il braccio mio conquise.* London: J.B. Cramer, Addison & Beale, [ca. 1824]. 7 pp.

309. ———. *Les brilliants de Malibran.* Arr. for the harp by N. C. Bochsa. London: Goulding & D'Almaine, [183–?]. 2 v. CONTENTS: Vol.1. The cavatina "Alma invitata"; Vol.2. The admired aria "Se m'abbandoni."

310. ———. [Caprice sur le recit du Caporal] *Caprice pour la harpe: sur le recit du Caporal (Air d'une nuit de la Garde Nationale).* Bordeaux: Filliatre et Neveu, [181–?]. 13 pp.

311. ———. *Les chants des Alpes: fantaisie à la Suisse for the harp: in which are introduced two favorite Swiss airs.* London: Latour, [183–?]. 7 pp.

312. ———. [Di tanti palpiti] *The favorite air, Di tanti palpiti: with variations for the harp.* London: Printed & sold by Chappell, [between 1819 and 1826]. 13 pp. Variations on a theme from Rossini's *Tancredi.*

313. ———. [Donald] *The favorite air of Donald: with variations & an introduction for the harp.* London: Chappell, [182–?]. 12 pp.

314. ———. *La dramatique à la Sontag: fantasia for the harp: introducing several melodies in Il Don Giovanni, the Terzetto and Preghiera in Otello, and Finale in Il Barbiere di Siviglia.* London: Goulding & D'Almaine, [183–?]. 7 pp.

315. ———. *L'élégante à la Sontag: fantasia for the harp: introducing Una voce poco fa, Rode's air, the favorite duet in Il Barbiere di Siviglia, and the Finale in La donna del lago.* London: Goulding & D'Almaine, [183–?]. 11 pp.

316. ———. [Etudes faciles, harp, op. 318] *Quarante etudes faciles, op. 318.* Revues et doigtées selon l'enseignement de Alphonse Hasselmans par R. Martenot. Paris: Leduc, [1946–1949]. 2 v. (Célèbres etudes pour la harpe)

317. ———. [Etudes faciles, harp, op. 318] *Quarante etudes faciles, op. 318.* Nouv. éd revues et doigtées selon l'enseignement de A. Hasselmans par R. Martenot. New York, N.Y.: Lyra Music Co., [197–?]. 2 v. (Célèbres études pour la harpe)

318. ———. [Etudes faciles, harp, op. 318, no. 13] *Etude no. 13, op. 318: pour la harpe.* Edited by Patricia John. Houston, Texas: Pantile Press, [198–?]. 1 p.

319. ———. [Etudes faciles, harp, op. 318, no. 24] *Etude no. 24, op. 318: pour la harpe.* Edited by Patricia John. Houston, Texas: Pantile Press, [198–?]. 2 pp.

320. ———. [Etudes faciles, harp, op. 318, no. 27] *Etude no. 27, op. 318: pour la harpe.* Edited by Patricia John. Houston, Texas: Pantile Press, [198–?]. 2 pp.

321. ———. [Etudes, harp. Selections] *Dix-huit études pour la harpe.* Révisions: Denise Mégevand. Paris: G. Billaudot, c1981. 49 pp. (La harpe)

322. ———. [Etudes, harp. Selections] *Etudes: [ten pieces].* Adapted for the non-pedal harp by Patricia John. Houston, Tex.: Pantile Press, 1980. 19 pp. [NP]

323. ———. [Etudes, harp. Selections] *Forty progressive studies for the harp.* New York: Fischer, c1900. 2 v.

324. ———. [Etudes, harp. Selections] *Vingt études: pour la harpe.* Paris: Costallat, n.d. 29 pp.

325. ———. [Etudes, harp. Selections] *Vingt etudes en deux suites.* Edition revue par A. Hasselmans. Paris: A. Leduc, c1953. 2 v. (Célèbres etudes pour la harpe)

326. ———. [Etudes, harp, op. 34] *Cinquante etudes, op. 34.* Nouv. éd. revues et doigtées selon l'enseignement de A. Hasselmans par R. Martenot. Paris: A. Leduc, c1948–1950. 2 v. (Célèbres etudes pour la harpe)

327. ———. [Etudes, harp, op. 34, no. 2] *Etude no. 2, op. 34: pour la harpe.* Edited by Patricia John. Houston, Texas: Pantile Press, [198–?]. 2 pp.

328. ———. [Etudes, harp, op. 145, no. 19] *Etude no. 19, op. 145: pour la harpe.* Edited by Patricia John. Houston, Texas: Pantile Press, [198–?]. 6 pp.

329. ———. [Exercices journaliers] *Cent-dix exercices journaliers: pour harpe.* Révision de Catherine Michel. Paris: G. Billaudot, c1977. 36 pp. (La harpe)

330. ———. [Exercises-etudes, op. 62] *Vingt-cinq exercises-etudes, op. 62.* Revues et doigtées selon l'enseignement de A. Hasselmans par R. Martenot. Paris: Leduc, [1946]. 63 pp. (Célèbres etudes pour la harpe)

331. ———. [Fantaisie brillante sur Sul margine d'un rio] *Grande fantaisie brillante, pour la harpe, sur l'air favori (Sul margine d'un rio).* Paris: Carli, [182–?]. 15 pp.

332. ———. [Fantaisie et variations brillantes sur Oh, rest thee babe] *Fantaisie et variations brillantes: pour la harpe: sur un air favori de Whitaker, Oh! rest thee babe!* Paris: Richault, [181–?]. 11 pp. Based on Whitaker's song inserted in *Guy Mannering* by Sir Henry Bishop and others.

333. ———. [Fantaisie et variations sur La ci darem la mano] *Fantaisie et variations sur le thème du joli duo La ci darem la mano: de l'opera de Don Juan: pour harpe.* Bordeaux: Filliatre et Neveu, [ca. 1818]. 11 pp.

334. ———. *Fantaisie et variations sur le trio favori "Ta Fanchette est charmante" de l'opera des Deux jaloux: pour la harpe.* London: Birchall, [182–?]. 11 pp. Theme is from Sophie Gail's opera *Les deux jaloux.*

335. ———. [Fantaisie et variations sur les couplets militaires de Virtuosi ambulanti] *Fantaisie et variations: pour la harpe ou piano: sur les couplets militaires de Virtuosi ambulanti (musique de Fioravanti).* [Paris]: Carli, 1812? or 1813? 10 pp. For harp or piano.

336. ———. [Fantaisie et variations sur les couplets militaires de Virtuosi ambulanti] *Fantaisie & variations on the military couplets in the opera of I virtuosi ambulanti composed by Fioravanti.* London: Birchall, [182–?]. 12 pp. For harp or piano.

337. ———. *Fantaisie et variations sur un air favori irlandais: pour la harpe.* Milan: J. Ricordi, [1823?]. 11 pp. Based on the Irish air "The groves of Blarney," also known, with words by Thomas Moore, as "The last rose of summer."

338. ———. [Fantaisie sur un air favori de H. R. Bishop] *Fantaisie: pour la harpe: sur un air favori de H. R. Bishop, Bid me discourse.* Paris: Richault, [1825?]. 11 pp. Based on H. R. Bishop's "Bid me discourse" from his *Twelfth night.*

339. ———. [Fantaisies, harp, no. 23] *Nouvelle fantaisie et variations pour la harpe sur un chant héroïque: composé par Lélu à l'occasion de la naissance du roi de Rome.* Paris: Lélu, [1816?]. 11 pp. "23eme fantaisie."

340. ———. *A fantasia: for the harp: in which is introduced a favorite Irish melody.* London: Chappell, [182–?]. 11 pp.

341. ———. *Fantasia à la Russe: for the harp: in which the above airs [A Cossack song, The bells of St. Petersburgh, A Russian waltz] are introduced.* London: Gow, [1823?]. 9 pp.

342. ———. [Fantasia with variations on Des petits oiseaux, harp] *Fantasia: for the harp: with variations on the favorite romance Des petits oiseaux.* London: Printed & sold by Chappell, [between 1819 and 1826]. 15 pp.

343. ———. *The favorite air, Di tanti palpiti: with variations for the harp.* London: Printed & sold by Chappell, [1818]. 13 pp. Variations on a theme from Rossini's *Tancredi.*

344. ———. *Les fleurs à la Pisaroni et à la Donzelli: fantasia for the harp: introducing the most favorite themes in La Donna del Lago.* London: Goulding & D'Almaine, [183–?]. 11 pp.

345. ———. *La folle: rondo à la valse sur la chanson française La folle.* London: T. Boosey, Foreign Musical Library, [183–]. 7 pp. (Élégances de l'Opéra Comique de Paris, no. 4)

346. ———. *Fra tante angoscie e palpiti: cavatine favorite, intercallée dans la Cenerentola, opéra de Rossini, op. 204: arr. avec variations pour la harpe.* Paris: V. Dufaut et Dubois, sucrs. de Mrs. Lulu, Bochsa père, et Mme. Duhan, [1824? or 1825?]. 9 pp. Variations on a theme by Michele Carafa.

347. ———. [French marches, no. 1] *The favorite French march: for the harp.* Newly arranged with additions & improvements. London: Chappell, [182–?]. 5 pp.

348. ———. [French marches, no. 2] *Second French march: for the harp.* London: Chappell, [1830?]. 4 pp.

349. ———. *Le garçon volage: contredanse arrangée en rondo pour la harpe avec introduction.* Paris: Pacini, [between 1810 and 1830?]. 9 pp.

350. ———. *God save the King: arranged with variations expressly for the harp.* [London: Skillern, 183–?]. 9 pp.

351. ———. *La gracieuse à la Sontag: the favorite finale and variations sung by Madlle. Sontag in La cenerentola.* Arr. for the harp by N. C. Bochsa. London: Goulding & D'Almaine, [183–?]. 9 pp.

352. ———. [Guaracha dance] *The favorite Guarache dance: with variations and an introduction: for the harp.* London: Printed & sold by Chappell, [1818?]. 9 pp.

353. ———. [Harp music. Selections] *Recueil de sonates et de variations: pour la harpe.* Révision, Catherine Michel. Paris: G. Billaudot, c1977. 35 pp. (La harpe) CONTENTS: 1ère Sonate; 3e Sonate; Thème varié.

354. ———. *Hommage aux mânes de J. L. Dussek: scène pour la harpe, opera 43.* Bordeaux: Filliatre et Neveu, [1812 or 1813]. 18 pp. For harp.

355. ———. *The imps' march: for the harp*. London: Goulding & D'Almaine, [183–?]. 9 pp.

356. ———. *Introduction founded on Handel's original recitative O let eternal honours and air From mighty kings*. London: Brewer, n.d. 5 pp.

357. ———. *Introductory exercises or studies: for the harp*. London: S. Chappell, 185–? 2 v. in 1.

358. ———. [March, harp, B♭ major] *A favorite march and polonoise: for the harp*. London: Printed & sold by Chappell & Co., [between 1819 and 1826]. 11 pp.

359. ———. [March in the Turkish style] *A favorite quick march (in the Turkish style): followed by Le pantalon: a French quadrille arr. as a rondo for the harp*. London: Printed & sold by Chappell & Co., [between 1819 and 1826]. 12 pp.

360. ———. *Martial fantasia: for the harp: with variations on the favorite air, Partant pour la Syrie*. London: Chappell, [1823?]. 13 pp.

361. ———. *Martial fantasia: for the harp: with variations on the favorite air, Partant pour la Syrie*. London: Latour, [1826?]. 13 pp.

362. ———. *Martial introduction and fantasia: for the harp: with the airs Charmante Gabrielle and My pretty page*. London: Printed by Goulding D'Almaine, [between 1823 and 1834]. 11 pp.

363. ———. *Menuet & gavotte favoris du ballet de Nina: avec introduction et variation pour la harpe*. Milan: J. Ricordi, [182–?]. 13 pp. Theme from the ballet by Louis Luc Loiseau Persuis.

364. ———. [Méthode de harpe, op. 60. Leçons progressives] *Cinquante leçons progressives: pour la harpe*. 1er cahier rev. Denise Megevand; 2e cahier rev. Catherine Michel. Paris: G. Billaudot, c1976. 2 v. (La harpe) CONTENTS: Vol.1. 1–25; Vol.2. 26–50.

365. ———. [Méthode de harpe, op. 60. Preludes, no. 7] *Prelude VII from oeuvre 60: pour la harpe*. Edited by Patricia John. Houston, Texas: Pantile Press, [1980?]. 8 pp.

366. ———. [Méthode de harpe, op. 60. Sonatas, no. 1] *Première sonate from oeuvre 60: pour la harpe*. Edited by Patricia John. Houston, Texas: Pantile Press, [1980?]. 4 pp.

367. ———. *Mexican march: for the harp: in which the new effects are introduced*. London: Goulding & D'Almaine, [183–?]. 8 pp.

368. ———. *Les montagnes suisses: the favorite Swiss air of the Simplon*. Arranged with variations for the harp by N. C. Bochsa. London: Mori & Lavenu, [183–?]. 7 pp.

369. ———. *Morceau d'expression dans le style de nocturne: pour la harpe*. Abergavenny, Gwent, Wales: Adlais, n.d. 5 pp.

370. ———. *My lodging is on the cold ground: a favorite melody, with an introduction and variations for the harp.* London: Royal Harmonic Institution, [ca. 1823]. 10 pp.

371. ———. [New French march] *The last new French march: for the harp.* London: Goulding & D'Almaine, 1832. 5 pp.

372. ———. *Pensées du Pirate: melange pour la harpe.* Milan: Ricordi, [1831?]. 11 pp.

373. ———. [Petit mélange sur Il crociato, no. 2] *Second petit melange: for the harp: on favorite airs from Il crociato in Egitto.* Milan: Ricordi, [1827?]. 13 pp. Bochsa's op. 276? Cf. Pazdirek.

374. ———. *Petit mosaique sur La création d'Haydn: contenant les plus célèbres mélodies de cet oratorio.* London: Brewer, n.d. 5 pp.

375. ———. *Petit souvenir sicilien et napolitain: pour la harpe: dans lequele sont introduits des mélodies siciliennes et napolitaines.* Mainz: Schott's & Söhne, n.d. 5 pp.

376. ———. *Petite pastorale: for the harp: introducing two airs from Henry R. Bishop's opera of Aladdin.* London: Goulding and D'Almaine, [183-?]. 7 pp.

377. ———. *Plaire sans effort: pettite esquisse for the harp: selected from Rossini's celebrated opera of Semiramide.* London: Mori & Lavenu, Chappell, [182-?]. 3 v.

378. ———. [Polish cavalry march] *Grand Polish cavalry march: for the harp.* London: Goulding & D'Almaine, [183-?]. 5 pp.

379. ———. [Pot-pourris, harp. Selections] *Tre pot-pourri: per arpa sola: sopra i motivi dell' opera La sonnambula del maestro V. Bellini.* Milan: Ricordi, [1834 or 1835]. 3 v.

380. ———. [Preludes, harp. Selections] *Preludes: for the harp.* London: Chappell, [1818?]. 17 pp.

381. ———. [Preludes, harp. Selections] *Preludes: for the harp.* London: Printed and sold by F.T. Latour, [ca. 1826]. 17 pp.

382. ———. [Preludes, harp. Selections] *Recueil de préludes: pour la harpe.* Révision, Catherine Michel. Paris: G. Billaudot, c1977. 33 pp. (La harpe) CONTENTS: 3ème prélude; 4ème prélude; 5ème prélude; 7ème prélude.

383. ———. *Quadrilliana: contradanse rondo: for the harp.* London: Goulding & D'Almaine, [183-]. 5 pp.

384. ———. *Quatre heures et cinq minutes: rondo des clochettes pour la harpe, op. 335.* Milan: Ricordi, [1840? or 1841?]. 9 pp.

385. ———. *Que ne suis-je la Fougère: air with variations for the harp.* London: Birchall, [183-?]. 7 pp.

386. ———. [Quick march, harp] *Les élégances de l'opéra comique de Paris: pour la harpe: no. 3, Quick march: founded on melodies in Auber's popular operas Fiorella and Le Serment*. London: T. Boosey & Co., [between 1816 and 1854]. 7 pp.

387. ———. *Le récit du caporal: a favorite French waltz: with variations and an introduction for the harp*. London: Printed & sold by Chappell, [1825? or 1826?]. 9 pp.

388. ———. *Rondeau à la Suisse: for the harp, on a favorite Swiss air: with an introduction in which is introduced a melody from the opera Die Schweizer Familie*. London: Latour, [183–?]. 7 pp.

389. ———. *Rondò alla barcarola: sopra un aria favorita nell' opera Il bravo: ridotta per arpa*. Milan: Ricordi, [1837]. 6 pp. Based on the aria "Il fasto e lo splendore" from Marliani's *Il bravo*.

390. ———. [Rondo sopra Giovinetto cavalier] *Rondò: per arpa: sopra l'aria favorita nel Crociato "Giovinetto cavalier" del Maestro Meyerbeer*. Milan: Ricordi, [1827 or 1828]. 9 pp. Based on the aria "Giovinetto cavalier" from Meyerbeer's *Crociato in Egitto*.

391. ———. [Russian air] *A Russian air: with variations for the harp*. London: Birchall, [182–?]. 9 pp.

392. ———. [Russian march] *Grand Russian march: for the harp*. London: Printed & sold by Chappell, [182–?]. 7 pp.

393. ———. *Sacred voluntary: for the harp: on favorite subjects from Handel's works: performed extempore at St. Patrick's Church, Dublin, in the oratorio given on installation of the Knights of St. Patrick by His Majesty George the Fourth*. London: Printed by Goulding & D'Almaine, [183–?]. 11 pp.

394. ———. [Se potesse un suona egual] *Mozart's favorite air, Se potesse un suona egual: with variations for the harp*. London: Chappell, [182–?]. 15 pp. Based on the aria "Könnte jeder brave Mann" from Mozart's *The Magic Flute*.

395. ———. [Sonatas, harp, E♭ major] *Grande sonate: for the harp*. Edited by Alice Lawson Aber. Ross, Calif.: Harp Publications, 1974. iii, 16 pp.

396. ———. [Sonatas, harp, op. 40, G minor] *Grande sonate favorite: pour la harpe, op. 40*. Paris: Carli, [181–?]. 23 pp.

397. ———. *Souvenir d'Irlande: a fantasia on the admired air Robin Adair: for the harp*. London: Chappell, [ca. 1826]. 10 pp.

398. ———. *Les souvenirs: a pathetic fantasia: for the harp*. London: Chappell, [1825?]. 16 pp.

399. ———. *Souvenirs de Rubini et du Pirata, no. 1: capriccio brillante pour la harpe*. Milan: Ricordi, [1830 or 1831]. 11 pp.

400. ———. *Sul margine d'un rio: a favorite air: with an introduction and brilliant variations for the harp.* London: Chappell, [1821?]. 14 pp.

401. ———. [Tanti palpiti] *The favorite air Di tanti palpiti: with variations for the harp.* London: Printed & sold by Chappell, [1818]. 13 pp. Variations for harp on a theme from Rossini's *Tancredi.*

402. ———. *Tartar divertimento: for the harp: in which is introduced the admired air The tartar drum.* London: Goulding & D'Almaine, [183–]. 7 pp.

403. ———. *La tempête: rondeau pour le harpe, op. 80.* Bordeaux: Filliatre et Neveu, [181–?]. 14 pp.

404. ———. *Le triumvirat des valses allemandes: en trois suites, op. 336.* Arr. pour la harpe par N. Ch. Bochsa. Mendrisio: C. Pozzi, [184–?]. 3 v. CONTENTS: 1. Strauss; 2. Marchand; 3. Lanner.

405. ———. *Tyrolese waltz: with variations for the harp.* London: Royal Harmonic Institution, [ca. 1825]. 9 pp.

406. ———. *Variations alla marziale: for the harp: on Auber's celebrated French national air.* London: Goulding & D'Almaine, n.d. 11 pp.

407. ———. [Variations de concert, op. 323] *Grandes variations de concert: pour la harpe, sur une marche de Rossini, op. 323.* Paris: Schonenberger, [183–?]. 21 pp.

408. ———. [Variations, harp. Selections] *Variations sur des thèmes de Mozart: 3 pièces pour harpe.* Revues et doigtées par Joëlle Bernard. Paris: Costallat, c1977. 27 pp. CONTENTS: Mon coeur soupire = Voi che sapete (du Mariage de Figaro); La ci darem la mano (Don Giovanni); Batti, batti o bel Masetto (Don Juan).

409. ———. [Variations, harp, op. 72] *Trois airs variés: pour la harp, oeu. 72.* Bordeaux: A. Filliatre et Neveu, [181–?]. 23 pp. CONTENTS: 1. Thème de la Cosarara; 2. Thème russe; 3. Gentil houzard.

410. ———. *When the wind blows: Bishop's favorite round in the Miller and his men: arr. for the harp, with an introduction.* London: Goulding, d'Almaine, [183–?]. 9 pp.

411. Boer, Jan den. *Farthing: for the Irish harp.* Amsterdam: Donemus, c1972. 1 leaf. [NP]

412. Boizard, Gilles. *Deux esquisses: pour harpe.* Paris: Éditions Rideau Rouge, c1969. 5 pp. CONTENTS: A l'estompe; A la pointe sèche.

413. Bolger, Mercedes, and Yeats, Gráinne, eds. *Sounding harps: music for the Irish harp: book one, for beginners to intermediate.* Dublin, Ireland: Cáirde na Cruite, 1990. 43 pp. [NP] CONTENTS: Dúnadána dorcha donn = Spinning song; Seán Buí = John Bull; Is umbó agus eiriú = Lullaby; Gheobhair, a pháiste = For you, my child; Oro, bhuachaillìn, seol do bhó = Young fellow, drive your cow; Tá'n Samhradh ag teacht = Summer is

coming; The sprightly widow; Níl sé'na lá = It is not day; Mallaí Bhán = Fair Molly; Éiníní = Little birds; Slow air; An cuimhin leat an oíche úd = Do you remember that night?; Giolla na Scríob = The wandering lad; Báidín Fheilimidh = Phelimy's boat; Con O'Leary's lament; A rúin, fan agam = My dear, stay with me; An Beinnsín luachra = The little bundle of roses; Sir Patrick Bellew; Im bím babaró = Work song (for three harps); An ghaoth aneas = The wind from the south; Thugamar féin an Samhradh linn = We brought the summer with us; Bog braon do'n tSeanduine = Warm a drop for the baby; Bean an Fhir Ruaidh = The red-haired man's wife; Pé'n Éirinn í = Whoever she may be; Seothóló thoil = Lullaby; Mo Ghile Mear = My bright prince; Fanny Power; Na Sióga = The fairies; Burn's march; Song of the chanter; William O'Flinn; Súgradh Beanntraí = The humours of Bantry; Ballinderry, for two harps.

414. Bolz, Harriett, ca. 1912–. *Narrative impromptu: for harp: street of dreams.* Washington, D.C.: Arsis Press, c1979. 7 pp.

415. Bon, Willem Frederik, 1940–1983. *Allégorie: pour harpe.* Amsterdam: Donemus, c1972. 12 pp.

416. Booth, Linda, 1937–1992. *In old Vienna.* Charlotte, N.C.: Pan Publications, c1984. 1 p.

417. Bosseur, Jean-Yves, 1947–. *Vingt fois: pour harpe celtique.* Paris: G. Billaudot, c1990. 4 pp. (La harpe) [NP]

418. Bouchaud, Dominig. *Blues: pour harpe ou harpe celtique.* Paris: A. Leduc, c1988. 3 pp. (Collection de pièces instrumentales destinées aux examens et concours des conservatoires et écoles de musique) [NP]

419. ———. *Panorama de la harpe celtique: 50 morceaux = Panorama of the Celtic harp: 50 pieces.* Collected and arranged by Dominig Bouchaud. Paris: Editions Musicales Transatlantiques, c1986. 47 pp. [NP]

420. ———. *Thème et variations: pour harpe ou harpe celtique.* Paris: A. Leduc, c1988. 3 pp. (Collection de pièces instrumentales destinées aux examens et concours des conservatoires et écoles de musique) [NP]

421. Bourguignon, Francis de, 1890–1961. *Ballade des dames de temps jadis: pour harpe chromatique, op. 50.* Brussels: CeBeDeM, c1964. 8 pp.

422. Bourland, Roger, 1952–. [Magical places] *Three magical places: (portrait of Monet): for solo harp.* Newton Centre, Mass.: Margun Music, c1982. 9 pp. CONTENTS: I. Charing Cross bridge; II. Poppy fields; III. Rouen Cathedral at dawn.

423. ———. *Postcard sonatas: for harp.* Newton Centre, Mass.: Margun Music, 1981. 5 pp. CONTENTS: 1. Flight; 2. Chastle; 3. Kescha; 4. Schubert; 5. Ourobouros.

424. Boussagol, Émile. *Romance sans paroles: pour harpe, op. 24.* Paris: Henry Lemoine & Co., n.d. 2 pp. music.

425. Boutry, Roger, 1932–. *Aquarelles: pour harpe*. Paris: Alphonse Leduc, c1967. 9 pp.

426. ———. *Cantilene: pour harpe*. Paris: Éditions Salabert, c1972. 3 pp.

427. Bovio, Auguste Angelo, 1824–1909. [Etudes, harp, op. 22] *Trenta studi per arpa, op. 22*. Milan: Tito di G. Ricordi, [ca. 1868?]. 95 pp.

428. ———. [Etudes, harp, op. 26] *Dodici studi: per arpa, op. 26*. Milan: G. Ricordi, n.d. 39 pp.

429. ———. [Etudes, harp, op. 40] *Ventisei studi: per arpa, op. 40: composti in continuazione ai 12 studi, op. 26*. Milan: G. Ricordi, [189–?]. 107 pp.

430. Bowen, York, 1884–1961. *Arabesque: for harp solo*. London: Goodwin & Tabb, c1932. 8 pp.

431. Bozza, Eugène, 1905–1991. *Evocations: aux bords du fleuve sacré: pour la harpe*. Paris: Leduc, c1954. 7 pp.

432. ———. *Improvisation sur le nom de Marcel Tournier: pour harpe*. Paris: A. Leduc, c1979. 9 pp.

433. ———. *Rondino et menuet*. Paris: Leduc, 1992. 8 pp.

434. Braal, Andries de, 1909–. *Drie-in-één: muziek voor 4 kleine harpen, kleine harp-solo, cello en kleine harp*. Amsterdam: Donemus, c1981. Score 9 pp. 1st movement for 4 harps; 2nd for harp solo; 3rd for harp and violoncello. [NP] CONTENTS: Preludio; Habanera; Nocturne.

435. ———. [Kleine harp als solo-en begeleidings instrument] *De kleine harp als solo-en begeleidings instrument*. Amsterdam: Donemus, c1971. Score 62 pp. Studies for harp solo, harp ensembles, & harp as an accompaniment instrument.

436. ———. *Triptiek I: voor de kleine harp*. Amsterdam: Donemus, c1977. 7 pp. [NP]

437. ———. *Triptiek II: voor de kleine harp*. Amsterdam: Donemus, c1977. 8 pp. [NP]

438. ———. *Triptiek III: voor de kleine harp*. Amsterdam: Donemus, c1977. 13 pp. [NP]

439. Braun, Yehezkiel, 1922–. [Devashot be-hufshah] *Pedals on vacation: for harp = Dvashot be-hufshah: le-nevel*. Tel Aviv: Israel Music Institute, c1966. 7 pp. [NP]

440. ———. *Fantasy: for harp*. Edited by Judith Liber. Tel Aviv: Israel Music Institute, c1990. 18 pp.

441. ———. [Sketches, harp] *Three sketches: for harp*. Tel Aviv: Israeli Music; New York: Leeds Music Corp., c1962. 11 pp.

442. Brenet, Thérèse, 1935–. *Madrepores: pour harpe celtique*. Paris: G. Billaudot, c1990. 2 pp. (La harpe) [NP]

443. ———. *Suite fantasque: pour harpe celtique.* Paris: G. Billaudot, c1983. 14 pp. (La harpe) [NP] CONTENTS: Et quasi tristes; Sous leurs déguise-ments fantasques; Ils n'ont pas l'air de croire à leur bonheur; Et leur chanson se mêle au clair de lune; Et sangloter d'extase les jets d'eau; Les grand jets d'eau sveltes parmi les marbres.

444. Brenta, Gaston, 1902–1969. *Dessin animé: pièce pour harpe.* Brussels: CeBeDeM, c1973. 7 pp.

445. ———. *Prelude et rondo: pour harpe.* Brussels: CeBeDeM, c1973. 8 pp.

446. Brief, Todd, 1953–. *Moments: for harp.* New York, N.Y.: American Composers Alliance, c1979. 5 pp.

447. ———. *Moments: for harp.* Vienna: Universal Edition, c1986. 7 pp.

448. Britain, Radie, 1903–. *Anima divina: for harp.* New York: Seesaw Music, c1973. 12 pp.

449. ———. *Reflection: for harp.* Hollywood: R.B. Brown Music Co., c1966. 4 pp.

450. Britten, Benjamin, 1913–1976. *Suite: for harp, op. 83.* Edited by Osian Ellis. London: Faber Music; New York: G. Schirmer, 1970. 15 pp. CON-TENTS: Overture; Toccata; Nocturne; Fugue; Hymn (St. Denio).

451. Broggi-Giannettani, A. M. *Variazioni e toccata sopra un tema di César Frank [sic]: per arpa.* Milan: Carisch, c1958. 17 pp.

452. Budd, Thomas. *Six divertimenti: for harp.* Edited by Margaret Thomas. Cardiff, Wales: University College Cardiff Press, c1986. 23 pp.

453. Buhr, Glenn. *Tanzmusik: 5 pieces for solo harp.* [S.l.]: Gandharva Editions, c1989. 25 pp. CONTENTS: Prelude; Recitativo; Tanzmusik; Cantilène élégiaque; Nocturne.

454. Bunting, Edward, 1773–1843, ed. *Six compositions including Carolan's Concerto: selected from the Bunting collection.* Suitable for harp or piano. Dublin: Walton's Piano and Musical Instrument Galleries (Publications Dept.) Ltd., n.d.

455. Burgon, Geoffrey, 1941–. *Beginnings: for harp.* Edited by David Watkins. London: Stainer & Bell, c1970. 12 pp. CONTENTS: Dawn; First sun; First rain; First plant; First fish; First bird; First beast; First man; Nocturne.

456. ———. [Nocturnes, harp] *Three nocturnes: for harp.* Pedalling by David Watkins. London; New York: Chester Music, c1978. 7 pp.

457. Burkhard, Willy, 1900–1955. *Vier Intermezzi: für Harpe, [op. 77a].* [Kassel]: Bärenreiter, c1964. 8 pp.

458. Busser, Henri, 1872–1973. *Ballade: en la bémol: pour harp à pédales.* Paris: Alphonse Leduc, n.d. 10 pp.

459. ———. *Impromptu sur des air japonais: pour harpe à pedales.* Paris: Leduc, [19—?]. 11 pp.

460. ———. *Impromptu sur des air japonais: pour harpe chromatique, op. 58.* Paris: Evette & Schaeffer, [1915]. 11 pp.

461. ———. *Pièce de concert: for the harp, op. 32.* Melville, N.Y.: Belwin Mills, [197–?]. 11 pp. (Kalmus harp series, no. 4679)

462. ———. *Pièce de concert: pour harpe, op. 32.* Paris: A. Leduc, n.d. 11 pp.

463. ———. *Prélude et danse: pour harpe.* Paris: Henry Lemoine & Cie., c1960. 12 pp.

464. Bussotti, Sylvano, 1931–. *Fragmentations: pour en jouer de harpes.* Florence: Bruzzichelli, c1963. 7 pp. For one harpist, two harps.

465. Cabezón, Antonio de, 1510–1566. *Glosados: del libro Obras de musica: para tecla, arpa y vihuela: (Madrid, 1578) de Antonio de Cabecon.* Recopiladas y puestas en cifra por Hernando de Cabecon; transcripcion y estudio de Maria A. Ester Sala; prologo de Macario Santiago Kastner. Madrid: Union Musical Española, 1980, c1974. viii, 281 pp.

466. ———. *Obras de musica: para tecla, arpa y vihuela.* Bearbeitet und herausgegeben von M. S. Kastner. New York: Schott, c1951. 48 pp. CONTENTS: Diferencias sobre el canto llano del Caballero; Pavana italiana—Diferencias sobre Las vacas; Duuiensela; Tiento del sexto tono; Motete glosado. Ave Maria de Josquin des Prés; Canción glosada. Ultimi mei suspiri de Philippe Verdelot; Canción glosada. Ardenti mei suspiri de Philippe Verdelot.

467. Cadman, Charles Wakefield, 1881–1946. *Romance in G♭ : harp solo.* Boston: Oliver Ditson, c1928. 9 pp.   .

468. Cage, John, 1912–1992. *In a landscape: for piano or harp solo.* New York: Edition Peters, c1960. 9 pp.

469. ———. *In a landscape: for piano or harp solo: 1948.* New York: Henmar Press, c1960. 7 pp.

470. ———. *Postcard from heaven: for 1–20 harps.* New York, N.Y.: Henmar Press, c1982. 20 parts.

471. Caggiano, Roberto. *Interludio e danza per un tragedia greca: per arpa.* Milan: Edizioni Curci, c1960. 5 pp.

472. Calbi, Otello, 1917–. *Due racconti: per arpa.* Milan: Edizioni Curci, c1967. 14 pp.

473. Caltabiano, Sebastiano. *Aria italiana.* Trascrizione per arpa di Maria Giulia Scimeca. Bologna: Edizioni Bongiovanni, c1958. 4 pp.

474. Calvo-Manzano, María Rosa, ed. *El arpa en el Renacimiento español.* [Compilación] María Rosa Calvo-Manzano. Madrid: Fundación Banco Exterior, 1986. 85 pp., 89–209 pp. (Colección investigaciones) Principally 16th-century Spanish works for harp.

475. ———. *Estampa cuatripartita: para arpa.* Madrid: Unión Musical Española, 1991. 55 pp.

476. ———. *La navidad de los niños: para arpa.* Madrid: Unión Musical Española, c1976. 27 pp.

477. ———. *El pequeno mundo de los ninos: coleccion de obras para arpa.* Madrid: Union Musical Española, c1971. 24 pp.

478. ———. *Retablo de Navidad: el pequeño nacimiento.* Madrid: Union Musical Española, c1980. 30 pp. CONTENTS: El sueño de José; José y María camino de Belén; En el portal de Belén; Jesús en el pesebre; El angel y los pastores; Ya es Navidad; La adoración de los pastores; La estrella de Oriente; El viaje de los Magos de Oriente; En el palacio de Herodes; La presentación en el templo; La adoración de los reyes; Los magos huyen de Herodes; Camino de Oriente; La envidia de Herodes; En angel visita a José; Los santos inocentes; La huida a Egipto; La familia de Nazaret; San José carpintero.

479. Cameron, William Truesdale, d. 1977. *Americana 928: harp solo.* Washington, D.C.: William Truesdale Cameron, n.d. 4 pp.

480. ———. *Ballade (Meditation).* New York: Lyon & Healy, c1938. 4 pp. For voice and piano, voice and harp or harp solo.

481. ———. *Caprice troubadour: harp solo.* Washington, D.C.: W.T. Cameron, [19—]. 2 leaves.

482. ———. *Colgan-Fassett: harp solo.* Washington, D.C.: William Truesdale Cameron, n.d. 4 pp.

483. ———. *Dance rhumba dance: harp solo.* Washington, D.C.: William Truesdale Cameron, n.d. 6 pp.

484. ———. *Dragonfly.* Washington, D.C.: William Truesdale Cameron, n.d. 2 pp.

485. ———. *Drifting snow.* Washington, D.C.: William Truesdale Cameron, c1939. 3 pp. "Practical for Irish harp." [NP]

486. ———. *Etude in G major: warm-up composition: exercise: harp solo.* Washington, D.C.: William Truesdale Cameron, n.d. 2 pp. [NP]

487. ———. *Evensong.* Washington, D.C.: William Truesdale Cameron, n.d. 3 pp. [NP]

488. ———. *Furioso.* Washington, D.C.: William Truesdale Cameron, n.d. 3 pp. [NP]

489. ———. *Humming-bird: harp solo.* Washington, D.C.: William Truesdale Cameron, n.d. 3 pp.

490. ———. *In the favor of God.* Washington, D.C.: William Truesdale Cameron, n.d. 4 pp.

491. ———. *Intermezzo.* Washington, D.C.: William Truesdale Cameron, n.d. 3 pp.

492. ———. *Moods of spring: harp solo.* Washington, D.C.: William Truesdale Cameron, n.d. 3 pp.

493. ———. *Nocturne.* Washington, D.C.: William Truesdale Cameron, n.d. 5 pp.

494. ———. *Petite gallop.* Chicago: Lyon & Healy, n.d. 2 pp.

495. ———. *Premier melodie.* Washington, D.C.: William Truesdale Cameron, n.d. 3 pp.

496. ———. *Reverie.* Washington, D.C.: William Truesdale Cameron, 1975. 3 pp.

497. ———. *Rodeo: harp solo.* Washington, D.C.: William Truesdale Cameron, n.d. 3 pp.

498. ———. *Romance.* Chicago: Lyon & Healy, c1937. 3 pp.

499. ———. *Serenade.* Washington, D.C.: William Truesdale Cameron, n.d. 3 pp. [NP]

500. ———. *Song of the bells: harp solo.* Washington, D.C.: W.T. Cameron, [1968?]. 3 leaves.

501. ———. *Spooks, ghosts and goblins: harp solo for Halloween.* Washington, D.C.: William Truesdale Cameron, n.d. 2 pp.

502. ———. *Springtime-caprice: harp solo.* Washington, D.C.: William Truesdale Cameron, n.d. 4 pp. [NP]

503. ———. *Tarantella: harp solo.* Washington, D.C.: William Truesdale Cameron, n.d. 3 pp.

504. ———. *Water-gate caprice.* Washington, D.C.: William Truesdale Cameron, n.d. 4 pp. [NP]

505. Campana, José Luis, 1949–. *Lust-ich 1: pour harpe seule.* Paris: G. Billaudot, c1986. 20 pp. (La harpe)

506. Campen, Ank van, 1932–, ed. *Muziek uit de 16e eeuw: vor keltische harp = Music of the XVIth century: for Celtic harp.* Edited by Ank van Campen. Hilversum: Harmonia, c1976. 24 pp. [NP]

507. Cantarelli, Giuseppe. [Monodimensione lirica, no. 2] *Monodimensione lirica n. 2: per arpa o pianoforte.* Ancona: Edizioni musicali Bèrben, c1973. 8 pp. For harp or piano.

508. Capanna, Robert, 1952–. *Phorminx: for solo harp.* New York: G. Schirmer, c1975. 8 pp.

509. Capelier, Michel. [Pièces faciles] *Dix pièces faciles: pour la harpe celtique.* Paris: G. Billaudot, c1979. 6 pp. (La harpe) [NP]

510. Caplet, André, 1878–1925. *Divertissements: pour la harpe.* Paris: Durand; Bryn Mawr, Pa.: Theodore Presser, 1925. 2 v. CONTENTS: I. A la française; II. A l'espagnole.

511. Capodaglio, Leonello. *Quattro preludi: per arpa o pianoforte, op. 23.* Padua: Zanibon, 1976. 4 pp.

512. Cardon, Jean Baptiste, 1760–1803. [Sonatas, harp, F minor] *Sonata: in fa minore.* London: Salvi Publications, c1983. 15 pp.

513. ———. [Sonatas, harp, violin, op. 7. no. 1] *Sonata no. 1: from Four sonatas for the harp, opus VII.* Edited by Alice Lawson. San Anselmo, Calif.: A. Lawson, 1970. 15 pp.

514. ———. [Sonatas, harp, violin, op. 7. no. 2] *Sonata no. 2: from Four sonatas for the harp, opus VII.* Edited by Alice Lawson. San Anselmo, Calif.: A. Lawson, 1970. 13 pp.

515. ———. [Sonatas, harp, violin, op. 7. no. 3] *Sonata no. 3: from Four sonatas for the harp, opus VII (1780).* Edited by Alice Lawson Aber. Ross, Calif.: Harp Publications, 1974. 13 pp.

516. ———. [Sonatas, harp, violin, op. 7. no. 4] *Sonata no. 4: from Four sonatas for the harp, opus VII (1780).* Edited by Alice Lawson Aber. Ross, Calif.: Harp Publications, 1974. 15 pp.

517. Cardon, Louis, 1747–1805. *Ah vous dirai je maman: a favorite French air, with variations for the harp.* Philadelphia: G. F. Blake, before 1820? 4 pp.

518. ———. *Ah vous dirai je mamman: French air with variations for the harp or piano forte.* Baltimore: G. Willig Jr., [185–?]. 5 pp.

519. Carles, Marc, 1933–. *Suite medievale: pour harpe celtique.* Paris: Editions Transatlantiques, c1976. 12 pp. [NP] CONTENTS: 1. Pastorale; 2. Sicilienne; 3. Pastourelle et choral; 4. Tambourin.

520. Carlson, Karl E., 1918–. *California delta songs: four exercise pieces for the pedal harp: featuring the glissando, arpeggio, and pedal changes.* Technical advice and editing by Phyllis Schlomovitz. Sunnyvale, Calif.: Harpress of California, c1976. 10 pp. CONTENTS: Delta night; Levee song; Tule whisperings; Magic river.

521. ———. *Songs of the king: suite for harp.* Technical advice and editing by Phyllis Schlomovitz. Sunnyvale, Calif.: Harpress of California, c1976. 5 pp. CONTENTS: Arthur's harp; Flowers for the queen; The knight's chorus; Now the king rests.

522. ———. *Thoughts of Nefertiti: harp solo.* Palo Alto, Calif.: Harpress of California, c1979. 3 pp.

523. Carolan, Turlough, 1670–1738. *Sette pezzi: per arpa.* Revisione di M. Vita. Milan: Edizioni Suvini Zerboni, c1970. 11 pp.

524. Carter, Elliott, 1908–. *Bariolage: harp solo from Trilogy.* United States: Hendon Music; Boosey & Hawkes, c1993. 10 pp.

525. Casadesus, Robert, 1899–1972. *Deux pièces: pour harpe, op. 20.* Doigtés de Marielle Nordmann. [Paris]: Gérard Billaudot, c1977. 15 pp. (La harpe) CONTENTS: Berceuse; Caprice.

526. Casamorata, Luigi Ferdinando, 1807–1881. *Divertimento: per arpa: sopra alcuni temi dell' opera La sonnambula del mo. V. Bellini.* Milan: Ricordi, [1831]. 11 pp.

527. Casella, Alfredo, 1883–1947. *Berceuse triste: pour harpe chromatique (ou piano).* Paris: Editions Salabert, c1911. 4 pp.

528. ———. *Berceuse triste, [op. 14]; and, Sarabande, op. 10: for chromatic harp or piano.* Boca Raton, Fla.: Masters Music Publications, 1990. 17 pp. Originally for chromatic harp.

529. ———. [Sarabande, harp, op. 10] *Sarabande: pour harpe chromatique (ou piano).* Paris; New York: Editions Salabert, c1910. 11 pp.

530. ———. [Sonatas, harp, op. 68] *Sonata: per arpa.* Milan: Edizioni Suvini Zerboni, [1946]. 19 pp.

531. Castelnuovo-Tedesco, Mario, 1895–1968. [Greeting cards. Arabesque, no. 2] *Second arabesque: on the name of Pearl Chertok: Greeting cards, op. 170, no. 45: for harp.* Hastings-on-Hudson, N.Y.: General Music Publishing Co., 1972. 7 pp.

532. ———. *Rhapsody for harp: "The harp of David," op. 209.* Hastings-on-Hudson, N.Y.: General Music Publishing Co., c1973. 15 pp.

533. Castérède, Jacques, 1926–. *Trois préludes: pour harpe.* Paris: A. Leduc, c1977. 17 pp.

534. Cattini, Umberto, 1922–. *Variazioni su un tema medioevale: per arpa.* Milan: Edizioni Curci, c1986. 11 pp.

535. Cecconi, Raffaele. *Impromptu.* [Santa Monica, Calif.]: Salvi, 1981. 4 pp.

536. Celis, Frits, 1929–. *Hymne aan August de Boeck van Merchtem: harp: op. 29.* Brussels: CeBeDeM, c1990. Score 10 pp.

537. Cella, Theodore, 1897–. *Pagano poeta: harp solo.* New York: International Music Co., c1922. 7 pp.

538. ———. [Week end suite. Moment of music] *A moment of music: from the Week end suite: for the Clark Irish harp.* New York: International Music Pub. Co., c1923. 2 pp. [NP]

539. Chailly, Luciano, 1920–. *Improvvisazione n. 4, op. 270: per arpa.* Florence: A. Forlivesi & C., c1963. 6 pp.

540. ———. *Priscogrammi: per arpa.* Rome: Boccaccini & Spada Editori, 1981. 8 pp.

541. Challan, Annie, 1940–. *Arcouest: pour harpe celtique (ou harpe).* Paris: Editions Aug. Zurfluh, c1986. 7 pp. (Collection Annie Challan) [NP]

542. ———. *Ballade: pour harpe.* Paris: Lido Melodies, c1970. 4 pp. (Collection de pièces instrumentales destinées aux examens et concours des conservatoires et ecoles de musique) [NP]

543. ———. *Brocéliande: pour harpe.* Paris: A. Leduc, c1983. 4 pp. (Collection de pièces instrumentales destinées aux examens et concours des conservatoires et ecoles de musique)

544. ———. *Cascades.* Paris: Chappell, c1970. 8 pp.

545. ———. *Danse de l'éventail et du parapluie: pour harpe.* Paris: A. Leduc, c1983. 4 pp. (Collection de pièces instrumentales destinées aux examens et concours des conservatoires et ecoles de musique)

546. ———. *Express: pour harpe celtique ou harpe.* Paris: Alphonse Leduc, c1984. 2 pp. (Collection de pièces instrumentales destinées aux examens et concours des conservatoires et ecoles de musique) [NP]

547. ———. *Glissons; and, Gym-tonic: pour harpe celtique.* Paris: A. Leduc, 1984. 3 pp. [NP]

548. ———. *Grand huit; and, Insomnie: pour harpe celtique.* Paris: A. Leduc, 1984. 2 pp. [NP]

549. ———. [Harp music. Selections] *Glissades; A deux mains; Remonte-pentes; A doigts croisées; Mélodie; Des accords: pour harpe celtique.* Paris: Lido Melodies, c1975. 7 pp. (The soloists' library) [NP]

550. ———. [Harp music. Selections] *Laura; Cascatelle; Promenade a Marly: pour harpe celtique.* [S.l.]: Lido Melodies, c1975. 7 pp. (The soloists' library) [NP]

551. ———. [Harp music. Selections] *Petite valse pour ma poupée: pour harpe; and, Ping-pong: pour harpe.* Paris: A. Leduc, c1983. 3 pp. (Collection de pièces instrumentales destinées aux examens et concours des conservatoires et ecoles de musique)

552. ———. [Harp music. Selections] *Prélude; Arpège; Gammes; Doigté croisé; Triolet; Mouvement perpétuel: pour harpe celtique.* Paris: Lido Melodies, c1975. 7 pp. (The soloists' library) [NP]

553. ———. *Romance pour Cendrillon: pour harpe.* Paris: A. Leduc, c1983. 3 pp. (Collection de pièces instrumentales destinées aux examens et concours des conservatoires et ecoles de musique)

554. Challoner, Neville Butler, b. 1784. [Sonatas, harp, op. 2] *Three sonatas: for the harp, op. 2.* London: Printed by Lavenue & Mitchell, [ca. 1805]. 19 pp. CONTENTS: E♭ major; F major; B♭ major.

555. ———. [Sonatas, harp, op. 2, no. 1] *Sonata no. 1: from Three sonatas for*

the harp, opus II. Edited by Alice Lawson Aber. Ross, Calif.: Harp Publications, c1974. 11 pp.

556. ———. [Sonatas, harp, op. 2, no. 2] *Sonata no. 2: from Three sonatas for the harp, opus II.* Edited by Alice Lawson Aber. Ross, Calif.: Harp Publications, c1974. 11 pp.

557. ———. [Sonatas, harp, op. 2, no. 3] *Sonata no. 3: from Three sonatas for the harp, opus II.* Edited by Alice Lawson Aber. Ross, Calif.: Harp Publications, c1974. 12 pp.

558. Chapuis, Auguste, 1858–1933. *David devant l'arche: pour harpe.* Paris: A. Durand & Fils, c1923. 3 pp.

559. ———. *Harpe éolienne: pour harpe.* Paris: A. Durand & Fils, c1923. 3 pp.

560. ———. *Sérénade: en quatre parties: pour harpe chromatique ou piano.* Paris: Durand, c1926. 4 v. CONTENTS: Entrée-cortège; Pantomime; Nocturne; Danses.

561. Charpentier, Louise. *La boîte à musique: pour harpe.* Paris: Alphonse Leduc, c1941. 4 pp.

562. ———. *Rapsodie: pour harpe.* Paris: Gérard Billaudot, c1987. 11 pp. (La harpe)

563. ———. *Suite française: pour harpe.* Paris: H. Lemoine, c1965. 30 pp. CONTENTS: Introduction et allegro grazioso; Bourrée; Tympanon; Andante; Pigaudon esplègle; Tu vas revenir, et mon coeur est plein de joie; Pièce en ut mineur dans le style ancien; Fuguetta.

564. Chatterton, John Balsir, 1805–1871. *Souvenir de Mozart: mélange for the harp: introducing favorite air in Il Don Giovanni.* London: Schott & Co., n.d. 13 pp.

565. Chauvel, Marjorie, 1922–. *Fantasyland: a suite for harp.* Palo Alto, Calif.: Encore Harp Service, c1984. 7 pp. CONTENTS: Enter the castle gates; Indian village; The world of to-morrow; Amusement park; The alpine slide; Farewell.

566. Chávez, Carlos, 1899–1978. *Invention III: for harp.* Melville, N.Y.: Belwin Mills, c1969. 8 pp.

567. Chaynes, Charles, 1925–. *Lyre: pour harpe celtique ou grande harpe.* Paris: A. Leduc, c1980. 19 pp. [NP]

568. Chertok, Pearl, 1918–1980. *Around the clock.* [Santa Monica, Calif.]: Salvi Publications, [197–?]. 15 pp. CONTENTS: Ten past two; Beige nocturne; Harpicide at midnight; The morning after.

569. ———. *Around the clock.* New York, N.Y.: Interstate Music, [1975?]. 14 pp. CONTENTS: Ten past two; Beige nocturne; Harpicide at midnight; The morning after.

570. ———. *Driftwood.* New York, N.Y.: Interstate Music, [19—]. 3 pp.

571. ———. *Seafoam.* New York, N.Y.: Interstate Music, [19—]. 4 pp.

572. ———. *Seafoam.* Santa Monica, Calif.: Salvi Publications, [197–?]. 4 pp.

573. Cheshire, John, 1839–1910. *Ariel's song: in A♭*. London: J.B. Cramer & Co., n.d. 5 pp.

574. ———. *Believe me if all those endearing young charms.* London: J.B. Cramer, n.d. 5 pp.

575. ———. *Bertie's mazurka: in B♭*. London: J.B. Cramer & Co., [18—?]. 5 pp.

576. ———. *Chanson originale.* London: J.B. Cramer & Co., n.d. 7 pp.

577. ———. *Cradle song.* London: J.B. Cramer & Co., Ltd., n.d. 4 pp.

578. ———. *Easy fantasia: Irish airs.* London: J.B. Cramer, n.d. 5 pp.

579. ———. *Ecstasy.* Boston: Oliver Ditson, c1912. 5 pp.

580. ———. *Ernani fantasia.* Arr. by John Cheshire. London: Cramer, [19—?]. 9 pp.

581. ———. *Fantasia on Scotch airs.* London: J.B. Cramer; New York: Chappell-Harms, n.d. 9 pp. (Cramer's album of harp music)

582. ———. *Fantasia: Rigoletto.* London: J.B. Cramer & Co., n.d. 5 pp.

583. ———. [Remembrance] *Harp solos: Remembrance; and, Twilight murmurs.* Boston: Oliver Ditson Co., c1912. 5, 5 pp.

584. ———. *Spanish dance.* Boston: Oliver Ditson, c1930. 8 pp.

585. ———. *Valse caprice: morceau brillante.* London: Edwin Ashdown, n.d. 13 pp.

586. Chevalier, A. L. (Antoine Louis), 1770–1823. *New quadrilles: with their proper figures in French and English: as performed at the public & private assemblies in New-York: arranged for the piano forte or harp.* New York: Published by Raymond Meetz; Philadelphia: G. E. Blake, [1819–1820]. 2 v. CONTENTS: Book 1. La nouvelle charmercy. La rausan. La moravilla. La derouault. La bonne Amazone. La wagram; Book 2. Ladolani. La surprise. La flocellière. L'auberge de bagniere. La victoire. Les trois bancs.

587. Chou, Wên-chung, 1923–. *Two Chinese folk songs: [for] harp solo.* New York: Edition Peters, c1964. 6 pp. This work is an arrangement of the composer's *Three folk songs for harp and flute;* only the first and last movements of that work are used in this composition.

588. Chrétien, Hedwige, b. 1859. *Intermezzo: pour harpe.* Paris: Evette et Schaeffer, c1922. 3 pp.

589. ———. *Sur le lac: harpe ou piano.* Paris: L. Jacquot & fils, c1932. 5 pp.

590. Ciarlone, Virginia. *Faust de C. Gounod: fantasia per arpa.* Milan: G. Ricordi, n.d. 33 pp.

591. Coelho, Diva Lyra. *Estudo de concerto: para harpa.* Brazil (S.l.): A. Nocera, n.d. 4 pp.

592. Coelho, Manuel Rodrigues, 1555 (ca.)–1635 (ca.). *Flores de musica: para o instrumento de tecla & harpa.* Transcricao e estudo de Macario Santiago Kastner. Lisbon: Fundaçao C. Gulbenkian, 1959–1961. Score (2 v.). (Portugaliae musica. Série A, 1, 3) For organ, harpsichord, virginal, clavichord, or harp.

593. ———. *Flores de música: para o instrumento de tecla & harpa.* Geneva: Editions Minkoff, 1986. 233 pp.

594. ———. [Flores de música. Selections] *Cinco tentos: extraidos das Flores de música: para o instrumento de tecla e harpa (Lisboa 1620).* Para serem executados em orgao, cravo, pianoforte ou harpa; revistos e editados por Santiago Kastner. Mainz: B. Schott's Söhne; New York: Associated Music Publishers, Inc., c1936. 42 pp. For organ, harpsichord, piano or harp. "The Tentos published in this volume correspond with the numbers 5, 7, 18, 19 and 23 of the complete work."

595. ———. [Flores de música. Selections] *Vier Susanas: oder Tentos über das chanson Suzanne un jour: für Tasteninstrumente oder Harfe = sur la chanson Suzanne un jour: pour clavier ou harpe = upon the song Suzanne un jour: for keyboard instruments or harp.* Bearbeitet und herausgegeben von M. S. Kastner. Mainz: Schott; New York: Associated Music Publishers, Inc., c1955. 25 pp. "Four paraphrases or tentos . . . composed upon Orlando di Lasso's *Chanson* . . . have been taken from his book *Flores de música para o instrumento de tecla e harpa.*"—Pref.

596. Cohen, Shimon. *Eight preludes: for harp (1983).* [Tel Aviv]: Israel Music Insitute, 1987. 27 pp.

597. Colaço Osorio-Swaab, Reine, 1889–. *Fantasia: voor harp.* Amsterdam: Donemus, 1949. 7 pp.

598. Colinet, Paul, 1954–. *Balade: for Celtic harp, opus 50.* Brussels: P. Colinet, c1991. 3 pp. [NP]

599. *A Collection of pedal harp music: consisting of marches, airs with variations, rondos, alegro's waltzer's, minuets, songs, &c. &c.* London: Weippert, [ca. 1800]. Score 49 pp. For solo harp, or voice with harp acc. Chiefly pieces by J. E. Weippert; includes pieces by L. Adam, J. F. X. Sterkel, and W. A. Mozart.

600. Concone, L. [Études progressives] *Études pour la harpe, op. 26: trente morceaux dans tous les genres: preludes, caprices et modulations d'une difficulté progressive.* Paris: Editions Costallat, n.d. 2 v.

601. ———. [Études progressives] *Trente études progressives: pour la harpe.* Paris: Gérard Billaudot, [197–?]. 2 v. (La harpe)

602. Constantinides, Dinos, 1929–. *Rhapsody: for solo harp.* New York: Seesaw Music, c1981. 6 pp.

603. Corri, Sophia, 1775–1847. [Rondos, harp] *The new German waltz: adapted as a rondo for the harp or piano forte.* London: Corri, Dussek & Co., [ca. 1799]. 3 pp.

604. ———. [Sonatas, harp, op. 2] *Trois sonates: pour la harpe, oeuvre 2.* Paris: Pleyel, [1797]. 16 pp. More likely composed by Sophia rather than J.L. Dussek. Cf. H.A. Craw, "A biography and thematic cat. of the works of J.L. Dussek" (Thesis, Univ. of Southern Calif., 1964). CONTENTS: 1. B♭ major; 2. G major; 3. C minor.

605. ———. [Sonatas, harp, op. 2, no. 1, B♭ major] *Grand sonata in B flat: for harp.* Annotated, fingered and edited for twentieth-century harp by Marcia X. Johnstone. South Pasadena, Calif.: M.X. Johnstone, c1955. 20 pp. (Harp-re-cords) More likely composed by Sophia rather than J.L. Dussek (Cf. H.A. Craw, "A biography and thematic cat. of the works of J.L. Dussek" [Thesis, Univ. of Southern Calif., 1964]).

606. ———. [Sonatas, harp, op. 2, no. 1, B♭ major] *Sonata I en si bémol majeur; and, Sonata II en sol majeur.* Restitutions de Catherine Michel. Paris: Heugel et Cie.; Editions Ouvrières, 1973. 16 pp. (L'Astrée: anthologie de la musique pour harpe, cahier 1) More likely composed by Sophia rather than J.L. Dussek (Cf. H.A. Craw, "A biography and thematic cat. of the works of J.L. Dussek" [Thesis, Univ. of Southern Calif., 1964]).

607. ———. [Sonatas, harp, op. 2, no. 1, B♭ major] *Sonata in B flat.* Ed. Jane B. Weidensaul. New York: Lyra Music Co., 1978. 9 pp. More likely composed by Sophia rather than J.L. Dussek (Cf. H.A. Craw, "A biography and thematic cat. of the works of J.L. Dussek" [Thesis, Univ. of Southern Calif., 1964]).

608. ———. [Sonatas, harp, op. 2, no. 3, C minor] *Sonata: for harp.* Edited by Nicanor Zabaleta. Mainz: B. Schott's Söhne; New York: Associated Music Publishers, Inc., c1954. 11 pp. The sonata is taken from Trois sonates pour harpe (Bibl. Nat. Paris. Vm9. 4103). More likely composed by Sophia rather than J. L. Dussek (H.A. Craw, "A biography and thematic catalog of the works of J. L. Dussek (1760–1812)" [Thesis, University of Southern California, 1964]). Craw D14 (op. 2, no. 3).

609. Corsin, 18th cent. *Sonata & an air with variations: for the harp.* Composed by Mr. Corsin. Philadelphia: Published by G. E. Blake, No. 13 South 5th Street, [between 1815 and 1817]. 11 pp.

610. Costello, Marilyn, ed. *Two original pieces: for harp.* Edited by Marilyn Costello. New York: Oxford University Press, c1984. 7 pp. Both works

composed for the Paris Conservatory sightreading examinations. CON-
TENTS: Solo for harp by César Franck. Solo for harp: "Morceau à
déchiffrer pour la harpe" by Léo Delibes.

611. Cousineau, Jacques-Georges, 1760–1836. [Sonatas, harp. Selections]
*Sonata I en mi bémol majeur; Rondo: en fa majeur; Sonate II [i.e. IV]: en si bémol
majeur: mouvement I.* Restitutions de Catherine Michel. Paris: Éditions
Ouvrières, c1973. 15 pp. (L'Astrée: anthologie de la musique pour
harpe, 2e cahier) The rondo is *Sonata no. 2.*

612. Cramer, Johann Baptist, 1771–1858. [Marche turque, harp] *Grand
Turkish march: for the harp or piano forte.* Baltimore: J. Cole, 18—. 2 pp.

613. ———. [Marche turque, harp, Eb major] *Marche turque: pour le harp ou
piano forte.* Philadelphia: G.E. Blake, [1808?]. 2 leaves.

614. ———. *Le petit rien.* Revision et doigtés pour la harpe de Denise
Mégevand. [Paris]: G. Billaudot, c1976. 5 pp. (La harpe)

615. Cras, Jean, 1879–1932. [Impromptus, harp] *Deux impromptus: pour
harpe (ou piano).* Paris, New York: Editions Salabert, c1926. 11 pp.

616. Craven, J. T., (John Thomas), b. 1796. [French march, harp] *The
celebrated French march: arr. for the harp.* London: Preston, [18—]. 3 pp.

617. Creston, Paul, 1906–1985. *Lydian song: for harp.* New York: Ricordi,
c1961. 11 pp. "Op. 55."

618. ———. *Olympia: rhapsody for harp solo, op. 94.* New York: G. Schirmer,
c1968. 15 pp.

619. Cunningham, Michael Gerald, 1937–. [Nocturnes, harp, op. 119]
Nocturnes: for harp, op. 119. New York: Seesaw Music, c1986. 8 pp. CON-
TENTS: Lengthening shadows; Rendezvous; Night clouds; Midnight
requiem; Dawn dusk.

620. ———. [Preludes, harp, op. 68] *Preludes: for harp, op. 68.* New York:
Seesaw Music, c1981. 9 pp.

621. Curtis-Smith, Curtis O. B., 1941–. [Pieces, harp] *Three pieces: for harp.*
S.l.: s.n., 1976. 16 pp.

622. Dalvimare, Martin Pierre, 1772–1839. *Fantaisie sur Mon coeur soupire:
avec huit variations: pour la harpe ou la piano.* Paris: Erard, n.d. 11 pp.

623. ———. [Sonatas, harp. op. 2] *Trois sonates: pour la harpe, oeuvre 2.* Paris:
Sieber, n.d. 24 pp.

624. ———. [Sonatas, harp, op. 18] *Trois grandes sonates: pour la harpe, oeuvre
18.* Paris: Chez Mlles Erard, [between 1800 and 1805]. 55 pp.

625. Damase, Jean Michel, 1928–. *Accordeon: pour harpe ou harpe celtique.*
Paris: Editions Musicales Transatlantiques, c1975. 2 pp. [NP]

626. ———. *Aubade: pour harpe.* Paris: Editions H. Lemoine, c1976. 13 pp.

627. ———. *Les chameaux: pour piano ou harpe*. Paris: Rideau Rouge, c1972. 2 pp.

628. ———. *Etude de concert: pour harpe*. Paris: H. Lemoine, c1951. 11 pp. Op. 14.

629. ———. [Etudes, harp] *Trente etudes: pour harpe*. Paris: Editions H. Lemoine, c1978. 2 v.

630. ———. [Etudes, harp] *12 études pour harpe*. Paris: Editions Henry Lemoine, 1991. 3 pp.

631. ———. *Harpe junior*. Paris: Lemoine, 1985. 2 pp.

632. ———. *L'insecte: pour piano ou harpe*. Paris: Rideau Rouge, c1972. 2 pp.

633. ———. *Introduction et toccata: pour harpe*. Paris: H. Lemoine, c1969. 6 pp.

634. ———. *Menuet boiteux: pour harpe celtique ou harpe*. Paris: Editions Musicales Transatlantiques, c1975. 3 pp. [NP]

635. ———. [Pièces, harp] *Deux pièces pour harpe celtique ou grande harpe*. Paris: Editions M. Combre, c1992. 5 pp. [NP] CONTENTS: Pour Gabrielle; Pour Pauline.

636. ———. *Pieces pour 1, 2 et 3 harpes celtiques (ou grande harpe)*. Courlay, France: Editions J.M. Fuzeau, 1988. Score (17 pp.). [NP]

637. ———. *Pluie: pièce facile pour harpe*. Paris: Editions Henry Lemoine, c1976. 3 pp.

638. ———. *Promenade: pour piano ou harpe*. Paris: Rideau Rouge, c1972. 2 pp.

639. ———. *Ritournelles: cinq courtes pièces pour harpe ou piano*. Paris: Henry Lemoine, c1972. 11 pp.

640. ———. *Sarabande: pour harpe, op. 8*. Paris: H. Lemoine, c1951. 7 pp.

641. ———. *Sicilienne variée: pour harpe*. Paris: H. Lemoine, c1966. 11 pp.

642. ———. *Vitrail: pour harpe celtique ou harpe*. Paris: Editions Musicales Transatlantiques, c1975. 2 pp. [NP]

643. Damon, Richard. *Suite: for harp*. San Mateo, Calif.: F.C. Publishing Co., c1987. 11 pp. (Solo series: harp) CONTENTS: Ballad; Portrait; Dance; Prelude; Sorrow; Whistling tune; Hymn.

644. D'Angeli Cattini, Alberta. *Fruscio di salici*. Bologna: Edizioni Bongiovanni, c1921. 7 pp.

645. David, Annie-Louise, 1891–1981, ed. *Album of solo pieces: for the harp*. Compiled and edited by Annie Louise David. Boston: Boston Music Co.; Bloomington, Ind.: Vanderbilt Music Co., [198–?], c1916. 2 v. CONTENTS: Vol.1. Prelude by W. Loukine. The music-box by Franz Poenitz.

Prayer; Will-o'-the-wisp by A. Hasselmans. Slumber-song by Gabriel Fauré. Marguerite at the spinning-wheel by Zabel. Polonaise by Margaret Hoberg.

Vol.2. Minuet by L. van Beethoven. Serenade by Christian Sinding. Aeolian harp; The brook by A. Hasselmans. Pattuglia Spagnuola by L. M. Tedeschi. Romance by A. Zabel. Harp solo from the opera Lucia di Lammermoor by Gaetano Donizetti, arr. by Albert Zabel.

646. ———, ed. *Album of solo pieces: for the harp.* Compiled and edited by Annie Louise David. Boston: Boston Music Co.; New York: G. Schirmer, c1916. 2 v. CONTENTS: Vol.1. Prelude by W. Loukine. The music-box by Franz Poenitz. Prayer; Will-o'-the-wisp by A. Hasselmans. Slumber-song by Gabriel Fauré. Marguerite at the spinning-wheel by Zabel. Polonaise by Margaret Hoberg.

Vol.2. Minuet by L. van Beethoven. Serenade by Christian Sinding. Aeolian harp; The brook by A. Hasselmans. Pattuglia Spagnuola by L. M. Tedeschi. Romance by A. Zabel. Harp solo from the opera Lucia di Lammermoor by Gaetano Donizetti, arr. by Albert Zabel.

647. ———. *Chorale in the style of Handel: for harp or piano.* Chicago, Ill.: Composers Press, c1960. 2 pp.

648. Davidson, Doris, 1924–. *Imaginations: tuneful fun and recital pieces to expand early grade harp skills: for non-pedal and pedal harps.* Edited by Ruth Berman Harris. White Plains, N.Y.: Sumark Press, c1990. 62 pp. [NP] CONTENTS: Woodpecker and cuckoo; Skating; Haunted house; Carousel; The echo; Hide and seek; Seesaw; Weaving; March; Picnic; Spinning wheel; The swing; Over the waves; Copy cat; Lament; Dancing bear; Jumping jacks; Peasant dance; Running down the lane; Dance of the Cossacks; Left turn; Minuet; Lullaby for Julianne; On the river; Leah's song; Cat and mouse; Summer breeze; Music box; Dreaming; Serenade; Maypole dance; Blarney fair; Rondo; Rachel's waltz; Ballerina; Black cat polka; Busybody; Gigue; Tarantella; The slide; Irish mail; Ballade; Julie's jig; Gaelic lullaby; Theme and variations.

649. Davies, Oliver, 1920–. *The popular Cambrian bacchanalian air of Glan meddwdod mwyn, or Good humoured and merry, with an introduction and variations for the harp.* Abergavenny: Adlais, c1977. 11 pp.

650. Dedman, Malcolm. *Elegy: for harp solo (1976).* [Paigles, Essex]: Anglian Edition, c1978. 4 pp. (Anglian new music series, ANMS 43)

651. ———. *Metamorphoses on the raga Puria dahaneshri: for harp solo.* Bradwell, Essex: Anglian Edition, c1983. 12 pp. (Anglian new music series, A.N.M.S. 131)

652. Defaye, Jean-Michel, 1932–. *Scherzando: pour harpe.* Paris: A. Leduc, c1979. 13 pp.

653. Delas, José Luis de, 1928–. *Obraz: für Harfe = for harp.* Cologne: Gerig, c1972. 16 pp.

654. Delaval, Madame. *Air russe: varié pour la harpe.* Paris: Mlles Erard, [180–?]. 7 pp.

655. Del Corona, Rodolfo. *Arabesque e Tarantella: per arpa.* Florence: Edizioni Musicali A. Forlivesi & C., c1971. 11 pp.

656. Delden, Lex van, 1919–1988. *Impromptu: voor harp, opus 48.* Amsterdam: Donemus, c1955. 7 pp.

657. ———. *Impromptu: harp solo, op. 48.* Amsterdam: Donemus, [1961]. Miniature score 26 pp. (Donemus audio-visual series, 1961/2) Also includes Sonate no. 2, violoncello solo by Henk Badings. Sonata, piano solo by Hans Henkemans.

658. ———. *Notturno: per arpa.* Amsterdam: Donemus, 1954. 2 pp.

659. ———. *Notturno: for solo harp.* South Croyden, Surrey: Lengnick, c1972. 4 pp.

660. Delerue, Georges, 1925–1992. *Fluide: pour harpe.* Paris: Editions Musicales Transatlantiques, c1973. 9 pp. Concours du Conservatoire National Superieur de Musique de Paris 1973.

661. Dello Joio, Norman, 1913–. *Bagatelles: for harp.* New York: Marks Music Corp., 1969. 9 pp.

662. Delmas, Marc, 1885–1931. *Prière: pour harpe.* Paris: J. Hamelle, n.d. 3 pp.

663. ———. *Prière: pour harpe.* London: Salvi Publications, c1991. 3 pp.

664. ———. *Theme et variations: pour harpe chromatique, op. 198.* Paris: Buffet-Crampon, c1925. 11 pp.

665. Del Tredici, David, 1937–. *Acrostic paraphrase: from Final Alice: harp solo.* [United States]: Boosey and Hawkes, c1983. 15 pp. Based on the "Acrostic song," the concluding aria from the composer's *Final Alice.*

666. Desangles, Anny, 1939–. *Souvenir à Montcalm: pour la harpe.* Paris: Editions musicales Alphonse Leduc, c1977. 7 pp.

667. Désargus, Xavier, 1768 (ca.)–1832. [Etudes, harp, op. 6] *Vingt quatre etudes: pour la harpe: sur les Folies d'Espagne, oeuv. 6.* Paris: Lemoine, n.d. 21 pp.

668. ———. [Etudes, harp, op. 6] *Vingt quatre études pour la harpe: sur les Folies d'espagne: pour exercer les deux mains de toutes les manières possibles, oeuvre 6.* Paris: Duhan, [181–?]. 21 pp.

669. Désenclos, Alfred, 1912–1971. *Fantaisie: pour harpe.* Paris: Durand; Philadelphia: Elkan-Vogel, c1964. 14 pp. "Morceau de Concours du Conservatoire National Supérieur de Musique de Paris (1964)."

670. De Sica, Manuel. [Momenti] *Tre momenti: per l'arpa: (Sonata)*. Milan: Ricordi, c1972. 16 pp.

671. Desserre, G. T. *Trois etudes: pour harpe*. Paris: Méridian, c1956. 4, 5, 4 pp. CONTENTS: Do bémol; Mi bémol; Sol bémol.

672. Detlefsen, Hans Christian. *Moai terék nliydang: harp solo*. Amsterdam: Donemus, c1983. 13 pp. CONTENTS: Ngok cière; Kouituhh; Aodha; Lyk oyumi dijòr; Sipat ayané.

673. Devčič, Natko, 1914–. *Structures transparentes: für Harfe*. Cologne: Gerig, c1967. 7 pp.

674. ———. *Structures volantes: für Harfe = for harp: 1971*. Cologne: Musikverlag Hans Gerig, c1975. 9 pp.

675. Devos, Gérard, 1927–. *Improvisation et allegro: pour harpe à pédales*. Paris: Hamelle, c1963. 11 pp.

676. ———, ed. *Pièces breves contemporaines: pour harpe*. Annotées et doigtées par Gérard Devos. Paris: Rideau Rouge, c1967–1971. 3 v. CONTENTS: Vol.1. Premiere romance sans paroles by Jacques Casterede. Adagietto; Fileuse Duo by Jean-Michel Damase. Berceuse pour la poupée chinoise; Les quatre doigts to triton by Gérard Devos. Bourée by Pierre-Max Dubois. Echo by Franz Tournier.
Vol.2. Alternances; Petite pastorale by Gérard Devos. Deuxième romance sans paroles by Jacques Castérède. Arabesque by Roger Boutry. Toccata by Alain Weber.
Vol.3. Pour les pédales by Gerard Devos. Air; Sérénade by Odette Gartenlaub. Pour les quatre doigts by Franz Tournier. Nocturne by Alain Weber. Accords; Arpèges by Roger Boutry. Romance by Pierre Max Dubois.

677. Dibdin, Henry Edward, 1813–1866. *Original march: for the harp*. Edinburgh: Purdie, [183–?]. 3 pp.

678. ———. *Rondoletto: for the harp*. Edinburgh: Paterson & Roy, [183- ?]. 3 pp.

679. Dibdin, Mary Ann, 1799–1886. *Fantasia for the harp on the favorite air O' twine a wreath of evergreen*. London: Goulding & D'Almaine, [183–?]. 11 pp.

680. ———. *Introduction and variations on an admired French waltz: for the harp*. London: Willis, [183–?]. 7 pp.

681. ———. *Marche à la grecque: for the harp: introducing some of the new effects*. London: Chappell, [1834?]. 5 pp.

682. Dizi, François-Joseph, 1780–1840. *Dans du Schall: musique de D. Steibelt variée pour la harpe*. Paris: Mlles. Erard, 181–? 7 pp.

683. ———. [Etudes, harp] *Quarante-huit études: pour la harpe*. Nouvelle éd.

en deux livres doigtée et corrigée par A. Hasselmans. Paris: H. Lemoine, c1959. 2 v.

684. ———. [Études, harp] *Quarantotto studi: per arpa.* Milan: G. Ricordi, c1922. 2 v.

685. ———. [Etudes, harp] *Quarante-huit études: pour la harpe.* Ed. Hasselmans. Reprint ed. New York: Lyra Music Co., [1978?]. 2 v. (61, 74 pp.).

686. ———. *Sonata-pastorale: in F-major: for harp.* Annotated, fingered, and edited for twentieth-century harp by Marcia X. Johnstone. South Pasadena, Calif.: Marcia X. Johnstone, c1955. 16 pp. (Harp-re-cords)

687. ———. *Tazah b'Tazah: an Indian air with variations.* Arranged for the harp by François Joseph Dizi. Edited by Alice Lawson. Walnut Creek, Calif.: Harp Publications, c1970. 9 pp.

688. Dobrodinský, Bedřich, 1896–. *Suita: pro harfu.* Prague: Státní nakl. Krásne literatury, hudby a umění, c1954. 15 pp.

689. Dobrokhotova, V. B., and Dobrokhotov, Boris Vasilevich, eds. *Sonaty, variatsii i fantazii, dlia arfy: arfovaia klassica.* Redaktory-sostaviteli: V. B. Dobrokhotova i B. V. Dobrokhotov. Moscow: Muzyka, 1964–.

690. Dobronić-Mazzoni, Rajka, ed. *Works for harp by Croatian composers.* Ed. by Rajka Dobronić-Mazzoni. [Zagreb?]: Croatian Composers' Association-Ars Croatica, 1993. 69 pp. CONTENTS: Six folk melodies: The girl raised a falcon; A little boat; It is raining; Wilt and fade, my violet; A sad rose; A handsome youth riding through the woods by Antun Dobronić. Sonata by Boris Papandopulo. Toccatina, op. 77 by Ivana Lang. Melancholy variations by Tomislav Uhlik. Enypnion by Ivo Josipovic. Illuminations by Dubravko Detoni.

691. Dodgson, Stephen, 1924–. *Ballade: [for solo harp].* Edited by Susan Drake. London: Oxford University Press, c1977. 8 pp.

692. ———. *Fantasy: for harp.* Edited by David Watkins. London: Stainer and Bell; New York: Galaxy Music Corp., c1972. 10 pp.

693. Dominguez, Alberto. *Frenesí: for pedal or troubadour harp.* [Arranged by Reinhardt Elster]. New York: Peer International, c1939. 2 pp. [NP]

694. ———. *Perfidia: for pedal or troubadour harp.* New York: Peer- Southern Concert Music, c1939. 2 pp. [NP]

695. Donatoni, Franco, 1927–. *Marches: due pezzi per arpa.* Milan: G. Ricordi, 1980, c1979. 8 pp.

696. Donceanu, Felicia, 1931–. *Inscription on a mast: ballad for harp.* New York: Lyra Music Co., 1991. 9 pp.

697. Donnellan, Muriel. *You are my inspiration.* S.l.: s.n., c1980. 3 pp.

698. Dubez, J. [Chansons sans paroles] *Deux chansons sans paroles: pour harpe.* Leipzig: Aug. Cranz, [19—?]. 7 pp.

699. Dubois, Pierre Max, 1930–. *Cordée: sonatine pour harpe.* Paris: G. Billaudot, c1980. 13 pp. (La harpe) "Morceau de concours du Conservatoire national supérieur de musique de Paris 1980."

700. ———. *Pour la harpe: deux pièces.* Paris: Editions Choudens, 1966. 7 pp. CONTENTS: La berceuse du petit loir; Danse de la girafe.

701. Dubois, Théodore, 1837–1924. *Aubade printanière: pour harpe.* Paris: Heugel & Cie., c1909. 9 pp.

702. Duchatz, W. *Lieber Augustine: a favorite German air.* London: J. Platts, 18—. 3 pp.

703. Duclos, Pierre, 1929–1974. *Toccata: pour harpe ou clavecin [by] François de Boisvallée.* Transcription de Paul Bonneau. Paris: Chappell, c1966. 3 pp. "Accompagnement d'orchestre à cordes ad lib."

704. Dulova, Vera, 1910–, ed. *Albom pec: dlia arfy.* Sostavlenie i redaktsiia Very Dulovoi. Moscow: Sov. kompozitor, 1979–. Music for harp or harp and other instruments by Russian composers.

705. Dumoulin, Maxime, 1893–1972. *Suite en mi, op. 2: pour piano ou harpe.* Paris: Editions Maurice Senart et Cie., c1921. 17 pp.

706. *Duncan Gray: a popular Scotch air: arranged with variations for the harp or piano forte.* London: R. Schroeder, [18—]. 2 pp. Theme with two variations.

707. Dussek, Johann Ladislaus, 1760–1812. [Concertos, harp, orchestra, op. 15, E♭ major. Rondo] *The plough boy: a favorite rondo for the pianoforte or harp.* Philadelphia: G.E. Blake; New York: R. Meetz, [between 1818 and 1820]. 7 pp. The tune is from *The farmer,* an opera by William Shield.

708. ———. [Sonatas, piano, op. 12, no. 2; arr.] *Dussek's sonata: with his celebrated variations to God save the king: for the piano-forte or harp.* Dublin: Published by Edmund Lee, [179–?]. 8 pp.

709. ———. [Sonatas, violin, violoncello, harp, op. 34, nos. 1, 2] *Deux grandes sonates, op. 34.* Edited by Catherine Michel. [Santa Monica, Calif.]: Salvi Publications, c1977. 43 pp. For harp. CONTENTS: Op. 34, no. 1, E♭ major; Op. 34, no. 2, B♭ major.

710. ———. [Sonatinas, harp] *Sest sonatin: pro harfu.* Red. Jan Racek; rev. Marie Zunová. Prague: Supraphon; Artia, 1956. xii, 19 pp. (Musica antiqua bohemica, 22)

711. ———. [Sonatinas, harp] *Six sonatinas: for the harp.* Edited by Lucile Lawrence and Dewey Owens. New York: Lyra Music Co., c1969. 23 pp.

712. ———. [Sonatinas, harp] *Six sonatines: for harp.* Edited by Josef Molnar. London: Salvi Publications, c1987. 21 pp.

713. Duykers, Elizabeth J. *Les souvenirs: for pedal or non pedal harp.* S.l.: s.n., c1974. 12 pp. [NP] CONTENTS: La valse dernière; Les adieux; Sans toi.

714. Dvořáček, Jiří, 1928–. *Hudba: pro harfu: ve trech vetách.* Prague: Panton, 1971. 15 pp.

715. Eben, Petr, 1929–. *Risonanza: per arpa sola.* Herausgegeben von Katharina Hanstedt. Kassel, New York: Bärenreiter, c1992. 11 pp. Based on the minuet from Mozart's *Don Giovanni.*

716. Ebenhöh, Horst, 1930–. [Stücke, harp, op. 51, no. 1] *Dreizehn Stücke: für Harfe, op. 51, 1.* Vienna: Robitschek, c1981. 13 pp.

717. ————. [Stücke, harp, op. 51, no. 2] *Sonate: für Harfe, op. 51/2.* Vienna: Robitschek, c1981. 22 pp.

718. Eberhard, Dennis, 1943–. *Especially: harp solo.* New York: C.F. Peters, c1988. 12 pp.

719. Echevarría, Victorino. *Capricho andaluz: para arpa.* Madrid: Union Musical Española, c1964. 11 pp.

720. Ehrlich, Abel, 1915–. *Una Linda de Marsilia: for harp (1977).* [Tel Aviv]: Israel Music Insitute, 1987. 17 pp.

721. Eitler, Esteban, 1913–1960. [Serie sentimental. Deseo] *Deseo: de la Serie sentimental: pieza para arpa.* Buenos Aires: Ediciones Musicales Politonia, c1945. 2 pp.

722. Ellis, Merrill, 1916–. *Pastorale.* [Santa Monica, Calif.]: Salvi, 1978. 3 pp.

723. Elouis, J. (Jean). [Selections] *First [-second] volume of a selection of favorite Scots songs: with accompaniments for the harp or pianoforte, which may be performed on these instruments either with the voice or without it as familiar lessons, to which are added several airs with variations.* Edinburgh: Sold by Messrs. Gow & Shepherd, Messrs. Muir Wood & Co., and by Robt. Birchall, London, [ca. 1807]. Score 2 v.

724. Enesco, Georges, 1881–1955. *Allegro de concert: pour harpe chromatique seule.* Paris: Enoch, [1955]. 7 pp.

725. ————. *Allegro de concert: pentru harpa.* Bucharest: Editura de Stat pentru Literatura si Arta, 1956. 7 pp.

726. Erdeli, K. A. (Kseniia Aleksandrovna), 1878–1971. [Exercises, harp] *Uprazhneniia: dlia arfy.* Moscow: Gos. muzykal'noe izd-vo, 1957. 22 pp. Exercises for harp.

727. ————. [Harp music. Selections] *Piat pes: dlia arfy.* Moscow: Gos. muzykal'noe izd-vo, 1960. 26 pp. CONTENTS: Tri preliudii; Elegiia; Variatsii na temu russkov narodnov pesni.

728. ————. [Legkikh pes v stile russkikh pesen] *Desiat' legkikh p'es v stile russkikh pesen: dlia arfy.* Moscow: Gos. muzykal'noe izd-vo, 1951. 13 pp. CONTENTS: 1. Prostaia pesenka; 2. Pechalnaia; 3. Veselaia; 4. Zadushev-naia; 5. Khorovodnaia; 6. Protiazhnaia; 7. Pliasovaia; 8. Ukrainskii tanets; 9. Pesnia; 10. Zakliuchitelnyi tanets.

729. Etchecopar, Marcel. *The old weathervane: four French ritournelles: for harp solo.* New York: M. Baron, c1942–1944. 4 v. CONTENTS: I. Northern: Le p'tit quinquin; II. Southern: Compere guilleri; III. Eastern: En passant par la Lorraine; IV. Western: Le petit navire.

730. Etcheverry, Maïté. *Exercices: pour la harpe celtique et la harpe sans pédales.* Paris: Billaudot, 1985–1991. 2 v. (22, 24 pp.). [NP] CONTENTS: Vol.1. Arpèges; Vol.2. Agilité; Vol.3. Gammes.

731. ———, comp. *Villanelles: 15 cantilènes médiévales pour harpe celtique sur des thèmes populaires bretons et irlandais.* [Compiled by] Maïté Etcheverry. Paris: Editions Choudens, c1974. 17 pp. [NP] CONTENTS: Alain le renard; Le faucon; La chanson de table; L'épouse du croisé; Les trois moines rouges; Le retour d'Angleterre; Les bleus; Le cygne; Le temps passé; Les ligueurs; La ceinture; La légende de Saint Roman; La ceinture de noce; Le baron de Jauioz; Marche de Brian Boru.

732. Eymieu, Henry, 1860–. *Romance sans paroles: pour harpe chromatique.* Paris: Henry Lemoine & Cie., n.d. 3 pp.

733. Farkas, Ferenc, 1905–. *Régi magyar táncok a XVII. századból = Dances hongroises du 17ème siècle.* Hárfára átírta Liana Pasquali. Budapest: Editio Musica, c1979. 12 pp. CONTENTS: Danse du Prince de Transylvanie; Danse hongroise; Chorea; Danse "Lapockás"; Chorea; Danse de Lázár Apor.

734. Farolfi, Giovanna. *Omaggio a Debussy: fantasia per arpa.* Santa Monica, Calif.: Salvi Publications, c1983. 7 pp.

735. Fauré, Gabriel, 1845–1924. *Une châtelaine en sa tour: pièce pour harpe, op. 110.* Paris: Durand, c1918. 7 pp.

736. ———. *Une châtelaine en sa tour—: pièce pour harpe, op. 110.* [New York, N.Y.?]: Lyra Music Co., [197–?]. 7 pp.

737. ———. [Impromptu, harp, op. 86, Db major] *Impromptu, [op. 86]: pour la harpe.* New York: Lyra Music, n.d. 13 pp.

738. ———. [Impromptu, harp, op. 86, Db major] *Impromptu: pour la harpe, op. 86.* Paris: Durand; Bryn Mawr, Pa.: Theodore Presser, 1904. 13 pp.

739. ———. [Impromptu, harp, op. 86, Db major] *Zwei Stücke = Deux pièces = Two pieces: für Harfe.* Hrsg. von Margarete Kluvetasch. Leipzig: Edition Peters, c1975. 23 pp. CONTENTS: Impromptu, op. 86; Une châtelaine en sa tour, op. 110.

740. *Favorite Swiss waltz: for the harp or piano forte.* New York: Firth & Hall, [between 1832 and 1847]. 1 leaf.

741. Feld, Jindrich, 1925–. *Toccata and passacaglia: for harp.* New York: G. Schirmer, c1980. 11 pp.

742. Ferrari Trecate, Luigi, 1884–1964. *Improvviso da concerto: per arpa.* Milan: Edizioni Suvini Zerboni, c1947. 7 pp.

743. Fine, Vivian, 1913–. *Variations: for harp.* New York, N.Y.: Lyra Music, 1965. 7 pp.

744. Finko, David, 1936–. *Mask: for harp.* Philadelphia: Dako Publishers, [1989?]. 4 pp.

745. Finzi, Graciane, 1945–. *Rythmes et sons: pour harpe.* Paris: Editions musicales transatlantiques, c1983. 6 pp.

746. Fischer, Jan, 1921–. *Čtyři etudy: pro solovou harfu: (1971) = Vier Etüden: für Harfe.* Prague: Supraphon, 1986. 15 pp.

747. Fisher, Alfred, 1942–. *Benediction: for harp.* New York: Seesaw Music, c1982. 4 pp.

748. Flagello, Nicolas, 1928–. *Sonata: for harp.* New York: Lyra Music Co., c1963. 24 pp.

749. Floritta, Maria. *Coscata: per arpa.* Milan: Casa Monzino & Garlandini, 1939. 12 pp.

750. Flothuis, Marius, 1914–. *Allegro con precisione, opus 75 nr. 4: per arpa sola.* Amsterdam: Donemus, c1979. 5 pp.

751. ———. *Berceuse brève: pour harpe,* op. 75, no. 1, 1963. Amsterdam: Donemus, c1989. 3 pp.

752. ———. [Easy studies, op. 87] *Six easy studies: for harp, opus 87.* Amsterdam: Donemus, c1986. 9 pp.

753. ———. *Molto lento: harp.* Amsterdam: Donemus, c1975. 3 pp.

754. ———. *Pour le tombeau d'Orphée: danse elegiaque pour harpe seule.* Amsterdam: Donemus, c1950. 7 pp.

755. ———. *Sonorités opposées: pour harpe seule,* op. 75, no 6. Amsterdam: Donemus, c1987. 4 pp.

756. Fontyn, Jacqueline, 1930–. *Intermezzo: per arpa.* London: Chappell, c1975. 5 pp.

757. ———. *Intermezzo: per arpa.* S.l.: POM, 1991. 7 pp.

758. Forst, Rudolf, 1900–1973. *From a railway carriage: for harp solo.* New York: Edition Musicus, c1944. 4 pp.

759. ———. *From a railway carriage.* West Babylon, N.Y.: Harold Branch Publishing, c1979. 3 pp.

760. ———. *Sequences: for solo harp.* Plainview, N.Y.: Harold Branch Publishing, c1976. 13 pp.

761. Fox, Charles, 1940–. *Ancient dance: (after Ravel): for harp.* New York: Peer International, c1968. 10 pp.

762. Françaix, Jean, 1912–. *Suite: pour harpe.* Mainz; New York: Schott, c1979. 23 pp. CONTENTS: Preludio; Capriccio; Sogno; Sarabande; Rondino; Élégie; Finale; Epilogue.

763. Franck, Maurice. *Suite: pour harpe.* Paris: Editions musicales trans-atlantiques, c1959. 12 pp. CONTENTS: Prélude; Scherzo; Improvisation; Final.

764. Franco, Johan, 1908–. *Suite agreste: for harp.* New York: American Composers Alliance, [19—]. 11 pp. (Composers facsimile edition) CONTENTS: Carillon; Pastorale; Musette; Berceuse; Contredanse.

765. Franco, José María, 1894–. [Pieces, harp, op. 60] *Dos piezas: para arpa, op. 60.* Madrid: Union Musical Española, [1963]. 5 pp. CONTENTS: Aria triste; Toccata.

766. ———. [Pieces, harp, op. 62–64] *Tres piezas: para arpa, op. 62, 63 y 64.* Madrid: Union Musical Española, [1963]. CONTENTS: Gallarda by A. Mudarra (Versión para arpa por Jose M. Franco). O quardame las vacas. Villancico variado.

767. ———. [Preludes, harp, op. 55] *Tres preludios: para arpa, op. 55.* Madrid: Union Musical Española, [1963]. 11 pp.

768. Frank, Andrew, 1946–. *Serenata: for harp.* Hillsdale, N.Y.: Mobart Music, [1987], c1985. 12 pp.

769. ———. *Sonata: for harp.* Newton Centre, Mass.: Margun Music, c1987. 20 pp. CONTENTS: Moderato; Notturno; Variations.

770. Franke, Horst, 1928–. *König David mit der Harfe: Trilogie für Harfe-Solo.* Frankfurt: Belcanto, c1989. 13 pp. CONTENTS: David mit der Konzert-harfe (Sänger der Psalmen); David und Bathseba (Liebeslied für Bath-seba); David in der Vollendung (Gotteslob der Ewigkeit).

771. Freed, Isadore, 1900–1960. *Promenade: for harp.* New York: Belwin, c1942. 5 pp.

772. Freedman, Robert M., 1934–. *Trois mémoires: solo pour la harpe.* Santa Monica, Calif.: Salvi Harps, c1979. 12 pp. CONTENTS: Des fleurs; De la joie; De la solitude.

773. Frid, Géza, 1904–. *Fuga: voor harpen, op. 62.* Amsterdam: Donemus, [1961?]. 9 pp.

774. Friou, Deborah, 1951–. *Harp exercises for agility and speed: for non-pedal and pedal harp.* Los Angeles, Calif.: Woods Music and Books Publishing, c1989. 93 pp. [NP]

775. Frojo, Giovanni. *Rêverie.* Napoli: R. Izzo, c1922. 6 pp.

776. Fuchs, Robert, 1847–1927. [Phantasie, harp, op. 85] *Phantasie: für Harfe, op. 85.* Vienna: Adolf Robitschek, [1909?]. 15 pp.

777. ———. [Phantasie, harp, op. 85] *Phantasie: for the harp, op. 85.* New York: Edwin F. Kalmus, [197–?]. 15 pp. (Kalmus harp series, no. 4682)

778. Fulton, DeWayne, 1932–. *Variations on a theme of Beethoven: for solo harp.* Santa Monica, Calif.: Salvi Harps, 1955. Score 9 pp.

779. ————. *Variations on a theme of Beethoven: for solo harp (or non-pedal harp),*
op. 1. Marina Del Rey, Calif.: Safari, c1989. 10 pp. [NP]

780. Gabucci, Agostino. *Preludio: per arpa.* [Rome: M. Alfredo, n.d.]. 3 pp.

781. Gabus, Monique, 1924–. *La harpe de Graziella: 10 pièces progressives pour*
harpe celtique ou grande harpe. Révision et doigtés, Odette Le Dentu. Paris:
Henry Lemoine, c1982. 16 pp. Originally for piano; adapted from piano
pieces for children. [NP] CONTENTS: Dans les montagnes; La petite
biehe; Crépuseule [sic] sur le lagon; Mélodie; Ritournelle bretonne; Le
jardin des tourterelles; Au bord du fleuve; Flûtes indiennes; Les jardins
flottants de Xoehimileo; La déesse des fleurs.

782. ————. *Images de Chine: 6 pièces progressives pour harpe celtique ou grande*
harpe. Paris: Gérard Billaudot, 1985. 15 pp. (La harpe) [NP] CON-
TENTS: Dans le parc de bambous; Un Français à Pékin; Paysage au bord
de l'eau; La danseuse T'ang; Pagode de l'harmonie céleste; Les cavaliers
du Sinkiang.

783. ————. *Sur les bords du Nil: 5 pièces pour grande harpe ou harpe celtique.*
Doigtés et conseils techniques: Huguette Géliot. Paris: Editions Henry
Lemoine, c1990. 12 pp. [NP] CONTENTS: Les oiseaux de la palmeraie;
Jardins au bord du Nil; Quand Nefertiti chantait; Un français en prom-
enade; Le petit âne du Caire.

784. Galais, Bernard, 1921–. [Morceaux, harp] *Huit morceaux en deux recueils*
pour harpe celtique ou harpe à pédales. Paris: Harposphere, c1988–. 2 v.
CONTENTS: 2. cahier. Barcarolle; Badinage; Melopée; Promenade.

785. ————. [Petits préludes, harp] *Vingt petits préludes: pour harpe.* Paris:
Harposphere, c1989. 4 v.

786. Galante, Carlo, 1959–. *The waning moon: poemetto notturno per arpa.*
Milan: Edizioni Suvini Zerboni, c1984. 5 pp. Based on poem by P.B.
Shelley.

787. Galeotti, Cesare, 1872–1929. *Légende, op. 139: pour harpe.* Paris: Enoch
& Cie., c1910. 12 pp.

788. ————. *Scherzo-caprice: pour harpe, op. 159.* Geneva: Henn, c1920. 10 pp.

789. Gallenberg, Robert, Graf von, 1783–1839. *Variations sur un air russe:*
pour la harpe. Milan: Jean Ricordi, n.d. 11 pp.

790. Gallon, Noël, 1891–1966. *Barcarolle: pour harpe.* Paris: Editions Salabert, c1932. 7 pp.

791. ————. [Etudes, harp] *Deux etudes: pour harpe.* Paris: Editions Philippo,
c1961. 14 pp. CONTENTS: Chromatisme; Moto perpetuo.

792. ————. *Fantaisie: pour harpe.* Paris: L. Rouhier; A. Leduc, c1921. 21 pp.
"Morceau imposé au concours du Conservatoire national de Paris en
1921."

793. Galuppi, Baldassare, 1706–1785. *Giga: für Harfe.* Ed. L. M. Magistretti. Frankfurt am Main: Zimmermann, c1914. 5 pp. (Des Harfenisten Konzert-Programm, No. 9)

794. Gamley, Douglas, 1924–. *Little suite for harp.* London: Studio G, c1970. 12 pp.

795. Garagusi, Nicola. *Gavotte antique: harp solo.* Detroit: Camara Music Pub., c1960. 7 pp.

796. Garcia, Digno. [Solos] *10 solos: for the harp.* Brussels: World Music Co., c1968. 26 pp.

797. Gartenlaub, Odette, 1922–. *Jeu: pour harpe celtique.* Paris: G. Billaudot, c1984. 3 pp. (La harpe) [NP]

798. ———. *Prelude: pour harpe celtique.* Paris: Gérard Billaudot, 1984. 3 pp. (La harpe) [NP]

799. ———. *Preparation au dechiffrage instrumental: volume F.* Paris: Éditions Rideau Rouge, c1975–1977. 2 v.

800. Garuti, Mario, 1957–. *Il vuoto e la vergine: fantasia per arpa.* Milan: Ricordi, 1988. 4 pp.

801. Gatayes, Guillaume Pierre Antoine, 1774–1846. [Potpourris, harp, no. 1, op. 6] *Premier potpourri, oeuvre 6e.* Paris: Augte. LeDuc, [1846?]. 7 pp.

802. ———. [Potpourris, harp, no. 3, op. 9] *Troisieme pot pourri: pour la harpe, oeuvre 9e.* Paris: Cochet, [1800 or 1801?]. 8 pp. Caption title: Fiez vous aux vains discours des hommes; 3me. pot-pourri par Gatayes.

803. ———. [Potpourris, harp, no. 4, op. 10] *Quatrième pot-pourri: pour harpe, oeuvre 10e.* Paris: LeDuc, [1806?]. 7 pp. Based on "Sous les yeux de la déesse" from *Les mystères d'Isis* by Louis Wenceslas Lachnith.

804. Gaubert, Philippe, 1879–1941. *Sarabande: pour harpe.* Paris: Durand, c1920. 4 pp.

805. Gebauer, Adolf, 1941–. [Episoden] *Fünf Episoden: für Harfe Solo.* Celle: Moeck Verlag, 1989. 16 pp.

806. ———. *Kinderträume: sechs kleine Stücke für Harfe solo (Irische Harfe oder Pedalharfe).* [Odenthal?]: Centraton Musikverlag, 1989. 10 pp. [NP]

807. Gelbrun, Artur, 1913–1985. *Introduction and arabesque: for harp: (1962).* Tel Aviv: Israel Music Institute, c1985. 12 pp.

808. ———. *Introduction and rhapsody: for harp.* Tel Aviv: Israel Music Institute, 1973. 11 pp.

809. Genzmer, Harald, 1909–. *Fantasie: für Harfe.* Frankfurt: H. Litolff's Verlag; New York: C.F. Peters, 1973. 11 pp.

810. Gianella, Louis, 1778?–1817. *[Collection of instrumental works for harp: a*

miscellaneous collection of original and arranged music for solo harp or for harp with various added accompaniments. London: s.n., 18—]. 1 v. (various pagings). Principally for solo harp, but with some added accompaniments for flute, piano, or violin. CONTENTS: Aria di ballo. Le badinage calabrien. L'elegante.

811. Gildon, J. (John). *Juliana: a favourite dance: arranged as a rondo for the harp or piano forte.* Baltimore: John Cole, [ca. 1822]. 3 pp.

812. ———. [March, harp] *Gildon's celebrated march: for the piano forte or harp.* London: J. Balls, [182–?]. 5 pp.

813. Gillmann, Kurt, 1889–1975. *Arabeske: [für] Harfe, op. 15.* Leipzig: J.H. Zimmermann, c1926. 5 pp.

814. ———. *Capriccio in Form eines Walzers: für Harfe Solo.* Hannover: A. Nagel, 1933. 7 pp.

815. ———. *Melodie: [für] Harfe, op. 10.* Leipzig: J.H. Zimmermann, c1926. 5 pp.

816. ———. *Suite im alten Stil: für Harfe solo.* Hannover: Verlag Adolph Nagel, c1936. 11 pp.

817. ———. *Walzer: [für] Harfe, op. 25.* Leipzig: J.H. Zimmermann, c1926. 7 pp.

818. Giuranna, Barbara, 1902–. *Sonatina: per arpa.* Milan: G. Ricordi, c1943. 13 pp.

819. Glanville-Hicks, Peggy, 1912–1990. *Sonata: for harp.* New York: Weintraub Music Co., c1953. 14 pp. CONTENTS: Saeta; Pastorale; Rondo.

820. Glière, Reinhold Moritsevich, 1875–1956. *Impromptu.* Ed. Tatiana Tauer. Marina Del Rey, Calif.: Safari Publications, 1992. 8 pp.

821. Glinka, Mikhail Ivanovich, 1804–1857. [Harp music. Selections] *Variations on a theme of Mozart; and, Nocturne.* Santa Monica, Calif.: Salvi Publications, [197–?]. 27 pp.

822. ———. [Nocturne, harp, E♭ major] *Nocturne: für Harfe.* Hamburg: H. Sikorski, c1972. 11 pp.

823. ———. [Nocturne, harp, E♭ major] *Nocturne: for harp.* New York: Lyra Music Co., c1975. 7 pp.

824. ———. [Nocturne, harp, E♭ major] *Nocturne.* Ed. Paul Hurst. Marina Del Rey, Calif.: Safari Publications, 1992. 8 pp.

825. ———. [Variatsii na temu Motsarta] *Mozart-Variationen: für Harfe.* Hamburg: H. Sikorski, c1972. 16 pp. Based on Papageno's bell tune from the finale to act 1 of *Die Zauberflöte*.

826. ———. [Variatsii na temu Motsarta] *Variations on a theme of Mozart: [Don Giovanni].* New York, N.Y.: Lyra Music, [1975?]. 17 pp. Includes two

versions of the variations, the version originally published about 1854 and the more recent edition.

827. Glyn, Gareth. *Triban: harp.* Abergavenny, Gwent, Wales: Adlais, c1978. 18 pp.

828. Godefroid, Dieudonné-Félix, 1818–1897. [Bois solitaire] *Romance without words: (Bois solitaire): harp solo.* Edited by Susann McDonald. [Bloomington, Ind.]: Musicworks-Harp Editions, c1982. 3 pp.

829. ———. *Carnaval de Venise, op. 184.* [Marina Del Rey, Calif.]: Safari, [198–?]. 18 pp.

830. ———. *Chant des exiles: pour harpe, op. 188.* Milan: G. Ricordi, n.d. 9 pp.

831. ———. *École mélodique: pour harpe: sur des mélodies de Schubert, op. 201.* Révision de Odette Le Dentu. Paris: Gérard Billaudot, c1979. 5 v. (La harpe) CONTENTS: Quand tu me vois souffrir; Sois toujours mes seules amours; Le désir; Les ris et les pleurs; La sérénade.

832. ———. [École mélodique. Quand tu me vois souffrir] *École mélodique: pour la harpe: 5 fantaisies sur des motifs favoris, [op. 201]. no. 1, Quand tu me vois souffrir.* Milan: Ricordi, [188–?]. 5 pp.

833. ———. [École mélodique. Sérénade] *École mélodique: pour la harpe: 5 fantaisies sur des motifs favoris, [op. 201]. No. 5, La sérénade.* Milan: Ricordi, [188–?]. 5 pp.

834. ———. *Étude de concert: en mi-bémol mineur, op. 193.* Paris: G. Ricordi, n.d. 7 pp.

835. ———. *Étude de concert: en mi-bémol mineur, op. 193: pour harpe.* New York: Lyra Music Co., n.d. 7 pp.

836. ———. *Étude de concert: en mi-bémol mineur: pour harpe, op. 193.* [Santa Monica, Calif.]: Salvi Publications, [198–?]. 7 pp.

837. ———. [Études caractéristiques. Danse des sylphes] *La danse des sylphes: étude caractéristique.* Leipzig: Schott, n.d. 11 pp.

838. ———. [Études caractéristiques. Danse des sylphes] *La danse des sylphes: (telle que l'auteur l'exécute dans ses concerts).* Nouv. éd. Paris: R. Deiss; Editions Salabert, [19—?]. 11 pp. (Oeuvres pour la harpe)

839. ———. [Études caractéristiques. Danse des sylphes] *La danse des sylphes.* Marina Del Rey, Calif.: Safari Publications, 1991. 11 pp.

840. ———. [Exercices, harp. Etudes mélodiques] *Vingt études mélodiques: pour la harpe, faisant suite aux exercises.* Paris: C. Hay, [19—]. 60 pp.

841. ———. [Exercices, harp. Etudes mélodiques] *20 études mélodiques.* Marina Del Rey, Calif.: Safari Publications, 1993. 58 pp.

842. ———. [Fidanzata del marinajo] *La fidanzata del marinajo: scène pour harpe, op. 192.* Milan: Ricordi, n.d. 13 pp.

843. ———. *La harpe éolienne.* Paris: R. Deiss, [18—?]. 5 pp.

844. ———. *La harpe eolienne.* Ross, Calif.: Harp Publications, [19—]. 7 pp.

845. ———. *La melancolie: etude caracteristique pour harpe.* Ross, Calif.: Harp Publications, [19—]. 7 pp.

846. ———. [Morceaux caractéristiques. Adieux] *Trois morceaux caractéristiques: no. 1, les adieux: romance sans paroles.* Mainz: B. Schott's Söhne, [188–?]. 7 pp.

847. ———. *Pensées musicales: pour la harpe: à placer entre les exercices & les 20 études mélodiques (d'une execution progressive).* Paris: Durdilly, Hayet, n.d. 22 pp.

848. ———. *Sois mes amours "sei mir gegrüsst," op. 201.* Mainz: B. Schott's Söhne, n.d. 5 pp.

849. ———. *Sur le lac (Nuit d'été): op. 191, pour la harpe.* Milan: G. Ricordi, n.d. 7 pp.

850. Golestan, Stan, 1875–1956. *Ballade roumaine: pour harpe.* Paris: Durand; Philadelphia: Elkan-Vogel, c1953. 10 pp.

851. Golubev, Evgenii Kirillovich, 1910–1988. *Arfa solo i v ensambliakh = The harp solo and in ensembles.* Moscow: Sov. kompozitor, 1990. Score 40 pp. The 1st work for high voice and harp; the 2nd for harp solo; the 3rd for 2 flutes and 2 harps. CONTENTS: Arfa: for harp and tenor, op. 91, no. 1; Nocturne: for harp solo, op. 91, no. 2; Quartet: for 2 flutes and 2 harps, op. 49.

852. Gombau, Gerardo, 1906–1967. *Apunte betico: harp solo.* Edited by Yvonne La Mothe Schwager. Berkeley, Calif.: Northern California Harpists' Association, c1951. 9 pp.

853. Goossens, Eugene, 1893–1962. [Ballades, harp] *Two ballades: for harp.* London: J. Curwen & Sons, c1924. 13 pp.

854. ———. [Ballades, harp] *Deux ballades: pour harpe.* Paris: Alphonse Leduc, 1960. 7 pp.

855. Grandjany, Marcel, 1891–1975. *Les agneaux dansent = Dancing lambs: for harp with or without pedals.* New York: O. Pagani, c1971. 6 pp. [NP]

856. ———. *Automne: pièce pour harpe.* Paris: Durand, c1927. 4 pp.

857. ———. [Bagatelles, harp, op. 22] *Bagatelles: op. 22, for harp.* New York: Edward B. Marks, c1941. 5 pp.

858. ———. [Chansons populaires françaises, harp] *Deux chansons populaires françaises: pièces faciles pour la harpe.* Paris: Durand; Philadelphia: Elkan-Vogel, c1913. 2 v. CONTENTS: Le bon petit roi d'Yvetôt; Et ron ron ron, petit patapon.

859. ———. *Children's hour: suite for harp, [op. 25].* New York: G. Schirmer,

c1950. 23 pp. CONTENTS: Into mischief; Little angel; Giddap pony; Playing in the garden; Parade; The sandman.

860. ———. *Children's hour: suite for harp, op. 25.* New York: Carl Fischer, Inc., c1950. 23 pp. CONTENTS: Into mischief = Espiègle; Little angel = Très sage; Giddap pony = Au trot; Playing in the garden = Jeux dans le jardin; Parade = Militaire; The sandman = Le marchand de sable.

861. ———. *Children's hour: suite for the harp, [op. 25].* 1966 edition. New York: Carl Fischer, Inc., c1966. 23 pp.

862. ———. *The Colorado trail: fantaisie for harp, op. 28.* New York: Associated Music Publishers, Inc., c1954. 11 pp.

863. ———. *Dans la forêt du charme et de l'enchantement: conte de fée: pour harpe, op. 11.* Paris: A. Durand & Fils, 1923. 10 pp.

864. ———. *Divertissement: pour harpe, op. 29.* Paris: Durand; Philadelphia, Pa.: Elkan-Vogel, c1963. 13 pp. Suite. CONTENTS: Canon; Fughetta; Final.

865. ———. [Enfants jouent] *Children at play = Les enfants jouent: pour la harpe, op. 16.* Paris: Durand, c1929. 11 pp.

866. ———. *The Erie canal: a fantasy for harp, op. 38.* Hollywood, Calif.: Composers Press, c1964. 7 pp.

867. ———. *Fantaisie: pour harpe: sur un thème de J. Haydn.* Paris: Editions Musicales Alphonse Leduc, c1958. 12 pp. CONTENTS: Introduction; Thème de Haydn; Variation I; Variation II; Variation III; Variation IV; Variation V.

868. ———. *Fileuse, op. 39.* New York: Lyra Music Co., 1990. 7 pp.

869. ———. *Frère Jacques: fantaisie pour harpe, op. 32.* Paris: Durand, c1957. 7 pp.

870. ———. *Harp album, op. 27.* New York: M. Baron Co., c1947. 18 pp. (Baron manuscript series) CONTENTS: 1. Greetings; 2. Zephyr; 3. In dancing mood; 4. A butterfly; 5. Deep river interlude; 6. The pageant begins; 7. On a western ranch; 8. Through the meadows.

871. ———. *Little harp book: 8 easy solos for harp (or harp without pedals).* New York: Carl Fischer, Inc., c1964. 15 pp. [NP] CONTENTS: Church choir; Hunting tune; Merry-go-round; Promenade (Modulation study); The see-saw; Rocking; Bonjour, Monsieur Rameau; Graduation parade.

872. ———. *Noël provençal: for harp, op. 24.* New York: Edward B. Marks Music Corp., c1941. 5 pp.

873. ———. *Old Chinese song: for harp, op. 23.* New York: E.B. Marks, c1941. 5 pp.

874. ———. *Pastorale: pour harpe sans pédales.* Paris: Editions Durand, 1971, c1912. 3 pp. [NP]

875. ———. *Petite suite classique: for harp.* New York: Carl Fischer, Inc., c1969. 12 pp. CONTENTS: Joyful overture (In the style of Purcell); Gigue (Remembrance of Kuhnau); Gavotte (Reverence to Lully); Siciliana (Aeolian mode); Passepied (Homage to the Couperins); Bourrée (In the style of Handel).

876. ———. *Petites pièces très faciles: pour la harpe, op. 7.* Paris: Alphonse Leduc, c1954. 8 pp.

877. ———. [Pièces faciles] *Trois pièces faciles = Three easy pieces: for harp.* New York: Lyra Music Co., c1943. 7 pp. CONTENTS: Nocturne; Rêverie; Barcarolle.

878. ———. *Préludes: pour harpe.* Paris: Editions Salabert, c1921. 5 pp.

879. ———. *Rhapsodie: pour la harpe.* Paris: Alphonse Leduc, c1923. 12 pp.

880. ———. *Souvenirs: poème pour harpe, op. 17.* [Paris: Durand, 1930]. 8 pp.

881. Grandjany, Marcel, 1891–1975, and Weidensaul, Jane B., 1935–. *First-grade pieces for harp: 18 solos for harp with or without pedals.* New York: Carl Fischer, Inc., c1965. 16 pp. [NP] CONTENTS: Drum and bugle; Patrol; Song; A little sad; The anvil; Just walking; Choral; Three o'clock; Treble clef song; Step by step; Lullaby for Violet; Little waltz; Midnight stars; Passing by; Barn dance memory; Melissa; El número uno.

882. Graziani, Maria Pia. [Esercizi, harp] *Tre esercizi: per arpa.* Milan: Carisch, c1976. 11 pp.

883. ———. *Studi facili: per arpa (con e senza pedali).* Milan: Carisch, c1978. 17 pp. [NP]

884. Graziani, V. M., 1825–1889. *Choeur dans l'introduction de l'opera Norma: varié pour la harpe.* Milan: J. Ricordi, [1834]. 14 pp. Ite sulcolle from Bellini's Norma.

885. Griffin, G. E. (George Eugene), 1781–1863. *A grand march: for the piano forte or harp.* London: Printed (for the author) by Clementi & Company, [between 1801 and 1806]. 5 pp.

886. Griffiths, Ann, 1934–. *Beth yw'r haf i mi? = What is summer to me?: fantasia on a Welsh folk song.* Abergavenny, Gwent, Wales: Adlais, c1973. 7 pp.

887. ———. *Cwlwm cymreig = A Welsh knot.* [Wales]: Adlais, 1978. 19 pp.

888. ———. [Delyn aur] *Y delyn aur.* Abergavenny, Gwent, Wales: Adlais, c1976. 7 pp. [NP]

889. ———. *Galarnad a dawns = Lament and dance: Irish harp.* Abergavenny, Gwent, Wales: Adlais, n.d. 5 pp. [NP]

890. ———. *Gwenni aeth i ffair pwllheli = [Sweet but simple Gwennie].* Abergavenny, Gwent, Wales: Adlais, c1973. 6 pp.

———. [Gwers i ddechreuwyr] *Saith gwers i ddechreuwyr: telyn = Seven lessons for beginners: harp.* See 37.

891. ———. [Telynor bach] *Y telynor bach = Le jeune harpiste = The young harpist.* Abergavenny: Adlais, c1974. 26 pp. Includes 7 pieces based on Welsh nursery tunes, each preceded by the Welsh words with English and French translations. Introduction and instructive notes in Welsh, English, and French. CONTENTS: Dau gi bach; Huna blentyn; Migildi, magildi; Ble'r ei di?; Yr ehedydd; Hen fenyw fach; Pedoli; Olé! by Gruffydd ap Llwyd; Alaw gyweirio by Ronald Stevenson.

892. Groot, Cor de, 1914–. *Au revoir: harpe (ou piano).* Amsterdam: Donemus, c1984. 8 pp.

893. ———. *Boerderij-muziek: 12 voorspeelstukjes voor de kleine- of ierse harp in Es: 1983.* Amsterdam: Donemus, c1983. 28 pp. For harp (or piano or accordion). CONTENTS: Het spiritueel ontbijt; Morgenzang; Balkanbrij; Promenade; Lam en veulen; Mysterie; Dansje op de deel; Met charmante klompen; Cortège en troubadour; Mini-mini (groet aan Joplin); Signal; Epiloog: het Avondmaal.

894. ———. *Les plaisirs à Queeckhoven: pour harpe.* Amsterdam: Donemus, c1983. 9 pp. "Une mémoire nostalgique en forme d'une barcarolle."

895. ———. *Souvenir de Dublin: for Irish harp (or piano solo).* Amsterdam: Donemus, c1983. 3 pp. [NP]

896. ———. *Suites: in E♭ for Irish (or non-pedal) harp.* Amsterdam: Donemus, c1983. 11 pp. [NP]

897. Grossi, Maria Vittoria, 1886–. *Esercizi tecnici: per i primi corsi di arpa.* Rome: De Santis, 1943. 40 pp.

———. *Metodo per arpa = Méthode pour harpe = Method for the harp = Harfenschule = Método para arpa.* See 39.

898. Gubitosi, Emilia, 1887–1972. *Fantasia: per arpa.* Milan: Edizioni Curci, [1963]. 21 pp.

899. Guerrini, Guido, 1890–1965. [Suore] *Le suore: tre bozzetti per arpa.* Bologna: F. Bongiovanni, [1939?]. 13 pp. Original imprint: Bologna: Pizzi & C. Editori, c1921. CONTENTS: La passeggiata nel chiostro; Pettegolezzo in refettorio; Nostalgie di novizze.

900. Guridi, Jesús, 1886–1961. [Alba seria] *La del alba seria.* Madrid: Unión Musical Española, c1960. 15 pp.

901. ———. *Colección para arpa.* Ed. and trans. María Rosa Calvo-Manzano. Madrid: Unión Musical Española, 1991. 15 pp.

902. ———. *Viejo Zortzico: (Zortzico Zarra): para arpa.* Madrid: Union Musical Española, c1960. 8 pp.

903. Gurov, L. S. *Capriccio on a Moldavian theme: for the harp.* New York: Edwin F. Kalmus, n.d. 14 pp. (Kalmus harp series)

904. Gustavson, Nancy, 1921–. *The magic road: six easy pieces for troubadour*

harp. Tempe, Ariz.: Nancy Gustavson, c1972. 12 pp. [NP] CONTENTS: A Magyar lament; The jade temple (Variation on a theme by Lou Harrison); Sakura; Mexican wedding song; Minuet; A Moorish garden.

905. ———. *The magic road: solos for pedal or non-pedal harp.* Santa Monica, Calif.: Salvi Publications, c1972. 12 pp. [NP] CONTENTS: A Magyar lament; The jade temple: variation on a theme by Lou Harrison; Sakura; Mexican wedding song; Minuet; A Moorish garden.

906. ———. *Pacific sketches: solos for troubadour or pedal harp.* Tempe, Ariz.: Nancy Gustavson, 1989, c1971. 12 pp. [NP] CONTENTS: Trav'ling on; Path to the sea; Rippling water; Autumn mood; Frolic.

907. ———. *Songs without words: solos for troubadour or pedal harp.* Tempe, Ariz.: N. Gustavson, c1973. 12 pp. [NP] CONTENTS: Cradle song; The blue rock; Love song; Riding on the wind.

908. ———. *Sparklers: solos for pedal harp.* Los Angeles, Calif.: Nancy Gustavson, c1975. 10 pp. CONTENTS: Cloud patterns; Sunny skies; Grams lullaby; The dancing imp; Great day.

909. ———. *Twilight waltzes: solos for pedal harp.* [Tempe, Ariz.]: N. Gustavson, 1993. 11 pp.

910. Gut, Serge. *Suite champêtre: pour harpe celtique.* Paris: G. Billaudot, 1977. 7 pp. (La harpe) [NP] CONTENTS: En gambadant; Le long de la rivière; Jour de vendages.

911. Hába, Alois, 1893–1973. [Sonatas, harp, op. 59] *Sonata: pro chromatickon harfu, op. 59.* Munich: Filmkunst-Musikverlag, [198- ?]. 15, 7, 6 pp.

912. ———. [Sonatas, harp, op. 60] *Sonata: pro diatonickon harfu, op. 60.* Munich: Filmkunst-Musikverlag, [198–?]. 7, 4, 8, 9 pp. [NP]

913. Haegeland, Eilert M., 1951–. *Intermezzo i folketone: for harpe (klaver).* Hamar: Noton, 1992. 4 pp. For harp or piano.

914. Haeussler, Joseph, 1768–1845. [Theme and variations, harp] *Tema s variacemi: arpa o piano = Thema und Variationen.* K vydání pripravil a úvodní studii napsal Zdeněk Culka. Prague: Supraphon, 1976. 15 pp. (Edice medailón, 5) Theme by Mozart.

915. ———. [Theme and variations, harp] *Theme with variations: theme ascribed to W. A. Mozart by Joseph Häussler. Variations: on Mozart's "Joseph Häussler" theme by Ank van Campen.* 1st work arr. Ank van Campen. Hilversum: Harmonia, c1980. 11 pp.

916. Hahn, Adam. *Schöne Erinnerung: fantasy for harp.* New York: Lyra Music, [197–?]. 5 pp.

917. Hajdu, Mihály, 1909–. [Koncertetüd, harp] *Ket koncertetüd: hárfára = Zwei Konzertetüden: für Harfe = Two concert studies: for harp.* Budapest: Editio Musica, c1983. 10 pp.

918. Haletzki, Paul, 1911–. *Römischer Brunnen: Konzertetüde für Harfe- (Klavier-) Solo.* Cologne: Riccardo-Ton-Verlag M. Richartz, c1966. 6 pp.

919. Hamel, Peter Michael, 1947–. [Miniaturen, no. 1] *Miniaturen: für Harfe: 1978/1980.* Kassel: Bärenreiter, 1982, c1980. 10 pp.

920. Handel, Darrell, 1933–. [Balloons] *Three balloons: for harp.* Paris: Salabert, c1977. 7 pp. CONTENTS: Blue; Yellow; Red.

921. ———. *Suzanne's animal music: pour harpe.* Paris: Editions Salabert, c1973. 7 pp. CONTENTS: The skunk; The black panther; An inchworm; In the fish bowl; The colt.

922. Handel, George Frideric, 1685–1759. [Pastorale et thème avec variations, harp] *Tema con variazioni: für Harfe oder Piano.* Herausgegeben von Hans Joachim Zingel. Mainz, New York: B. Schott's Söhne, c1956. 7 pp. For harp or piano.

923. Hansen-Jamet, Renée. *Variations sur un thème mineur: pour la harpe.* Paris: Leduc, c1946. 14 pp.

924. Hardin, Louis, 1916–. *Music for little hands: troubadour harp, book 1: pieces in the Greek modes: for harp or keyboard.* By Moondog (Louis Hardin). [S.l.: J. Goebel, 197–?]. 8 pp. [NP]

925. ———. *Pastorale.* Written by Louis Hardin, a.k.a. Moondog. [S.l.: s.n.], c1971. 4 pp. For harp.

926. Harpa, Gisele. *Six morceaux: pour la harpe.* Paris: Editions Henry Lemoine, c1978. 15 pp. CONTENTS: La cascade enchantée; Premier aveu; Cet ours tout blanc; Ma première valse; Je te jouerai de la harpe; Souvenir de voyage.

927. Harries, David, 1933–. *Three stanzas: for harp, [op. 8].* [Edited by David Watkins]. London: Stainer & Bell, c1973. 8 pp.

928. Harrington, Henry, 1727–1816. *Harrington's easy lesson for the piano forte or harp.* Second edition. New York (29 Chatham Street, New York): E. Riley, [1820?]. Score ([1], 2–3, [1] pp.).

929. Harris, Ruth Berman, 1916–. *Miniatures.* Transcribed & composed for pedal & non-pedal harp by Ruth Berman Harris. White Plains, N.Y.: Sumark Press, 1976. 12 pp. [NP] CONTENTS: Excerpt from En bateau by Debussy. Theme from Chopin etude, op. 10, no. 3. Spring by R. Berman Harris. Debby's waltz by R. Berman Harris. Lucia di Lammermoor by G. Donizetti.

930. Harrison, Lou, 1917–. *From music for Bill and me: [for] harp.* [S.l.: s.n., 196–?]. 2 leaves.

931. ———. *Music: for harp.* [Santa Monica, Calif.]: Salvi, c1978. 12 pp. CONTENTS: Jahla: in the form of a ductia to pleasure Leopold Stokowski

on his ninetieth birthday; Avalokiteshvara; Music for Bill & me; Beverly's troubadour piece; Serenade; Sonata in Ishartum: for small harps.

932. Hartway, James John, 1944–. *Basho: for harp*. Grosse Pointe Pk., Mich.: Hard Wall Pub. Co., 1990. 17 pp.

933. Harty, Hamilton, 1879–1941. *Spring fancies: two preludes for harp solo*. London: Novello, c1915. 2 v.

934. Hartzell, Eugene, 1932–. *Monologue 15: Air and variations: for harp = Harfe solo*. Vienna: Doblinger, c1986. 9 pp.

935. Hasselmans, Alphonse, 1845–1912. *Au monastère: esquisse pour la harpe, op. 29*. Paris: Durand & Fils, n.d. 5 pp.

936. ———. *Aubade: pour la harpe, op. 30*. Paris: Durand, [19—]. 5 pp.

937. ———. *Ballade: pour la harpe*. Paris: A. Leduc, [19—]. 11 pp.

938. ———. *Ballade: pour la harpe*. Ross, Calif.: Harp Publications, [19—]. 11 pp.

939. ———. *Barcarolle: pour la harpe, op. 7*. Paris: Durand, [19— ?]. 7 pp.

940. ———. *Berceuse: pour harpe, op. 2*. Paris: Durand, [19—]. 7 pp.

941. ———. *Berceuse: pour harpe*. Paris: Billaudot, c1986. 7 pp. (La harpe)

942. ———. *Chanson de mai: romance sans paroles pour la harpe, op. 40*. Paris: Durand, [19—]. 7 pp.

943. ———. *Chanson de mai: romance sans paroles pour la harpe, op. 40*. [London]: Salvi Publications, 1990. 7 pp.

944. ———. *Chasses: petite pièce caractéristique pour la harpe, op. 36*. Paris: Durand, [19—]. 5 pp.

945. ———. *Confidence: romance sans paroles pour la harpe, op. 24*. Paris: Durand, [19—]. 5 pp.

946. ———. *Conte de Noël = A Christmas story, op. 33: pour la harpe*. Paris: G. Billaudot, c1982. 8 pp. (La harpe)

947. ———. *Élégie, op. 54: pour la harpe*. Paris: Durand & Fils, n.d. 7 pp.

948. ———. *Élégie, op. 54: pour harpe*. Paris: G. Billaudot, c1991. 7 pp. (La harpe)

949. ———. [Etude mélodique, harp, op. 35] *Etude mélodique: pour la harp, op. 35*. Paris: Durand, [19—]. 5 pp.

950. ———. [Etudes, harp, op. 37, B♭ major] *Etude en si-bémol majeur: pour la harpe, op. 37*. Paris: A. Durand, [189–?]. 7 pp.

951. ———. *Feuilles d'automne: 3 improvisations faciles pour la harpe*. Paris: Durand, [19—]. 8 pp. CONTENTS: Sérénade mélancolique, op. 45; Crépuscule, op. 46; Calme, op. 47.

952. ———. *Fileuse: etude caracteristique pour la harpe, op. 27*. Paris: Philippo, c1892. 10 pp.

953. ———. *Fileuse: Marguerite au rouet: étude caractéristique pour la harpe, op. 27*. Paris: Éditions M. Combre, n.d. 10 pp.

954. ———. *Fileuse: Marguerite au rouet: étude caractéristique pour la harpe, op. 27*. Paris: S. Chapelier, c1892. 10 pp.

955. ———. *Follets: caprice-étude pour la harpe, op. 48*. Paris: Durand, [19—]. 7 pp.

956. ———. *Gitana: caprice pour la harpe*. Paris: A. Durand & Fils, n.d. 11 pp.

957. ———. *Gitana: caprice pour la harpe*. Ross, Calif.: Harp Publications, [19—]. 9 pp.

958. ———. *Gitana: caprice pour la harpe*. New York, N.Y.: Salvi Harps, [19—]. 9 pp.

959. ———. *Gitana: caprice for the harp, op. 21*. New York: Kalmus, [197–?]. 11 pp. (Kalmus harp series, no. 4684)

960. ———. *Gitana: caprice pour la harpe*. Paris: G. Billaudot, c1982. 11 pp. (La harpe) "Op. 21."

961. ———. *Gnomes: caprice caractéristique pour la harpe, op. 49*. Paris: A. Durand & Fils, n.d. 5 pp.

962. ———. *Gnomes: caprice caractéristique pour la harpe, op. 49*. Paris: Billaudot, 1991. 7 pp.

963. ———. *Gondoliera: 2e barcarolle pour la harpe, op. 39*. Paris: Durand, [19—]. 5 pp.

964. ———. *Gondoliera, op. 39: 2e barcarolle pour harpe*. Paris: G. Billaudot, c1991. 7 pp. (La harpe)

965. ———. *Guitare: pièce caractéristique: pour la harpe*. Paris: Alphonse Leduc, n.d. 7 pp.

966. ———. *Guitare: pièce caractéristique: pour la harpe*. Paris: Gay, [1900?]. 7 pp.

967. ———. *Harpe d'Eole: nocturne pour la harpe, op. 32*. Paris: Leduc, [19—]. 7 pp.

968. ———. *Lamento: pour la harpe, op. 23*. Paris: Durand & Fils, [19—]. 5 pp.

969. ———. *Mazurka: pour la harpe, op. 31*. Paris: Durand, [19—]. 5 pp.

970. ———. *Menuet: pour la harpe, op. 34*. Paris: Durand, [19—]. 5 pp.

971. ———. *Nocturne: pour la harpe, op. 43*. Paris: Durand, [19—]. 5 pp.

972. ———. *Orientale: pour la harpe, op. 38*. Paris: Durand, [19—]. 9 pp.

973. ———. *Patrouille: petite marche caractéristique pour harpe.* Paris: Edition S. Chapelier, n.d. 5 pp.

974. ———. *Patrouille: petite marche caractéristique pour harpe.* Paris: Noël, [19—]. 5 pp.

975. ———. *Patrouille: petite marche caractéristique pour harpe.* Paris: L. Philippo, Editeur, [19—?]. 5 pp.

976. ———. *Petite berceuse: pour harpe.* Paris: Alphonse Leduc, c1961. 2 pp.

977. ———. *Petite valse, op. 25: pour la harpe.* Paris: G. Billaudot, c1985. 5 pp. (La harpe)

978. ———. [Petites bluettes] *Trois petites bluettes.* Paris: Gay & Tenton, n.d. 8 pp. CONTENTS: Istorietta; Ländler; Carillon.

979. ———. [Petites bluettes] *Trois petites bluettes: pour la harpe.* [New York?]: Lyra Music, [19—]. 8 pp. CONTENTS: Istorietta; Ländler; Carillon.

980. ———. [Petites bluettes] *Trois petites bluettes: pour la harpe.* Paris: Alphonse Leduc, c1950. 8 pp. CONTENTS: Istorietta; Ländler; Carillon.

981. ———. [Petites pièces faciles] *Trois petites pièces faciles: pour la harpe.* Paris: Durand; Bryn Mawr, Pa.: T. Presser, 1971. 7 pp. CONTENTS: Rêverie; Rouet; Ronde de nuit.

982. ———. [Petites pièces faciles] *Trois petites pièces faciles: pour la harpe.* Paris: Gérard Billaudot, [1986], c1985. 7 pp. (La harpe) CONTENTS: Rêverie; Rouet; Ronde de nuit.

983. ———. [Préludes, harp] *Trois préludes: pour la harpe.* Paris: Durand, [19—]. 3 v.

984. ———. *Prière: pour harpe.* Paris: René Gilles, n.d. 7 pp.

985. ———. *Prière: pour harpe.* Paris: Éditions Salabert, c1895. 7 pp.

986. ———. *Prière: pour harpe.* Paris: Magasin de musique du Conservatoire, [19—]. 7 pp.

987. ———. *Reverie: esquisse poètique d'après la Mignon de Goethe: pour harpe.* Paris: Leduc, 1891. 5 pp.

988. ———. *Romance: pour harpe.* Paris: Éditions S. Chapelier, [18—?]. 7 pp.

989. ———. *Romance: pour harpe.* Paris: A. Noel, [18—?]. 7 pp.

990. ———. [Romances sans paroles] *Deux romances sans paroles: pour harpe.* Paris: Louis Rouhier, n.d. 7 pp.

991. ———. [Sérénade, harp, op. 5] *Sérénade: pour harpe, op. 5.* Paris: Philippo, [189–?]. 7 pp.

992. ———. *La source, op. 44: étude pour la harpe.* [Santa Monica, Calif.]: Salvi Publications, [197–?]. 11 pp.

993. ———. *Valse de concert: pour harpe.* Paris: L. Philippo, n.d. 9 pp.

994. ———. *Valse de concert: pour harpe.* Paris: Noël, [19—]. 9 pp.

995. Hässy, Günter, 1944–. *Sechs romantische Stücke: für Harfe solo, op. 96a.* Pulheim: G. Hässy, c1991. 16 pp.

996. Haubenstock-Ramati, Roman, 1919–1994. *Cathedrale: für Harfe.* Vienna: Alleiniger Vertrieb, Universal Edition, c1988. 8, 17 leaves. For 1–16 harps.

997. Haubiel, Charles, 1892–1978. [Miniatures, harp. Madonna] *Madonna.* Edited by Lucien Thomson. Northbrook, Ill.: Composers Press, c1953. 2 pp.

998. ———. [Miniatures, harp. Mystery] *A mystery.* Edited by Lucien Thomson. New York: Composers Press, c1953. 2 pp.

999. ———. [Miniatures, harp. Snowflakes] *Snowflakes.* Edited by Lucien Thomson. New York: Composers Press, c1953. 5 pp.

1000. ———. [Preludes, harp] *Four preludes: for harp.* Northbrook, Ill.: Composers Press, c1973. 7 pp.

1001. Hayakawa, Masaaki, 1934–. *Zwei impromptus: für Harfe = for harp.* Frankfurt: Zimmermann, c1984. 11 pp.

1002. Healey, Derek, 1936–. *Wake up!, op. 56: for harp.* S.l.: s.n., c1979. 9 pp.

1003. Hearne, John, 1937–. *Fra Eyjafiroi: for harp.* Abergavenny: Adlais, 1969. 5 pp.

1004. Heilmann, Harald, 1924–. *Sonata: per arpa.* Frankfurt am Main: W. Zimmermann, c1973. 15 pp.

1005. Hekster, Walter, 1937–. *Night journey: for harp solo.* Amsterdam: Donemus, 1990. 3 pp.

1006. Henry, Bénigne. [Sonatas, harp, no. 1, E♭ major] *Premiere sonate: pour la harpe: suivie d'un air varié, oeuvre IIme.* Paris: Corbaux, [1815?]. 15 pp. "Air italien" for harp: pp. 9–15.

1007. Henson-Conant, Deborah, 1953–. *Nataliana.* Ellensburg, Wash.: F.C. Publishing Co., c1987. 10 pp. (Solo series: harp)

1008. Herbert, Perig. *An dorgenn: pour harpe celtique.* Paris: A. Leduc, c1983. 3 pp. (Collection Carrousel) [NP]

1009. Herchet, Jorg, 1943–. *Komposition (I-III): für Harfe solo.* Herausgegeben von Katharina Hanstedt. Kassel: Bärenreiter, c1992. 16 pp.

1010. Heulyn, Meinir. *Telyn y werin.* [Wales]: Adlais, c1975–1976. 2 v. [NP] CONTENTS: Vol.1. Codiad yr Ehedydd; Merch Megan; Cader Idris; Blaenhafren; Llwyn Onn; Clychau'r Cantre; Cainc y Datgeiniaid; Caru Doli; Morfa Rhuddlan; Gwenynen Gwent; Y Ferch o'r Scêr; Moel yr Wyddfa; Llanofer; Y Bardd yn ei Awen.

Vol.2. Nos Galan; Pant Corlan yr Wyn; Pen Rhaw; Eryri Wen; Mathafarn; Tôn Alarch; Cainc Dafydd Broffwyd; Wyres Megan; Serch Hudol; Yr Hufen Melyn; Mwynder Corwen.

1011. ———, ed. *Telynor llys a chastell: casgliad o alawon gwerin ac alawon telyn mewn trefniadau gwreiddiol = A collection of Welsh harp airs and folksongs.* Y Fenni, Gwent: Adlais, c1981. 18 pp. CONTENTS: Rhyfelgyrch Capten Morgan; Dafydd y garreg wen; Y fwyalchen; Rhyfelgyrch Gwyr Harlech; Tros y garreg; Ymadawiad y brenin; Y ferch o blwy' Penderyn; Ar hyd y nos; Y deryn pur; Y gog lwydlas; Si hei lwli, 'mabi.

1012. Hindemith, Paul, 1895–1963. *Sonate: für Harfe.* Mainz: B. Schott's Söhne; New York: Associated Music Publishers, Inc., c1940. 15 pp.

1013. Hobbs, Christopher, 1950–. *Harp star-pieces.* London: Experimental Music Catalogue, [196–]. 12 pp.

1014. Hoberg, Margaret. *Clouds.* S.l.: Joe Nicomede, c1921. 2 pp.

1015. ———. *Country dance.* Boston: Arthur P. Schmidt, c1917. 5 pp.

1016. ———. *Lazy lane.* S.l.: Joe Nicomede, c1918. 2 pp.

1017. ———. *Log cabin sketches: two suites for the harp.* Boston: Oliver Ditson Co., c1920. 2 v. CONTENTS: Summer; Winter.

1018. ———. *Song without words.* Boston: Arthur P. Schmidt, c1917. 7 pp.

1019. ———. *Suite: for harp.* Boston: Ditson, c1912. 19 pp.

1020. ———. *Sunset on the lake.* S.l.: Joe Nicomede, c1921. 2 pp.

1021. Hochbrucker, Christian 1733-ca. 1799. *Sonate: en sol majeur: pour harpe, [op. 1], no. 6.* Restitution et révision de France Vernillat. Paris: Editions Ouvrières, 1969. 10 pp. (L'Astree: collection de musique instrumentale classique)

1022. Hoddinott, Alun, 1929–. *Fantasy: [for harp], op. 68, no. 2.* London: Oxford University Press, 1972. 7 pp.

1023. ———. *Sonata: for harp, [op. 36].* London: Oxford University Press, 1967. 15 pp.

1024. ———. *Suite: for harp, [op. 52].* London: Oxford University Press, c1968. 12 pp. CONTENTS: Capriccio; Sarabanda; Giga.

1025. Hoffman, Joel, 1953–. *Sonata: for harp.* New York: Galaxy Music Corp., c1984. 19 pp.

1026. Holden, Smolett, ed. *A collection of old established Irish slow & quick tunes.* Arranged for the harp, piano forte or bagpipes. Dublin: S. Holden, [1804–1806]. 2 v. (36, 39 pp.).

1027. Holliger, Heinz, 1939–. *Sequenzen über Johannes I, 32: für Harfe.* Mainz: B. Schott's Söhne, 1965. 8 pp. "This piece can be played between two versions of *Moblie for oboe and harp* (Edition Schott 5384)."

1028. Holst, Gustavus. *Fleuve du tage: with variations for the harp*. London: G. Holst, [182–?]. 5 pp. "No. 2 of Popular airs for the harp."

1029. ———. *Will you come to the bower?: a popular air with variations for the harp*. London: Royal Harmonic Institution, [18—]. 9 pp.

1030. Holst, M. (Matthias), 1767–1854. *The jubilee rondo: for the harp or piano forte*. London: Printed by W. Hodsoll, 1810? 7 pp.

1031. Holý, Alfred, 1866–1948. *Am Spinnrad: Charakterstück Es-dur: für Harfe, op. 3*. Berlin: Carl Simon, c1896. 14 pp.

1032. ———. *Elegie: für Harfe solo, op. 17A*. Berlin: Carl Simon, c1912. 7 pp.

1033. ———. [Etudes, harp, op. 20] *Twelve studies: for harp, op. 20*. Berlin: Carl Simon, c1912. 32 pp.

1034. ———. *Evening at home: four easy pieces for the harp, op. 24*. Boston: Oliver Ditson, c1918. 9 pp.

1035. ———. *Fantasiestück: g moll: für Harfe, op. 8*. Berlin: Carl Simon, c1897. 13 pp.

1036. ———. *Idyll, op. 4, no. 1*. Berlin: Carl Simon, c1896. 7 pp.

1037. ———. *Impromptu, Des-dur: für Harfe, op. 11*. Berlin: Carl Simon, c1902. 13 pp.

1038. ———. *In toyland: op. 30, six easy pieces*. Reprint ed. New York: Lyra Music Co., [1979?]. 12 pp.

1039. ———. [Kleine Stücke, op. 12, no. 1] *Drei kleine Stücke, op. 12, no. 1*. Bayreuth: Carl Giessel, c1901. 9 pp.

1040. ———. [Kleine Stücke, op. 12, no. 1] *Drei kleine Stücke, op. 12, no. 1*. Leipzig: Jul. Heinr. Zimmermann, c1901. 9 pp.

1041. ———. [Lyrische Stücke] *Three lyric pieces: for the harp, op. 1*. New York: Edwin F. Kalmus, [197–?]. 11 pp. (Kalmus harp series, no. 4685) CONTENTS: Erzählung; Wiegenliedchen; Gondellied.

1042. ———. [Lyrische Stücke] *Three lyric pieces: for the harp, op. 1*. Melville, N.Y.: Belwin Mills, [198–?]. 11 pp. (Kalmus string series, 4685) CONTENTS: Erzählung; Wiegenliedchen; Gondellied.

1043. ———. *Mazurka: for harp, op. 28*. New York: Carl Fischer, c1922. 11 pp.

1044. ———. *Noël: Canzoncina a Maria Vergine: berceuse*. Brooklyn, N.Y.: Edition Le Grand Orgue, [195–?]. 7 pp.

1045. ———. [Sketches, harp, op. 25] *Three sketches: for the harp, op. 25*. Boston: Oliver Ditson, c1918. 5 pp.

1046. ———. [Studies, harp, op. 26] *Twenty-four easy studies: for the harp = Vingt quatre études faciles*. New York: Lyra Music Co., n.d. 20 pp.

1047. ———. [Studies, harp, op. 26] *Twenty-four easy studies: for the harp, op. 26.* Boston: Ditson, c1918. 20 pp.

1048. ———. [Technische Studien] *Technical studies: for harp = Technische Studien: für Harfe.* Vienna, New York: Universal Edition, c1923. 2 v. CONTENTS: Vol.1, nos. 1–331; Vol.2, nos. 332–691.

1049. ———. [Tonbilder] *Zwei Tonbilder: für Harfe, op. 4.* Berlin: Carl Simon, c1896. 7 pp.

1050. ———. [Vortragsstücke] *Drei Vortragsstücke: für Harfe, op. 7.* Berlin: Carl Simon, c1897. 2 v. CONTENTS: Arabeske; Herbstlied; Spanischer Tanz.

1051. Hook, Mr. (James), 1746–1827. *Le ruisseau: a favorite bagatelle for the harp or piano forte.* London: Bland & Wellers, n.d. 3 pp.

1052. Hoor, Emanuel. *Prelude: pour harpe chromatique.* Leipzig: C.F.W. Siegel, n.d. 7 pp.

1053. Houdy, Pierick, 1929–. *Jeux de mains, jeux d'esprit: pour petite ou grande harpe.* [Santa Monica, Calif.]: Salvi, 1979. 20 pp. [NP]

1054. ———. *Sonate: pour harpe.* Paris: Alphonse Leduc, c1955. 11 pp.

1055. ———. *Telenn: sonate pour harpe sans pédales.* Santa Monica, Calif.: Salvi Publications, c1983. 11 pp. [NP]

1056. Hovhaness, Alan, 1911–. *Nocturne: for harp, op. 20, no. 1.* New York, N.Y.: C.F. Peters, c1966. 6 pp.

1057. ———. [Sonatas, harp, op. 127] *Sonata: harp solo, [op. 127].* New York: C.F. Peters, c1957. 12 pp.

1058. ———. [Sonatas, koto, op. 110] *Two sonatas: for koto (cheng or harp), op. 110.* New York: C. F. Peters, c1963. 5 pp.

1059. ———. *Suite: for harp, op. 270.* New York: Associated Music Publishers, Inc., 1974. 16 pp.

1060. Hua, Lin, and Chang, Shao-Lei, arrs. *The cherry blossoms.* Transcribed Lin Hua, Shao-Lei Chang; edited by Aristid Von Würtzler. Santa Monica, Calif.: Salvi Publications, c1983. 4 pp.

1061. ———, arrs. *The voice of youth: for solo harp.* Transcribed Lin Hua, Shao-Lei Chang; edited by Aristid Von Würtzler. Santa Monica, Calif.: Salvi Publications, c1983. 5 pp.

1062. Huber, Georg Walter. *Valse caprice: [für Harfe Solo], op. 12.* [Liepzig: J.H. Zimmermann], c1902. 9 pp.

1063. Huber, Nicolaus A., 1939–. *Turmgewächse: für Harfe = Tower growths: for harp.* Wiesbaden: Breitkopf & Härtel, c1984. 12 leaves.

1064. Huber, Rupert. *Conductus: für Harfe und Orgel by Rupert Huber.* AnRa:

für Harfe by *Johannes Kotschy*. Salzburg: Arbeitsgemeinschaft der Eigenverleger, c1987. Score 33 pp. 1st work for harp and organ; 2nd work for harp solo.

1065. Huber, Walter Simon, 1898–1978. *Andante religioso, op. 5*. Leipzig: Zimmermann, c1902. 7 pp.

1066. Hughes, Pamela. *The playful unicorn*. Houston: Pantile Press, c1976. 5 pp. [NP]

1067. Hugon, Georges, 1904–1980. *Fantaisie: pour harpe*. Paris: Editions Musicales Transatlantiques, c1970. 8 pp.

1068. Hujsak, Joy, 1924–. [Easy birthday pieces] *Two easy birthday pieces: for non-pedal harp*. La Jolla, Calif.: Mina-Helwig Publishing Co., c1982. 2 pp. [NP] CONTENTS: Happy birthday; Well...

1069. ———. *Lullaby for Kirstie: harp solo*. La Jolla, Calif.: Mina-Helwig Publishing Co., c1981. 2 pp.

1070. ———. [Minis for first lesson] *Two mini's [sic] for first lesson*. La Jolla, Calif.: Mina-Helwig Publishing Co., n.d. 2 pp. [NP] CONTENTS: Grass hoppers; Jack jump over the candlestick.

1071. ———. *Song of the birds = El cant del ocells: solo for harp*. La Jolla, Calif.: Joy Hujsak, c1982. 6 pp.

1072. ———, arr. *A trilogy of hymns: solos for harp*. Arr. Joy Hujsak. La Jolla, Calif.: Mina-Helwig Publishing Co., c1982. 4, 4, 2 pp. CONTENTS: A mighty fortress; Fairest Lord Jesus; Abide with me.

1073. Hummel, Bertold, 1925–. *Andantino: für Harfe, op. 77e*. Hamburg: N. Simrock, c1987. 3 pp.

1074. ———. *Im Tempo eines Walzers*. Hamburg: N. Simrock, 1990. 2 pp.

1075. Hummel, Johann Nepomuk, 1778–1837. *Three sets of variations: for the piano forte or harp, opera 1*. [London]: Preston & Son, [1800]. 11 pp. CONTENTS: 1. The plough boy; 2. A German air; 3. La belle Catherine.

1076. Huré, Jean, 1877–1930. *Première sonate: pour piano [ou harpe chromatique]*. Paris: A.Z. Mathot, c1920. 13 pp.

1077. Hurník, Ilja, 1922–. *Tance pro harfu = Danze per arpa*. Prague: Panton, 1990. 12 pp.

1078. Huston, T. Scott, 1916–1991. *Suite of three*. New York: G. Schirmer, c1966. 15 pp. CONTENTS: Eulogy; Dance; Improvisation.

1079. Hyndman, Bonnie, 1915–. *More pieces for Tara: intermediate for non-pedal harp*. La Mesa, Calif.: Bonnie Hyndman, c1985. 11 pp. [NP] CONTENTS: Reverie; Jimmy O'Rourke; Prelude; Lotus blossom; Interlude.

1080. ———. [Pieces for Tara] *Ten pieces for Tara: easy to intermediate pieces for non-pedal harp*. La Mesa, Calif.: [Bonnie Hyndman], c1981. 20 pp. [NP] CONTENTS: Perpetual three; Louise; Glide a bit; Little serenade; Remembrance; Exhibit; Country tune; View of the chateau; Summer song; Asilomar.

1081. Iakhnina, Evgeniia Iosifovna, 1918–. *Akvareli: tsikl p'es dlia arfy.* Moscow: Sov. kompozitor, c1976. 23 pp. For harp.

1082. Ibert, Jacques, 1890–1962. [Pièces, harp] *Six pièces: pour harpe à pédales.* Paris: Alphonse Leduc, c1917–1918. 6 v. CONTENTS: 1. Matin sur l'eau; 2. Scherzetto; 3. En barque le soir; 4. Ballade; 5. Reflets dans l'eau; 6. Fantasie.

1083. ———. *Reflections = Reflets dans l'eau: pour harpe à pédales.* Orem, Utah: SARO Publishing Co., n.d. 32 pp.

1084. Ingebos, Louise Marie. *Modes: pour harpe seule.* Paris: Jobert, c1980. 9 leaves.

1085. Inglefield, Ruth K. *Lieder for Laura: easy pieces for small fingers: non-pedal or pedal harp.* Santa Monica, Calif.: Salvi Publications, c1982. 10 pp. [NP] CONTENTS: Memories; Someday; By the green pond; Mysterious; Fireworks; After the fireworks.

1086. ———. *Solos for Sonja: easy pieces for small fingers: non-pedal or pedal harp.* [Santa Monica, Calif.]: Salvi Publications, c1976–1982. 2 v. [NP] CONTENTS: Vol.1. Waterfall; Jump and run; Falling leaves; Spinning top; Dancing fingers; Rain; Elephant parade.
Vol.2. Nocturne; Berceuse; Sarabande; Psalm; Lament; Improvisation.

1087. ———. *Songs for Sonja: easy pieces for small fingers: for troubadour or Irish harp.* [Santa Monica, Calif.]: Salvi Publications, c1972. 2 v. [NP] CONTENTS: Vol.1. Up and down; Fun song; Marching; Two at a time; Swinging song; Both hands; Crossing over; Over and over; Three finger dance; Wider and wider; Playing together; Somersault song; Sliding song.
Vol.2: Four-finger song; Merry-go-round; To the last stop; Up and down the mountain; Little waltz; Lullabye; Not sleepy; Skating; Skipping along; A song with a sharp; Dancing; Kittens playing; Very hard song; Rolling waves.

1088. Isambert, Muriel, 1949–. *Trois pièces: pour harpe celtique.* Brest: Centre Breton d'art populaire, 1983. 15 pp. [NP] CONTENTS: Yeun elez; Me a zavo eun dourell; A hader.

1089. Ishii, Maki, 1936–. [Toki no hirameki] *A gleam of time: for harp solo, op. 53 (1983).* Celle: Moeck, 1985. 9 pp.

1090. Jacoby, Hanoch, 1909–. *Canzona: harp solo.* Tel Aviv: Israeli Music Publications; New York: Leeds Music Corp., 1962. 7 pp.

1091. Jacquet, H. Maurice, 1885–1954. *Cantique à l'ancienne.* Paris: Éditions de la Sirène, c1920. 7 pp.

1092. ———. *The cuckoo clock: composition for piano or harp in olden style, op. 1.* Boston: C.C. Birchard, c1927. 6 pp.

1093. ———. *Papillons gris = Gray butterflies.* Boston: C.C. Birchard, c1927. 13 pp.

1094. Jay, Charles. *Divertissement: pour harpe.* Paris: Alphonse Leduc, c1968. 6 pp.

1095. Jersild, Jörgen, 1913–. *Fantasia: per arpa sola.* Copenhagen: Wilhelm Hansen Musik-Forlag, c1977. 11 pp. (Libro d'arpa, v. 4)

1096. ———. *Pezzo elegiaco.* Copenhagen: Wilhelm Hansen Musik-Forlag, c1969. 20 pp. (Libro d'arpa, v. 1)

1097. John, Patricia, 1916–. *Americana: suite [for] harp.* Houston: Pantile Press, c1978. 3 v. in 1. CONTENTS: Preamble; A time of snow; Imago ignato = Unknown image.

1098. ———. *Aprille: music for harp alone.* Houston, Texas: Pantile Press, c1969. 7 pp.

1099. ———. *Circles.* Houston, Tex.: Pantile Press, 1991. 4 pp.

1100. ———. *The gothic harp and its music.* Houston, Tex.: The Pantile Press, c1987. 23 pp. Collection of music for the gothic harp from the 13th–16th centuries. CONTENTS: Rondel (XIII cent.); Lai d'yseut (XIV cent.); Rondel (XIII cent.) by Anon. 5 branles; Gaillarde; Tourdion by Attaingnant.

1101. ———. *Henriette: un portrait: music for harp alone.* Houston, Tex.: Pantile Press, c1974. 9 pp.

1102. ———. *Let's play: harp (pedal or non-pedal).* Houston, Texas: Pantile Press, 1975. 3 v. [NP] CONTENTS: Clown dance; Arithmetic; Canoe.

1103. ———. *Mnemosyne: music for harp alone.* Houston, Texas: Pantile Press, c1969. 7 pp.

1104. ———. *Paradigm for the harp.* Houston, Tex.: Pantile Press, 1992. 7 pp.

1105. ———. *Prelude to summer.* Houston, Tex.: The Pantile Press, c1990. 7 pp.

1106. ———. *Sea anemones: harp (pedal or non-pedal).* Houston, Tex.: The Pantile Press, 1982. 3 pp. [NP]

1107. ———. *Sea changes: suite of three pieces for harp alone.* New York: Pantile Press, c1968. 11 pp. CONTENTS: Fog off pelican spit; Summer squall; Surf.

1108. ———. *Serenata: for harp.* Houston, Tex.: Pantile Press, c1981. 5 pp.

1109. ———. *Sonnerie = Bells.* Houston, Tex.: The Pantile Press, c1990. 3 pp. For harp solo (pedal or non-pedal). [NP]

1110. ———. *Tachystos = Swift: music for one or several harps.* Houston, Texas: Pantile Press, c1971. 14 pp.

1111. ———. *The voyage of the Elissa: harp (pedal or non-pedal).* Houston, Tex.:

The Pantile Press, c1985. 10 leaves. [NP] CONTENTS: The bosun's whistle; The Curlew; Serenia; The Narwhal; Scrimshaw.

1112. ———. *The wind rose: harp (pedal or non-pedal)*. Houston, Tex.: The Pantile Press, c1983. 2 pp. [NP]

1113. Jolas, Betsy, 1926–. *Tranche: pour harpe seule*. Paris: Heugel, 1968. 2 pp.

1114. Jolivet, André, 1905–1974. [Prélude, harp] *Prélude: pour harpe*. London: Boosey and Hawkes, c1966. 4 pp.

1115. Jollet, Jean-Clément. [Petits mouvements] *Trois petits mouvements: pour harpe celtique*. Paris: G. Billaudot, c1990. 8 pp. (La harpe) [NP]

1116. Jones, Edward, 1752–1824. *Maltese melodies: or, National airs, and dances usually performed by the Maltese musicians at their carnival, & other festivals: with a few other characteristic Italian airs & songs: to these are annex'd a selection of Norwegian tunes, never before published: and to which are added basses for the harp or piano forte*. London: Printed for the Editor, [ca. 1800]. 40 pp.

1117. ———. *The musical and poetical relicks of the Welsh bards: preserved by tradition, and authentic manuscripts, from remote antiquity, never before published. To the tunes are added variations for the harp, harpsichord, violin, or flute. With a choice collection of the pennillion, epigrammatic stanzas, or, native pastoral sonnets of Wales, with English translations. Likewise a history of the bards from the earliest period to the present time, and an account of their music, poetry, and musical instruments, with a delineation of the latter*. London: Robert Morley and Co., 1985. xii, 78 pp. Arr. for keyboard instrument or harp, many pieces with figured bass. Facsimile reprint of the 1784 London edition. A second volume was published in 1802 under title *The bardic museum*; and a third volume, in 1820, under the title *Hên ganiadau cymru*.

1118. Jones, Elsbeth M. *Tannau teifi: alawon telyn*. [Aberystwyth]: Cyhoeddwyd gan yr Awdur, 1978. 16 pp. [NP] CONTENTS: Pen dinas; Plascrug; Yr hafod; Craig y pistyll; Cwmystwyth; Llwyn yr eos; Craig yr efail; Blodau glyn dyfi.

1119. Jongen, Joseph, 1873–1953. *Valse: pour harpe, op. 73*. Brussels: Chez l'auteur, 1924. 10 pp.

1120. ———. *Valse: pour harpe, op. 73*. Brussels: CeBeDeM, c1987. 8 pp.

1121. Kanno, Yoshihiro. *Transparent mirror: for harp*. Tokyo: Ongaku No Tomo, c1988. 20 pp.

1122. Kastner, Alfred, 1870–1948. [Esquisses, harp] *Deux esquiesses: pour harpe*. Leipzig: J.H. Zimmermann, c1913. 11 pp. CONTENTS: Mélancholie; Joie.

1123. ———. [Étude de concert, harp, no. 1] *Première étude de concert: pour harpe, op. 17*. Paris: Henry Lemoine & Cie., c1912. 11 pp.

1124. ———. [Etudes, harp, op. 2] *Ten etudes: for the harp, op. 2.* New York: Kalmus, [197–?]. 33 pp. (Kalmus harp series, no. 4686)

1125. ———. [Etudes, harp, op. 7] *Zwei Etüden, op. 7.* Leipzig: Friedrich Hofmeister, [189–?]. 11 pp.

1126. ———. [Leichte Übungen] *50 leichte Übungen f. Pedalharfe, op. 11.* Leipzig: Wilhelm Zimmermann, n.d. 2 v. [NP] CONTENTS: Vol.1. Übung 1–25 (ohne Pedale); Vol.2. Übung 26–50 (mit Pedalen).

1127. ———. [Leichte Übungen. Selections] *25 easy studies.* Rev. and ed. Kathy Bundock Moore. Ellensburg, Wash.: F.C. Publishing Co., 1993. 48 pp.

1128. ———. [Morceaux faciles] *Deux morceaux faciles (sans pedales): [pour] harpe, op. 10.* Leipzig: J.H. Zimmermann, [190–?]. 8 pp. [NP]

1129. Kastner, Macario Santiago, 1908-, ed. *Sette pezzi: per arpa: dei secoli XVII e XVIII tratti da antichi manoscritti spagnoli e portoghesi.* Trascrizione in notazione moderna e revisione di M. S. Kastner. Milan: Edizioni Suvini Zerboni, 1972. 21 pp. CONTENTS: Paseos by di Anonimo; Aria e menuete ayrozo by di A. Principe. Partita by Anon. Tocata para el harpa by di A. Corelli. Tocata segunda; Sonata en sol mayor by J. Rodriguez. Sonata para arpa by Anon.

1130. Kelkel, Manfred, 1929–. *Melancolia & Mirabilis: zwei Stücke für Harfe solo, op. 23.* Berlin: Bote & Bock, c1978. 7 pp.

1131. Keller, Ginette, 1925–. *Vibrations: pour harpe celtique.* Paris: G. Billaudot, c1990. 5 pp. (La harpe) [NP]

1132. Kessner, Daniel, 1946–. *Sonatina: for solo harp: 1969.* New York: Alexander Broude Inc., c1971. 11 pp.

1133. Khachaturian, Aram Ilich, 1903–1978. [Pièces, harp] *Deux pièces: pour harpe.* [Paris]: Le Chant du Monde, c1975. 15 pp. CONTENTS: Danse orientale; Toccata.

1134. ———. [Pièces, harp] *Two pieces: for the harp.* Edited by Vera Dulova. [London]: Salvi Publications, [198–?]. 11 pp. CONTENTS: Oriental dance; Toccata.

1135. Khristova, Milina, ed. *Piesi: za arfa ot bulgarski kompozitori.* Sustavila i redaktirala Milina Khristova. Sofia: Nauka i izkustvo, 1972. 35 pp. CONTENTS: Tri etiuda; Preliud by D. Tupkov. Pastoral i tants by St. Ikonomov.

1136. Kikta, V. (Valerii Grigorevich), 1941–. [Harp music. Selections] *Proizvedeniia: dlia arfy.* Moscow: Sov. kompozitor, 1985. 112 pp. CONTENTS: Iz Ossiana; Diptakh po skulpturam A. Burdelia; Romanticheskie variatsii na temu Stanislava Liudkevicha; Sonata lamento; Bylinnye zvukoriady; Fantaziia na temy opery P. I. Chaikovskogo "Pikovaia dama"; U tleiushchego kamina.

1137. ———. [P'esy po skulpturam burdelia] *Dve p'esy po skul'pturam burdelia, soch. 46 (1972).* Redaktsiia O. G. Erdeli. Moscow: Muzyka, c1980. 19 pp. CONTENTS: Safo; Umiraiushchii kentavr.

1138. King, Harold C., 1895–. *Introduzione e toccata: per arpa.* Amsterdam: Donemus, c1966. 14 pp.

1139. Klebe, Giselher, 1925–. *Alborada: per arpa sola, op. 77.* Kassel: Bärenreiter, c1977. 20 pp.

1140. Kleemann, Hans, 1883–1958. [Präludium und Chaconne, harp, op. 29, C minor] *Präludium und Chaconne, op. 29: für Harfe solo (c-Moll).* Leipzig: Hofmeister, c1955. 7 pp.

1141. Klein, Virginia, ed. *Playing the masters: for the troubadour or pedal harp.* [Ed. by Virginia Klein]. Dallas: Little Pub. House, 1974–. 4 v. [NP]

1142. Kleinsinger, George, 1914–1982. *Pavane for Seskia: for harp.* Edited by Pearl Chertok. New York: Tetra Music Corp., c1977. 4 pp.

1143. Knight, Judyth, 1936–. *Fiesta: for solo harp.* Edited by Sioned Williams. London: Lopes Edition, c1988. 6 pp.

1144. Koch, Erland von, 1910–. *Monolog 12: harpa: [La primavera].* Stockholm: Carl Gehrmans Musikförlag, c1978. 10 pp.

1145. Koch, Frederick, 1923–. *Hexadic dance: for harp solo.* New York: Seesaw Music, c1972. 7 pp.

1146. Kogbetlieva, L., ed. *Pesy sovetskikh kompozitorov = Character pieces by Soviet composers: for harp.* Edited by L. Kogbetlieva. Moscow: Muzyka, 1988. 63 pp.

1147. Köhler, Wolfgang, 1923–. *Variationen: für Harfe uber ein Thema von Joh. Seb. Bach in der Bearbeitung von Johannes Brahms, opus 62.* Berlin: Verlag Merseburger, c1984. 15 pp. (Edition Merseburger, 2072) Theme by J.S. Bach (Chaconne from solo violin Partita, BWV 1004) as arranged by Brahms for piano, left hand.

1148. Kohn, Karl, 1926–. *Son of prophet bird: paraphrase for solo harp.* New York: Carl Fischer, Inc., c1977. 15 pp. Based on the composer's earlier composition *The prophet bird.*

1149. Kong, Chen. *Landscape in the sunset: for solo harp.* Edited by Aristid Von Würtzler. Santa Monica, Calif.: Salvi Publications, c1983. 8 pp.

1150. *Kontsertnye p'esy: dlia arfy.* Moscow: Izd-vo "Muzyka," 1972. 64 pp. CONTENTS: Sonata by Tailleferre. Variatsii, soch. 30 by Salzedo. Rondo-sonata by Baltin. Sonata by Smirnova.

1151. Kostelanetz, André, 1901–1980. *Lake Louise: harp solo.* Boston: Oliver Ditson, c1928. 3 pp.

1152. Kreiss, Hulda E., 1924–, ed. *Compositions of David Loeb, Hulda E. Kreiss,*

Rudolf Forst. [Ed. by Hulda E. Kreiss]. Delray Beach, Fla.: Accentuate Music, 1989. Score 33 pp. CONTENTS: Norse song by Schumann, tr. Kreiss. Pushkin's love song by Adolf G. H. Kreiss. Evening prayer from Hänsel and Gretel by Humperdinck, tr. Kreiss. From a railway carriage; Sequences by Forst. Partita for trombone and harp by Loeb.

1153. Krenek, Ernst, 1900–1991. *Sonata: for harp.* Kassel: Bärenreiter, c1959. 8 pp.

1154. Kresky, Jeffrey, 1948–. *Vox clamantis: for solo harp.* New York: American Composers Alliance, c1976. 7 pp. (Composers facsimile edition)

1155. Kröll, Georg, 1934–. *Passamezzo: für Harfe = for harp.* Cologne: Gerig, c1983. 4 pp.

1156. Krumpholz, Jan Křtitel, 1742–1790. *Air et variations: para arpa.* Revision, Nicanor Zabaleta. Madrid: Unión Musical Española, c1986. 13 pp.

1157. ———. [Harp music. Selections] *Oeuvres choisies: pour harpe.* Edition par Marie-Françoise Thiernesse-Baux. Paris: Heugel, c1982. 2 v. (vii, 215 pp.). (Le pupitre, L.P. 63-L.P. 64) Pref. by M.-F. Thiernesse-Baux in French and English. CONTENTS: Vol.1. 12 préludes et petits airs: op. 2; 2e sonate de l'op. 3; 6e sonate de l'op. 8; 6e concerto op. 9.
Vol.2. 1re symphonie op. 11; 2e symphonie op. 11; 1re sonate de l'op. 15; 2e sonate de l'op. 15: Scène de demi-caractère; Andante de Haydn.

1158. ———. [Preludes, harp. Selections] *Préludes: 1 (la bémol majeur); 6 (sol mineur); 10 (la mineur): pour harpe.* Restitution et révision de France Vernillat. Paris: Editions ouvrières, 1969. 18 pp. (L'Astrée: collection de musique instrumentale classique)

1159. ———. [Recueil de petits airs variés, harp, op. 10. Variations on an air by Mozart] *Variations on an air by Mozart: for the harp: from Recueil de petits airs variés, op. X.* Ross, Calif.: Harp Publications, c1970. 7 pp. The air is from Mozart's Serenade in D major "The Haffner."

1160. ———. [Recueil de petits airs variés, harp, op. 10. Variations on an air of Marlborough] *Variations on an Air of Marlborough: for the harp: from Recueil de petits airs variés, op. X.* Edited by Alice Lawson. San Anselmo, Calif.: A. Lawson, 1970. 5 pp.

1161. ———. [Recueil de petits airs variés, harp, op. 10. Variations on the air Jay du bon tabac] *Variations on the air Jay du bon Tabac: for the harp: from Recueil de petits airs variés, op. X.* Edited by Alice Lawson. San Anselmo, Calif.: A. Lawson, 1970. 5 pp.

1162. ———. [Sonatas, harp, B♭ major] *Sonata: pro harfu: B-dur.* Revidovala M. Zunová. V Kutne Hore: Ceska Hudba, [19—?]. 6 pp.

1163. ———. [Sonatas, harp, B♭ major] *Sonata: in B♭ major: for harp.* Amsterdam: Broekmans & Van Poppel, c1969. 10 pp.

1164. ———. [Sonatas, harp, C minor] *Sonata no. VI: in C minor: for harp.* Annotated, fingered and edited for twentieth-century harp by Marcia X. Johnstone. [S.l.]: Marcia X. Johnstone, 1955. 26 pp.

1165. ———. [Sonatas, harp, op. 12] *Quatre sonates non difficilles: pour la harpe seule ou avec accompagnement d'un violon et violoncelle.* London: R. Birchall, between 1789 and 1819. parts. For harp solo or harp, violin, and violoncello.

1166. ———. [Sonatas, harp, op. 12] *Quatre sonates non difficiles: pour la harpe seule, ou avec acc. d'un violon et violoncelle, oeuvre 12.* Nouv. éd. Paris: B. Viguerie, [181–]. 3 parts. For harp; or, harp, violin, and violoncello.

1167. ———. [Sonatas, harp, op. 12] *Four sonatas: for the harp, opus 12.* Edited by Alice Lawson. San Anselmo, Calif.: A. Lawson, c1970. 12, 11, 10, 10 pp. CONTENTS: No. 1, F major; no. 2, E♭ major; no. 3, G major; no. 4, F major.

1168. ———. [Sonatas, harp, op. 13] *Four sonatas for the harp, opus XIII: practicable also for the piano with table of adaptation by the composer.* Edited by Alice Lawson Aber. Ross, Calif.: Harp Publications, 1974. 6, 13, 11, 13 pp. CONTENTS: No. 1, B♭ major; no. 2, E♭ major; no. 3, C major; no. 4, G major.

1169. ———. [Sonatas, harp, op. 13] *Quatre sonates d'une difficulté graduelle: pour la harpe, praticables sur le forte piano, avec acc. d'un violin ad lib., oeuvre 13me.* Paris: H. Naderman, [18—?]. 2 parts. For harp; or, piano and violin.

1170. ———. [Sonatas, harp, op. 15, no. 1, F major] *Sonate: für Harfe.* Hrsg. von Hans J. Zingel. Mainz: B. Schott's Söhne; New York: Associated Music Publishers, Inc., c1966. 19 pp.

1171. ———. [Sonatas, harp, op. 18, no. 1, D minor] *Sonata no. 1: from Two sonatas for the harp in the form of scenes of different character, practicable also for the piano, opus XVIII.* Edited by Alice Lawson Aber. Ross, Calif.: Harp Publications, 1974. iii, 7 pp.

1172. ———. *Variations on a theme of Haydn.* [Santa Monica, Calif.]: Salvi, 1977. 8 pp.

1173. Krzywicki, Jan. *Starscape: for solo harp.* Philadelphia: Jan Krzywicki, 1983. 9 pp.

1174. Kufferath, Jeanne Adrienne. *Deux pièces pour harpe.* Paris: Senart, n.d. 7 pp. CONTENTS: Simple histoire; Autrefois.

1175. Kunst, Jos, 1936–. *Outward bound: for harp solo.* Amsterdam: Donemus, c1971. 9 pp.

1176. Kunze, Hugo. *Fantasie helvetica, op. 5, no. 1.* Leipzig: Jul. Heinr. Zimmermann, c1917. 11 pp.

1177. Kushida, T. *Remember.* [China]: s.n., [1978?]. 8 pp.

1178. Kvandal, Johan, 1919–. *Sonata: for solo harp: the Heming ballad = Sonate: for harpe solo: Ballade om Hemingen unge, op. 63.* Oslo: Norsk Musikforlag, c1984. 11 pp.

1179. Kymlicka, Milan, 1936–. *Simple music: for harp.* Ed. Erica Goodman. [S.l.]: Cantus Publishing Co., 1985. 9 pp.

1180. Labarre, Théodore, 1805–1870. [Étude, harp, op. 30] *Grande étude: pour la harpe: composée de huit caprices, op. 30.* Révue et doigtée par Alph. Hasselmans. Paris: C. Joubert, [190–?]. 28 pp.

1181. ———. [Etude, harp, op. 30] *Grande etude, op. 30: pour la harpe: composée de huit caprices.* Revue et doigtée par Alphonse Hasselmans. Paris: Gérard Billaudot, c1982. 28 pp. (La harpe)

1182. ———. *Fantaisie et variations sur la ballade de Zampa: pour la harpe.* Paris: J. Meissonnier, n.d. 13 pp.

1183. ———. [Fantaisie et variations sur la romance du Pré aux clercs] *Fantaisie et variations: pour la harpe: sur la romance du Pré aux clercs de F. Herold, op. 63.* Mainz: Fils de B. Schott, [1833? or 1834?]. 13 pp.

1184. ———. [Fantaisie sur les motifs de l'opéra de Gustave] *Fantaisie: pour la harpe: sur les motifs de l'opéra de Gustave, ou, Le bal masqué de D. F. E. Auber, op. 66.* Mainz: Fils de B. Schott, [1833? or 1834?]. 11 pp.

1185. ———. [Fantasia, harp, op. 39] *Brilliant fantasia: for the harp, op. 39: introducing the three much admired Irish melodies Sly Patrick, The Moreen and Nora Creena.* London: Goulding & D'Almaine, [183–?]. 13 pp.

1186. ———. [Méthode complète de harpe. Etudes, nos. 1–20] *Twenty etudes for the harp.* Abergavenny, Gwent: Adlais, c1985. 29 pp.

1187. ———. *Ricordanza dei Puritani: fantaisie pour la harpe, op. 72.* Milan: J. Ricordi, [1835 or 1836]. 11 pp.

1188. ———. *Sonate de concert: pour la harpe, op. 92.* Mainz: B. Schott, [1821?]. 12 pp.

1189. ———. *Souvenirs irlandais: fantaisie pour la harpe, op. 32.* Paris: Brandus, [183–?]. 14 pp. CONTENTS: Introduction; Tema con variazioni; Adagio; Finale.

1190. Lancen, Serge, 1922–. *Récréation: pour harpe ou harpe celtique.* Paris: Editions Musicales Hortensia, c1974. 2 pp. [NP]

1191. ———. *Rêverie: pour harpe ou harpe celtique.* Paris: Éditions Musicales Hortensia, c1974. 2 pp. [NP]

1192. ———. *Si j'étais = If I were = Wäre ich.* Paris: Lido Melodies, c1982. 7 pp. CONTENTS: No. 37, Beethoven; no. 38, Grieg; no. 39, Tchaikowski.

1193. Landes, Bernard William, 1915–. *The fountain.* New York: Emerson Music Publications, 1950.

1194. Langer, Hans-Klaus, 1903–. [Fantasien, harp] *Tre fantasie: per arpa.* Berlin: Edition Corona, c1979. 11 pp. (Dokumentation ostdeutscher Komponisten)

1195. Lantoine, Louis, 1951–. *Trois études en forme de—: pour harpe.* Paris: Harposphere, c1989. 2, 9, 7 pp.

1196. Lanzi, Alessandro, 1936–. *Quattro pezzi per arpa.* Milan: Edizioni Suvini Zerboni, c1967. 12 pp.

1197. Laparra, Raoul, 1876–1943. *Rythmes espagnols: pour harpe chromatique.* Paris: Enoch, c1913. 17 pp.

1198. Lapitino, Francis J., 1879–1949. *Fantasia on melodies of Stephen Foster: Old folks at home and Massa's in the cold, cold ground, op. 25.* Transcribed for harp solo by Francis J. Lapitino. New York: International Music Pub. Co., [19—?]. 8 pp.

1199. ———. *Fedora gavotte.* Boston: O. Ditson, c1912. 7 pp.

1200. ———. *The harp.* New York: International Music, n.d. 11 pp.

1201. ———. *Valse caprice.* New York: International Music Pub. Co., c1917. 4 pp.

1202. ———. *Valse impromptu in C major, op. 4.* [Boston]: O. Ditson, c1914. 7 pp.

1203. La Presle, Jacques de, 1888–1969. *Le jardin mouillé: pour la harpe.* Paris: Alphonse Leduc, c1913. 12 pp.

1204. Larhantec, Marie-Annick. *Mouvements à la corde lisse: pour harpe celtique.* Paris: Gérard Billaudot, c1974. 13 pp. [NP] CONTENTS: Dialogue de Korrigans; Merlin au berceau; Chanson de Quête du Trégor; An durzunell = La tourterelle; Le moulin; Le baron de Javioz; An alarc'h = Le cygne; L'anneau de viviane; Promenade dans les chemins creux; Les bergers; Révérences; Marv Pontkallek = La mort de Pontcallec.

1205. Larivière, Edmond, 1811–1842. [Etudes, op. 9] *Exercices et etudes: pour la harpe, op. 9.* Revues et doigtées selon l'enseignement de Alphonse Hasselmans, par Raphaël Martenot. Paris: A. Leduc, c1946. 30 pp.

1206. ———. [Etudes, op. 9] *Exercices et etudes: pour la harpe.* Revues et doigtées selon l'enseignement de Alphonse Hasselmans. [New York]: Lyra Music Co., [196–?]. 30 pp.

1207. ———. *Fantaisie brillante: pour la harpe: sur l'opéra Lucie de Lamermoor de Donizetti, opera 22.* Paris: Bernard Latte, n.d. 13 pp.

1208. ———. *La folle: romance de Grisar: variée pour la harpe, op. 12.* Paris: B. Latte, [183–]. 11 pp.

1209. ———. *Les laveuses du couvent: caprice pour la harpe: sur la romance d'Albert Grisar, op. 15.* Paris: Bernard Latte, n.d. 12 pp.

1210. Larsen, Libby, 1950–. *Theme and deviations.* St. Paul, Minn.: Minnesota Composers Forum, c1973. 11 pp.

1211. ———. *Traige: three Irish moods for harp.* S.l.: s.n., c1977. 19 pp. CONTENTS: Suantraige (Sleep music); Goltraige (Grief music); Gentraige (Joy music).

1212. Laruelle, Jeanne Marie, 1934–. *Chansons et danceries: pour harpe celtique.* Paris: Jeanne Marie Laruelle, c1976. 8 pp. [NP] CONTENTS: Chansons: Légende; Chanson à bercer; Madrigal; Ballade. Danceries: Entrée-prélude; Ballerie; Allemande; Bransle gay.

1213. ———. *Châteaux: pour harpe celtique ou grande harpe.* Paris: J.M. Laruelle, c1982. 8 pp. [NP] CONTENTS: Le manoir; Le castel; Le donjon.

1214. ———. *Danses et toccata: pour harpe celtique.* Paris: Jeanne Marie Laruelle, c1964. 8 pp. [NP] CONTENTS: Rigaudon; Sarabande; Chaconne; Toccata.

1215. ———. *Joies: pour harpe celtique ou grande harpe.* Paris: Jeanne Marie Laruelle, c1977. 2 pp. CONTENTS: Joie de l'aube; Joie de midi; Joie du soir.

1216. ———. *Pavane: pour piano, clavecin ou grande harpe.* Paris: Jeanne Marie Laruelle, c1977. 2 pp. For piano, harpsichord or pedal harp.

1217. ———. *Printemps: pour harpe celtique ou grande harpe.* Paris: J.M. Laruelle, c1982. 2 pp. [NP] CONTENTS: Pervenche; Primevère; Perceneige; Pensée.

1218. Latour, T. *The blue bell of Scotland: with new variations for the piano forte or harp.* Baltimore: John Cole, [18—?]. 3 pp.

1219. Laurent, F. *Les souvenirs: collection d'airs variés pour la harpe.* Milan: J. Ricordi, [1823 or 1824]. 2 v. CONTENTS, Vol.2: Le carnaval de Venise; Duo dell'Italiana in Algeri, by Rossini; La ci darem la mano, by Mozart.

1220. Lavry, Marc, 1903–1967. *Five lyrical pieces: harp solo.* New York: Leeds Music Corp., [19—]. 15 pp. CONTENTS: Marche grotesque; Chant d'amour; Melodie orientale; Berceuse; Chanson orientale.

1221. Lawrence, Lucile, 1907–, ed. *Solos: for the harp player.* Selected and edited by Lucile Lawrence. New York: G. Schirmer, 1966. 72 pp. CONTENTS: Pavane by Anon., arr. Salzedo, Italian pavane by Antonio de Cabezón, arr. Lawrence. Fuga by Antonio de Cabezón, arr. Lawrence. Giga by Arcangelo Corelli, arr. Salzedo. Sarabande from Sonata VII, op. 5 by Arcangelo Corelli, arr. Owens. Gavotte by Arcangelo Corelli, arr. Owens. Rigaudon by Jean-Philippe Rameau, arr. Salzedo. Tambourin by Jean-Philippe Rameau, arr. Salzedo. Siciliano from Sonata in E♭ for flute and cembalo by Johann Sebastian Bach, arr. Owens. Chaconne by Marie-

Auguste Durand, arr. Salzedo. First arabesque by Claude Debussy, arr. Salzedo. Zarabanda from Partita in C by Joaquín Turina, arr. Stephanie Rappa-Curcio. Two Chinese folk songs by Chou Wen-Chung. Berceuse by Nicolas Flagello. Looking glass river by Rudolf Forst. Five preludes by Alojz Srebotnjak.

1222. Lawrence, Lucile, 1907–, and Salzedo, Carlos, 1885–1961. *The art of modulating = L'art de moduler: for harpists, pianists, organists: including modulating formulas, examples of modulations, extensions, cadenzas, and a complete illustration of harmonic fluxes (formerly called glissandi) by Lucile Lawrence and Carlos Salzedo; followed by ten fragments of dances and five easy characteristic pieces for harp by Carlos Salzedo.* New York: G. Schirmer, 1950. 61 pp.

————. *Method for the harp: fundamental exercises with illustrations and technical explanations = Méthode pour la harpe: exercises fondamentaux avec illustrations et explications techniques by Lucile Lawrence and Carlos Salzedo. Fifteen preludes for beginners = Quinze préludes pour commençants by Carlos Salzedo.* See 50.

————. *Pathfinder studies: for the troubadour or Irish-type harp.* See 51.

1223. Lebano, Felice, 1867–1916. *Tristesse: romance sans paroles pour la harpe.* Milan; New York: G. Ricordi, [19—?]. 7 pp.

1224. *Lectures a vue: de la Fédération Nationale des Unions de Conservatoires Municipaux de Musique.* Paris: Editions M. Combre, c1979. 14, 9 pp. [NP] CONTENTS: Grande harpe; Petite harpe.

1225. Le Dentu, Odette, 1900–, ed. *Variations sur un thème de Mozart: pour la harpe celtique.* Auteur inconnu (18e–19e siècle); [édité] par O. Le Dentu. Paris: G. Billaudot, c1980. 7 pp. (La harpe)

1226. Ledet, Marlene Shepard. *Of rhymes and seasons: a beginning collection of solo pieces for the troubadour harp or the folk harp.* Chicago: Lyon & Healy Harps, c1985. 32 pp. [NP] CONTENTS: C is next to D; C is played with A; Look-alikes; Twin Gs; Stepping stones; Rocking; Down to the windy sea; Thumbs up, fingers down; Good position; Heavenly lights; Finding notes; The seasons; Left hand excursion; Riding the waves; A tangled web; Back to school; October; Pumpkins winking; Yellow moon; Black cats; Thanks-giving holidays; Pumpkin pies; Turkeys gobble; Falling leaves; Jingle bells; Jolly old Saint Nicholas; Silent night; The first Noel; Hark! the herald angels sing; Winter's delight; Wintertime; Valentine; Springtime; Blue-birds nest; Clever fingers; March winds blow; Spring flowers; Raindrops; May days; Spanish lullaby; The gristmill; The music box; The first etude.

1227. Leduc, Jacques, 1932–. *Trois impromptus: pour harpe diatonique, op. 16.* Brussels: CeBeDeM, c1967. 17 pp. [NP]

1228. Leeuw, Ton de, 1926–. *The four seasons: for harp.* Amsterdam: Donemus, c1964. 10 pp.

1229. Legg, James. *Soliloquy: for solo harp.* New York: Associated Music Publishers, Inc., c1983. 6 leaves.

1230. Legley, Vic, 1915–. *Suite: per arpa, op. 72, no. 1.* Antwerp: Uitgave Metropolis, c1972. 10 pp.

1231. Lejet, Edith, 1941–. *Métamorphoses: pour harpe.* Paris: Editions musicales transatlantiques, c1982. 7 pp.

1232. Lémann Cazabón, Juan, 1928–. *Sonata: para arpa.* [Santiago]: Universidad de Chile, Instituto de Extension, [19—]. 11 pp.

1233. Lemeland, Aubert, 1932–. *Élégie: pour harpe celtique.* Paris: Editions Françaises de Musique, Technisonor, c1974. 2 pp. [NP]

1234. Leonardo, Josef. *Scherzo: for harp.* Philadelphia: Elkan-Vogel, c1935. 7 pp.

1235. Leroux, Philippe, 1959–. *Histoire de pas; and, Histoire de furtive: pour harpe celtique.* Paris: G. Billaudot, 1990. 3 pp. For Celtic harp. [NP]

1236. ———. *Histoire filante: pour harpe celtique.* Paris: G. Billaudot, 1990. 3 pp. For Celtic harp. [NP]

1237. Lesur, Daniel, 1908–. *Marine: pour harpe.* Paris: Editions Choudens, c1978. 11 pp. "Oeuvre imposée au Concours du Conservatoire National Supérieur de Musique de Paris (1978)."

1238. Lesur, Daniel, 1908–, and Werner, Jean Jacques, 1935–, eds. *1er recueil d'oeuvres pour harpe.* Dirigée par Daniel-Lesur et Jean-Jacques Werner. Paris: G. Billaudot, 1991. 12 pp. (Collection panorama) CONTENTS: Chanson pour Sylvia by Annie Challan. Menuet by Pierre Villette. Enfantines by Dominique Probst. Trois pièces by Denise Megevand. Etude no. 1 by Zarko Princic.

1239. ———, eds. *2e recueil d'oeuvres pour harpe.* [Compiled by] Daniel Lesur and Jean Jacques Werner. Paris: G. Billaudot, c1990. 23 pp. (Collection panorama) CONTENTS: Presque rien, des nuages? by Gérard Condé. Danse sorcière by Bernard Andrès. L'eau qui dort by Gilles Silvestrini. Quarante quatre by Jean-Yves Bosseur. Jeu by Naji Hakim.

1240. ———, eds. *3e recueil d'oeuvres pour harpe.* Dirigée par Daniel-Lesur et Jean-Jacques Werner. Paris: G. Billaudot, 1991. 20 pp. (Collection panorama) CONTENTS: Etude fantasy by Dinu Ghezzo. Caprice by Dieter Acker. Feuilles en automne by Dia Succari. Orphée by Christophe Looten. Etude pour les sonorités variées by Masayuki Nagatomi.

1241. *Lieder und Tänze für die Volksharfe (Tiroler Harfe).* Munich: Musikverlag Josef Preissler, c1964. 30 pp. CONTENTS: Lechtaler Walzer; Halbwalzer; Harfenpolka; Gemütlicher Ländler; Eisenkeil Walzer; Alpbacher Tanzl; Zillertaler Polka; Mühlviertler Arien; Spinnradl: aus dem Mühlviertel Oberösterreich; Zillertaler Boarischer; Der Summa is uma: Volksweise;

Ein alter Steyrisher: aus dem Rasperwerk; Ländlerische Spielmusik; D'r Hirtebue; Der Vorderkaiserfeldner; Im schönen Kaisertal: Ländler; Bauernmenuett; Bergmändle: Ländler aus Hindelang; Der Altausseer: Walzer; Moarhofer Marsch; Die schöne Weis'; Nanei Ländler; Unterinntaler Tanzl; Hochreis Polka; In der Kiefer: Walzer; Steyrischer Ländler; Tiroler Herzen: Ländler; Auf der Griesner Alm: Bayerischer Polka; Zillertaler Harfenländler; Lant it luck!: Tanzweise aus dem Allgäu; In der Klostermühle: Boarischer aus Dietramszell.

1242. Liviabella, Lino, 1902–1964. *Minuetto: per arpa.* Rome: Edizioni de Santis, 1940. 3 pp.

1243. Llácer Pla, Francisco, 1918–. *Preludio místico: para arpa.* Valencia: Piles, c1981. 8 pp.

1244. Llewelyn, Thomas David, 1828–1879. *Llyfr alawon poced = Pocket tune book.* Ed. and arr. by Robin Huw Bowen. Aberystwyth: Gwasg Teires, 1990. 20 pp.

1245. Loeb, David, 1939–. *Sonata: for harp solo.* Plainview, N.Y.: Accentuate Music, c1983. 10 pp.

1246. Lomon, Ruth, 1930–. *Dust devils: for solo harp.* Washington, D.C.: Arsis Press, c1976. 8 pp. CONTENTS: The whorl; The eye; The jinn.

1247. Longo, Alessandro, 1864–1945. [Pezzi, harp, op. 51] *6 pezzi: per arpa, op. 51.* Milan: G. Ricordi, c1910. 35 pp.

1248. ———. *Suite in tre pezzi: per arpa, op. 47.* Milan: G. Ricordi & Co., c1910. 15 pp. CONTENTS: Gavotta; Andantino; Studio.

1249. ———. *Tema con variazioni: per arpa, op. 50.* Milan: Ricordi, c1910. 11 pp.

1250. Lorenzi, Giorgio, 1846–1922. *Il destino: gran valzer di concerto.* Florence: Bratti, [190–?]. 8 pp.

1251. Loudová, Ivana, 1941–. [Solo pro Krale Davida] *The harp of King David: harp solo.* Dobbs Ferry, N.Y.: General Music Publishing Co., c1977. 9 pp.

1252. ———. *Solo pro Krale Davida: [for harp].* 1st ed. Prague: Panton, c1977. 9 pp.

1253. Louie, Alexina, 1949–. *From the eastern gate.* [S.l.]: Alexina Louie, 1985. 21 pp.

1254. Loukine, Woldemar. [Ballade, harp, no. 2, op. 16] *Deuxième ballade, op. 16.* Paris: Henry Lemoine & Cie., n.d. 7 pp.

1255. ———. *Grande sonate: c-moll: pour harpe seule, op. 10.* Moscow: P. Jurgenson, 1907. 19 pp.

1256. ———. *Idyll: moment musical, op. 26.* New York: International Music Pub. Co., c1913. 3 pp.

1257. ———. *Intermezzo: harp solo [in E minor], op. 28.* New York: International Music Pub. Co., c1914. 4 pp.

1258. ———. *Legende.* Moscow, Leipzig: P. Jurgenson, 1906. 7 pp.

1259. Louvier, Alain, 1945–. *Chimère: pour harpe.* Paris: A. Leduc, c1974. 4 pp. "For student harpists in the elementary or middle levels of instruction."

1260. Lovelace, William, 1960–. *Quatre-vingt six.* Ellensburg, Wash.: F.C. Publishing Co., 1993. 3 pp.

1261. ———. [Tanzende Bächlein] *Das tanzende Bächlein.* San Mateo, Calif.: F.C. Publishing Co., c1989. 6 pp. (Solo series: harp)

1262. Lo Vetere, Italo, 1940–. [Piccoli canoni, harp] *Dodici piccoli canoni: senza pedali: per arpa.* Milan: Edizioni Curci, c1979. 6 pp. [NP]

1263. ———. *Preludio, scherzino e postludio: per arpa.* Milan: Carisch, 1981. 7 pp.

1264. Lupi, Roberto, 1908–1971. *Partita: per arpa: (da intavolature per liuto della metà del secolo XVII).* Milan: Carisch, 1942. 7 pp.

1265. Maayani, Ami, 1936–. [Makamat] *Maqamat: for harp.* Tel Aviv: Israeli Music Publications, [1936]. 19 pp.

1266. ———. [Makamat (1980)] *Maqamat: pour harpe seule.* New version, 1980. New York, N.Y.: Lyra Music Co., c1984. 7 pp.

1267. ———. *Passacaglia dans le style oriental.* New York: Lyra Music Co., 1976. 11 pp.

1268. ———. [Pieces, harp] *Five pieces for the young harpist.* New York: Lyra Music Co., c1977. 10 pp.

1269. ———. *Sonate: pour harpe seule.* New York, N.Y.: Lyra Music Co., c1980. 18 pp.

1270. ———. *Toccata: for harp.* Tel Aviv: Israel Music Institute, c1962. 15 pp.

1271. ———. *Tokatah: le-nevel = Toccata: for harp.* 2nd ed. rev. Tel Aviv: Israel Music Institute, c1969. 12 pp.

1272. Maghini, Ruggero, 1913–1977. [Suites, harp, no. 1] *Suite: per arpa.* Milan: Edizioni Suvini Zerboni, c1950. 20 pp.

1273. ———. [Suites, harp, no. 2] *Suite breve: per arpa: 2. suite.* Milan: Edizioni Suvini Zerboni, c1958. 16 pp.

1274. Magistretti, Luigi Maria, d. 1956. [Esercizi giornalieri] *Cinquantuni esercizi giornalieri: per arpa: ad uso dei concertisti = 51 daily exercises: for harp: for advanced players.* Milan: Ricordi, c1918. 25 pp.

1275. Maingueneau, Louis, 1884–1950. [Sonatas, harp] *Sonata: pour harpe.* Paris: Durand & Cie., c1946. 21 pp.

1276. Makhov, Viktor Ivanovich, 1905–. [Adagio, harp] *Adazhio: dlia arfy.* Moscow: Gosudarstvennoe Izdatelstvo, 1959. 5 pp.

1277. Mamy, Jacques. [Pièces breves, harp] *Six pièces breves: pour harpe celtique.* Paris: Editions Max Eschig, c1978. 10 pp. [NP] CONTENTS: 1. Prélude; 2. Invention; 3. Invocation; 4. Courante; 5. Reflet; 6. Ronde.

1278. ———. *Suite gaelique: pour harpe ou harpe celtique.* Paris: Henry Lemoine, c1974. 13 pp. [NP] CONTENTS: Cantilène; Dentelle; Lac; Brumes; Gigue.

1279. Mannino, Franco, 1924–. *Tre canzoni: per arpa, op. 205.* Rome: Boccaccini & Spada, c1980. 8 pp.

1280. Marc, Edmond. *Poème antique: pour harpe.* Paris: Henry Lemoine & Cie., c1961. 8 pp.

1281. Marcianò, Sergio. *Quattro partite: per arpa: sopra il corale An Wasserflüssen Babylon.* Bergamo, Italy: Edizioni Carrara, 1980. 8 pp.

1282. Marcland, Patrick, 1944–. *Stretto: pour harpe.* Paris: Éditions musicales transatlantiques, c1978. 5 pp.

1283. Marcucci, Ferdinando, 1800–1871. *Ah non giunge: cavatina nella Sonnambula del Vo. Bellini: ridotta per arpa, con variazioni brillanti e giocose.* Milan: Ricordi, [1836]. 15 pp.

1284. ———. *Aria finale: Qual cor tradisti: nell' opera Norma [di] Bellini: ridotta per arpa, con introd. e variazioni.* Milan: Ricordi, [1837]. 11 pp.

1285. ———. *Divertimento: per arpa: sopra alcuni motivi dell' opera Il profeta del M. Cav. Meyerbeer, op. 29.* Florence: Stab. musicale de F. Lorenzi, [185–?]. 12 pp.

1286. ———. [Fantaisie sur les plus jolis motifs d'Anna Bolena] *Fantaisie: pour la harpe sur les plus jolis motifs d'Anna Bolena de Donizetti.* Milan: Ricordi, [1835?]. 12 pp.

1287. ———. [Fantaisie sur Tu sordo ai miei lamenti] *Fantaisie: pour la harpe sur l'air favori Tu sordo ai miei lamenti de Rossini.* Paris: Magasin de musique de Pacini, [1830? or 1831?]. 13 pp.

1288. ———. [Fantasia sopra diversi motivi dell' opera Lucrezia Borgia] *Fantasia per arpa sopra diversi motivi dell' opera Lucrezia Borgia del Mo. Donizetti.* Milan: Ricordi, [1837]. 23 pp.

1289. ———. [Fantasia sull' aria Bello ardir d'un congiurato] *Fantasia: per arpa con variazioni e rondo finale, sull' aria Bello ardier d'un congiurato del M. cav. Donizetti.* Milan: Ricordi, [1838?]. 10 pp. The theme is from Donizetti's *Marino Faliero.*

1290. ———. *Oh mattutini albori: cavatine della Donna del lago de Rossini: variée pour la harpe.* Milan: Ricordi, [1831?]. 8 pp.

1291. ———. *Variazioni sopra un tema favorito: per arpa.* Milan: Ricordi, [1836]. 9 pp.

1292. Marek, Czeslaw, 1891–. *Deux pièces romantiques: pour harpe, op. 31 (1930).* Winterthur: Verlag der Zentralbibliothek Zürich in Kommission bei Amadeus Edition; New York: Eulenburg, 1977. 19 pp. (Schweizerische Musikbibliothek: Einzelkomponisten, MCz 31)

1293. Marescotti, André François, 1902–. *Mouvement: pour harpe.* Paris: Jobert, c1941. 11 pp.

1294. Mari, Pierrette, 1929–. *D'une amphore oubliée s'echappent des sirènes = Sirens flow from a forgotten amphora = Sirenen entweichen aus einer vergessenen Amphora.* Pédales indiquées par O. Le Dentu. Paris: Société d'Editions Musicales Internationales, c1979. 3 pp.

1295. Mariatti, Franco. *Sonatina: per arpa.* Milan: Edizioni Curci, c1978. 5 pp.

1296. Marin, Marie Martin Marcel de, b. 1769. *Essay upon an air of the Molinarella: varied in all the known styles of music, such as the Chinese, Polish, French, Scotch, Sicilian, Turkish, Cossacks, Russian, Arabic, Grecian, Tartar, and the Italian cantabile, also God save the King, and four favorite Scotch and Welsh airs, adapted for the harp, opera 11th.* London: Muzio Clementi & Co., 1800.

1297. ———. [Favorite airs] *Three favorite airs: for the harp: with variations & a march, op. 13.* London: Clementi Banger Hyde Collard & Davis, ca. 1800. 16 pp.

1298. ———. [New grand sonata] *A new grand sonata: for the harp.* London: Clementi, Banger, Hyde, Collard and Davis, ca. 1800? 13 pp.

1299. ———. [Progressive sonatinas] *Six progressive sonatinas: for the harp: interspersed with some easy preludes, containing also a table for the theory of the pedal.* London: Clementi Banger Hyde Collard, ca. 1800? 32 pp.

1300. ———. [Sonatinas] *Three sonatinas: for the harp, op. 10.* London: John Longman, Clementi & Co., 1800. 26 pp.

1301. Marischal, Louis, 1928–. *Petit caprice: pièce pour harpe.* Paris: Editions Chappell, c1970. 4 pp.

1302. Maros, Miklós, 1943–. *Trifoglio: per arpa.* Stockholm: Svensk musik, 1988. 8 pp.

1303. Maros, Rudolf, 1917–. *Suite: for harp.* New York: Southern Music Publishing Co., c1968. 12 pp. CONTENTS: Notturno; Toccata; Naenia; Rondo.

1304. Marsh, Roger, 1949–. *Heaven haven: for harp: composer's facsimile score.* Borough Green, Kent: Novello, c1983. 11 pp.

1305. Marshall, Pamela, 1954–. *Dances for the morning: for harp.* New York: Seesaw Music, c1976. 5 pp. CONTENTS: For the sunrise; For the morning birds; For the morning rain; Morning spell.

1306. Martelli, Henri, 1895–1980. [Divertissement, harp, op. 86] *Divertissement: pour harpe, op. 86.* Paris: Ricordi, c1956. 14 pp.

1307. ————. [Scherzando, harp, op. 102] *Scherzando: pour harpe, [op. 12].* Paris: M. Eschig, c1968. 11 pp.

1308. Martin y Coll, Antonio, ca. 1660–ca. 1740, and Sagasta Galdós, Julián, eds. *Tonos de palacio: música per la tecla, arpa i vihuela (segles XVI-XVII): de la colleció de Fr. Antonio Martin y Coll.* Estudio i transcripció, Julian Sagasta Galdós. Barcelona: Edicions del Conservatori Superior de Música del Liceu, 1981. 64 pp. (Florilegi "Liceu", 2) Pieces for keyboard, harp, or vihuela, believed to be by one anonymous composer, from the collection *Flores de música.* Contains marizápalos, pavanas, folias, españoletas, pasacalles, tamborileros, vacas, alonches, canciónes and "passajes para hacer las manos."

1309. Martinez Chumillas, Manuel. *Dos piezas translucidas: para arpa.* Madrid: Union Musical Española, c1977. 5 pp.

1310. Martino, Ralph. *Soliloquy: for harp.* New York: Lyra Music Co., c1967. 5 pp.

1311. Marzuki, Marilyn S., 1942–, and Kaplan, Barbara, eds. *Harp album: repertoire primer.* Lebanon, Ind.: Studio P/R, c1976. 119 pp. "For pedal & non-pedal harps." Included are second harp or piano parts for some of the pieces. [NP] CONTENTS: Falling water; Cantilever by M. Marzuki. Passacaglia in C minor by J. S. Bach. The Moldau by B. Smetana. Allegro spirtuoso from Symphony no. 104 by F. J. Haydn. Scarborough Fair. Shenandoah. All creatures of our God and King. Thumbtime by M. Marzuki. Il était une bergère. When the saints go marching in. Plaisir d'amour by J. Martini. Merry widow waltz by F. Lehár. Les pâtés toutes chauds. Finale from Symphony no. 4 by P. I. Tchaikovsky. In the meadow stood a little birch tree. Allegretto from Symphony no. 7 by L. van Beethoven. Du liegst mir im Herzen. La bamba. Amazing grace. Annual greetings. Intermezzo after Brahms, op. 117. Jeanie with the light brown hair by S. C. Foster. Bobo leh me 'lone. Allegro ma non troppo from Symphony no. 1 by J. Brahms. Sixteenth birthday by M. Marzuki. Kalevalainen sävelmä. Deh vieni alla finestra by W. A. Mozart. Air con variazione by G. F. Handel. Auf dem Strom by F. Schubert. Michael, row the boat ashore. Moscow nights by V. Soloviev-Sedoy. Frère Jacques. Feierlich und gemessen from Symphony no. 1 by G. Mahler. Andantino from Symphony no. 4 by P. I. Tchaikovsky. How lovely is thy dwelling place from A German requiem by J. Brahms. Dies irae. Ave Maria by Bach-Gounod. Black is the color of my true love's hair. Der Leiermann by F.

Schubert. Bourrée I from Solo cello suite IV by J. S. Bach. The boundless expanse of the sea. Allegretto grazioso from Symphony no. 2 by J. Brahms. Shule aroon. Polovetsian dances by A. Borodin. Overture from La forza del destino by G. Verdi. Give five by M. Marzuki. Scene from Swan lake by P. I. Tchaikovsky. The entertainer by S. Joplin. Barbara's blues by M. Marzuki. Frozen moments by G. Nelson. Londonderry air.

1312. Masetti, Enzo. *Cucù: per arpa.* Bologna: Edizioni Bongiovanni, c1925. 7 pp.

1313. Mason, Derrick. *Minuet, nocturne and impromptu: for harp.* London: Keith Prowse Music Publishing Co., Ltd., c1967. 7 pp.

1314. Mathias, William, 1934–1992. *Improvisations: for harp, opus 10.* London: Oxford University Press, c1964. 7 pp.

1315. ———. *Santa Fe suite: for harp.* Oxford; New York: Oxford University Press, c1990. 18 pp. CONTENTS: Landscape; Nocturne; Sun dance.

1316. Matthews, Colin, 1946–. *Little suite: for harp.* Edited by Osian Ellis. London: Faber; New York: G. Schirmer, 1981. 7 pp.

1317. Maurat, Edmond. *Sept miniatures d'époque: pour harpe, op. 3.* Paris: Éditions Max Eschig, c1967. 11 pp.

1318. Maxwell, Robert, 1921–. *Ebb tide.* New York: Robbins Music Corp., c1953. 5 pp.

1319. ———. *Ebb tide.* New York: Maxwell Music Corp., c1953. 9 pp.

1320. ———. *From a seed.* New York, N.Y.: Maxwell Music Corp., c1988. 5 pp.

1321. ———. *Harping on a harp.* New York: American Academy of Music, c1948. 4 pp. (Modern harp series)

1322. ———. *Harping on a harp.* London: Salvi International, c1948. 4 pp.

1323. ———. *The little burro.* New York, N.Y.: Maxwell Music Corp., c1988. 5 pp.

1324. ———. *Slippery tune on a sticky bass.* New York, N.Y.: Maxwell Music Corp., c1988. 5 pp.

1325. Maxwell, Robert, 1921–, and Malneck, Matty, 1904–. *Shangri-la.* New York: Maxwell Music Corp., c1946. 7 pp.

1326. Mayer, William, 1925–. *Appalachian echoes: for harp solo.* New York, N.Y.: Gaudia Music and Arts, c1991. 7 pp. CONTENTS: Appalachian echoes; Wild horses.

1327. Mayr, Giovanni Simone, 1763–1845. *Suite: für Harfe.* Zum ersten Mal hrsg. von Heinrich Bauer. Frankfurt: H. Litolff; New York: C.F. Peters, c1974. 16 pp.

1328. McClintock, Robert, 1946–. *Ode: for harp.* Sacramento, Calif.: Robert McClintock, c1982. 12 pp.

1329. McDonald, Susann, 1935–, and Wood, Linda, 1945–. *Haiku: for the harp.* Bloomington, Ind.: Musicworks-Harp Editions, c1986. 36 pp. CONTENTS: A stray cat Asleep on the roof In the spring rain; A flash of lightning! The sound of dew Dripping down the bamboo; Sacred music at night; Into the bonfires Flutter the tinted leaves; Being chased, The firefly Hides in the moon; Sweeping the garden, The snow is forgotten By the broom; Striking the fly, I hit also A flowering plant; The sparrows Are playing hide and seek Among the tea flowers; The old pond; A frog jumps in, The sound of water; After the moon-viewing, My shadow walking home Along with me; Even among insects, in this world, Some are good at singing, Some bad; Dance from one blade of grass To another, Pearls of dew; Distant lights; There they live This autumn night.

1330. ———. *Harp solos: graded recital pieces.* [Bloomington, Ind.]: Musicworks-Harp Editions, c1982. 5 v. CONTENTS: Vol.1. Moonlight; Little prelude; Stars; Reverie; Chorale; Concert etude.
Vol.2. Interlude; Serenade; Ballade; Processional.
Vol.3. Russian lullaby; Alpine waltz; Koto in the temple; Bagpipe jig.
Vol.4. Sonatina in classical style; Two guitars; Toccata (Sabre danse).
Vol.5. Crystalis; Nocturne; Petite suite.

1331. McGuire, Edward. *Prelude 10: for solo harp.* Glasgow: Scottish Music Publishing, 1986. 10 pp.

1332. Mchedelov, M. (Mikhail). [Etudes, harp] *Piat' etiudov.* Moscow: Gos. muzykal'noe izd-vo, 1959. 30 pp.

1333. ———. [Harp music. Selections] *Variatsii na temu Paganini; Na prazdnike: iz siuity "V Gruzii"; Tri preliudii; Skertsino: dlia arfy = Variations on Paganini's theme; At a festivity: from the suite "In Georgia"; Three preludes; Scherzino: for harp.* Moscow: Muzyka, 1986. 47 pp.

1334. ———. *V Gruzii: siuita dlia arfy.* Moscow: Gos. muz. izd-vo, 1952. 26 pp.

1335. McKay, Neil, 1924–. *World(s): three pieces for solo koto or harp.* Delaware Water Gap, Pa.: Shawnee Press, c1979. 2 v. CONTENTS: Pengawit; Ai; Veränderungen.

1336. Mégevand, Denise, 1947–. *Ballade celtique: harpe celtique.* Paris: Technisonor, c1973. 4 pp. [NP]

1337. ———. *Harpeurs: harpe celtique.* Paris: Technisonor, c1973. 3 pp. [NP]

1338. ———. *Perspectives I et II: pour harpe celtique.* Paris: G. Billaudot, 1992. 11 pp. [NP]

1339. ———. [Pieces, harp] *Dix pièces: pour harpe celtique ou grande harpe.* Paris: Editions Intersong, c1974. 29 pp. [NP] CONTENTS: Le paradis; Prophetie de gwenc'hlan; La tourterelle; Ronde bretonne; Danse du glaive; Prélude; Air varié; Errance; Berceuse; Déploration.

1340. ———, arr. *Variations sur des thèmes bretons: 10 pièces pour harpe celtique ou grande harpe.* Paris: Intersong-Editions Tutti, c1974. 29 pp. [NP] CONTENTS: Le paradis; Prophetie de Gwenc'hlan; La tourterelle; Ronde bretonne; Danse du Glaive; Prélude; Air varié; Errance; Berceuse; Déploration.

1341. Meineke, C. (Christopher), 1782–1850. *Walze with variations: for the harp or piano forte.* Baltimore: Printed (for C.M.) & sold at Carrs Music Store 36 Baltimore Street, [between 1808 and 1813]. 4 pp.

1342. Mengelberg, Karel, 1902–. *Soneria, romanza e mazurca: per arpa.* Amsterdam: Donemus, c1958. 8 pp.

1343. Mennin, Peter, 1923–1983. *Cadenza capricciosa: from Reflections of Emily: for solo harp.* New York: G. Schirmer, c1979. 6 pp.

1344. Merlet, Michel, 1939–. *Passacaille: pour harpe: ostinato de J. S. Bach.* Paris: A. Leduc, c1972. 11 pp. Based on the ostinato of J. S. Bach's Passacaglia, BWV 582, C minor.

1345. Meyer, Friedrich Karl. *Adagio patetico, and waltz of the Black Forest: for the harp.* London: Published by the author, [18—?]. 11 pp. (Porte-feuille de pièces d'un genre brillant, et d'autres différens styles, pour la harpe, no. 6)

1346. ———. *Air & polonaise: for the harp.* London: S. Chappell, [between 1830 and 1834]. 11 pp.

1347. ———. *L'alba: fantasia and grand march: for the harp.* London: Royal Harmonic Institution, [between 1820 and 1826]. 5 pp.

1348. ———. *Andante and brilliant scherzando: for the harp.* London: Printed for the author, [18—?]. 9 pp. (Porte-feuille de pièces legères et amusantes pour la harpe, no. 2) Also called F. K. Meyer's Scherzando, no. 2.

1349. ———. *Auld Robin Gray: divertimento for the harp.* London: Royal Harmonic Institution, [between 1820 and 1826]. 7 pp.

1350. ———. *Delia: divertimento for the harp.* London: Royal Harmonic Institution, [between 1820 and 1826]. 7 pp.

1351. ———. *Fantasia and brilliant variations on the favorite Scotch air Thou art gane awa: for the harp.* London: S. Chappell, [between 1826 and 1830]. 13 pp. (Porte-feuille de pièces d'un genre brillant, et d'autres différens styles, pour la harpe, no. 5)

1352. ———. *Fantasia and variations on the favorite Scotch air Saw ye my father: for the harp.* London: Printed for the author, [18— ?]. 7 pp. (Porte-feuille de pièces legères et amusantes pour la harpe, no. 4)

1353. ———. *A favorite march and waltz: for the harp: inscribed to Miss White, of the Hall, Tuxford.* London: Printed for the author, [18—?]. 10 pp. (Porte-feuille de pièces legères et amusantes pour la harpe, no. 8)

1354. ———. *Grand fantasie on a celebrated German air: for the harp.* London: J. B. Cramer, Addison & Beale, [between 1824 and 1844]. 11 pp. (Portefeuille de pièces d'un genre brillant, et d'autres différens styles, pour la harpe, no. 1)

1355. ———. *Martial introduction and rondoletto: for the harp.* London: Printed for the author, [18—?]. 5 pp. (Porte-feuille de pièces legères et amusantes pour la harpe, no. 3)

1356. ———. *Mary's dream: divertimento for the harp.* London: Royal Harmonic Institution, [between 1820 and 1826]. 7 pp.

1357. ———. *Il pensieroso: an air with variations for the harp.* London: Royal Harmonic Institution, [between 1820 and 1826]. 11 pp.

1358. ———. *Progressive lessons and preludes: for the harp.* Edited by David Watkins. London: The Clive Morley Collection, [198–?]. 19 pp.

1359. ———. *The rising of the lark: a Welch air: with variations and la chasse: for the harp.* London: J. B. Cramer, Addison & Beale, [between 1824 and 1844]. 11 pp.

1360. ———. *Serenade du troubadour: no. 2: for the harp: with ad libitum accompaniment for the piano forte, flute & violoncello.* London: S. Chappell, [between 1830 and 1834]. Score 7 pp.

1361. ———. [Sonata, harp, C minor] *Sonata: for the harp: composed and dedicated to Miss Goldsmid.* London: Royal Harmonic Institution, [between 1820 and 1826]. 13 pp.

1362. Meyer, Philippe-Jacques, 1737–1819. *The bush aboon traquair: a favorite Scotch air with variations for the harp, no. 39.* London: Birchall, n.d. 4 pp.

1363. ———. [Lessons, harp. Selections] *Four original lessons: for the harp.* Edited by David Watkins. London: The Clive Morley Collection, [198–?]. 23 pp.

1364. ———. *A rose tree in full bearing: a favorite air with variations for the harp.* London: R. Birchall, [1810?]. 3 pp. "No. 27."

1365. ———. [Sonatas, harp, op. 3, no. 6] *Sonate: für Harfe.* Herausgegeben von Hans J. Zingel. Mainz: B. Schott's Söhne, c1966. 11 pp.

1366. Migot, Georges, 1891–1976. *Sonate luthée: pour la harpe.* Paris: Leduc, c1953. 23 pp.

1367. Milhaud, Darius, 1892–1974. *Sonate: pour harpe.* Paris: Eschig, c1972. 11 pp.

1368. Milligan, Samuel, ed. *Fun from the first!: with the Lyon-Healy troubadour harp.* Chicago: Lyon-Healy, c1962. 2 v. [NP] CONTENTS: Vol.1. Antrim fair; Merrily we roll along; Do, do, l'enfant do; March; Anything you can do; Westminster bells; Little Johnnie three-note; Dublin bells; Let me teach you Frère Jacques; Round dance; Lazy Mary; Eleven, twelve, thirteen; Waltz; The goose girl; Good King Wenceslaus; Silent night; Tantum ergo; Concerdi laetitia; Jasmine flower; Drink to me only with thine eyes; Dutch mariner's hymn; Kol slaven; The northern princess; There stands a little man (from Hansel and Gretel).

Vol.2. Robin loves me; Noel; Giga; The royal oak; In the month of May; Paván; Air; Vesper hymn; The purple bamboo; O sanctissima; When love is kind; Kremser; The first Noel; Deck the halls; Early one morning; Album leaf.

1369. ———, ed. *Medieval to modern: repertoire for the Lyon-Healy troubadour harp.* Collected and edited by Samuel Milligan. Chicago: Lyon-Healy, c1962. 2 v. "Selected compositions from the 12th century to the present, arr. for harp . . . easy to moderately difficult." [NP] CONTENTS: Vol.1. Lai et Rotrouenge. Jesu Criste's milde moder. Tiento IX by Alonso Mudarra. Air from Festes de l'Été by Michel Pinolet de Monteclair. Rugier, glosado de Antonio by Antonio de Cabezon. The new sa-hoo by Giles Farnaby. Andiam, mio tesoro. Little prelude in F major by Johann Sebastian Bach. Minuet by Carl Philipp Emanuel Bach. Soeur Monique by François Couperin (le Grand). Air varié by George Frideric Handel. Minuet by Jean Jacques Rousseau. Allegro moderato from Sonatina in G by Franz Joseph Haydn. Tambourin by Louis Claude Daquin. La paloma by Sebastián Yradier. Choral by Robert Schumann. Dondon's sleep from the opera Coq d'or by Nicolas Rimsky-Korsakov.

Vol.2. Air and rondo (Portrait charmant; Le garçon volage) by Robert Nicolas Charles Bochsa. Greensleeves. Spanish dance by Georges Bizet. Sonatina in classic style by Samuel O. Pratt. Weinachtsglocken, op. 36, no. 1 by Neils Wilhelm Gade. Les pifferari = The fifers by Charles Gounod. Scotch air. Welsh penillion melodies (Breuder bywyd = The frailty of life. Gywydd y gof = The blacksmith's song). Three traditional Welsh airs (Breuddwyd y frenhines = The royal dream. Craig y tyle = Winter has come. Llwyn onn = The ash grove. La paloma azúl = The blue dove).

1370. Mills, Verlye, d. 1983. *Harp cues: for radio.* New York: E. Ascher, c1943. 16 pp.

1371. ———. *Harp with a beat.* Melville, N.Y.: MCA/Mills, c1975. 38 pp.

Mills, Verlye, d. 1983, and Castellucci, Stella. *Rhythm: for harp.* See 54.

1372. Miroglio, Francis, 1924–. *Moires: pour harpe.* Paris: Salabert, c1985. 8 pp. "Morceau de concours du Conservatoire national supérieur de musique de Paris pour l'année 1985."

1373. ———. *Rumeurs: harpe celtique ou harpe diatonique.* Paris: Amphion, c1980. 3 pp. [NP]

1374. Molino, Louis, 1792–1846. *Introduzione and andante: varied for the harp.* London: C. Wheatstone & Co., [18—]. 7 pp.

1375. Möller, Arnold, 1912–. *Elegie: für Harfe solo.* Frankfurt: Zimmermann, c1983. 4 pp.

1376. Molnar, Josef, 1929–. *Colors: suite for solo or multiple harps.* Palo Alto, Calif.: Harpress of California, c1986. Score 9 pp. CONTENTS: Red; Yellow; Blue; Green; Orange; Lilac; Beige; Colors.

1377. ———. *Itsuki no komori uta by Molnar. Der Lindenbaum by Schubert.* [Arr. by Josef Molnar]. [Japan]: s.n., n.d. Score 11 pp. Includes 2 versions of the 1st work: one for harp solo and 1 for 4 Irish harps; 2nd work is for harp solo. [NP]

1378. ———. [New age pieces] *Two new age pieces: for solo harp.* Palo Alto, Calif.: Harpress of California, c1990. 5 pp. CONTENTS: Lights; Waves.

1379. Monsigny, Pierre-Alexandre, 1729–1817. [Operas. Selections; arr.] *Mélange: pour la harpe: sur differents thêmes favoris, oeuvre 39.* Tirés des opéra du célèbre Monsigny par Charles Bochsa fils. Paris: Carli, [181–]. 13 pp. Includes themes from Monsigny's Félix and Le roi et le fermier.

1380. Montani, P. L. *La conola.* New York: International Music Co., c1922. 7 pp.

1381. Montesquieu, Odette de, 1908–. *Prélude: pour la harpe.* Paris: Gay, [196–?]. 4 pp.

1382. ———. *Valse humoresque: pour la harpe.* Paris: Gay & Cie., [1937?]. 4 pp.

1383. Mooney, Janet Thompson. *In a glass garden.* Columbus, Ohio: Wheeler Music Publishers, c1983. 2 pp.

1384. Moran, Peter K., d. 1831. *Robin Adair: a favorite Irish melody the introductions and variations for the harp or piano forte.* New York: W. Dubois, [between 1817 and 1821]. Score 9 pp.

1385. ———. *Stantz waltz: with variations for the harp or piano forte.* New York: John Paff, [181–?]. 5 pp.

1386. ———. *Stantz waltz: with variations for the piano-forte or harp.* Philadelphia: J.G. Klemm, 1823 or 4. 5 pp.

1387. ———. *Stantz waltz: with variations for the piano-forte or harp.* Baltimore: J. Cole, 183–? 3 pp.

1388. ———. [Swabian air] *Moran's favorite variations to the Suabian air: for the harp or piano forte.* New York: Wm. Dubois, [181–?]. 5 pp.

1389. ———. [Swiss waltz] *A favorite Swiss waltz: with variations for the harp or piano forte.* Baltimore?: J. Cole?, 18—. 1 p.

1390. ———. [Swiss waltz] *Favorite Swiss waltz: with variations for the harp or piano forte.* New York: John Paff, [181–]. 5 pp.

1391. ———. [Swiss waltz] *A favorite Swiss waltz: with variations for the harp or pianoforte.* Phildelphia: G. Willig, 1817? 5 pp.

1392. ———. [Swiss waltz] *Favorite Swiss waltz.* New York: Wm. Dubois, 1817 or 18. 5 pp.

1393. ———. [Swiss waltz] *A favorite Swiss waltz.* New York: E. Riley, ca. 1819. 5 pp.

1394. ———. [Swiss waltz] *A favorite Swiss waltz: with variations for the piano or harp.* New York: E.S. Mesier, [after 1826]. 6 pp.

1395. Morel, Jean-Marie, 1934–. *Cinq interludes d'un Roméo et Juliette: pour harpe.* Paris: Editions musicales transatlantiques, c1979. 11 pp.

1396. Moreno Gans, José. *Invenciones: para arpa.* Madrid: Union Musical Española, c1965. 7 pp.

1397. ———. *Melodia no. 4: para arpa.* Madrid: Union Musical Española, c1969. 2 pp.

1398. ———. *Nocturno: para arpa.* Madrid: Union Musical Española, c1969. 8 pp.

1399. ———. *Sonata: para arpa: en si menor.* Madrid: Unión Musical Español, c1974. 17 pp.

1400. Morgan, Melissa, 1957–. *Erin's harp.* San Diego, Calif.: Melissa Morgan, c1983. 26 pp. [NP]

1401. Mortari, Virgilio, 1902–1993. *Incantesimi: per arpa.* Milan: Curci, c1974. 10 pp. CONTENTS: Visione; L'arpa stregata.

1402. ———. [Pezzi, harp] *Tre pezzi: per arpa.* [Diteggiatura di Elena Zaniboni]. Milan: Edizione Curci, c1977. 19 pp. CONTENTS: Preludio; Dittico; Allegro fantastico.

1403. ———. *Sonatina prodigio: per arpa.* Milan: Carisch, c1939. 5 pp. (Composizioni scelte per arpa)

1404. ———. *Studi galanti: per arpa (o pianoforte).* Florence: A. Forlivesi, n.d. 10 pp.

1405. Moss, Piotr, 1949–. *Ad libitum: 26 sequences: pour harpe celtique.* Paris: Gérard Billaudot, c1985. 11 leaves. (La harpe) [NP]

1406. ———. [Istanti] *Tre istanti: per arpa sola.* Warszawa: ZAIKS, c1974. 14 pp. (Contemporary Polish music: series of solo compositions)

1407. Mourant, Walter, 1910–. *Apostrophe: [for] harp solo.* New York: Composers Facsimile Edition, c1965. 6 pp.

1408. ———. *In a Japanese garden: [for] harp solo.* New York: Composers Facsimile Edition, c1968. 3 pp.

1409. ———. *Manhattan suite: harp solo.* New York: American Composers Alliance, c1963. 6 pp. (Composers facsimile edition) CONTENTS: Penthouse lullaby; Rendezvous in Yorkville; After hours.

1410. ———. *Manhattan suite: harp solo.* New York: Hendon Music, c1966. 16 pp. CONTENTS: Prelude; Intermezzo; Dance.

1411. ———. *Ode in the mixolydian mode: [for] harp solo.* New York: Composers Facsimile Edition, c1969. 6 pp.

1412. Munkel, Heinz. *Impromptu und Elegie für Harfe Solo.* Elegie auch auf der Irischen Harfe spielbar. Odenthal: Centraton Musikverlag, 1989. 4 pp. [NP]

1413. ———. [Preludes, harp] *Zwei préludes: As-dur/as-moll: für Harfe.* Frankfurt: Wilhelm Zimmermann, c1953. 7 pp.

1414. *Musette de Nina: pour la harpe.* Philadelphia: Published by G.E. Blake, [between 1810 and 1814]. [4] pp. Variations on the Allegretto in the overture to *Nina,* by Dalayrac.

1415. *Musette de Nina: pour la harpe ou forte piano.* Philadelphia: G. Willig, [ca. 1816]. [4 pp.] For harp or piano, with four numbered variations. Variations on the Allegretto in the overture to *Nina,* by Dalayrac.

1416. *Musette de Nina: with variations for the harp or piano forte.* Baltimore: J. Cole, 1826? 3 pp.

1417. Naderman, François Joseph, 1773 (ca.)-1835. [Airs variées, harp, op. 21] *Recueil d'airs varies: pour la harpe, oeuvre 21.* Paris: Naderman, [180–?]. 41 pp. CONTENTS: La Biondina; Charmante Gabrielle; Le bon Roi Dagobert.

1418. ———. [Divertissements, harp, no. 1] *Premier divertissement, ou potpourri: chiffré pour la harpe à l'usage des commencants.* Paris: Naderman, [182–?]. 9 pp.

1419. ———. [Etudes et préludes, harp] *Etudes et préludes.* [Ed. de] Schuëcker; révision de Odette Le Dentu. Paris: G. Billaudot, c1980. 3 v. (La harpe) CONTENTS: Vol.1. 30 etudes progressives; Vol.2. 24 préludes; Vol.3. 18 etudes de haut niveau.

1420. ———. [Etudes, exercises et préludes, harp, op. 93] *Etudes, exercises et préludes, op. 93.* Paris: Costallat & Cie., n.d. 106 pp. (Enseignement de la harpe) (École de harpe, part 3)

1421. ———. [Fantaisie et variations, harp, op. 61] *Fantaisie et variations: pour la harpe, oeuvre 61.* Paris: Naderman, 181–?]. 11 pp.

1422. ———. [Fantaisie sur Lison dormait] *Lison dormait dans un bocage: fantaisie, avec introduction et coda pour la harpe, oeuv. 67.* Paris: Naderman, [181–?]. 15 pp. Based on the air by N. Dezède.

1423. ———. [Fantasies, harp, op. 52, no. 1] *Fantaisie: pour la harpe sur l'air O Peseator, oeuvre 52, no. 1.* Paris: Naderman, [181–?]. 11 pp.

1424. ———. [Harp music. Selections] *Douze etudes et un thème varié: pour la harpe celtique.* Revision et adaptation: O. Le Dentu. Paris: G. Billaudot, c1978. 17 pp. (La harpe) [NP]

1425. ———. [Harp music. Selections] *Etuden und Praeludien: für Harfe.* In progressiver Reihenfalge ausgewählt, revidirt und mit genauer Fingersatz und Pedalbezeichnung versehen von Edmund Schuëcker. Leipzig: Carl Merseburger, [192–]. 3 v. CONTENTS: Vol.1. 30 fortschreitende Etuden; Vol.2. 24 Präludien; Vol.3. 18 Etuden für höhere Ausbildung.

1426. ———. [Harp music. Selections] *Nadermann pour harpe celtique (ou harpe).* Adaptation et doigtés de Annie Challan. Paris: Editions Aug. Zurfluh, c1988. [NP]

1427. ———. *Introduction and the favorite air Pauvre Jacques: with variations for the harp.* London: Rutter & M. Carthy, n.d. 5 pp.

1428. ———. [J'ai vu Lise hier au soir] *The favorite air J'ai vu Lise hier au soir.* Arr. for the harp by Naderman. London: Printed & sold by J. Platts, [ca. 1827]. 7 pp. Theme and variations.

1429. ———. *Petite fantasie: on favorite airs in Rossini's opera La gazza ladra.* Arr. for the harp by F. J. Naderman. Milan: J. Ricordi, [1827?]. 9 pp.

1430. ———. *Portuguese air: with variations for the harp.* London: Rutter & McCarthy, n.d. 11 pp.

1431. ———. [Pot-pouri, harp, no. 2] *Deuxième pot-pouri: suivi de Plaisir d'amour: varié pour la harpe.* S.l.: Marchand de Musique Rue du Roule, n.d. 29 pp.

1432. ———. [Pot-pouri, harp, no. 3] *Troisième pot-pouri: suivi d'un air varié pour la harpe.* S.l.: Marchand de Musique Rue du Roule, n.d. 28 pp.

1433. ———. [Sonatas, harp, op. 17] *Trois nouvelles sonates pour la harpe, op. 17.* Recueillies et revues par Pierre Jamet. Paris: Gérard Billaudot, c1979. 3 v. (La harpe) CONTENTS: Vol.1. 1ere sonate en mi-bémol majeur; Vol.2. 2e sonate en fa; Vol.3. 3e sonate en si-bémol majeur.

1434. ———. [Sonatas, harp, op. 47, no. 2, F major] *Trois sonates: précédées de trois préludes: pour la harpe, oeuvre 47, no. 2.* Paris: Naderman, [181–?]. 25 pp.

1435. ———. [Sonates progressives, harp, op. 92] *Sieben progressive Sonatinen.* Marina Del Rey, Calif.: Safari Publications, n.d. 45 pp.

1436. ———. [Sonates progressives, harp, op. 92] *Sieben progressive Sonatinen: für Harfe, op. 92.* Neue, revidierte, mit genauen Fingersatz und Pedalbezeichnungen versehene Ausgabe von Edmund Schuëcker. Leipzig: C. E. W. Siegel, [ca. 1900]. 2 v. CONTENTS: Vol.1: No. 1, E major; no. 2, C minor; no. 3, B major; no. 4, G minor. Vol.2: No. 5, F major; no. 6, D minor; no. 7, C major.

1437. ———. [Sonates progressives, harp, op. 92] *Sept sonates progressives:*

pour la harpe. Revues et doigtées selon l'enseignment de Alphonse Hasselmans par Raphael Martenot. Paris: A. Leduc, c1925. 51 pp.

1438. ———. [Sonates progressives, harp, op. 92] *Sept sonates progressives: pour la harpe.* Revues et doigtées selon l'enseignement de Alphonse Hasselmans. [New York, N.Y.]: Lyra Music Co., [197–?]. 51 pp.

1439. ———. [Suites, harp, op. 45, no. 1. Gentil houzard] *Gentil houzard: suivi de la marche de Tamerlan, variés pour la harpe: 1ere. suite de l'oeuvre 45.* Paris: Naderman, [181–?]. 10 pp.

1440. ———. *Theme and variations no. 1: for the Clark Irish harp.* New York: International Music Co., c1921. 5 pp.

1441. ———. *Variations on the air L'oiseau chantant.* Santa Monica, Calif.: Salvi Publications, c1978. 11 pp.

1442. Nagayo, Sueko, 1950–. *Myukesu: hapu soro no tame no = Mucus: for solo harp.* Tokyo: Ongaku No Tomo Sha, c1972. 19 pp. (Contemporary Japanese music series, 107) Issued as suppl. to Ongaku geijutsu, 1973, v. 31, no. 1.

1443. Narimanidze, Niko. *Variatsii: na temu gruzinskoi narodnoi pesni Chela: dlia arfy.* [Redaktsiia T. Vymiatninoi]. Moscow: Sov. kompozitor, 1978. 31 pp.

1444. Natra, Sergiu, 1924–. *A book of Hebrew songs: for harp.* Tel Aviv, Israel: Israel Music Institute, c1979. 25 pp.

1445. ———. *Prayer: for harp.* Tel Aviv: Israel Music Institute, 1972. 12 pp.

1446. ———. *Prayer: for harp.* 2nd ed. Tel Aviv: Israel Music Institute, c1978. 12 pp.

1447. ———. *Sefer shirim ivriyim: l'nevel = A book of Hebrew songs: for harp.* Tel Aviv: Israel Music Institute, 1979. 25 pp. (Eliezer Peri educational music series)

1448. ———. *Sonatina: for harp.* Tel Aviv: Israel Music Institute, c1964. 18 pp.

1449. ———. *Sonatina: for harp.* [2nd rev. ed.]. Tel Aviv: Israel Music Institute, 1978. 18 pp.

1450. Negrea, Martian, 1893–1973. *Patru piese: pentru harpa.* Bucharest: Editura de Stat pentru Literatura si Arta, n.d. 18 pp.

1451. Nicoletta, Eleanor J. *Dance of the marionettes: Irish harp solo.* New York: International Music Co., c1922. 3 pp. [NP]

1452. Nicoletta, Frank A. *Caprice (Eleanor).* New York: International Music Pub., c1918. 4 pp.

1453. ———. *Oriental: intermezzo.* New York: International Music Pub. Co., c1917. 5 pp.

1454. Nieland, Herman. *Theme with variations in old style: for harpsichord or harp.* Amsterdam: Broekmans & Van Poppel, c1964. 6 pp.

1455. Noda, Teruyuki, 1940–. *The dream of Endymion: for harp solo.* Tokyo, Japan: Ongaku No Tomo Sha, c1986. 12 pp. Composed 1983–1984; revised 1985.

1456. ———. *Hymn: for harp solo.* Tokyo: Academia Music Ltd., c1973. 12 pp.

1457. Nodaïra, Ichirô, 1953–. *Messages I: pour harpe.* Paris: Lemoine, 1985. 12 pp.

1458. Novák, Milan, 1927–. *Sonata: pre harfu = Sonate: für Harfe.* Bratislava: Opus, c1985. 25 pp.

1459. Oberthür, Charles, 1819–1895. *Ah be not sad: harp.* New York: Browne & Buckwell, n.d. 5 pp.

1460. ———. *Air russe: le sarafan, op. 207.* Mainz: B. Schott's Söhne, n.d. 9 pp.

1461. ———. *Alpen-Lieder: Gesänge aus dem bayerischen Oberland, op. 308.* Mainz: B. Schott's Söhne, n.d. 7 pp.

1462. ———. *Andalusia: bolero brillant pour la harpe.* London: Edwin Ashdown, n.d. 8 pp.

1463. ———. *Bel chiaro di luna: impromptu, op. 91.* Leipzig: Friedrich Hofmeister, n.d. 11 pp.

1464. ———. *The blind girl.* New York: Browne & Buckwell, c1864. 7 pp.

1465. ———. *Bonnie Scotland: fantaisie brillante for the harp, op. 115.* London: Edwin Ashdown, [189–?]. 21 pp.

1466. ———. *Clouds and sunshine, op. 219.* Mainz: B. Schott's Söhne, [18–?]. 15 pp.

1467. ———. *A dream of by-gone days: melody.* Mainz: B. Schott's Söhne, n.d. 9 pp.

1468. ———. *Elegie: Lagrima sulla tomba di Parish Alvars, op. 38.* London: Wessel & Co., n.d. 13 pp.

1469. ———. *Erin, oh! Erin: melodie irlandaise favorite, op. 183.* London: Schott & Cie., n.d. 11 pp.

1470. ———. *A fairy legend, op. 182.* Mainz: B. Schott's Söhne, n.d. 11 pp.

1471. ———. *Fantasia on Il trovatore de Verdi, op. 144.* London: Edwin Ashdown, n.d. 9 pp.

1472. ———. *Fantasie über E. Humperdinck's Hänsel und Gretel: für Harfe.* Mainz: B. Schott's Söhne, c1895. 11 pp.

1473. ———. *La grâce: impromptu pour la harpe.* New York: J.F. Browne, ca. 1858? 7 pp. "Op. 123."

1474. ———. *The harp that once through Tara's halls = Harfe die einst in Tara's Hallen erklang, op. 187.* Leipzig: Friedrich Hofmeister, n.d. 9 pp.

1475. ———. *Hommage à Schubert: trois mélodies favorites: pour harpe seule, op. 89.* London: Edwin Ashdown, n.d. 3 v.

1476. ———. *The keel row: fantasia for the harp, op. 166.* London: Edwin Ashdown, n.d. 9 pp.

1477. ———. *Meditation: a musical sketch composed for the harp, op. 153.* Dresden: Louis Bauer, n.d. 11 pp.

1478. ———. *Meditation, op. 153.* Leipzig: Friedrich Hofmeister, 188–? 11 pp.

1479. ———. [Morceaux caractéristiques] *Trois morceaux caractéristiques: pour la harpe, op. 121.* London: Edwin Ashdown, n.d. 3 v. CONTENTS: La gitana; Mélodie mazurque; La gazelle.

1480. ———. [Morceaux caracteristiques, harp. no. 5] *Six morceaux caracteristiques: harp. No. 5. The gypsy girl.* New York: Browne & Bucknell, 1867. 7 pp.

1481. ———. [Musical illustrations, harp] *Three musical illustrations: for the harp.* Mainz: B. Schott's Söhne, n.d. 3 v. CONTENTS: The troubadour; Serenade; Soldier's delight.

1482. ———. [Musical poems] *Two musical poems: for the harp, op. 351.* London: Edwin Ashdown, n.d. 2 v. CONTENTS: In twilight hour; In fairyland.

1483. ———. *Nun's prayer = La prière de la réligieuse = Der Nonne Gebet, op. 54.* Mainz: B. Schott's Söhne, n.d. 5 pp.

1484. ———. *Le papillon: caprice pour la harpe, op. 317.* Paris: Lacombe, n.d. 7 pp.

1485. ———. *Partant pour la Syrie: French national song: harp.* New York: J.F. Browne, c1867. 7 pp.

1486. ———. *Le passé et l'avenir: poèsie musicale pour la harpe.* Paris: Lemoine & Fils, n.d. 5 pp.

1487. ———. [Preludes, harp] *24 preludes: for the harp.* New York: Carl Fischer, [ca. 1900?]. 15 pp.

1488. ———. *Seaside rambles: four musical sketches, op. 158.* London: Edwin Ashdown, n.d. CONTENTS: Sea nymphs; Murmuring waves; My bark glides through the silver wave; Water sprites.

1489. ———. *Silvana: air de ballet composé pour la harpe, op. 311.* London: Chappel & Co., n.d. 7 pp.

1490. ———. *Songs without words = Lieder ohne Worte.* London: Edwin Ashdown, n.d. 18 v.

1491. ———. *Souvenir de Boulogne: nocturno, op. 30.* London: Schott, ca. 1850? 14 pp.

1492. ———. *Souvenir de Lucia di Lammermoor, op. 188.* Leipzig: Friedrich Hofmeister, n.d. 9 pp.

1493. ———. *Sur la parade: petit march pour le harpe.* Leipzig: C.F. Kahnt, n.d. 7 pp.

1494. ———. *Sur la rive de la mer = Am Meeresstrande: impromptu pour la harpe, op. 117.* Leipzig: Otto Junne, n.d. 9 pp.

1495. Orgad, Ben-Zion, 1926–. *Taksim: harp solo.* Tel Aviv: Israeli Music Publications, c1962. 12 pp.

1496. Orr, Buxton, 1924–. *Three diatonic preludes: for harp.* [Ed. by Sidonie Goossens]. London: Oxford University Press, c1967. 9 pp.

1497. Orrego Salas, Juan, 1919–. *Variations on a chant, op. 92: solo harp.* Bloomington, Ind.: Frangipani Press, c1986. 13 pp.

1498. Orthel, Léon, 1905–. [Bagatelles, harp, op. 67] *Vijf bagatellen voor harp, opus 67.* Amsterdam: Donemus, c1974. 14 pp.

1499. ———. *Petite suite: harpe, op. 69.* Amsterdam: Donemus, c1977. 11 pp.

1500. ———. [Schizzetti] *Cinque schizzetti: arpa, op. 82.* Amsterdam: Donemus, c1977. 9 pp.

1501. Ortiz, Alfredo Rolando, 1946–. [Harp music. Selections] *From harp to harp, with love = De harpe à harpe, avec amour.* Corona, Calif.: A.R. Ortiz, c1983.

———. *Latin American harp music and techniques: for pedal and non-pedal harpists.* See 60.

———. *Latin American harp music and techniques: for pedal and non-pedal harpists.* 2nd ed., rev. and enlarged. See 61.

1502. Osieck, Hans, 1910–. *Sonatine: for harp solo.* Amsterdam: Donemus, c1968. 14 pp.

1503. Osokin, M. (Mikhail), 1903–. [Preludes, harp, op. 54] *Dvadtsat chetvertyi preliudii: dlia arfy, soch. 54.* Moscow: Sov. kompozitor, 1973. 54 pp. 24 preludes for harp.

1504. ———. [Sonatas, harp, op. 59] *Sonata: dlia arfy, soch. 59; Kontsertnyï duet: dlia arfy i fleïty, soch. 50.* Moscow: Sov. kompozitor, c1979. 43 pp. 1st work for harp; 2nd work for flute and harp.

1505. Owen, Eleri. *Llety'r bugail.* Wales: Eleri Owen, 1979. 20 pp. CONTENTS: Porth-y-castell; Llety'r bugail; Tir iarll; Twyn-yr-fen; Cerrig llwydion; Tyderwen; Argoed; Coed derw; Dolfedw.

1506. Owen, Geraint Lloyd; Meirion, Mona, and Jones, Nan. *Tant i'r plant.*

Wales: Gwasg Gwynedd, 1981. 27 pp. Each work acc. by a Welsh poem. CONTENTS: Hawys; Elliw; Gwenan; Manon; Betsan; Ffion; Caryl; Elin; Siwan; Awen; Angharad.

1507. Owens, Dewey. [Impressions on pedal patterns] *Twelve impressions on pedal patterns: for young harpists.* New York: Lyra Music Co., c1974. 10 pp.

1508. ———. [Pieces, harp] *Six pieces: for harp (with or without pedals).* New York: Lyra Music Co., c1971. 11 pp. Promenade; Pastorale; Carillon; Jig (in baroque style); Etude in G (study for left hand); Spanish elegy. [NP]

1509. Owens, Dewey, and Murphy, Olive. *Three Irish pieces.* Arranged for Irish, troubadour or pedal harp. New York: Charles Colin, c1964. 3 pp. [NP] CONTENTS: The girl I left behind me; The Sligo fancy; The pet of the pipers.

1510. Palau Boix, Manuel, 1893–1967. *Danza y copla del ausente: para arpa.* Madrid: Union Musical Española, c1972. 5 pp.

1511. Palmer, Lynne Wainwright, 1919–. *Classical suite: for harp alone.* [Santa Monica, Calif.]: Salvi, 1977. 24 pp.

1512. ———. *Harp à la mode.* Ellensburg, Wash.: F C Publishing Co., 1992. 20 pp. [NP]

1513. ———. *Procession for Janet.* Santa Monica, Calif.: Salvi Publications, c1982. 2 pp.

1514. ———. *Shades of blue; and, A snatch of jazz.* Santa Monica, Calif.: Salvi Publications, c1981. 6 pp.

1515. ———. *Sounds I and II.* [San Mateo, Calif.]: F.C. Publishing Co., 1987. 7 pp.

1516. ———. *Troubadour trek.* San Mateo, Calif.: F.C. Publishing Co., [1987], c1986. 9 pp. [NP] CONTENTS: Hunt and peck; Second chance; Third dimension; Four-in-hand; Five by five; Sixth sense; Seven up; Eight ball.

1517. Panormo, Francis, 1764–1844. *The bird waltz: for the harp or piano forte.* Albany, N.Y.: R.S. Meacham, [18—]. 3 pp.

1518. ———. *The bird waltz: for the piano forte or harp.* Philadelphia: G. E. Blake, 18—. 3 pp.

1519. ———. *The bird waltz: for the harp or piano forte.* Philadelphia: Published by Bacon & Co., 181–. 3 pp.

1520. ———. *The bird waltz: harp or piano forte.* Baltimore: G. Willig, 182–. 3 pp.

1521. ———. *The bird waltz: for the harp or piano forte.* Baltimore: J. Cole, 1827? 3 pp.

1522. ———. [Variations, harp, op. 11] *Six favourite airs with variations: for the harp or piano forte, op. XI.* [London]: The author, [180–?]. 33 pp. The beggar girl; Blue bell of Scotland; Maid of Lodi; In the dead of the night; Over the water to Charlie; Fresh and strong the breeze was blowing.

1523. Papp, Lajos, 1935–. *Ricercare: per arpa*. Budapest: Editio Musica, c1970. 11 pp.

1524. Paret, Betty. *Berceuse de noël*. New York: MCA Music, c1939. 1 p. (Very first harp pieces)

1525. ———, arr. [Harp book, no. 1] *First harp book*. [Compiled and arranged by] Betty Paret. New York: G. Schirmer, c1942. 37 pp. CONTENTS: Harp song; Big brown bear; Autumn leaves; Elephant; Copy-cat; Waltz; Alphabet song; Swinging; Jumping; Wooden-shoe dance; Cuckoo; Rocking; Russian tune; Star dance; Scale snippets; Sur le pont d'Avignon; Long, long ago; Pussy cat; Folk-song; Swedish folk-dance; The jolly peasant; Rondo; Rain song; Lavender's blue; The keys of heaven; En roulant; Lota; Barbara Allen; Night song; Shepherd's cradle-song; The bluebells of Scotland; A riddle; The wonderful inn; Le bon petit roi d'Yvetot; The keel row; The judge's dance; Song of the evening bell; Hymn of Thanksgiving; Jardin d'amour; O'Carolan's air; Andante from the Surprise symphony by Haydn; Waltz, op. 77, no. 2 by Schubert; The foggy dew; Leezie Lindsay; Drink to me only; All through the night; German dance, op. 33, no. 7 by Schubert; Flowers in the valley; Wi' a hundred pipers.

1526. ———, arr. [Harp book, no. 1] *First harp book*. [Compiled and arranged by] Betty Paret. New York: Lyra Music Co., [1980?], c1942. 37 pp. CONTENTS: See 1525.

1527. ———, arr. [Harp book, no. 2] *Second harp book*. [Compiled and arranged] by Betty Paret. New York, N.Y.: Lyra Music Co., c1966. 41 pp. CONTENTS: Deep in the forest; Evening song by J. J. Rousseau; While bagpipes play from the Peasant cantata by J. S. Bach; The Queen's music; Lolotte's complaint; Theme from sonata by W. A. Mozart; Three sea sketches. Dolphins in the waves; The bell buoy rings; The white gull's flight by Betty Paret; Minuet from Don Giovanni by W. A. Mozart; Skye boat song; Sonatina (1st movement) by Clementi; Troubadour's song by Betty Paret; Valse gracieuse by W. A. Mozart; Hornpipe by Henry Purcell; Sarabande by G. F. Handel; 16th century Spanish dance; Minuet from VIth French suite by J. S. Bach; Air by Henry Purcell; Prelude by J. S. Bach; Sarabande by Corelli; The Lord's prayer by Malotte; To a wild rose by Edward MacDowell; Allegretto by Haydn; Nocturne by Schumann; Alabama lullaby (based on the folk song Go to sleepy) by Betty Paret; Chorale from St. Matthew passion by J. S. Bach; Harlequin from The carnival suite by Henry Closson.

1528. ———. *Harp solos*. New York: Sprague-Coleman, c1939–41. 3 v. in 1. CONTENTS: The hunt is up; Jungle scenes; Londonderry air.

1529. ———. *Very first harp pieces.* New York: Sprague-Coleman, c1939. 3 v. in 1. CONTENTS: Moonlight; I hear a harp; Berceuse de Noel.

1530. Parfenov, N. G. (Nikolai Gavrilovich), 1893–1942. *Malen'kaia siuita: dlia arfy.* Moscow: Muzgiz, 1938. 15 pp.

1531. ———. *Variations on a theme of Corelli: for harp.* Moscow: Gosudarstvennoe, 1935. 12 pp.

1532. Parish-Alvars, Elias, 1808–1849. *Barcarole.* Edited by John Thomas. London: Gould & Bolttler, [19—?]. 9 pp. (Parish Alvars' compositions for the harp, 11)

1533. ———. *Danse des fées: morceau caractéristique pour harpe, op. 76.* Paris: Henry Lemoine et Cie., n.d. 12 pp.

1534. ———. *La danse des fées, op. 76.* Marina Del Rey, Calif.: Safari Publications, 1993. 13 pp.

1535. ———. *Fantasia on themes from Weber's Oberon, op. 59.* Abergavenny, Gwent: Adlais, c1979. 25 pp.

1536. ———. *The Greek pirates chorus, from Byron's Corsair: march composed for the harp.* London: T. Boosey & Co.'s Foreign Musical Library, [ca. 1870]. 5 pp.

1537. ———. *Introduction et variations sur un thème du l'opera I Capuleti et Montecchi de Bellini, op. 40.* Milan: Ricordi, [1838?]. 7 pp.

1538. ———. *Lucia de Lammermoor fantasie, op. 79.* Marina Del Rey, Calif.: Safari Publications, 1992. 26 pp.

1539. ———. [Mandoline] *La mandoline: grande fantaisie pour harpe.* Revision de Martine Geliot. Paris: Gérard Billaudot, c1977. 19 pp. (La harpe)

1540. ———. [Mandoline] *Grand study in imitation of the mandoline.* Abergavenny, Gwent: Adlais, c1979. 21 pp.

1541. ———. [Mandoline] *Grand study in imitation of the mandoline.* London: Salvi Publications, c1990. 17 pp.

1542. ———. *Marche favorite du sultan.* Edited by John Thomas. London: Hutchings & Romer, [19—?]. 7 pp. (Parish Alvars' compositions for the harp, 15)

1543. ———. *Marche pour la harpe d'après une mélodie napolitaine, oeuv. 87.* Milan: Ricordi, n.d. 5 pp.

1544. ———. *La plainte d'une jeune fille.* Edited by John Thomas. London: Hutchings & Romer, [19—?]. 7 pp. (Parish Alvars' compositions for the harp, 18)

1545. ———. *Prayer: from Mosé in Egitto.* Abergavenny, Gwent: Adlais, [198–?]. 9 pp. Adapted from Rossini.

1546. ———. *Rêveries, op. 82.* Marina Del Rey, Calif.: Safari Publications, n.d. 23 pp.

1547. ———. *Romances: for the harp.* Edited by David Watkins. [England]: The Clive Morley Collection, [198–?]. 3 v.

1548. ———. *Romances: for the harp: book 1.* Edited by John Thomas. Marina Del Rey, Calif.: Safari, 1990. 35 pp. Reprint. CONTENTS: Nos. 1–12.

1549. ———. *Romances: for the harp: book 2.* Edited by John Thomas. Marina Del Rey, Calif.: Safari, 1990. 31 pp. Reprint. CONTENTS: Nos. 13–24.

1550. ———. [Romances, harp. Selections] *Six romances sans paroles.* Mainz: Schott's Söhne, [19—?]. 2 v.

1551. ———. [Romances, harp. Selections] *Three romances: for harp.* [Edited] by Samuel O. Pratt. New York: Colin, c1966. 9 pp. (Pratt music library series of masterworks originally for harp)

1552. ———. [Serenade, harp, op. 73] *Serenade, op. 73.* Ed. by Susanna Mildonian. New York: Lyra Music, c1975. 8 pp.

1553. ———. [Serenades, harp, op. 83, B♭ major] *Sérénade: pour harpe, op. 83.* Paris: Gérard Billaudot, c1975. 9 pp. (La harpe)

1554. ———. [Serenades, harp, op. 83, B♭ major] *Sérénade.* Abergavenny, Gwent: Adlais, [198–?]. 9 pp.

1555. ———. *Souvenir de Portici.* Edited by John Thomas. London: Gould & Bolttler, [19—?]. 5 pp. (Parish Alvars' compositions for the harp, 12)

1556. ———. *Souvenir de Taglioni: pas original de l'auteur, dans le ballet La fille du Danube, op. 88.* Mainz: Fils de B. Schott, 1846. 7 pp.

1557. ———. [Souvenirs des opéras italiens. Ernani] *Souvenirs des opéras italiens: no. 1 [sur des motifs d']Ernani [de Verdi]: arr. dans un style facile et brillant pour la harpe.* Milan: Ricordi, [1845]. 14 pp. Parish-Alvars' op. 77. Cf. Franz Pazdirek, *Universal-Handbuch der Musikliteratur* (Vienna: Pazdirek, 1904–1910).

1558. ———. [Voyage d'un harpiste en Orient. Air hebreu de Philopopolis] *Air hebreu de Philopopolis.* Edited by John Thomas. London: Hutchings & Romer, [19—?]. 5 pp. (Parish Alvars' compositions for the harp, 3)

1559. ———. [Voyage d'un harpiste en Orient. Air hebreu de Philopopolis] *Hebrew air.* Abergavenny, Gwent: Adlais, [198–?]. 5 pp. "Op. 62, no. 3."

1560. ———. [Voyage d'un harpiste en Orient. Bulgarian gipsy dance] *Bulgarian gipsy dance.* Edited by John Thomas. London: Hutchings & Romer, [19—?]. 5 pp. (Parish Alvars' compositions for the harp, 1)

1561. ———. [Voyage d'un harpiste en Orient. Papagallo] *Il papagallo.* Edited by John Thomas. London: Gould & Bolttler, [19—?]. 9 pp. (Parish Alvars' compositions for the harp, 7)

1562. ———. [Voyage d'un harpiste en Orient. Papagallo] *Il papagallo, op. 85.* Marina Del Rey, Calif.: Safari Publications, 1993. 9 pp.

1563. ———. [Voyage d'un harpiste en Orient. Sérenade] *Sérenade.* Edited by John Thomas. London: Hutchings & Romer, [19—?]. 9 pp. (Parish Alvars' compositions for the harp, 16)

1564. ———. [Voyage d'un harpiste en Orient. Sultan's parade march] *The sultan's parade march.* Edited by John Thomas. London: Hutchings & Romer, [19—?]. 5 pp. (Parish Alvars' compositions for the harp, 5)

1565. Parrott, Ian, 1916–. *Ceredigion: three pieces with interludes: for harp.* Cardiff: University of Wales Press, c1962. 11 pp.

1566. Parry, Enid. *Castell Caerdydd: for harp.* Cardiff, Wales: University Council of Music and the University of Wales Press Board, c1959. 6 pp.

1567. ———. [Piece, harp] *Darn: i'r delyn = Piece: for harp.* Swansea, England: Snell & Sons, c1951. 5 pp.

1568. ———. [Prelude, harp] *Preliwd: i'r delyn = Prelude: for harp.* Swansea, England: Snell & Sons, c1951. 3 pp.

1569. ———. [Rondo, harp, B♭ minor] *Rondo: for harp.* Cardiff, Wales: University Council of Music and the University of Wales Press Board, c1960. 7 pp.

1570. Parry, John, 1710–1782. [Lessons, harp] *Four lessons; Sonata.* Abergavenny, Gwent: Adlais, 1981. xi, 23 pp. Facsimile edition of the original publication (1761) with commentary by Ann Griffiths.

1571. ———. [Lessons, harp] *Four sonatas: for harp (1761).* Ed. Sioned Williams. [Santa Monica, Calif.]: Salvi, 1981. 40 pp.

1572. ———. *Llyfr alawon poced John Parry Ddall, Rhiwabon = pocket tune-book.* Aberystwyth: Gwasg Teires, 1991. 20 pp. [NP]

1573. Partos, Oedoen, 1907–1977. *Improvisation and niggun: harp solo.* Tel Aviv: Israeli Music Publications; New York: Leeds, 1959. 16 pp.

1574. ———. *Mizmor: for harp (1975).* [Tel Aviv]: Israel Music Institute, 1987. 12 pp.

1575. Pascal, Claude, 1921–. *Musique: pour harpe.* Paris: Durand; Philadelphia: Elkan-Vogel, c1960. 13 pp.

1576. Patachich, Istvan, 1922–. *Balcanophonia: per arpa.* Budapest: Editio Musica, c1983. 12 pp.

1577. ———. *Contorni: per arpa.* Budapest: Editio Musica, c1971. 12 pp. CONTENTS: Grafica; Tempera; Incisione.

1578. Patlaenko, Eduard Nikolaevich, 1936–. *Geometricheskie variatsii: dlia arfy.* Moscow: Sov. kompoz, c1974. 23 pp.

1579. Patorni-Casadesus, Régina. [Eau qui court] *L'eau qui court: pour harpe chromatique*. Paris: Choudens, 1937. 3 pp.

1580. Patterson, Paul, 1947–. *Spiders: harp solo*. London: Universal Edition, c1985. 19 pp. "Originally written as Three bagatelles." CONTENTS: The dancing white lady; The red-backed spider; The black widow; Tarantula.

1581. Pauer, Jiří, 1919–. [Partita, harp] *Suita: pro harfu (1947)*. 2d ed. Prague: Panton, 1983, c1966. 17 pp.

1582. Paulus, Stephen, 1949–. [Divertimento, harp, orchestra. Berceuse] *Berceuse: for harp solo: from Divertimento for harp and chamber orchestra*. Totowa, N.J.: European American Music Corp., c1982. 1 part (5 pp.). Excerpt from the suite, playable as unacc. solo.

1583. Pay'r, Robert. [Technische Studien] *887 technische Studien für Harfe = Technical studies for the harp*. Leipzig: Ludwig Doblinger, c1912. 4 v.

1584. Pehrson, Joseph. *Etude moderne: for harp solo*. New York: Seesaw Music, c1983. 11 pp.

1585. Pennisi, Francesco, 1934–. *Madame Récamier: due capricci per arpa*. Milan: Ricordi, 1981. 11 pp.

1586. ———. [Piccole rapsodie] *Due piccole rapsodie: per arpa*. Milan: G. Ricordi, c1983. 6 pp.

1587. Perrachio, Luigi, 1883–1966. [Pezzi, harp] *Tre pezzi: per arpa*. Milan, New York: G. Ricordi & Co., c1926. 17 pp. CONTENTS: Gagliarda; Romanesca; Passemezzo.

1588. ———. [Sonate popolaresche italiane, no. 1] *Cinque sonate popolaresche italiane: sonata 1a.: per arpa*. Milan: Carisch, c1938. 17 pp. (Composizioni scelte per arpa)

1589. Perrotta, Vincenzo. *Poemetto: per arpa*. Padua: Edizioni G. Zanibon, c1940. 4 pp.

1590. Persichetti, Vincent, 1915–1987. [Parables, no. 7] *Parable: for solo harp*. Bryn Mawr, Pa.: Elkan-Vogel, c1973. 23 pp. Op. 119.

1591. Petit, Jacques, 1928–1982. *Bleu nuit: pour harpe*. Paris: Éditions Rideau Rouge, c1976. 4 pp.

1592. Petrassi, Goffredo, 1904–. *Flou: per arpa*. Milan: Edizioni Suvini Zerboni, c1981. 10 pp.

1593. Petrić, Ivo, 1931–. *Preludij: za harfo; Scherzino: za harfo = Prelude: for harp; Scherzino: for harp*. Frankfurt am Main: W. Zimmermann, c1965. 5 pp.

1594. Petrini, François, 1744–1819. *Te bien aimer: romance de Plantada, oeuvre 45*. Arr. pour la harpe avec variations par F. Petrini. Paris: Naderman, [181–?]. 9 pp.

1595. ———. *Variations.* New York: Lyra Music Co., c1967. 6 pp.

1596. Petrini, Henri, b. ca. 1775. *Etude de la main gauche: contenant douze airs connus, arr. pour la harpe, oeuv. 9.* Paris: s.n., ca. 1800. 10 pp.

1597. Philippe, Y. *Fantaisie: pour harpe.* Paris: Gay & Tenton, c1928. 11 pp.

1598. ———. *Les naïades: pour harpe.* Paris: Louis Rouhier, c1925. 5 pp.

1599. ———. *Nuit vénitienne: pour harpe.* Paris: Louis Rouhier, c1925. 6 pp.

1600. Phillips, Richard. *Le jardin secret d'Elodie: six pieces pour harpe ou harpe celtique.* Paris: Éditions M. Combre, c1988. 10 pp. [NP] CONTENTS: Pres du rosier; Le dolmen; La chanson d'Elodie; Old England; Chant d'Irlande; Comme au temps jadis.

1601. Pick-Mangiagalli, Riccardo, 1882–1949. *Capriccio, op. 65: per arpa.* Milan: Carisch, 1941. 10 pp.

1602. ———. *Sarabanda: per arpa, op. 69.* Milan: Carisch, 1942. 5 pp.

1603. ———. *Sfumature: per arpa, op. 70.* Milan: Carisch, 1942. 5 pp.

1604. Pierce, Alexandra, 1934–. *Maola: for harp.* New York: Seesaw Music, c1977. 8 pp.

1605. Pierné, Gabriel, 1863–1937. *Impromptu-caprice: pour la harpe.* Edition de concert. New York: Lyra Music Co., [19—]. 9 pp.

1606. ———. *Impromptu-caprice: pour la harpe, op. 9.* Edition de concert. Paris: Alphonse Leduc, [1965]. 9 pp.

1607. Pillois, Jacques, 1877–1935. [Pièces, harp] *Deux pièces.* [Transcription pour harpe à pédales par Marcel Grandjany]. Paris: Editions M. Senart, c1928. 7 pp. CONTENTS: 1. A la manière de Lully (Gavotte); 2. A la manière de Fauré (Romance sans paroles).

1608. Pinkham, Daniel, 1923–. *Vigils: harp solo.* Edited by Carol Baum. Boston: Ione Press, 1982. 15 pp.

1609. Pinto, Angelo Francis, d. 1948. [Adirondacks sketches. Lake scene] *The lake scene: from The Adirondacks sketches: suite for harp solo, op. 52.* New York: International Music Pub. Co., c1915. 8 pp.

1610. ———. [Adirondacks sketches. Pastoral reverie] *Pastoral reverie: from The Adirondacks sketches, suite for harp solo [in G major], op. 53.* New York: International Music Pub. Co., c1915. 7 pp.

1611. ———. [Adirondacks sketches. Sunset] *Sunset (tone poem): from The Adirondacks sketches, suite for harp solo [in A♭ minor], op. 50.* New York: International Music Pub. Co., c1915. 4 pp.

1612. ———. *Believe me if all those endearing young charms: petite paraphrase for harp solo.* New York: International Music, c1916. 7 pp.

1613. ———. [Floral thoughts. Rosemary] *The rosemary from The floral thoughts: suite for harp solo [in E minor], op. 54.* New York: International Music Pub. Co., c1915. 5 pp.

1614. ———. *Impromtu* [sic]: *Aeolian harp sounds in the forest: from The romantic suite for harp solo, op. 64.* New York: International Music, c1915. 9 pp.

1615. ———. *Paraphrase on The sweetest story ever told.* Boston: Oliver Ditson Co., c1920. 8 pp.

1616. ———. *Petite berceuse: [for] harp solo [in B♭ major].* New York: International Music Pub. Co., 1914. 5 pp.

1617. ———. *Reve apres le bal: scherzo for harp solo [in D minor].* New York: International Music Pub. Co., c1911. 7 pp. "Harp or piano."

1618. ———. *Serenade capricciosa.* New York: International Music Pub., c1913. 4 pp.

1619. ———. *Suite religioso: for harp solo.* New York: International Music Co., c1921. 11 pp. CONTENTS: Come ye disconsolate; Silent night; Abide with me; Nearer my God to thee; Old hundred; Adeste fideles; See the conquering hero comes.

1620. ———. *Tarantella: in C minor: improvised from the Naderman Étude.* New York: International Music, c1911. 7 pp.

1621. Pitfield, Thomas, 1903–. [Miniatures, harp] *Eleven miniatures: for harp.* London; New York: Edition Peters, c1976. 10 pp. CONTENTS: 1. First little jig; 2. First ostinato; 3. Imitation; 4. First little waltz; 5. Second little jig; 6. Cossak lullaby; 7. Third little jig; 8. Second ostinato; 9. Fourth little jig; 10. Second little waltz; 11. Rippling.

1622. ———. [Sonatina, harp] *Harp sonatina.* New York: Hinrichsen, c1958. 7 pp.

1623. Piva, Franco. *Recitativo II: per arpa.* Milan: Carisch, c1983. 5 pp.

1624. Pizzo, Giuseppe. [Suites, harp, no. 1. Elegie] *Elegie: from Suite no. 1: harp solo.* New York: International Music Pub., c1922. 9 pp.

1625. Plakidis, P. (Petr), 1947–. *Meditation: pour harpe.* Paris: Alphonse Leduc, c1992. 7 pp.

1626. Pleyel, Ignaz, 1757–1831. *Rondo: pour la harpe ou piano-forte, op. 51.* Offenbach a/M: Jean André, n.d. 5 pp.

1627. Poenitz, Franz, 1850–1913. *Abendfrieden, op. 77, no. 1; Nocturne, op. 77, no. 2.* Leipzig: Zimmermann, c1907. 7 pp.

1628. ———. *Gebet = Prière: für Harfe, op. 67, no. 1.* Berlin: Carl Simon, c1902. 2 pp.

1629. ———. *Klange aus der Alhambra: fantasia, op. 68.* Bayreuth: Carl Giessel, c1902. 11 pp.

1630. ———. [Leichte Stücke] *Drei leichte Stücke: Standchen, op. 29, no. 1.* Berlin: Carl Simon, n.d. 4 pp.

1631. ———. *Maskenscherz, op. 78.* Leipzig: J.H. Zimmermann, c1913. 10 pp.

1632. ———. *Nordische Ballade: Es moll, op. 33: für Harfe.* Berlin: Carl Simon, 1892. 19 pp.

1633. Polansky, Larry, 1954–. *Another you: 17 variations for solo harp.* [S.l: s.n.], [198–]. 15 pp.

1634. Poliart, Jean-Louis. *Piece: pour harpe* = *Stuk: voor harp.* Ostend: Andel, [198–]. 4 pp.

1635. Polin, Claire C. J., 1926–. *Eligmos archaios: (ancient winding roads which lead to the heart of man . . .): landscapes for solo harp.* New York: Seesaw Music, c1973. 11 pp.

1636. ———. *Summer settings: harp solo.* New York: Lyra Music Co., 1967. 5 pp.

1637. Pollet, Benoît, d. 1818. [Sonatas, harp, no. 2] *Deuxième sonate.* Sans pedales, jouable sur grande harpe ou harpe celtique. Paris: Billaudot, 1982. 13 pp. (La harpe) [NP]

1638. Pollini, Francesco, 1763–1846. *Capriccio e aria con variazioni: per arpa.* Rev. Mirella Vita. Milan: Edizioni Suvini Zerboni, [1968]. 19 pp.

1639. ———. *Tema e variazioni: per arpa.* Rev. Mirella Vita. Milan: Edizioni Suvini Zerboni, c1968. 10 pp.

1640. Poot, Marcel, 1901–. *Impromptu: pour harpe.* Paris: Editions musicales A. Leduc, c1964. 8 pp.

1641. Popesco, Marie-Monique. *Facettes: 8 pièces pour grande harpe ou harpe celtique.* Paris: G. Billaudot, c1992. 11 pp. [NP]

1642. Poser, Hans, 1917–1970. [Preludes, harp] *Drei Preludes: für Harfe.* Wolfenbüttel: Möseler Verlag, c1970. 11 pp.

1643. Posse, Wilhelm, 1852–1925. [Grosse Konzert-Etüden] *Eight great concert-studies: for harp.* New York: Lyra Music Co., [19—]. 38 pp.

1644. ———. [Grosse Konzert-Etüden] *Acht grosse Konzert-Etüden: für Harfe* = *Eight great concert-studies: for harp.* Frankfurt a.M.: W. Zimmermann, c1957. 8 v. (Musik für Harfe: Schulwerke)

1645. ———. *Improvisationen: für Harfe solo.* Frankfurt: Zimmermann, n.d. 11 pp.

1646. ———. [Kleine Characterstücke] *5 kleine Characterstücke.* Mainz: B. Schott's Söhne, n.d. 9 pp. CONTENTS: Menuett; Wellenspiel; Am Abend; Lied ohne Worte; Turkischer Marsch.

1647. ———. [Kleine Stücke] *Sechs kleine Stücke: für Harfe.* Leipzig: Jul. Heinr. Zimmermann, c1910. 17 pp.

1648. ———. *Tarantella.* [Santa Monica, Calif.]: Salvi Publications, c1977. 5 pp.

1649. ———. *Thema mit Variationen: für Harfe.* Leipzig: Jul. Heinr. Zimmermann, c1919. 15 pp.

1650. ———. *Variationen über Der Karneval von Venedig: für Harfe.* Leipzig: Jul. Heinr. Zimmermann, c1919. 15 pp.

1651. ———. *Variationen über Der Karneval von Venedig: für Harfe.* Marina Del Rey, Calif.: Safari, 1989. 15 pp.

1652. ———. [Waltzer, harp, no. 1] *Walzer.* Leipzig: Jul. Heinr. Zimmermann, c1912. 9 pp.

1653. ———. [Waltzer, harp, no. 2] *Walzer: Es-dur: für Harfe solo.* Frankfurt: Zimmermann, c1912. 7 pp.

1654. Possio, Gianni, 1953–. *Notturno: per arpa.* Milan: Rugginenti Editore, c1986. 7 pp.

1655. Pozzoli, Ettore, b. 1873. *Studi di media difficoltà = Etudes de moyenne difficulté = Studies of moderate difficulty: per arpa.* Milan: Ricordi, 1975, c1947. 70 pp.

1656. Praag, Henri C. van, 1894–1968. *Arphia-sonatine: voor harp-solo.* Amsterdam: Donemus, c1954. 12 pp.

1657. Pratesi, Mira. *I canti della speranza: 5 canti ebraici per arpa; I canti di nozze: 6 melodie ebraiche per arpa.* Milan: Edizioni Musicali La Palmierama, c1987. 17 pp. CONTENTS: I canti della speranza: All'angolo del villaggio; La rondine chiamerà; Perchè verranno; Noi ci saremo; Apritemi le porte della giustizia. I canti di nozze: La novia entre flores; Convite del fin de la boda; Hallazgo del espose; La cena del desposado; Duelos y alegria de la esposa; Alabanza de la esposa.

1658. Pratt, Rosalie Rebollo, 1933–, ed. *Music for dauphines and troubadours.* Collected and edited by Rosalie R. Pratt. Orem, Utah: SARO Publishing Co., n.d. 37 pp. CONTENTS: In toyland: suite for harp. Dolly's cradle song; Harlequin; Columbine; Procession; Dolly's dance; Oriental by Alfred Holy. Theme with variations; Intermezzo; Petite valse lente by Joh. Snoer. Dance of the little page by Domenico Sodero. A jolly old tar by Van Veachton Rogers. The jester by Philip Sevasta. Sonata in classic style by Samuel Pratt. Bird waltz by Francis Panormo.

1659. Pratt, Rosalie Rebollo, 1933–, and Pratt, Samuel O., 1925–1985, eds. *Danses pour la dauphine.* Collected and edited by Rosalie R. Pratt and Samuel O. Pratt. Orem, Utah: S.O. Pratt, [19—]. 36 pp. CONTENTS: The golden goose; The wild colonial boy; Die Lorelei; Kira's waltz; Little brown flower; My love has a shay; Black is the color of my true love's hair; The British grenadiers; How sweet the winds do blow; I love my love; My love's a wild bird; The streets of Laredo; Round waltz; Sicilian dance; He's gone away; Goodbye old paint; You can never change a woman's mind; Soaring; Cake walk; The rose and the nightingale; Alborado; The little fountain (includes part for second harp).

1660. ———, eds. *Danses pour la dauphine.* Collected and edited by Rosalie R. Pratt and Samuel C. Pratt. Chicago, Ill.: Lyon & Healy, c1966. 36 pp. CONTENTS: See 1659.

1661. ———, eds. *The harpist's companion.* Collected and edited by Rosalie R. Pratt and Samuel C. Pratt. Upper Montclair, N.J.: SARO Publishing Co., n.d. 40 pp. (Eighteenth-century harp music, Book 2) CONTENTS: Sonata by Boieldieu. Sonata in E♭ by Cardon. Air with variations and Rondo pastorale by Mozart. Sonata in G major by Haydn.

1662. Pratt, Samuel O., 1925–1985. *Alborado: for harp.* New York: Colin, c1966. 6 pp.

1663. ———. [Harp music. Selections] *Five preludes and other pieces: for harp solo.* Upper Montclair, N.J.: SARO Publishing Co., [1975]. 35 pp. CONTENTS: Prelude I; Prelude II; Prelude III; Prelude IV; Prelude V; La Gitana morra; Toccata; Harp elegy; Intermezzo.

1664. ———. *The little fountain.* New York: New Sounds in Modern Music, c1965. 6 pp.

1665. ———. [Preludes, harp] *Five preludes: harp.* New York: Colin, c1966. 16 pp. (Pratt music library series of masterworks originally for harp) CONTENTS: 1. Ariel; 2. To a little dead bird; 3. Ondine; 4. Homage to S. Rachmaninoff; 5. Clouds.

1666. Prokofiev, Sergey, 1891–1953. *Piece: for harp; Prelude, op. 12, no. 7: for harp or piano.* Santa Monica, Calif.: Salvi Publications, n.d. 9 pp.

1667. ———. *Piece: for harp.* [Ed. by V. Dulova]. New York, N.Y.: Lyra Music Co., c1970. 3 pp.

1668. Ptaszynska, Marta, 1943–. *Arabeska: na harfe solo = Arabesque: for harp solo.* Warszawa: Agencja Autorska, c1979. 12 pp. (Contemporary Polish music: series of solo compositions)

1669. ———. [Bagatelles, harp] *Six bagatelles: for harp.* Bryn Mawr, Pa.: T. Presser, c1992. 11 pp.

1670. Purcell, Henry, 1659–1695. [Purcell's ground, Z. S122] *Ground: in F: with variations: for harp or troubadour harp.* Edited by Lucien Thomson. [U.S.A.]: Barger & Barclay; Salvi Publications, c1963. 7 pp. Originally for unspecified instrument; authorship by Purcell doubtful. [NP]

1671. ———. [Purcell's ground, Z. S122] *Ground in F with variations.*

Transcribed for harp with or without pedals by Lucien Thomson. Santa Monica, Calif.: Salvi Publications, c1978. 7 pp. Originally for unspecified instrument; authorship by Purcell doubtful. [NP]

1672. ———. [Purcell's ground, Z. S122] *Purcell's ground: in F major.* Edited by Lucien Thomson. New York: Lyra Music, 1978. 8 pp. [NP]

1673. Raksin, David, 1912–. *The psalmist: harp solo.* Los Angeles, Calif.: Western International Music, 1964. 4 pp.

1674. Ramovs, Primoz, 1921–. *Cirkulacije: za harfo = Circulations: for harp.* Ljubljana [Slovenia]: Drustvo slovenskih skadateljev; Cologne: Hans Gerig, 1973. 13 pp.

1675. ———. *Improvizacije: za harfo = Improvisations: for harp.* Ljubljana [Slovenia]: Društvo slovenskih skladateljev, 1983. 12 leaves.

1676. Rands, Bernard, 1935–. [Formants, no. 1] *Formants I: les gestes.* London: Universal Edition, c1966. 6 pp.

1677. Raphling, Sam, 1910–. *Dance no. 1: for harp.* New York: Lyra Music, c1964. 4 pp.

1678. Raukhverger, Mikhail Rafailovich, 1901–. [Pes, harp] *Deviat p'es: dlia arfy.* Moscow: Sov. kompozitor, 1973. 31 pp.

1679. Raxach, Enrique, 1932–. *Danses pythiques: pour harpe.* Amsterdam: Donemus, c1993. 10 pp.

1680. Read, Gardner, 1913–. *Jungle gardens by moonlight: for harp, op. 54, no. 2a.* New York: Seesaw Music, c1971. 5 pp.

1681. ———. *Sea-scapes: for harp, op. 46.* New York: Seesaw Music, c1971. 5 pp.

1682. Redway, Laurance D. *Prelude in D♭ : for piano (or harp).* New York: Carl Fischer, c1912. 5 pp.

1683. Rees-Rohrbacher, Darhon. *Fantasy on Ode to joy.* Buffalo, N.Y.: Dragonflower Music, 1990. 4 pp. [NP]

1684. ———. [Festival preludes] *Three festival preludes: on Mussorgsky, Bach, and Handel.* Buffalo, N.Y.: Dragonflower Music, 1992. 8 pp.

1685. ———. *Kymation: for pedal or lever harp.* Buffalo, N.Y.: Dragonflower Music, 1992. 4 pp. [NP]

1686. Reiner, Karel, 1910–1979. [Suite, harp] *Suite: for harp: 1964.* [S.l.]: General Music Publishing Co., c1978. 16 pp.

1687. ———. [Suite, harp] *Suita: pro harfu: 1964.* Prague: Panton, 1978. 16 pp.

1688. Renié, Henriette, 1875–1956. *Ballade fantastique: d'après Le coeur révélateur d'Edgar Poe: pour harpe.* Paris: L. Rouhier, 1912. 19 pp.

1689. ———. [Ballades, harp, no. 2] *2e ballade: pour harpe.* Paris: Leduc, c1949. 14 pp.

1690. ———. *Contemplation: pour harpe.* Paris: H. Lemoine, [19—]. 5 pp.

1691. ———. *Danse des lutins: pour harpe.* [London]: Salvi Publications, n.d. 10 pp.

1692. ———. *Danse des lutins: pour harpe.* Paris: A. Leduc, c1949. 10 pp.

1693. ———. *Esquisse: pour harpe.* [New York: Salvi Publications, n.d.]. 3 pp.

1694. ———. *Esquisse: pour harpe.* Ross, Calif.: Harp Publications, [19—]. 3 pp.

1695. ———. *Feuille d'automne: esquisse: pour harpe.* Paris: L. Rouhier, c1912. 4 pp.

1696. ———. *Feuille d'automne: esquisse: pour harpe.* London: Salvi Publications, c1990. 4 pp.

1697. ———. *Feuillets d'album: pour harpe.* Paris: H. Lemoine, [19—?]. 7 pp. CONTENTS: Esquisse; Dans d'autrefois; Angelus.

1698. ———. *Feuillets d'album = Album leaves.* [Edited by Marcel Grandjany.] New revised edition. New York: Edward B. Marks Music Corp., c1943. 7 pp.

1699. ———. *Gran'mère raconte une histoire: petite pièce très facile pour la harpe sans pédales.* Paris: A. Leduc, c1940. 3 pp. [NP]

1700. ———. *Légende: d'après Les elfes de Leconte de Lisle: pour harpe.* Paris: A. Leduc, c1949. 17 pp.

1701. ———. *Pièce symphonique: en trois episodes: pour harpe.* Paris: L. Rouhier, c1913. 12 pp.

1702. ———. *Pièce symphonique: en trois episodes.* Marina Del Rey, Calif.: Safari Publications, 1991. 12 pp.

1703. ———. [Pièces brèves] *Six pièces: pour harpe.* New York: Lyra Music, [19—]. 2 v. CONTENTS: 1ere suite: Conte de Noël; Recueillement; Air de danse. 2e suite: Invention dans le style ancien; Rêverie; Gavotte.

1704. ———. [Pièces brèves] *Six pièces brèves: pour harpe.* Paris: A. Leduc, c1919. 2 v. CONTENTS: 1ère suite: Conte de Noël; Recueillement; Air de danse. 2e suite: Invention dans le style ancien; Rêverie; Gavotte.

1705. ———. [Pièces, harp] *Six pièces: pour harpe.* Paris: L. Rouhier, [19—?]. 2 v. CONTENTS: [Vol.1]. Menuet; Au bord du ruisseau; Petite valse. [Vol.2]. Air ancien; Lied; Valse mélancolique.

1706. ———. [Pièces, harp] *Six pièces: pour harpe.* New York: Lyra Music Co., [19—]. 2 v. CONTENTS: 1re suite: Menuet; Au bord du Ruisseau; Petite valse. 2e suite: Air ancien; Lied; Valse mélancolique.

1707. ———. [Pièces, harp] *Six pièces: pour harpe.* Paris: A. Leduc, c1957. 2 v. CONTENTS: 1re suite. Menuet; Au bord du ruisseau; Petite valse. 2e suite: Air ancien; Lied; Valse mélancolique.

1708. ———. *Promenade matinale: 2 pièces pour harpe.* Paris: Rouhier, c1923. 2 v. CONTENTS: Au loin, dans la verdure, la mer calme et mystérieuse; Dans la campagne ensoleillée, la rosée scintille.

1709. Reschofsky, Sándor, 1887–. *Valsette; e, Piccola serenata: per arpa.* Budapest: Editio Musica, c1981. 4 pp.

1710. Revel, Pierre, 1901–. *Impromptu: pour harpe.* Paris: A. Leduc, c1965. 7 pp.

1711. Rice, Joyce, 1940–. *Valley tunes: 16 original compositions for lever harp: for advanced beginner to advanced intermediate players.* Los Angeles: J. Rice, c1992. 30 pp. [NP]

1712. Richards, Mary, 1787–1877. *Llyfr alawon poced = Pocket tune-book.* Aberystwyth: Gwasg Teires, 1991. 20 pp. [NP]

1713. Richardson, J. S. *Rondo alla scozzese: The dukes dang o'er my Daddie O: for the harp or piano forte.* Philadelphia: Published by G. E. Blake, [between 1814 and 1841]. 2 leaves.

1714. Rieunier, Jean Paul, 1933–. *Vibrations: pour harpe.* Paris: Editions Salabert, c1984. 10 pp.

1715. Righini, Vincenzo, 1756–1812. *Twelve dances and marches in character: for the quadrille: at the close of the Berlin carnival, 1799.* London: R. Birchall, [ca. 1800?]. 21 pp.

1716. Riley, Dennis, 1943–. [Preludes, harp] *Six preludes: harp solo.* New York: C.F. Peters, c1989. 15 pp.

1717. Rivier, Jean, 1896–1987. *Nocturne; et, Impromptu: pour harpe.* Paris: Editions Salabert, c1962. 8 pp.

1718. Robarts, I. *Six airs: for the harp: adapted for beginners (including one with variations) and a march.* London: Printed & sold for the authoress by Birchall, [181–?]. 8 pp.

1719. Roberts, Ceinwen. *Tinc a thonc.* Gorffennaf: Argraffiad Cyntaf, 1977. 20 pp. [NP] CONTENTS: Ail fys yn unig; Pwy sy'n copio?; Mor hapus yw; Gee, ceffyl Bach; Iesu tirion; Croen y ddafad felan; Clychau'r nadolig; Tawel nos; Ymadawiad y brenin; Mozart, Wolfgang Amadeus. Diolch a chân; Pwt ar y bys; Amrywiad; Breuddwyd y frenhines; Ffarwel i blwy llangower; Si hei lwli, mabi; Robin Goch.

1720. Roberts, Mair. *Maes y delyn.* S.l.: s.n., n.d. 20 pp. CONTENTS: Arglwydd y Ddawns; Ble'r ei Di?; Boneddwr Mawr o'r Bala; Cainc Dafydd Broffwyd; Calennig; Dacw Mam yn Dwad; Dau Gi Bach; Ganed Bachgen; Deryn y Bwn; Draw yn y Preseb; Heno Heno; Heddwch (Shalom);

Mae gennyf Ebol Melyn; Mi welais Jac y Do; Patapan; Pedoli, pedoli; Y Deryn Bach Syw; Y Gelynen.

1721. Robertson, Kim, arr. [Wind shadows, no. 1] *The music from Wind shadows: a collection of traditional and original music for harp.* Santa Barbara, Calif.: Folk Mote Music, c1983. 20 pp. [NP] CONTENTS: March of King Laois. Morgan Magan; Eleanor Plunkett. Arran boat song. Spagnoletta by Praetorius. Carolan's dream by Conollan. Lament by Carolan. Lauda. Casey's hornpipe. Bittersweet II by Kim Robertson. Give me your hand. Skye boat song.

1722. ———, arr. [Wind shadows, no. 2] *The music from Wind shadows II.* Winona, Minn.: Hal Leonard Publishing Corp., c1987. 78 pp. [NP] CONTENTS: Arise and get dressed; Banish misfortune; Black nag; Bridget Cruise; Butterfly jig; Castle of Dromore; The foggy dew; Hornpipe; Jig; Kathleen ashore; Lark on the strand; The last rose of summer; Minstrel boy; Mon ami; My thousand treasures; O'Connell's lamentation; Star of the County Down; Tuza.

1723. Robinson, Gertrude Ina, b. 1868. *Advanced lessons: for the harp: comprising preludes in minor keys, glissandos and solos in characteristic forms for harp according to the famous Hasselmans method.* New York: Carl Fischer, Inc., 1913. 60 pp.

1724. ———. [Advanced melodic and progressive studies] *Twenty advanced melodic and progressive studies: for harp.* New York: Carl Fischer, c1921. 86 pp.

1725. ———, arr. *Excerpts & solos: for small harp (Irish harp).* New York: Fischer, c1923. 29 pp. [NP] CONTENTS: March of the gnomes by Robinson; Happy farmer = Fröhlicher Landmann by Schumann; Nearer, my God, to Thee by Mason; Melody by Parkhurst; Drink to me only with thine eyes; Butterfly waltz by Robinson; Holy night (i.e., Silent night) [by Gruber]; Menuetto from Don Giovanni by Mozart; Medley of Irish melodies (Introduction; Believe me if all those endearing young charms; Wearing of the green; Erin, the tear and the smile in thine eyes) by Moore; In the time of roses (Hoffnung) by Reichardt; The fairies' dream by Robinson; Intermezzo sinfonico from Cavalleria rusticana by Mascagni.

1726. ———. *The fairies dream: harp solo [in G flat major].* New York: International Music Pub. Co., c1913. 5 pp.

1727. ———. *First lessons for the harp: comprising a series of graded technical exercises and melodious studies according to the famous Hasselmans method.* New York: Carl Fischer, Inc., c1912. 63 pp.

1728. ———. [Melodic and progressive etudes] *Twenty melodic and progressive etudes: for harp.* New York: Carl Fischer, c1914.

1729. ———. *Original compositions & adaptations: for the harp*. Boston: Fischer, c1916. 33 pp.

1730. Rochberg, George, 1918–. *Ukiyo-e = Pictures of the floating world: for solo harp*. Bryn Mawr: T. Presser Co., c1976. 14 pp.

1731. Rodio, Rocco, fl. 1550–1600. *Cinque ricercate [e] una fantasia: per organo, clavicembalo, clavicordo o arpa*. Revisione e trascrizione in notazione moderna di Macario Santiago Kastner. Padua: Editore Guglielmo Zanibon, c1958. 31 pp. For organ, harpsichord, clavichord, or harp.

1732. ———. [Libro di ricercate. Selections] *Cinque ricercate, una fantasia: per organo, clavicembalo, clavicordo o arpa*. Revisione e transcrizione in notazione moderna di Macario Santiago Kastner. Padua: Zanibon, c1958. 31 pp. For organ, harpsichord, clavichord, or harp.

1733. Rodrigo, Joaquín, 1901–. *Impromptu: para arpa*. Madrid: Union Musical Española, c1963. 5 pp.

1734. Roe, Betty, 1930–. *A garden of herbs: harp solo*. S.l.: Thames, c1987. 8 pp. CONTENTS: Thyme; Rosemary; Iris florentina; Summer savoury; Tarragon; Anise; Nettle.

1735. Roger-Ducasse, 1873–1954. *Barcarolle: pour harpe*. Paris: Durand, c1907. 8 pp.

1736. ———. *Basso ostinato: pour harpe chromatique*. Paris: Durand & Fils, c1923. 8 pp.

1737. Rogers, Van Veachton, 1864–1937. *Barcarole, op. 17*. New York: Carl Fischer, c1916. 1 p.

1738. ———. *The dance of the gnomes*. Washington, D.C.: William Truesdale Cameron, c1908. 5 pp.

1739. ———. *Eccentric dance: pantomime*. Providence, R.I.: Van Veachton Rogers, c1922. 3 pp.

1740. ———. *Fleurette: for piano or harp*. Boston: C.W. Thompson & Co., c1900. 5 pp.

1741. ———. *A jolly old tar: for the Clark Irish harp*. New York: International Music Pub. Co., c1923. 2 pp. [NP]

1742. ———. *Lullaby*. Washington, D.C.: William Truesdale Cameron, n.d. 1 p.

1743. ———. *Modern dance*. Washington, D.C.: William Truesdale Cameron, c1922. 5 pp.

1744. ———. *Valse Albania*. Washington, D.C.: William Truesdale Cameron, c1910. 5 pp.

1745. ———. *Wooden shoe dance*. New York: Lyon & Healy, c1913. 2 pp.

1746. Rolle, Johann Heinrich, 1718–1785. *Allegro e presto*. Leipzig: Jul.

Heinr. Zimmermann, c1914. 11 pp. (Des Harfenisten Konzert-Programm)

1747. Romm, Roza Davydovna, 1916–. *Sonatina: for the harp.* New York: E.F. Kalmus, [19—]. 19 pp. (Kalmus harp series, no. 4687)

1748. Ropartz, Joseph Guy Marie, 1864–1955. *Impromptu: pour la harpe.* Paris: Durand, c1927. 7 pp.

1749. Rorem, Ned, 1923–. *Sky music: ten pieces for solo harp.* [New York]: Boosey and Hawkes, c1976. 23 pp. Theme with variations.

1750. Rose, Beatrice Schroeder. *The enchanted harp: 10 easy descriptive pieces for the non-pedal or pedal harp with a supplement for a second harp.* New York, N.Y.: Lyra Music Co., c1974. 8 pp. [NP] CONTENTS: Jack and the giant; The prince and Cinderella; The shepherdess and the chimney-sweep; Peter Rabbit; Snow White; Seven dwarfs; The clock and the mouse; The gold-spinners; The magic canary; The princess on the glass hill (for pedal harp only).

1751. Rosenberger, Otto. *Musik für Harfe nach alt-italienischen Sätzen = Harp music based on movements of old Italian works.* Wilhelmshaven: Heinrichshofen's Verlag, c1965. 11 pp.

1752. Rosenfield, Joyce. *Favorite fables: for harp with or without pedals.* New York: Franco Colombo, c1967. v. [NP]

1753. ———. *Sonatina.* Ed. Lucien Thomson. [Ellensburg, Wash.]: F.C. Publishing Co., 1988. 12 pp.

1754. Rosetti, Francesco Antonio, ca. 1750–1792. [Sonatas, harp, K. IV, 13] *Six harp sonatas, op. 2.* Susann McDonald edition. Tucson, Ariz.: Nuove Music, c1976. 42 pp.

1755. ———. [Sonatas, harp, K. IV, 13. Allegro assai] *Sonate: für Harfe, [op. 2, no. 2].* Herausgegeben von Hans J. Zingel. Mainz: B. Schott's Söhne, c1966. 12 pp.

1756. Ross, John, 1763–1837. [Auld lang syne] *The favorite Scotch air, Auld langsyne: with variations for the piano forte or harp composed by D. Ross.* New York: J.L.Hewitt, [18—?]. Score 6 pp.

1757. ———. [Auld lang syne] *The favorite Scotch air, Auld langsyne: with variations for the piano forte or harp composed by D. Ross.* New York: W. DuBois, [1818]. Score 6 pp.

1758. ———. [Auld lang syne] *The favorite Scotch air, Auld langsyne: with variations for the piano forte or harp composed by D. Ross.* New York: Engraved, printed, and sold by E. Riley, [1820?]. Score 6 pp.

1759. ———. [Auld lang syne] *The favorite Scotch air Auld lang syne.* Philadelphia: G.E. Blake, 1821? 6 pp. Variations for harp.

1760. ———. [Auld lang syne] *The favorite Scotch air, Auld langsyne: with variations for the piano forte or harp composed by D. Ross.* Philadelphia: Published by John G. Klemm, [1823–1831]. Score 6 pp.

1761. ———. *Auld lang syne: with variations for the piano forte or harp.* Boston: C. Bradlee, 183–? 4 pp.

1762. Rossini, Gioacchino, 1792–1868. *Allegretto: per arpa.* Rev. Mirella Vita. Milan: Edizioni Suvini Zerboni, c1968. 2 pp.

1763. ———. *Sonata: für Harfe.* Hrsg. von Marcela Kozikova, Lucile Johnson. Mainz; New York: Schott, c1978. 7 pp.

1764. Rota, Nino, 1911–1979. *Sarabanda e toccata: per arpa.* Milan: G. Ricordi, c1955. 8 pp.

1765. Rothmüller, Aron Marko, 1908–1993. [Aforizmi] *Aphorismes: pour harpe = Aphorisms: for harp = Aphorismen: für Harfe.* Zagreb, Yugoslavia: Edition Omanut, c1936. 6 pp.

1766. Rothstein, Sue. *Animals on the harp: a suite of 6 easy harp solos.* Santa Monica, Calif.: Salvi Publications, n.d. 6 pp. [NP] CONTENTS: Camel train; The happy frog; Butterfly; Little kitten come and play; The frolicking lambs; Seagull.

1767. Rotondi, Umberto, 1937–. *Cinque episodi: per arpa.* Milan: Edizioni Suvini Zerboni, c1966. 15 pp.

1768. Roubanis, Nicholas. *Phormigx: syllogē asmatōn, thrēskeutikōn hymnōn kai aplopoiēmeno systēma mousikēs anagnōseōs = Harp: Greek songs, hymns and sight-reading lessons.* New York: N. Roubanis, 1950. 55 pp.

1769. Roussel, Albert, 1869–1937. *Impromptu: pour harpe, [op. 21].* Paris: Durand; Bryn Mawr, Pa.: T. Presser, c1919. 7 pp.

1770. ———. *Impromptu: pour harpe, [op. 21].* New York: Lyra Music Co., [198–?]. 7 pp.

1771. Rozen, Giora. *Empty box, empty voice: for harp (1982).* [Tel Aviv]: Israel Music Institute, 1985. 20 pp.

1772. Rubbra, Edmund, 1901–1986. *Pezzo ostinato: for solo harp, op. 102.* London: A. Lengnick & Co., c1959. 7 pp.

1773. ———. *Transformations: for solo harp, op. 141.* Edited and fingered by Ann Griffiths. South Croydon, Surrey: A. Lengnick, c1979. 13 pp.

1774. Rubin, Mark Abramovich. *Khrestomatiia: pedagogicheskogo repertuara dlia arfy.* Sostavitel' M. Rubin. Moscow: Gosudarstvennoe Muzykal'noe Izdatelstvo, 1960. 2 v. Studies and exercises.

1775. ———, ed. *P'esy sovetskikh kompozitorov: dlia arfy.* Sostavitel i red. M. Rubin. Moscow: Muzyka, c1982. 19 pp. (Tvorchestvo molodykh) CONTENTS: Preliudiia by V. Ekimovskii. Inventsiia-val's by O. Magidenko. Posviashchenie Debiussi by A. Vustin. Dve p'esy by D. Smirnov.

1776. ———, ed. *P'esy sovetskikh kompozitorov: dlia arfy.* Sostavitel M. Rubin. Moscow: Muzyka, c1972. 47 pp.

1777. Rudzinski, Witold, 1913–. *Largo, aria e toccata: per arpa sola.* Kraków: Polskie Wydawn. Muzyczne, c1970. 7 pp.

1778. Ryterband, Roman, 1914–. *Two images: for harp solo.* San Diego, Calif.: Music Graphics Press, 1943. 4, 6 pp. CONTENTS: Song of olden times = Un air d'autrefois; At sunset beneath the palms = Le soir sous les palmiers.

1779. ———. *Two images: for harp solo.* [Palm Springs, Calif.?]: C. Ryterband, c1980. 6 pp. CONTENTS: Song of olden times = Un air d'autrefois; At sunset beneath the palms = Le soir sous les palmiers.

1780. Saint Pierre de Newbourg, comte. *Studies: for the harp.* London: Pearce, 18—. 37 pp.

1781. Saint-Saëns, Camille, 1835–1921. *Fantaisie: pour harpe, op. 95.* Paris: Durand; Philadelphia, Pa.: Elkan-Vogel, 1949. 15 pp.

1782. Salmenhaara, Erkki, 1941–. [Ballad kantele] *Balladi; Inventio: kanteleelle tai harpulle.* Hameenlinna, Finland: Jasemusiikki, c1985. 10 pp. For kantele or harp.

1783. Salvi, Alberto, 1893–1983. *Serenata.* New York: International Music Pub. Co., c1923. 5 pp.

1784. Salzedo, Carlos, 1885–1961. *Chanson chagrine: for harp.* Edited by Dewey Owens. New York: Lyra Music Co., c1985. 4 pp.

1785. ———. *Christmas harp collection.* London: Boosey and Hawkes, [1980?], c1956. 36 pp. CONTENTS: Short fantasy on a noël provençal; Short fantasy on a Neapolitan carol; Short fantasy on a Catalan carol; Short fantasy on a Basque carol; Concert variations on Deck the halls; Concert variations on Good King Wenceslas; Concert variations on O Tannenbaum; Paraphrase on It came upon a midnight clear; Paraphrase on Angels we have heard on high; Paraphrase on Greensleeves; Paraphrase on O little town of Bethlehem; Paraphrase on We three kings of orient are.

1786. ———. *Conditioning exercises: for beginners and advanced harpists as well as for touring harpists = Exercices d'assouplissement: pour harpistes commençants et avancés ainsi que pour harpistes en tournées.* New York: G. Schirmer, c1955. 11 pp.

1787. ———. *Dixie parade: concert fantasy for harp.* New York: Southern Music Publishing Co.; Hamburg: Peer Musikverlag, c1966. 8 pp.

1788. ———. *Fraicheur = Zephyrs: for harp alone, or several harps in unison.* New York: G. Schirmer, c1933. 5 pp.

1789. ———. *The harpist's daily dozen.* New York: G. Schirmer, c1929. 11 pp. (Schirmer's scholastic series, v. 213)

1790. ———. *The harpist's daily dozen.* New York: Lyra Music, c1966. 11 pp.

1791. ———. *Jolly piper: concert fantasy [on the theme of The sailor's hornpipe]: for harp.* New York: Southern Music Publishing Co., c1959. 9 pp.

1792. ———. [Method for the harp. Chanson dans la nuit] *Chanson dans la nuit = Song in the night.* New York: Lyra Music, c1966. 6 pp.

1793. ———. *Modern study of the harp = L'étude moderne de la harpe.* New York: G. Schirmer, c1917. 53 pp.

1794. ———. [Morceaux, harp] *Trois morceaux: pour harpe seule.* Paris: Leduc, c1913. 3 v. CONTENTS: Ballade; Jeux d'eau; Variations sur un thème dans le style ancien.

1795. ———. *Paraphrase on Liszt's Second Hungarian rhapsody: for harp.* New York: G. Schirmer, c1961. 8 pp.

1796. ———. *Paraphrase on Liszt's Second Hungarian rhapsody.* Chicago: Lyon & Healy, 1987, 1961. 8 pp. (Lyon & Healy treasury of harp music)

1797. ———. [Petits préludes intimes] *Cinq petits préludes intimes: pour harpe seule.* New York: Lyra Music, [19—]. 14 pp. CONTENTS: Tendrement ému; Rêveusement; Profondement quiet; Très recueille; En procession.

1798. ———. [Petits préludes intimes] *Cinq petits préludes intimes: pour harpe seule.* New York: International Music, c1921. 14 pp.

1799. ———. [Petits préludes intimes] *Preludes intimes: five easy preludes for harp.* New York: Boosey and Hawkes, c1954. 15 pp.

1800. ———. *Poem of the little stars: for harp.* New York: International Music Pub. Co., c1923. 3 pp.

1801. ———. *Prelude fatidique: for the harp.* New York: G. Schirmer, c1956. 5 pp.

1802. ———. *Prélude fatidique; and, Suite of eight dances: for the harp, complete in one volume.* New York: Charles Colin, c1965. 28 pp. CONTENTS: Suite of eight dances: Gavotte; Menuet; Polka; Siciliana; Bolero; Seguidilla; Tango; Rumba.

1803. ———. *Prélude fatidique; and, Suite of eight dances: for the harp.* New York: Lyra Music Co., c1971. 28 pp. CONTENTS: See 1802.

1804. ———. *Prelude for a drama: for one or several harps.* New York: M. Baron, c1951. 7 pp.

1805. ———. *Prelude in the nature of an octave study: an untitled manuscript.* New York: Lyra Music Co., c1985. 4 pp. Performance notes by Dewey Owens.

1806. ———. [Preludes, harp] *Five preludes: for harp alone: first series.* New York: Composers' Music Corp.; Carl Fischer, Inc., c1924. 1 v. (various pagings). CONTENTS: Quietude; Iridescence; Introspection; Whirlwind; Lamentation.

1807. ———. *Recessional: for harp solo.* New York: International Music, c1922. 7 pp.

1808. ———. *Scintillation: for harp.* Philadelphia: Elkan-Vogel, c1937. 19 pp.

1809. ———. *Scintillation: for harp.* New York: Charles Colin, c1964. 19 pp.

1810. ———. *Scintillation.* New York: Lyra Music Co., c1973. 19 pp.

1811. ———. *Scintillation: for harp.* [London]: Salvi Publications, c1989. 19 pp.

1812. ———. *Short stories in music: for young harpists.* Philadelphia: Elkan-Vogel, c1935. 2 v. CONTENTS: Vol.1. The dwarf and the giant; The kitten and the limping dog; Rocking horse; On donkey-back; Rain drops; Madonna and Child; Memories of a clock; Night breeze. Vol.2. On stilts; Pirouetting music box; Behind the barracks; At church; Goldfish; The mermaid's chimes; Skipping rope.

1813. ———. *Sketches for harpist beginners = Esquisses pour la harpe à l'usage des commençants: for harp or Irish harp.* Philadelphia: Elkan-Vogel, c1954–1959. 11, 12 pp. "There are no pedal changes in the course of these pieces." [NP] CONTENTS: Vol.1. Rock me, mommy; Imitation; Echo; Huntsman's horns; Lost in the mist; Hurdy-gurdy; Poor doggy; Tuneful snuff-box; Pagan rite; Beethoven at school. Vol.2. The organist's first steps; A young violinist; Falling leaves; Royal trumpeters; A lonely bell; Baby on the swing; Mourners; On the tight rope; Pierrot is sad; Choral.

1814. ———. *Suite of eight dances: for the harp.* New York: G. Schirmer, 1953. 8 v. CONTENTS: See 1802.

1815. ———. *Suite of eight dances.* [New 1986 ed.]. Chicago: Lyon & Healy, c1986. 24 pp. (Lyon & Healy treasury of harp music) CONTENTS: See 1802.

1816. ———. *Tiny tales: for harpist beginners = Petits contes: pour la harpe à l'usage des commençants: first and second series.* Philadelphia, Pa.: Elkan-Vogel, c1936. 2 v. "There are no pedal changes in the course of these pieces." [NP]

1817. ———. *Tiny tales for harpist beginners = Petits contes pour la harpe à l'usage des commençants.* New York, N.Y.: Lyra Music Co., c1970. 2 v. For harp or Irish harp. [NP]

1818. ———. *Traipsin' thru Arkansaw: fantasy on the theme of The Arkansas traveller.* New York: Southern Music Pub. Co., c1955. 9 pp.

1819. ———. *Turkey strut: concert fantasy on the theme of Turkey in the straw.* New York: Southern Music Pub. Co., c1961. 9 pp.

1820. ———. *Variations sur un thème dans le style ancien, [op. 30].* New York: Lyra Music Co., n.d. 16 pp.

1821. ———. *Variations sur un thème dans le style ancien: pour harpe seule.* Paris: Alphonse Leduc, c1913. 16 pp. "Op. 30."

1822. ———. *Variations on a theme in the ancient style.* New 1989 ed. Chicago: Lyon & Healy, 1989. 23 pp. (Lyon & Healy treasury of harp music)

Salzedo, Carlos, 1885–1961, and Lawrence, Lucile, 1907–. *Pathfinder to the harp = Guide pour la harp: and supplement, Pathfinder studies: for the troubadour or Irish-type harp.* See 76.

1823. Samuel-Rousseau, Marcel, 1882–1955. *Variations pastorales sur un vieux Noël: pour la harpe.* Paris: Alphonse Leduc, c1919. 16 pp.

1824. Sancan, Pierre, 1916–. *Thème et variations: pour harpe.* Paris: Durand, c1975. 14 pp.

1825. Sanders, Julia L., 1951–. *In a Japanese tea garden: for pedal or non-pedal harp.* Houston, Tex.: Julia Sanders, 1988. 3 pp. [NP]

1826. ———. *Japanese lullaby: for pedal or non-pedal harp.* Houston, Texas: Julia Sanders, c1991. 3 pp. [NP]

1827. ———. *Japanese waterlily: for pedal or non-pedal harp.* Houston, Texas: Julia Sanders, c1991. 3 pp. [NP]

1828. ———. *The lost princess: advanced solo for folk harp.* Edmonds, Wash.: Paradise Music, c1989. 2 pp. [NP]

1829. ———. *March orientale: for a pedal or non-pedal harp.* Houston, Tex.: Julia Sanders, c1988. 3 pp. [NP]

1830. ———. *New age tango: solo for pedal harp.* Houston, Tex.: Julia Sanders, c1988. 3 pp.

1831. ———. *New Orleans stomp.* Ellensburg, Wash.: F.C. Publishing Co., 1991. 6 pp.

1832. ———. *Prelude orientale: pentatonic solo for folk harp.* Edmonds, Wash.: Paradise Music, c1988. 2 pp. [NP]

1833. ———. *Spanish dance: solo for pedal harp.* Houston, Tex.: Julia Sanders, c1988. 3 pp.

1834. ———. *Waltz in C.* Ellensburg, Wash.: F.C. Publishing Co., 1990. 2 pp.

1835. Schafer, R. Murray, 1933–. [Patria, no. 4. Crown of Ariadne] *The crown of Ariadne: for solo harp with percussion.* Bancroft, Ont.: Arcana Editions, c1980. 13 pp. The harpist prerecords portions on tape and also plays the percussion instruments. CONTENTS: Ariadne awakens; Ariadne's dance; Dance of the bull; Dance of the night insects; Sun dances; Labyrinth dance (Theseus & Ariadne).

1836. Schäffer, Boguslaw, 1929–. *Fünf kurze Stücke: für Harfe = Five short pieces: for harp solo.* Celle: Moeck, 1974. 11 pp.

1837. Schauss, Ernst. *Notturno: für Harfe.* Berlin: Afas-Musikverlag H. Dünnebeil, c1941. 5 pp.

1838. Scherchen-Hsiao, Tona, 1938–. *Once upon a time: pour harpe.* Paris: Amphion; Toronto: Kerby, c1979. 3 pp.

1839. Schibler, Armin, 1920–1986. *Fantaisie concertante: pour harpe seule, op. 79.* Munich: Ahn & Simrock, c1964. 13 pp.

1840. Schidlowsky, León, 1931–. *Five pieces: for harp.* Edited by Judith Liber. Tel Aviv: Israel Music Institute, c1990. 12 pp.

1841. ———. *Koloth = Voices: for harp.* Tel Aviv: Israel Music Institute, 1972. 11 pp.

1842. Schifrin, Lalo, 1932–. *Continuum: for solo harp.* New York: Associated Music Publishers, Inc., 1970. 8 pp.

1843. Schliepe, Ernst Heinrich, 1893–. [Variationen und Fuge, harp, op. 25] *Variationen und Fuge über ein altes Lied In stiller Nacht: für Harfe, Werk 25.* Leipzig: W. Zimmermann, [19—]. 19 pp.

1844. Schlomovitz, Phyllis, 1917–. *Fantasie on a fourteenth-century air.* Palo Alto, Calif.: Harpress of California, c1982. 11 pp.

1845. Schmidt, Eric, 1907–. *Six etudes: pour harpe.* Revues et doigtées par Pierre Jamet. Paris: A. Leduc, c1954. 16 pp.

1846. Schmitt, Florent, 1870–1958. [Pièces, harp, op. 57] *Deux pièces: pour harpe chromatique (ou piano).* Paris: Durand et Cie., c1913. 2 v. CONTENTS: Lande; Tournoiement.

1847. Schmitt, Meinrad. *Konzertetüde 1984: Das Mahl der Harpyen: für Harfe.* S.l.: Vereinigung deutscher Harfenisten e.V., 1990. 11 pp. CONTENTS: König Phineus; Die Harpyien; Die Söhne des Nordwinds.

1848. ———. [Miniaturen] *Drei Miniaturen: für Harfe: 1979.* Kassel: Merseburger, c1986. 4 pp. (Music für Harfe)

1849. ———. *Moment musical: für Harfe.* S.l.: Vereinigung deutscher Harfenisten e.V., 1990. 9 pp.

1850. ———. *Rhapsodie: für Harfe.* S.l.: Vereinigung deutscher Harfenisten e.V., 1990. 7 pp.

1851. Schocker, Paul. *Lonely shepherd: for harp solo.* Easton, Pa.: Paul Schocker, c1964. 3 pp.

1852. ———. *Lullaby: for harp solo.* Easton, Pa.: Paul Schocker, c1965. 3 pp.

1853. Schonthal, Ruth, 1924–. *Interlude: for harp.* Washington, D.C.: Sisra Publications, c1987. 5 pp.

1854. Schubert, Erich, 1913–. *Harfen-Duos: spielbar für 2 Harfen, auch für 1 Harfe und ein anderes Instrument, 1. Stimme auch für Solo-Harfe.* Traunstein,

Germany: Verlag Musikhaus Fackler, c1981. 2 parts (12 pp. each). For two harps, harp and another instrument, or solo harp. CONTENTS: Die Moosjungfer: Tiroler Lied; Bergfee-Walzer; Da Zuagroaste: Walzer; Harfenliesl: Rheinländler; Marienwalzer; Da Z'sammbastlte: Landler.

1855. ———. *Harfenmusik aus Tirol: acht neue Tänze für ein und zwei Harfen.* Traunstein, Germany: Verlag Musikhaus Fackler, c1982. 16 pp. and 1 part. CONTENTS: Almerisch-Landlerisch; Achenwalder Harfenländler; Brixlegger Harfenständchen; Bernauer Landler; Landlerische Tanzweisen; Kramsacher Boarischer (for 2 harps); Mariataler Landler (for 2 harps); Der Verhinderte.

1856. Schuëcker, Edmund, 1860–1911. *Am Springbrunnen: Characterstück für Harfe, op. 15.* Leipzig: Breitkopf & Härtel, 1891. 9 pp.

1857. ———. [Ballade, harp, no. 1, op. 5] *Erste Ballade: für Harfe, op. 5.* Leipzig: Breitkopf & Härtel, [189–]. 11 pp.

1858. ———. *Barcarole, op. 38.* Leipzig: W. Zimmermann, c1900. 13 pp.

1859. ———. *Elisabeth-gavotte, op. 37.* Bayreuth: C. Giessel, c1900. 5 pp.

1860. ———, ed. *Etüden und Melodien-Album: book 1.* Marina Del Rey, Calif.: Safari Publications, n.d. 39 pp. A collection by various composers edited by Schuëcker.

1861. ———. [Etüden-Schule] *Etüden-Schule des Harfenspielers: Sammlung von Etüden jeder Stilart vom ersten Anfang bis zur höchsten Ausbildung, op. 18.* Für den Unterricht bearbeitet mit genauem Fingersatz und Pedalbezeichnung versehen von Edmund Schuëcker. Neue Auflage. Leipzig: Carl Merseburger, [189–?]. 3 v. CONTENTS: Vol.1. *25 kleine Etüden für die Elementar- und Unterstufe:* Thema mit Variationen, Es dur by Robert Nicolas Charles Bochsa. Allegretto Es dur; Allegretto B dur by Edmund Schuëcker. Moderato C dur (2 works) by Federigo Fiorillo. Allegretto con moto F dur; Andante con moto Es dur; Andante con moto C dur by Edmund Schuëcker. Moderato Des dur by Federigo Fiorillo. Allegro As dur; Moderato F moll by Edmund Schuëcker. Allegro moderato F dur; Andante Ges dur; Allegro As dur; Maestoso Es dur; Moderato G dur by Federigo Fiorillo. Allegro D moll; Allegro moderato B dur; Andante grazioso non troppo lento As dur; Andante sostenuto B moll; Andante, G moll; Andante ma non troppo F dur; Moderato C dur by Robert Nicolas Charles Bochsa. Moderato B dur by Federigo Fiorillo. Andante espressivo As dur by Edmund Schuëcker.

    Vol.2. *12 Etüden für die Mittel- und Oberstufe:* Thema mit Variationen in Etuden-Form Des dur by François Joseph Nadermann. Allegretto Ges dur; Allegro moderato Es dur; Allegro ma non troppo Es dur; Andante sostenuto B moll; Allegro G moll; Andante con moto C dur by Edmund Schuëcker. Andante ma non troppo Es dur by François Joseph Nadermann. Allegro scherzando G dur by Edmund Schuëcker. Andante

amabile Es dur by François Joseph Nadermann. Allegro con moto Es
moll; Allegro con fuoco D moll by Edmund Schuëcker.

Vol.3. *12 Etüden im brillanten Stil:* Allegro molto C dur; Allegretto F dur;
Allegro con fuoco Ges dur; Allegro moderato F dur; Andante molto
espressivo As dur; Allegro ma non troppo G moll; Allegro di molto Ces
dur; Moderato Es dur; Moderato Es dur; Allegro moderato B dur; Allegro
di molto Es dur; Moderato Ges dur; Allegro con spirito F moll by Edmund
Schuëcker.

1862. ———. [Etüden-Schule. Book 2] *Etüden-Schule des Harfenspielers: book
2.* Marina Del Rey, Calif.: Safari Publications, 1992. 43 pp.

1863. ———. [Etüden-Schule. Selections] *Sammlung von Etüden: für Harfe,
op. 18.* In Auswahl neu herausgegeben von Wolf Buchholz. Kassel: Verlag
Merseburger Berlin, c1983. 48 pp. CONTENTS: Thema mit Variationen
Es-dur by Nicolas Bochsa. Moderato C-dur; Moderato C-dur by Federigo
Fiorillo. Thema mit Variationen in Etüdenform Des-dur by François
Joseph Nadermann, bearbeitet von Edmund Schuëcker. Allegretto Es-
dur; Allegretto B-dur; Allegretto con moto F-dur; Andante con moto Es-
dur; Allegro As-dur; Moderato f-moll; Allegro ma non troppo Es-dur;
Andante sostenuto b-moll; Andante con moto C-dur by Edmund
Schuëcker.

1864. ———. [Etudes, harp, op. 8] *Etüden- und Melodien-Album: für Harfe:
Sammlung auserwählter Stücke, Etüden usw. in progressiver Reihenfolge,
Originale sowie Bearbeitungen, zum Gebrauche beim Unterrichte.* Leipzig:
Hofmeister, [19—]. 4 v.

1865. ———. [Etudes, harp, op. 36] *Sechs Virtuosen-Etuden, op. 36.* Bayreuth:
Carl Giessel, c1900. 31 pp.

1866. ———. *Fantaisie-appassionato, op. 35.* Leipzig: J.H. Zimmermann,
c1900. 19 pp.

1867. ———. *Fantasia de bravura: für Harfe, op. 11.* Leipzig: Breitkopf &
Härtel, [189–]. 17 pp.

1868. ———. *Fantasie-Caprice, op. 14.* Leipzig: Breitkopf & Härtel, [1891].
19 pp.

1869. ———. *Henrica: Nocturno, op. 41.* Leipzig: J.H. Zimmermann, c1902.
11 pp.

1870. ———. *Impromptu: für Harfe allein, op. 13.* Leipzig: C.E.W. Siegel, n.d.
14 pp.

1871. ———. *Marcia fantastica, op. 43: [für] Harfe.* Leipzig: Carl
Merseburger, [19—?]. 11 pp.

1872. ———. [Mazurkas, harp, op. 12] *Mazurka: für Harfe, op. 12.* Leipzig:
Breitkopf & Härtel, [189–]. 7 pp.

1873. ———. [Mazurkas, harp, op. 12] *Mazurka, op. 12.* Marina Del Rey, Calif.: Safari, c1989. 7 pp. Reprint.

1874. ———. [Mazurkas, harp, op. 33, A minor] *Mazurka: (no. 2), op. 33.* Leipzig: Friedrich Hofmeister, [19—]. 6 pp.

1875. ———. *Menuett, op. 32.* Leipzig: Friedrich Hofmeister, n.d. 7 pp.

1876. ———. *Nocturne: für Harfe, op. 7.* Leipzig: C.F.W. Siegel, n.d. 11 pp.

1877. ———. [Phantasiestücke] *Zwei Phantasiestücke: für Harfe componirt, op. 4.* Leipzig: Breitkopf & Härtel, n.d. 11 pp.

1878. ———. *Serenade: für Harfe allein, op. 10.* Leipzig: C.F.W. Siegel, n.d. 7 pp.

1879. ———. [Stücke, harp, op. 29] *Drei Stücke, op. 29.* Leipzig: Breitkopf & Härtel, c1896. 11 pp. CONTENTS: No. 1. Intermezzo; no. 2. Consolation; no. 3. Walzer.

1880. ———. *Träumerei, op. 44: [für] Harfe.* Leipzig: Carl Merseburger, [19—?]. 9 pp.

1881. Schuetze, Carl. [Fantasias, harp, F major] *Fantasia: the last rose of summer: harp solo [in F major].* New York: International Music Pub. Co., c1914. 7 pp.

1882. ———. *In the garden: a composition for harp.* New York: G. Schirmer, c1911. 7 pp.

1883. ———. *A spring thought.* New York: International Music Pub. Co., [192-?]. 3 pp. "Harp or piano solo."

1884. Schuller, Gunther, 1925–. *Fantasy: for solo harp.* New York: Associated Music Publishers, Inc., c1969. 11 pp.

1885. Sciarrino, Salvatore, 1947–. *L'addio a trachis: per arpa.* Milan: Ricordi, 1984, c1980. 3 pp.

1886. Sciortino, Patrice, 1922–. *Astralité: pour harpe.* Paris: EFM/Technisonor, c1974. 17 pp.

1887. ———. *Brin: pour harpe celtique ou harpe.* Paris: Éditions Musicales Hortensia, c1976. 2 pp. [NP]

1888. Selmi, Giuseppe, 1908–. *Improvviso: sul ritmo e sul canto del cuccu: per arpa.* Rome: Edizioni EDI-PAN, c1981. 5 pp.

1889. Sendrez, Michel. *Notes pour un portrait: pour harpe.* Paris: Gérard Billaudot, c1989. 12 pp. (La harpe)

1890. Sevasta, Philip. *Dance characteristic: thema of Bellotta: harp solo [in G minor].* New York: International Music Pub. Co., c1915. 4 pp.

1891. ———. [Marionetts ballet suite. Jester] *The jester: from the Marionetts ballet suite: for the Clark Irish harp.* New York: International Music Pub. Co., c1923. 2 pp. [NP]

1892. Sevriens, Jean. *Astre: for harp.* Amsterdam: Donemus, 1990. 4 pp.

1893. Shaw, Harriet. *A reverderla.* New York: International Music Pub. Co., c1923. 3 pp.

1894. Sheinfeld, David, 1906–. *Dualities: for harp.* [Palo Alto, Calif.]: San Andreas Press, c1976. 14 pp.

1895. Sheppard, C. James (Charles James), 1943–. *Garden of earthly delights: for prepared harp.* New York: Seesaw Music, c1978. 6 pp. Includes instructions for performance; a long strip of cotton and several plastic knives with serrated cutting edges are needed.

1896. Sheriff, Noam, 1935–. *Invention: for harp.* Tel Aviv: Israel Music Institute, c1969. 7 pp.

1897. Siegmeister, Elie, 1909–1991. *American harp: suite for solo harp.* Bryn Mawr, Pa.: T. Presser Co., [1976], c1971. 16 pp. CONTENTS: Reverie; Dance; Ballad; Celebration.

1898. Silverman, Faye-Ellen, 1947–. *Volcanic songs.* New York: Seesaw Music, c1984. 11 pp.

1899. Silvestri, Constantin, 1913–1969. *Sonata: per arpa, op. 21, Nr. 1.* Mainz: B. Schott's Söhne, 1964. 17 pp.

1900. Simoncelli, Giulia Principe. *Trittico: per arpa.* Milan: Edizioni Curci, c1971. 26 pp. CONTENTS: Omaggio a Rossini; Meditazione; I burattini di Mangiafuoco.

1901. Skalkottas, Nikos, 1904–1949. *Echo: for harp or piano.* Newton Centre, Mass.: Margun Music, 1980. 3 pp.

1902. Slavicky, Klement, 1910–. *Musica per arpa (1972).* Ed. by Dagmar Platilova. Prague: Panton, 1986. 15 pp. CONTENTS: Intermezzo lirico; Intermezzo responsoriale; Capriccio burlesco.

1903. Slonimsky, Nicolas, 1894–. *Russian toccata.* Santa Monica, Calif.: Salvi Publications, n.d. 9 pp.

1904. Snoer, Johannes, 1868–1936. *Abendlied: für Harfe solo.* [Frankfurt]: Zimmermann, [1988?]. 5 pp. Reprint; originally pub. ca. 1918.

1905. ———. *Capriccio marcial und Intermezzo: [für] Harfe, op. 104.* Leipzig: J.H. Zimmermann, c1913. 5 pp.

1906. ———. *Colonial days: gavotte.* New York: International Music Pub. Co., c1923. 2 pp.

1907. ———. *Études dans le style brilliant, op. 40.* Ed. Denise Megevand. Paris: G. Billaudot, 1991. 48 pp.

1908. ———. *Fantaisie: morceau de concert pour les jeunes harpistes, op. 65.* Leipzig: Aug. Cranz, n.d. 10 pp.

1909. ———. *Fantaisie-Caprice: für Harfe, op. 19.* Bremen: Praeger & Meier, n.d. 9 pp.

1910. ———. *Im Walde: fünf leichte Stücke zum Konzert- und Solovortrag: für Harfe, op. 106.* Leipzig: J.H. Zimmermann, c1913. 3 v. CONTENTS, Vol.1: Morgenstimmung = Fantaisie du matin; Vol.3. Am Bach = Près du ruisseau.

1911. ———. [Kleine Stücke] *Drei kleine Stücke: für die Harfe, op. 7.* Leipzig: Rob. Forberg, n.d. 11 pp.

1912. ———. [Leichte Salonstücke] *Zwei leichte Salonstücke: für Harfe, op. 52.* Leipzig: J.H. Zimmermann, [c1899?]. 2 v. in 1. CONTENTS: Capriccio marcial; Capriccio melodieux.

1913. ———. *Paraphrase aus Rheingold von Richard Wagner: für Harfe.* London: Schott, n.d. 7 pp.

1914. ———. *Phantasie über das Niederländische Volkslied Wien Neerlandsch bloed: [für] Harfe, op. 51.* Leipzig: J.H. Zimmermann, [c1899?]. 11 pp.

1915. ———. *Phantasie über zwei Weihnachtslieder, op. 59.* Leipzig; New York: Breitkopf & Härtel, c1905. 7 pp. (Breitkopf & Härtel's Bibliotheken für Blas-, Schlag- u.a. Instrumente)

1916. ———. [Romance, harp, op. 102] *Romance: [für] Harfe, op. 102.* Leipzig: Jul. Heinr. Zimmermann, c1913. 6 pp.

1917. ———. [Studies, harp] *20 Harfenstudien: für die linke Hand: für Anfänger, op. 22.* Leipzig: D. Rahter, 1905. 17 pp.

1918. ———. *Suite no. 1: for the Irish or concert harp.* New York: International Music, c1921. 7 pp. [NP] CONTENTS: Andante pastorale; Theme with variations; Intermezzo; Petite valse lente.

1919. ———. [Tägliche Übungen, harp, op. 46] *Tägliche Übungen: für angehende Harfenspieler: eingerichtet für einfache oder Doppel-Pedalharfe ohne Benutzung der Pedale, op. 46.* Leipzig: Steingräber; New York: Edw. Schuberth, [189–?]. 15 pp. [NP]

1920. ———. *Valse de concert: [für] Harfe, op. 105.* Leipzig: J.H. Zimmermann, c1913. 7 pp.

1921. Sodero, Carlo. *Mazurka de concert, op. 31.* New York: International Music Pub., c1919. 7 pp.

1922. ———. *Papillon: etude-caprice, op. 33.* New York: International Music Pub. Co., c1923. 5 pp.

1923. Sodero, Domenico. *Fantasia drammatica: per arpa, op. 70.* New York: International Music Pub. Co., c1923. 18 pp.

1924. ———. *Impressione.* New York: International Music Pub. Co., c1917. 7 pp.

1925. ———. [Little ballet suite. Dance of the little page] *Dance of the little page: from The little ballet suite.* New York: International Music Pub. Co., c1923. 2 pp. Cover: "From the Clark Irish harp suite." [NP]

1926. ———. *Scherzo: harp solo, op. 57.* New York: International Music, c1915. 9 pp.

1927. Soubeyran, Robert. *Pièces: pour harpe.* Paris: Choudens, c1981. 7 pp.

1928. Soulage, Marcelle, 1894–. *Petites pièces pour harp à pédales: Choral; Danse.* Paris: Rouart, Lerolle et Cie., c1917. 3, 3 pp.

1929. Spohr, Louis, 1784–1859. [Fantasies, harp, op. 35, C minor] *Fantasie c-moll: für Harfe, op. 35.* Herausgegeben von Hans Joachim Zingel. Santa Monica, Calif.: Salvi Publications, n.d. 9 pp.

1930. ———. [Fantasies, harp, op. 35, C minor] *Fantasie: c-moll: für Harfe, op. 35.* Hrsg. von Hans Joachim Zingel. Kassel: Bärenreiter, 1954. 9 pp.

1931. ———. [Fantasies, harp, op. 35, C minor] *Fantasie: for harp, op. 35.* [Edited by Dewey Owens]. New York, N.Y.: Lyra Music Co., c1976. 8 pp.

1932. ———. [Fantasies, harp, op. 35, C minor] *Fantasia: for the harp, op. 35.* Edited by John Thomas; revised by Ann Griffiths. Abergavenny, Gwent: Adlais, 1989. 9 pp.

1933. ———. [Variations, harp, op. 36, F major] *Variations sur l'air Je suis encore dans mon printemps = I am still so young.* Reviewed and corrected by W. Posse. Frankfurt am Main: Musikverlag W. Zimmermann, c1968. 11 pp. (Musik für Harfe) The theme is by Méhul.

1934. Sporck, Georges, 1870–1943. [Impromptus, harp, no. 1] *Impromptu: en la-bémol pour harpe.* Paris: Editions Max Eschig, c1936. 15 pp.

1935. ———. [Impromptus, harp, no. 2] *2me impromptu: en la-bémol mineur pour harpe.* Paris: Editions Max Eschig, c1938. 12 pp.

1936. Srebotnjak, Alojz, 1931–. *Preludji: za harfo.* Zagreb [Croatia]: Naklada saveza kompozitora Jugoslavije, [1960?]. 20 pp.

1937. Stahl, Ernst, fl. 1900. *Les adieux, op. 41.* Leipzig: J.H. Zimmermann, c1901. 7 pp.

1938. ———. *An der Quelle, op. 50.* [Leipzig: J.H. Zimmermann, 1900?]. 7 pp.

1939. ———. *Marguerite: Gavotte-caprice, op. 56.* [Leipzig: J.H. Zimmermann, 1900?]. 9 pp.

1940. ———. [Serenade, harp, op. 42] *Serenade, op. 42.* [Leipzig: J.H. Zimmermann, 1900?]. 7 pp.

1941. Standing, Vida. *Evening hour: harp solo [in C♭ major].* [New York]: International Music Pub. Co., c1912. 6 pp.

1942. Starer, Robert, 1924–. *Prelude: for harp.* New York: Peer International, c1950. 5 pp.

1943. Stefan, Josef Antonín, 1726–1797. *Six concertos pour clavecin ou harpe avec accompagnement de violons, dont il y en a ad libitum, op. 3.* Rotterdam: Accardi, 1986.

1944. Stefano, Salvatore de, 1887–1981. *Petite suite oriental.* New York: International Music Co., c1921. 6 pp.

1945. ———. *Souvenir d'Italie (Petite barcarolle): harp solo [in Db major].* New York: International Music Pub. Co., c1914. 4 pp.

1946. ———. *Tenerezza.* New York: International Music Pub. Co., c1921. 2 pp.

1947. Steffens, Walter, 1934–. *Sarahs Traumstündchen: sechs Stücke für Irische Harfe = Sarah's little daydream: six pieces for Celtic harp, op. 59.* Berlin: N. Simrock, 1991. 4, 7 pp. [NP]

1948. Steibelt, Daniel, 1765–1823. *A favorite Spanish air: for the harp or piano forte.* London: Printed by Goulding, [ca. 1810]. 3 pp.

1949. Steil, W. Henry. *Fantaisie ecossaise: for the harp: on the air O Nanny wilt thou gang with me.* London: Chappell, [18—]. 10 pp.

1950. ———. [Lullaby] *The favorite air of Lullaby: arr. for the harp.* London: Goulding, D'Almaine, Potter & Co., [18—]. 9 pp.

1951. ———. *My lodging is on the cold ground: Scotch air with variations for the harp.* London: Goulding, D'Almaine, Potter & Co., [18—]. 7 pp.

1952. Sternefeld, Daniel, 1905–. *Etude-passacaglia: voor diatonische of chromatische harp = pour harpe diatonique ou chromatique.* Brussels: CeBeDeM, c1980. 10 pp.

1953. Stevens, Halsey, 1908–1989. *Prelude: for harp.* New York: Peer International, 1968. 3 pp.

1954. ———. [Slovakian folksongs] *Six Slovakian folksongs: for solo harp.* New York: Peer International, c1976. 6 pp. CONTENTS: Poza bučki, poza les = Beyond beeches, beyond woods; Opila som sa, ňevem d'e = Where did I get so tipsy?; Šipová ružička = Wild rose; Hori, hori, čierne hori = Black mountains; Ej, hora, hora = Hey, mountain, mountain; Zaprelo sa d'iouča = The girl that barred the door.

1955. ———. [Sonatinas, harp] *Sonatina: for harp solo.* New York: American Composers Alliance, c1957. 13 pp. (Composers facsimile edition)

1956. ———. [Sonatinas, harp] *Sonatina: for harp.* New York: Peer International, 1969. 18 pp.

1957. Stivell, Alan, 1944–. *Na reubairean: fantaisie sur un thème gaélique.* Paris: Intersong, c1973. 3 pp.

1958. ———, arr. *Renaissance de la harpe celtique.* Paris: Éditions Intersong/ Tutti, c1972. CONTENTS: Vol.2. Gaeltacht. Port ui Mhuirgheasa; Airde cuan; Na reubairean; Caitlin Triall; Heman dubh; Struan Robertson; The little cascade; Port en Deorai; Gaëlic waltz; Braigh loch iall; Mélodie manxoise; Marv pontkalleg; Eliz iza; Ys.

1959. Strategier, Herman, 1912–. [Pieces, harp] *Five pieces: for harp.* Amsterdam: Donemus, c1986. 17 pp.

1960. ———. *Suite: for harp-solo.* Amsterdam: Donemus, c1962. 19 pp. CONTENTS: Prelude; Dance; Impromptu; Scherzo; Final-dance.

1961. Stuckey, Anna B., 1898–1993. [Humming bird] *Etude: The humming bird: harp solo.* S.l.: s.n., c1979. 5 pp.

1962. ———. *Noche en Mexico: solo for harp or piano.* S.l.: s.n., c1979. 4 pp.

1963. Succari, Dia, 1938–. *Sur l'étang.* Paris: Harposphère, c1987. 4 pp. For Celtic harp. [NP]

1964. Surtel, Maarten, 1958–. *Etude: —et le chant de son corps—: pour harp.* Amsterdam: Donemus, c1991. 5 pp.

1965. Szalonek, Witold, 1927–. [Sketches, harp] *Three sketches: for harp.* New York: Seesaw Music, c1972. 3 pp.

1966. ———. [Sketches, harp] *Trzy szkice = Three sketches: na harfe solo.* Kraków: Polskie Wydawn. Muzyczne; New York: Seesaw Music, 1979, c1972. 5 leaves.

1967. Szonyi, Erzsébet, 1924–. *Fantasy: for harp.* Budapest: Editio Musica, c1987. 4 pp.

1968. Szymańska, Iwonka B., 1943–. [Essays] *Dwa eseje: na harfe = Two essays: for harp.* Wyd. 1. Warszawa, Poland: Agencja Autorska, c1986. 12 pp. (Contemporary Polish music: Series of solo compositions)

1969. Tacuchian, Ricardo, 1939–. *Ritos (1977): für Harfe solo = for harp solo.* Bad Schwalbach: Edition Gravis, 1984, c1982. Score 10 leaves.

1970. Tailleferre, Germaine, 1892–1983. *Sonate: pour harpe.* Paris: Nouvelles Editions Meridian, c1957. 13 pp.

1971. Taira, Yoshihisa, 1937–. *Sublimation: pour harpe.* Paris: Editions Rideau Rouge, c1973. 5 pp.

1972. Takemitsu, Toru, 1930–. *Stanza II: for harp and tape.* Paris; New York: Editions Salabert, c1972. 3 pp.

1973. Tal, Josef, 1910–. *Dispute: for harp.* Edited by Judith Liber. Tel Aviv: Israel Music Institute, c1990. 12 pp. (Harp music in Israel)

1974. ———. *Intrada: harp solo.* Tel Aviv: Israeli Music Publications, c1959. 7 pp.

1975. ———. *Intrada: harp solo.* New York: Leeds Music Corp., c1959. 7 pp.

1976. ———. *Structure: for harp solo.* Tel Aviv: Israel Music Institute, c1962. 12 pp.

1977. Taxman, Barry, 1922–. *Three pieces: for solo harp.* Ross, Calif.: Harp

Publications, c1974. 4 pp. CONTENTS: Meditation; Chordal piece; Flight.

1978. Tcherepnin, Alexander, 1899–1977. *Quatre caprices diatoniques: pour harpe = Vier diatonische Capricen: für Harfe, opus posthum.* Frankfurt: M.P. Belaieff, c1984. 5 pp.

1979. Tedeschi, L. M. (Luigi Maurizio), 1867–1944. *Al ruscello: studio di concerto per arpa, op. 36.* Leipzig: W. Zimmermann, c1902. 15 pp.

1980. ———. *Anacreontica, op. 44.* Leipzig: J.H. Zimmermann, c1914. 11 pp.

1981. ———. *Angelus, op. 42.* Leipzig: J.H. Zimmermann, c1914. 7 pp.

1982. ———. *Chiarafonte, op. 47: capriccio per arpa.* Leipzig: Jul. Heinr. Zimmermann, c1924. 11 pp.

1983. ———. [Compositions, harp] *Sei composizioni: per arpa.* Milan: Carisch, 1927. 6 v. CONTENTS: Mignonnette; Preludio; Storiella a Bebè (Bluette); Pierrot innamorato (Serenata); Ritornello triste; Presso il mulino (Improvviso).

1984. ———. *Etude impromptu: pour harpe, op. 37.* Leipzig: Jul. Heinr. Zimmermann, c1906. 7 pp.

1985. ———. *Marionette: humoresque pour harpe, op. 31.* Leipzig: Wilhelm Zimmermann, n.d. 6 pp.

1986. ———. *Pattuglia spagnuola, op. 32.* Leipzig: J.H. Zimmermann, c1903. 7 pp.

1987. ———. *Presque rien, op. 43.* Leipzig: J.H. Zimmermann, c1914. 5 pp.

1988. ———. *Suite, op. 34.* Leipzig: W. Zimmermann, c1902. 27 pp.

1989. Templeton, Alec, 1910–1963. *Rigodon.* New York: Lyra Music Co., c1964. 4 pp.

1990. ———. *Sicilienne.* New York: Lyra Music Co., c1964. 4 pp.

1991. Theumann, M. *Fantaisie sur quatre thèmes russes: pour harpe, op. 11.* Leipzig: Zimmermann, c1914. 11 pp.

1992. Theumann-Schetochina. *Rhapsodie hongroise: pour la harpe.* Leipzig: Jul. Heinr. Zimmermann, c1911. 8 pp.

1993. Thiele, Siegfried, 1934–. *Raumspiele: für Harfe solo.* Herausgegeben von Katharina Hanstedt. Kassel: Bärenreiter, c1992. 11 pp.

1994. Thomas, John, 1826–1913. [Adleisiau'r rhaeadr] *Echoes of a waterfall: caprice for the harp.* London: A. W. Cannon, [187–?]. 10 pp.

1995. ———. *Adleisiau'r rhaeadr: difyrrwch i'r delyn = Echoes of a waterfall: caprice for the harp.* Abergavenny, Gwent: Adlais, 1986. 11 pp.

1996. ———. *Autumn: for the harp.* Boston: Percy Ashdown, n.d. 11 pp.

1997. ———. *Eolian sounds: for the harp.* London: Gould & Bolttler, [19—].
16 pp.

1998. ———. [Ffarwel y telynor i'w enedigol wlad] *The minstrel's adieu to his
native land: an original melody.* London: Edwin Ashdown, n.d. 7 pp. (Welsh
melodies for the harp)

1999. ———. *Ffarwel y telynor i'w enedigol wlad = The minstrel's adieu to his
native land.* Abergavenny, Gwent, Wales: Adlais, n.d. 7 pp.

2000. ———. [Ffarwel y telynor i'w enedigol wlad] *Minstrel's adieu to his
native land: pour harpe.* [Rev. Martine Géliot]. Paris: Gérard Billaudot,
c1977. 7 pp. (La harpe)

2001. ———. *Rêverie: for the harp.* London: Gould & Bolttler, [19—]. 13 pp.

2002. ———. *Rhapsody: for the harp.* Abergavenny, Gwent, Wales: Adlais, n.d.
11 pp.

2003. ———. *Riding over the mountain: an original melody: for harp.* Santa
Monica, Calif.: Salvi Publications, c1983. 8 pp.

2004. ———. [Romances, harp] *Four romances: for the harp.* London:
Hutchings & Romer, [19—]. 4 v. CONTENTS: The tear; The smile; The
parting; The remembrance.

2005. ———. *The seasons: for the harp.* London: Hutchings & Romer,
[19—]. 4 v. CONTENTS: Spring; Summer; Autumn; Winter.

2006. ———. *The seasons: for the harp.* Abergavenny: Adlais, 1983. 4 v.
CONTENTS: See 2005.

2007. ———. *Serch hudol = Love's fascination: harp.* Santa Monica, Calif.: Salvi
Publications, c1983. 5 pp.

2008. ———. *Le soir: premier impromptu: for the harp.* London: Hutchings &
Romer, n.d. 7 pp.

2009. ———. *The spinning-wheel: characteristic study for the harp.* London:
Gould & Bolttler, [19—?]. 7 pp.

2010. ———. *Staccato movement: for the harp.* London: Hutchings and Romer,
n.d. 5 pp.

2011. ———. [Studies, harp] *Six [i.e. Twelve] studies: for the harp.* London:
Gould & Bolttler, [18—]. 2 v.

2012. ———. [Studies, harp. Selections] *Dewis dethol: o ymarferiadau telyn =
Selected studies: for the harp.* Abergavenny, Gwent: Adlais, c1975. 32 pp.
"The four studies selected for this volume are taken from the series of
twelve studies in two books originally published by Hutchings and Romer,
being numbers 4 and 6 from Series 1, and 9 and 12 from Series 2."

2013. ———. *Tyrolienne: characteristic piece for the harp.* London: Hutchings &
Romer, n.d. 9 pp.

2014. ————. *Tyrolienne: characteristic piece for the harp.* Abergavenny, Gwent, Wales: Adlais, n.d. 9 pp.

2015. Thomas, Mansel, 1909–. *Variants on an ancient Welsh melody: Yr hen erddygan.* Abergavenny, Gwent, Wales: Adlais, c1976. 17 pp. CONTENTS: Introduction; Sarabande (Variant I); Toccata (Variant II); Processional (Variant III); Impromptu (Variant IV); Siciliano (Variant V); Theme & epilogue.

2016. Thomas de Sancta Maria, fray, d. 1570. *Veinticinco fantasías del Arte de tañer fantasia: para organo, clave o arpa.* Realizacion en notacion moderna por Jose y Lupe de Azpiazu. Madrid: Union Musical Española, c1965. 28 pp.

2017. Thomson, Lucien, 1913–. [Pieces, harp. Ebbing tide] *Ebbing tide.* New York: Lucien Thomson, c1987. 2 pp. [NP]

2018. ————. [Pieces, harp. Song at night] *Song at night.* New York: Lucien Thomson, c1987. 2 pp. [NP]

2019. ————, and Lovelace, William, 1960–. *First day of spring: for pedal or non-pedal harp.* [New York?: William M. Lovelace], c1989. 2 pp. [NP]

2020. Tisné, Antoine, 1932–. *Particule: pour harpe: d'après le poème de David Niemann.* Paris: G. Billaudot, c1985. 14 pp. (La harpe)

2021. Tocchi, Gianluca, 1901–. *Dodici studi: per arpa.* Diteggiatura di Ada Ruata Sassoli. Rome: Edizioni De Santis, 1945. 2 v.

2022. Tomasi, Henri, 1901–1971. *Invocation et danse: pour harpe.* Paris: A. Leduc, 1969. 7 pp.

2023. Tomchin, A. (Arkadii). *Sonata: dlia arfy.* Leningrad: Sov. kompozitor, 1987. 18 pp.

2024. Tommasini, Vincenzo, 1880–1950. *Sonata: per arpa.* Milan: G. Ricordi, c1939. 17 pp.

2025. Tôn-Thât, Tiêt, 1933–. *Chu ky III: pour harpe.* Paris: Jobert, c1978. 12 pp.

2026. Torgerson, Helena Stone. *Bourée: pour harpe.* Paris: A. Durand & Fils, c1927. 3 pp.

2027. ————. *Contentement: pour harpe.* Paris: A. Durand & Fils, c1927. 7 pp.

2028. ————. *Etude pour la main gauche = Study for the left hand: pour la harpe.* Paris: Durand, c1913. 5 pp.

2029. ————. *Papillon = A butterfly: pièce pour harpe.* Paris: Durand, 1913. 4 pp.

2030. ————. [Petite canons] *Six petite canons: etudes: easy and progressive.* New York: International Music Pub. Co., c1915. 2 pp.

2031. ———. *Rêverie = Revery: pièce pour harpe.* Paris: Durand, c1913. 7 pp.

2032. ———. *Valse de concert = Concert waltz: pour harpe.* Paris: A. Durand & Fils, c1927. 7 pp.

2033. Toulmin, Alfred F. *Petite fantasie: Robin Adair & Kate Kearney.* New York: J. F. Browne, c1863. 9 pp.

2034. Tournier, Marcel, 1879–1951. *Air à danser: petite pièce brève et facile pour la harpe.* Paris: Éditions Max Eschig, c1976. 4 pp.

2035. ———. *Au hasard des ondes: nouvelles images pour la harpe, [op. 50].* Brussels: H. Lemoine, c1953. 47 pp. CONTENTS: Au Japon; En Chine; En Afrique; En France; En Scandinavie; En Roumanie; En Italie.

2036. ———. *Berceuse: petite pièce brève & facile: pour la harpe.* Paris: Max Eschig, c1913. 3 pp.

2037. ———. *Berceuse russe: pour harpe, op. 40.* Paris: Éditions Henry Lemoine, c1932. 3 pp.

2038. ———. *Ce que chante la pluie d'automne: lied pour la harpe, op. 49.* Paris: Henry Lemoine & Cie., c1947. 8 pp.

2039. ———. *Encore une boîte à musique: pour harpe, op. 43.* Paris: H. Lemoine & cie., 1935. 4 pp.

2040. ———. *Etude de concert: au matin: pour la harpe.* Paris: Alphonse Leduc, c1940. 8 pp.

2041. ———. *Féerie: prélude et danse: pour la harpe.* Paris: Alphonse Leduc, c1920. 16 pp.

2042. ———. *Fresque marine: pour la harpe.* Paris: Henry Lemoine & Cie., c1946. 12 pp.

2043. ———. *Images: pour harpe.* Paris: Editions Henry Lemoine, c1925–1932. 4 v. CONTENTS: *1re suite* [op. 29]: Clair de lune sur l'etang du parc = Moonlight in a pool; Au seuil du temple = On the temple's threshold; Lolita, la danseuse = Lolita, the dancer. *2e suite* [op. 31]: Les enfants à la crèche = Children by Christmas crib; L'etrange cavalier = The strange rider; La marchande de frivolités = Frivolity's merchant. *3e suite* [op. 35]: Les anesses grises sur la route d'El-Azib = Grey donkeys on the road to El-Azib; Danseuse à la fontaine d'Aïn- Draham = Dancer at the fountain of Aïn-Draham; Soir de fête à Sedjenane = Evening fête at Sedjenane. *4e suite* [op. 39]: La volière magique = The magical aviary; Cloches sous la neige = Bells in the snow; La danse du moujik = The dance of the moujik.

2044. ———. *Jazz-band: pour la harpe, op. 33.* Paris: Editions Henry Lemoine, c1926. 7 pp.

2045. ———. [Nöels] *Six Nöels pour la harpe, op. 32.* Paris: H. Lemoine & Cie., c1926. 8 pp.

2046. ———. *Pastels du vieux Japon: pour harpe, op. 47*. Paris: Editions Henry Lemoine, c1947. 8 pp. CONTENTS: Berceuse du vent dans le cerisiers; Le koto chante pour l'absent; Le danseur au sabre.

2047. ———. [Petites pièces brèves et faciles] *Deux petites pièces brèves et faciles: pour la harpe*. Paris: Editions Max Eschig, 1976, c1913. 3 pp. CONTENTS: Soupir; Offrande.

2048. ———. *Pièces nègres: pour harpe, op. 41*. Paris: Editions Henry Lemoine, c1935. 9 pp. CONTENTS: Berceuse nègre; La jeune fille au voile; Ronde des négrillons.

2049. ———. [Preludes, harp, op. 16] *Quatre preludes: pour harpe*. Paris: Edition Maurice Senart, c1917. 9 pp.

2050. ———. [Preludes, harp, op. 16] *Quatre préludes: pour harpe*. Paris: Louis Rouhier, c1920. 9 pp.

2051. ———. [Preludes, harp, op. 16] *Quatre préludes: pour harpe, [op. 16]*. Paris: A. Leduc, c1955. 9 pp.

2052. ———. [Preludes, harp, op. 16] *Quatre preludes pour harpe, [op. 16]*. New York: Lyra Music, [1955?]. 9 pp.

2053. ———. [Rouet enchanté] *Le rouet enchanté: pour harpe*. Paris: Henry Lemoine & Cie., c1937. 15 pp.

2054. ———. *Scherzo romantique: pour harpe, op. 38*. Paris: Editions Henry Lemoine, c1932. 13 pp.

2055. ———. [Sonatinas, harp, no. 1, op. 30] *Sonatine: pour harpe, op. 30*. Paris: Lemoine, c1924. 23 pp.

2056. ———. [Sonatinas, harp, no. 2, op. 45] *Deuxieme sonatine: pour harpe, op. 45*. Paris: Editions Henry Lemoine, c1945. 24 pp.

2057. ———. *Thème et variations: pour la harpe*. Paris: Alphonse Leduc, c1913. 22 pp.

2058. ———. *Vers la source dans le bois: pour la harpe*. Paris: Alphonse Leduc, 1922. 8 pp.

2059. Trabaci, Giovanni Maria, 1580 (ca.)-1647. [Ricercate, libro 1–2] *Ricercate, canzone franzese: libro primo [1603]; Secondo libro de ricercate: [1615]*. Florence: Studio per edizioni scelte, 1984. 2 v. (Archivum musicum. Collana di testi rari, 56) Facsimiles of the prints of Costantino Vitale, Naples, 1603 (book 1) and of Giovanni Giacomo Carlino, Naples, 1615 (book 2). For performance by harpsichord, organ, harp, consort of viols, lutes, or other combinations of instruments.

2060. Tremblot de la Croix, Francine, 1938–. *Trois îles: pour harpe*. Paris: Billaudot, 1981. 8 pp. "Morceau de concours du Conservatoire national supérieur de musique de Paris 1981." CONTENTS: Orthuz: danse du pêcheur; Aran: berceuse irlandaise; Lesbos: jeux.

2061. Trépard, Emile, 1870–. *Chauves souris: pièce pour harpe.* Paris: L. Grus, n.d. 5 pp.

2062. Trneček, Hanuš, 1858–1914. *Dalibor fantasie, op. 75.* Leipzig: Zimmermann, c1915. 19 pp. Based on themes from Smetana's opera *Dalibor.*

2063. ———. *Furiant: für Harfe, op. 77.* Leipzig: Wilhelm Zimmermann, [19—]. 11 pp.

2064. ———. *Furiant, op. 77.* Marina Del Rey, Calif.: Safari Publications, 1993. 11 pp.

2065. ———. *Novellette, op. 30.* [Leipzig: J.H. Zimmermann, 1900?]. 11 pp.

2066. ———. *Novellette, op. 30.* Marina Del Rey, Calif.: Safari Publications, 1993. 11 pp.

2067. ———. [Rhapsodies, harp, no. 1, op. 74] *Erste Rhapsodie, op. 74.* Leipzig: W. Zimmermann, c1915. 19 pp.

2068. ———. [Rhapsodies, harp, no. 1, op. 74] *Erste Rhapsodie, op. 74.* Marina Del Rey, Calif.: Safari Publications, 1993. 19 pp.

2069. ———. *Schubert-fantasie: für Harfe, [op. 7].* Bayreuth: Giessel, n.d. 17 pp.

2070. ———. *Variationen: F dur: auf ein lustiges Thema, op. 73.* Leipzig: Jul. Heinr. Zimmermann, c1915. 19 pp.

2071. Trotter, Louise, 1927–. *Mission in space: descriptive suite for harp.* Houston, Tex.: Louise Trotter, 1989. 12 pp. CONTENTS: Countdown and liftoff; Moonscape; Spacewalk; Touchdown!

2072. Turner, Robert, 1920–. *Little suite: for harp.* New York: Peer International, c1971. 13 pp. CONTENTS: Prelude; Melody; Waltz; Fantasy.

2073. Turok, Paul, 1929–. *Sonatina: for harp.* New York: G. Schirmer, c1980. 15 pp. Op. 51, no. 1.

2074. Tutino, Marco. *Improvviso: per arpa.* Milan: Edizioni Suvini Zerboni, c1982. 5 pp.

2075. Tutton, James Rufus. *Six preludes for the harp.* London: The author, [185–?]. 6 pp.

2076. Twinn, Sydney. *Two pieces.* London: Hinrichsen, c1961. 7 pp. CONTENTS: Pastourelle; Esquisse.

2077. Tyre, Marjorie, 1910–. *Etude.* San Mateo, Calif.: F.C. Publishing Co., c1988. 2 pp. (Solo series: harp)

2078. Ugoletti, Paolo. *Al suo orologio in una notte insonne: per arpa.* Milan: Edizioni Suvini Zerboni, c1982. 8 pp.

2079. Vachey, Henri, 1930–. *Marche pour deux fois quatre petits doigts: pour harpe celtique ou à pédales = March for twice four little fingers.* Paris: A. Leduc, c1972. 3 pp. [NP]

2080. ———. [Prelude, harp] *Prelude: pour harpe.* Paris: Alphonse Leduc, c1966. 4 pp.

2081. Valenza, Michelangelo. *Santa Lucia: canzone napolitana: piccola fantasia.* Milan: G. Ricordi, n.d. 9 pp.

2082. Vallier, Jacques, 1922–. *Sonatine: pour harpe.* Toulouse: Verseau, c1979. 8 pp.

2083. Vamos, Grace Becker, 1898–. *Fountainbleau suite: harp solo.* New York: Lyra Music Co., c1967. 12 pp. CONTENTS: Palace lake; Summer night; Forest.

2084. ———. *Gypsy: for harp solo.* Ross, Calif.: Harp Publications, c1975. 4 pp.

2085. ———. *Legend of the redwoods: for harp solo.* [Edited by Anne Louise David]. Ross, Calif.: Harp Publications, c1950. 9 pp. "Prize-winning composition, 1949 competition, Northern California Harpists' Association."

2086. ———. *Legend of the redwoods: for harp.* Rev. ed. San Francisco, Calif.: Vamos Publications, [198–?], c1950. 9 pp.

2087. Van Appledorn, Mary Jeanne, 1927–. *Sonic mutation: for harp.* Edited by Gail Barber. Washington, D.C.: Sisra Publications, c1988. 9 pp.

2088. Van Buskirk, Carl. *Music: for harp.* [S.l.: s.n., 1955]. 13 pp.

2089. Van Hulse, Camil, 1897–. [Suite, harp, op. 141] *Suite: for harpe, op. 141.* Tucson, Ariz.: Camil Van Hulse, c1966. 21 pp. CONTENTS: Preludio; Nostalgia; Marcia; Toccata.

2090. Vaughan, Clifford, 1893–. *Revery: harp solo.* Los Angeles, Calif.: Western International Music, 1967. 4 pp.

2091. Velez Camerero, E. *Pilveran: capricho para arpa.* Rev. y dig. de Ma. Rosa Calvo Manzano. Madrid: Union Musical Española, c1973. 16 pp.

2092. Vercoe, Elizabeth, 1941–. *Parodia: sopra Lasciate mi morire.* New York: American Composers Alliance, c1983. 9 pp. "*Parodia* is a fantasy on the Monteverdi madrigal 'Lasciate mi morire.' Although not strictly a Renaissance-style parody, all five voices of the original appear in quotation or in various levels of disguise."

2093. Verdalle, Gabriel, fl. 1898–1912. *A Capri: (Tarentella).* Leipzig: J.H. Zimmermann, c1915. 9 pp.

2094. ———. *Adagio, op. 7.* Leipzig: J.H. Zimmermann, c1898. 5 pp.

2095. ———. [Air de ballet, no. 4] *Quatrième air de ballet.* Leipzig: J.H. Zimmermann, c1915. 9 pp.

2096. ———. *Amoroso, op. 76.* Leipzig: J.H. Zimmermann, c1901. 6 pp.

2097. ———. [Aubade, harp, op. 4] *Aubade, op. 4.* [Leipzig: J.H. Zimmermann, 19—]. 7 pp.

2098. ———. *Badinage, op. 73.* Leipzig: J.H. Zimmermann, c1901. 6 pp.

2099. ———. *Barcarolle, op. 10.* [Leipzig: J.H. Zimmermann, 19—]. 5 pp.

2100. ———. *Berceuse, op. 79.* Leipzig: W. Zimmermann, c1901. 5 pp.

2101. ———. *Butterflies: morceau characteristique [pour] harpe.* New York: International Music Pub. Co., c1913. 5 pp.

2102. ———. *Capricciosa: (valse lente).* Leipzig: J.H. Zimmermann, c1914. 11 pp.

2103. ———. *Childish march, op. 45.* Leipzig: J.H. Zimmermann, c1900. 5 pp.

2104. ———. *Danse slave, op. 40.* Leipzig: J.H. Zimmermann, c1900. 7 pp.

2105. ———. *Doux songe, op. 34: Harfe.* Bayreuth: C. Giessel, c1900. 7 pp.

2106. ———. [Impromptus, harp, no. 2] *Deuxième impromptu.* Leipzig: J.H. Zimmermann, c1915. 9 pp.

2107. ———. *Invocation, op. 33.* Leipzig: J.H. Zimmermann, c1900. 5 pp.

2108. ———. *Légende bretonne, op. 41.* Bayreuth: C. Giessel, Jr., c1900. 6 pp.

2109. ———. *Leggenda d'amore, op. 46.* Leipzig: C. Giessel, Jr., c1900. 5 pp.

2110. ———. *Leggenda d'amore, op. 46: für Harfe solo.* [Frankfurt]: Zimmermann, [198–?]. 5 pp.

2111. ———. *Lucciola, op. 39: [für] Harfe.* Bayreuth: C. Giessel, c1900. 7 pp.

2112. ———. [Mazurka, harp, op. 9] *Mazurka, op. 9.* Leipzig: J.H. Zimmermann, c1903. 7 pp.

2113. ———. [Morceaux, harp. En rêve] *En rêve!* Paris: Leduc, c1905. 5 pp.

2114. ———. *On the lake.* Leipzig: J.H. Zimmermann, c1915.

2115. ———. *Petite marche, op. 3.* Leipzig: J.H. Zimmermann, c1898. 6 pp.

2116. ———. *Primavera, op. 67.* Leipzig: J.H. Zimmermann, c1901. 7 pp.

2117. ———. *Recueillement, op. 43.* Leipzig: J.H. Zimmermann, c1900. 5 pp.

2118. ———. *Remembrance, op. 42.* Leipzig: J.H. Zimmermann, c1900. 5 pp.

2119. ———. *Romance sans paroles, op. 6.* Leipzig: J.H. Zimmermann, c1898. 4 pp.

2120. ———. *Saltarelle, op. 23.* Bayreuth: C. Giessel, Jr., 1898. 7 pp.

2121. ———. *Scherzetto, op. 87.* Leipzig: J.H. Zimmermann, c1901. 9 pp.

2122. ———. *Sérénade, op. 5.* [Leipzig: J.H. Zimmermann, 19—]. 5 pp.

2123. ———. *Sevillana, op. 27.* Leipzig: J.H. Zimmermann, c1900. 7 pp.

2124. ———. *Valse caprice, op. 8: [pour] harpe.* Leipzig: W. Zimmermann, c1903. 7 pp.

2125. ———. *Valse lente, op. 19.* [Leipzig: J.H. Zimmermann, 19—]. 7 pp.

2126. ———. *Vision: harp solo [in A♭ major].* New York: International Music Pub. Co., c1913. 5 pp.

2127. Vergnault, Michel. *Ballade et ronde: pour harpe.* Paris: Editions L. Philippo et M. Combre, c1974. 2 pp.

2128. Vernier, Jean Aimé, b. 1769. [Airs variés, harp, op. 6] *Six airs variés: pour la harpe: tirés des opéras du Petit matelot, de L'amour filial, de La famille indigente, [etc.].* Paris: Les frères Gaveaux, [180–?]. 26 pp.

2129. ———. [Allégro] *Deux allégro: avec acc. de violon: suivis de deux airs variés arr. pour la harpe, oeuvre 40.* Paris: Naderman, [181–?]. 2 parts. 1st work for harp and violin; 2nd work for harp.

2130. ———. [Fantaisie avec six variations sur la romance de Cendrillon] *Fantaisie avec six variations: pour la harpe: sur la romance de Cendrillon,* op. 49. Musique de Nicolo [Isouard]. Arr. par Vernier. Paris: L'auteur, [181–?]. 15 pp.

2131. ———. [Harp music. Selections] *Vive Henry IV, Charmante Gabrielle, et un air des Mystères d'Isis: variés pour la harpe.* Paris: Naderman, [1812?]. 14 pp.

2132. ———. [Potpourris, harp, no. 8] *Huitième pot-pourri: pour la harpe.* Paris: Cousineau, 181–? 13 pp.

2133. ———. [Potpourris, harp, no. 9, op. 45] *Neuvième pot-pourri: pour la harpe: dans lequel se trouve la Romance des Deux journées variée, oeuvre 45.* Paris: Gaveaux ainé, [between 1812 and 1832]. 17 pp.

2134. ———. [Variations, harp, op. 49] *Airs variés: pour la harpe, oeuvre 49: 1ère. livraison.* Paris: Vernier, [1814?]. 17 pp.

2135. Vick, Lloyd. *Fragment: or, The gentle harp: solo for the harp.* Ross, Calif.: Harp Publications, c1974. 10 pp.

2136. ———. *Wedding piece: for Michelle on her wedding day.* Palo Alto, Calif.: Harpress of California, c1978. 6 pp.

2137. ———. *Winter dreams: tone poem for harp solo.* Palo Alto, Calif.: Harpress of California, c1982. 9 pp.

2138. Vierne, Louis, 1870–1937. *Rhapsodie: pour harpe, op. 25.* Paris: Rouhier, 1911. 12 pp.

2139. Viotti, Giovanni Battista, 1755–1824. *Sonate: pour la harpe.* [Santa Monica, Calif.]: Salvi, 1978. 29 pp.

2140. Vito, Edward, 1902–1990. [Pieces, harp] *Two pieces: for harp.* New

York: Composers Press, c1954. 2 v. CONTENTS: Etude in C major; Gigue in olden style.

2141. Vito, Joseph, 1887–. [Etudes, harp] *Twenty etudes: for harp*. New York: Belwin, 1946. 40 pp.

2142. ———. *Impromptu: for harp*. New York: Belwin, c1942. 11 pp. (Classics for concert harp)

2143. ———, arr. *The old refrain*. Transcribed for harp by Joseph Vito. New York, N.Y.: Belwin, c1942. 7 pp. (Classics for concert harp, no. 12)

2144. Voigtländer, Lothar, 1943–. *Nocturne en trois modes: für Harfe solo*. Herausgegeben von Katharina Hanstedt. Kassel: Bärenreiter, c1992. 7 pp.

2145. Voirpy, Alain, 1955–. *Cinq pièces: pour harpe(s)*. Paris: Éditions Henry Lemoine, c1986. 8 pp. (Carte blanche) For one or more harps.

2146. Von Würtzler, Aristid, 1930–. *Brilliant romantic etude: for harp*. Hastings-on-Hudson, N.Y.: General Music Publishing Co., c1976. 16 pp.

2147. ———. *Canto amoroso*. San Mateo, Calif.: F.C. Publishing Co., c1989. 2 pp. (Solo series: harp)

2148. ———. *Caprice de concert*. Ellensburg, Wash.: F.C. Publishing Co., 1990. 13 pp.

2149. ———. *Concert improvisation*. New York: Lyra Music Co., c1966. 7 pp.

2150. ———. *Dance of puppets*. New York, N.Y.: Lyra Music Co., c1966. 2 pp.

2151. ———. *Fantasia española*. Ellensburg, Wash.: F.C. Publishing Co., 1993. 13 pp.

2152. ———. *Little tale*. [Ellensburg, Wash.]: F.C. Publishing Co., 1989. 2 pp.

2153. ———. *Little tale for boys*. Santa Monica, Calif.: Salvi Publications, c1983. 4 pp.

2154. ———. *Meditation: for solo harp*. Santa Monica, Calif.: Salvi Publications, c1983. 5 pp.

2155. ———. *Minuet: also for non-pedal harp*. Santa Monica, Calif.: Salvi Publications, c1984. 4 pp. [NP]

2156. ———. *Modern sketches: yesterday, today, tomorrow: for solo harp*. New York: Southern Music Pub. Co., c1974. 23 pp.

2157. ———. *Old dance*. New York, N.Y.: Lyra Music Co., c1966. 3 pp.

2158. ———. *Old dance: also for non-pedal harp*. Santa Monica, Calif.: Salvi Publications, c1983. 3 pp. [NP]

2159. ———. *Paraphrase from Lucia di Lammermoor: [for solo harp]*. Hastings-on-Hudson, N.Y.: General Music Publishing Co., c1976. 10 pp.

2160. ———. *Paraphrase from Rigoletto.* Ellensburg, Wash.: F.C. Publishing Co., 1991. 15 pp.

2161. ———. *Puppet dance: also for non-pedal harp.* Santa Monica, Calif.: Salvi Publications, c1983. 2 pp. [NP]

2162. ———. *Variations on a theme of Corelli: for harp solo.* Dobbs Ferry, N.Y.: General Music Pub. Co., c1968. 14 pp. Theme from Corelli's Gavotte from Sonata in F for violin, op. 5, no. 10.

2163. ———. *Viennese episode.* Ellensburg, Wash.: F.C. Publishing Co., 1993. 8 pp.

2164. Voynow, Sara Kaieolani. *Bichromation: for solo harp.* [S.l.]: SKVS Music Publications, c1987. 4 pp.

2165. Vries Robbé, Willem de, 1902–. [Arabesques, harp, no. 1] *Arabesque: pour harpe à pedales.* Amsterdam: Donemus, c1974. 6 pp.

2166. ———. [Arabesques, harp, no. 2] *Deuxieme arabesque: harpe.* Amsterdam: Donemus, c1974. 7 pp.

2167. Wagenaar, Bernard, 1894–1971. *Four vignettes: for harp.* Philadelphia: Elkan-Vogel, [1965]. 10 pp. CONTENTS: Prelude; Dance; The Angelus; Toccatina.

2168. Wagner, Joseph Frederick, 1900–1974. *Fantasy sonata: in one movement: for harp solo.* New York: Lyra Music Co., c1964. 16 pp.

2169. Walter, Fried, 1907–. *Sonatine: für Harfe.* Frankfurt a.M.: W. Zimmermann, c1957. 11 pp. CONTENTS: Junge Birken = Young birches; Japanischer Kirschbaum = Japanese cherry-tree; Unter den Eichen = Under the oaks.

2170. Walter-Khune, Catherine. *Fantasie on a theme from Tchaikovsky's Eugene Onegin.* Marina Del Rey, Calif.: Safari Publications, 1992. 18 pp.

2171. Walters, Gareth, 1928–. *Three impromptus: for harp.* Chesham, Bucks, England: G. Ricordi & Co., c1970. 16 pp. CONTENTS: Prelude; Aria; Toccata.

2172. Washburn, Gary, 1946–. *Study: for harp.* New York: Seesaw Music, c1974. 5 pp.

2173. Watkins, David, 1938–, ed. *Anthology of English music: for the harp.* Edited by David Watkins. London: Stainer and Bell; [S.l.]: Galaxy Music Corp., c1972–73. 4 v. Contains original works and arrangements. CONTENTS: Vol.1. (1550–1650): A toy. Giles Farnaby's dreame; His rest (galliard); Tell mee, Daphne by Giles Farnaby. Alman by Thomas Morley. Pavana by William Byrd. Praeludium; Praeludium (Dor.) by John Bull. Lachrimae antiquae pavan; My Lady Hunsdon's puffe by John Dowland. The fall of the leafe; Alman by Martin Peerson. Alman I; Alman II by

Robert Johnson. The Lady Hatton's galliard by Orlando Gibbons. Watkins ale.

Vol.2. (1650–1750): Sarabande; Ground by William Croft. Suite no. 1 in G (Z. 660); Round O (Z. T684); Air (Z. T676); Ground (Z. D222); Hornpipe (Z. T683); Hornpipe (Z. T685); Suite no. 8 in F (Z. 669) by Henry Purcell. Mortlack's ground by John Blow.

Vol.3. (1750–1800): Sonata in D major by John Parry. Sonata no. 3 in G major; Sonata no. 3 in G minor; Sonata no. 7 in A major by T. A. Arne.

Vol.4. (1800–1850): Nocturne in D minor; Nocturne in B♭ by John Field. Romance in A♭ ; Romance in F; Serenade; Introduction, cadenza and rondo by Elias Parish-Alvars.

2174. ———. *Dance suite.* [Santa Monica, Calif.]: Salvi, 1979. 10 pp.

2175. ———. *Petite suite: for harp.* London: United Music Publishers, c1962. 12 pp. CONTENTS: Prelude; Nocturne; Fire dance.

2176. ———. *Petite suite: for harp.* Revised edition. London: United Music Publishers, Ltd., c1984. 12 pp. CONTENTS: Prelude; Nocturne; Fire dance.

2177. ———. [Pieces, harp] *Six pieces: for harp (or piano).* London: Boosey and Hawkes, c1989. 12 pp. [NP] CONTENTS: Prelude; Berceuse; Gigue; The nightingales; Nocturne; Dance.

2178. Weber, Alain, 1930–. *Chant de biwa: estampe pour harpe.* Paris: A. Leduc, 1971. 6 pp.

2179. ———. *Harpalpha: pour harpe celtique.* Paris: Editions musicales transatlantiques, 1978. 4 pp. [NP]

2180. ———. *Volutes: pour harpe celtique.* Paris: G. Billaudot, c1992. 3 pp. [NP]

2181. Weiner, Stanley, 1925–. *Sonatine: für Harfe, op. 74.* Hamburg: Sikorski, c1978. 14 pp.

2182. Weinzweig, John, 1913–. *Fifteen pieces: for harp.* Edited by Judy Loman. [S.l.: John Weinzweig], c1983. 58 pp. CONTENTS: Shadows; Quick march; Reverie; Quarks; Just dreamin'; Fine time; Bluenote; Around and around; Arioso; Why not?; Do you remember?; Echoes; All those woes! (Shakespeare); Conversations; Satellite serenade.

2183. Weippert, John Erhardt, 1739–1820. [First book of preludes] *A first book of preludes for the pedal harp: with a collection of marches, airs, rondos, waltzes, op. 22.* London: s.n., n.d. 27 pp.

2184. Werner, Jean Jacques, 1935–. [Croix et le carre] *La croix et le carre: pour harpe celtique.* S.l.: Editions Françaises de Musique, c1974. 11 pp. [NP]

2185. ———. *Encore me souviens d'un matin: trois pièces pour harpe (sans l'emploi des pédales).* Paris: Les Editions Ouvrières, c1974. 6 pp. (Le verseau: collection de musique instrumentale contemporaine) [NP]

2186. ———. *Nocturnal: pour harpe.* Paris: Editions Transatlantiques, c1976. 8 pp.

2187. ———. [Pièces modales] *Cinq pieces modales: pour harpe.* Paris: Editions Musicales Transatlantiques, c1971. 8 pp.

2188. Wilder, Alec, 1907–1980. [Pieces, harp] *Three pieces: for solo harp.* Newton Centre, Mass.: Margun Music, 19—. 2, 4, 3 pp. CONTENTS: Dream; Dance; Frolic.

2189. ———. [Pieces, harp] *Dance, dream and frolic: for harp.* Hastings-on-Hudson, N.Y.: General Music Publishing Co., c1974. 9 pp.

2190. ———. [Pieces, harp] *Dance, dream and frolic: for harp.* S.l.: Joshua Corp, c1974. 9 pp.

2191. Williams, Grace, 1906–1977. *Hiraeth.* Cardiff: University of Wales Press, c1961. 3 pp.

2192. Winters, Geoffrey, 1928–. *Journeys, op. 80: for Celtic harp or pedal harp: ten easy solos.* With fingering by Danielle Perrett. London: N. Simrock, c1988. 11 pp. [NP] CONTENTS: 1. Hill tune; 2. Jog trot; 3. Left out; 4. Waltz variations; 5. Clip- clop; 6. At anchor; 7. Anticipation; 8. Celtic rag; 9. Gliding; 10. Cruising.

2193. ———. *Tributaries: for harp solo, op. 79.* London: N. Simrock, c1984. 15 pp. (Elite edition, 3197)

2194. Woods, Sylvia, 1951–. *The harp of Brandiswhiere: narrative and suite for Celtic harp inspired by tales of the legendary harper.* Los Angeles, Calif.: Woods Music, c1982. 59 pp. [NP] CONTENTS: The legend; In the forest; Dialogue with a brook; Lament; Gypsy mirage; Gourenspur; The harper's vision; Morning calm; Forest march; Metamorphosis; Brandiswhiere's triumphant return.

2195. ———, arr. *Songs of the harp: 20 songs about harps and harpers.* Arranged for all harps by Sylvia Woods. Los Angeles, Calif.: Woods Music and Books Publishing, c1979. 48 pp. [NP] CONTENTS: Let now the harp. The mountain minstrel. Strike the harp. The bard's lament. Now strike the harp gladly. David of the white rock. The nobleman's wedding. The bard of Armagh. Songs of Thomas Moore: My gentle harp; The legacy; Shall the harp then be silent; The wandering bard; Sing, sweet harp; The minstrel boy; Dear harp of my country; The origin of the harp; The harp that once. The night dance. Two sisters. Little David.

2196. Wrochem, Johann G. von, 1938–. *Drei Kompositionsstudien: für Harfe solo: für Xenia.* Berlin: J.G. von Wrochem, c1986. 12 pp.

2197. Wurmser, Lucien. *Guirlandes: pour harpe chromatique*. Paris: Editions musicales Evette, c1927. 15 pp.

2198. Wynne, David, 1900–1983. *Prelude and dance: for harp*. Cardiff: University of Wales Press, c1967. 11 pp.

2199. Yamanouchi, Tadashi, 1935–. *Pour harpe*. Tokyo: International Music Publishers, Co., Ltd., c1965. 14 pp. CONTENTS: La muse jouant la cithara à Hélicon; Le musicien jouant la harpe—Bahram Gur chassant avec Azadé.

2200. Yannay, Yehuda, 1937–. *Coloring-book: for the harpist: also stick-ons and cut-outs*. Champaign, Ill.: Media Press, c1972. 5 leaves. (Media Press series 1: music for small groups, v. 4) Chance composition.

2201. Yun, Isang, 1917–. *In balance: für Harfe solo (1987)*. Berlin: Bote & Bock, c1988. 10 pp.

2202. Zabaleta, Nicanor, 1907–1993, ed. *Spanish masters of the 16th and 17th century: for harp*. [Edited by] Nicanor Zabaleta. Mainz: B. Schott's Söhne; New York: Associated Music Publishers, Inc., c1954. 7 pp. CONTENTS: Pavane and variations by Antonio de Cabezón. Romance by Francisco Fernandez Palero. Hachas by Lucas Ruiz de Ribayaz.

2203. Zabel, Albert, 1834–1910. [Am Springbrunnen] *Am Springbrunnen, op. 23*. St. Petersburg: W. Bessel, [189–?]. 13 pp.

2204. ———. [Am Springbrunnen] *La source = Am Springbrunnen, op. 23*. New York: Lyra Music, c1962. 12 pp.

2205. ———. [Am Springbrunnen] *La source = Llygad y ffynnon = Am Springbrunnen, op. 23*. Revised and edited by Ann Griffiths. Abergavenny, Gwent: Adlais, c1988. 13 pp.

2206. ———. [Am Springbrunnen] *La source = Am Springbrunnen, op. 23*. [London]: Salvi Publications, [1990?]. 12 pp.

2207. ———. *Ballade in drei Episoden: für Harfe, op. 20*. Leipzig: Fr. Kistner, n.d. 13 pp. CONTENTS: Die Erwartung am See; Die Begegnung; Der Abschied.

2208. ———. *La capricieuse, op. 32*. Moscow: W. Bessel et Cie., n.d. 7 pp.

2209. ———. *Chanson de pecheur: barcarolle, op. 24*. Leipzig: W. Bessel & Cie., n.d. 5 pp.

2210. ———. *Chanson de pêcheur: barcarolle, op. 24*. [London]: Salvi Publications, 1990. 4 pp.

2211. ———. *Le desire = Zhelanie: romance, op. 17*. Petrograd: W. Bessel, n.d. 5 pp.

2212. ———. [Études de concert, harp, no. 1, E♭ major] *Etude*. Leipzig: J.H. Zimmermann, c1900. 7 pp.

2213. ———. [Études de concert, harp, no. 3, E♭ major] *Élégie fantastique, op. 11*. Petrograd: Bessel, n.d. 9 pp.

2214. ———. [Études de concert, harp, no. 3, E♭ major] *Etude*. Leipzig: J.H. Zimmermann, c1900. 7 pp.

2215. ———. *Fantaisie sur les motifs de l'opéra Faust de Ch. Gounod*. Leipzig: Breitkopf & Härtel, n.d. 19 pp.

2216. ———. *Fantaisie sur les motifs de l'opéra Faust de Ch. Gounod*. Marina Del Rey, Calif.: Safari Publications, n.d. 19 pp.

2217. ———. [Grosse Konzert-Etüden. Selections] *Three concert etudes: for the harp*. Edited by Alice Lawson. San Anselmo, Calif.: A. Lawson, c1970. 6, 7, 6 pp.

2218. ———. [Grosse Konzert-Etüden. Selections] *Drei grosse Konzert-Etüden: für Harfe*. [Frankfurt]: Zimmermann, [1988?]. 19 pp. Reprint; originally pub. ca. 1900.

2219. ———. [Harp music. Selections] *Compositions: pour la harpe*. Edited by David Watkins. [England]: The Clive Morley Collection, [198–?]. 27 pp. CONTENTS: Romance sans paroles, op. 31; Am Springbrunnen (La source), op. 23; Marguerite douleureuse au rouet (no. 2), op. 26.

2220. ———. [Harp music. Selections] *Masterpiece collection*. Marina Del Rey, Calif.: Safari Publications, n.d. 51 pp. CONTENTS: Murmure de la cascade; La source; Un moment heureux (romance); Chanson de pêcheur (barcarolle); Marguerite douleureuse au rouet (no. 2); Le désir; Élégie fantastique; Rêve d'amour.

2221. ———. *Legende: morceau fantastique pour harpe, op. 18*. Leipzig: D. Rahter, n.d. 11 pp.

2222. ———. *Marguerite au rouet, op. 19*. Leipzig: W. Bessel & Cie., n.d. 9 pp.

2223. ———. *Marguerite au rouet = Marguerite at the spinning wheel, op. 19*. London: Salvi Publications, [198–?]. 9 pp.

2224. ———. *Marguerite douleureuse au rouet, op. 26*. Moscow: W. Bessel et Cie., c1910. 7 pp.

2225. ———. *Marguérite douleureuse au rouet, no. 2, op. 26*. London: Salvi Publications, [198–?]. 7 pp.

2226. ———. *Un moment heureux: romance, op. 27*. Leipzig: Breitkopf & Härtel, n.d. 3 pp.

2227. ———. *Un moment heureux: romance, op. 27*. St. Petersburg: W. Bessel, [189–?]. 5 pp.

2228. ———. *Murmure de la cascade: esquisse musicale, op. 29*. Leipzig: W. Bessel & Cie., n.d. 7 pp.

2229. ———. *Warum fragment, op. 28*. New York: W. Bessel, n.d. 5 pp.

2230. Zafred, Mario, 1922–1987. *Sonata: per arpa.* Rome: Boccaccini & Spada, c1979. 18 pp.

2231. Zagwijn, Henri, 1878–1954. *Ballade: per arpa solo.* Amsterdam: Donemus, c1948. 7 pp.

2232. ———. *Elegia e capriccio.* New York: C.F. Peters, c1950. 14 pp.

2233. Zanettovich, Daniele, 1950–. *Stravaganze: per arpa.* Undine, Italy: Pizzicato Edizioni Musicali, c1987. 6 pp.

2234. Zbinden, Julien François, 1917–. *Trois esquisses japonaises: pour harp, op.* 72. Paris: Gérard Billaudot, c1986. 17 pp. (La harpe) CONTENTS: Kamakura; Miyajima; Himeji.

2235. Zecchi, Adone, 1904–. *Giovedi grasso: bizzarria per arpa.* Bologna: Bongiovanni, c1939. 4 pp.

2236. ———. *Musiche per un balletto immaginario: suite per arpa.* Bologna: Edizioni Bongiovanni, 1954. 15 pp. CONTENTS: Danza solistica; Passo a due; Valzer in tutu; Danza generale.

2237. ———. *Trittico.* Milan: A. & G. Carisch, 1926. 14 pp. CONTENTS: Preludio; Serenata; Bisbigli.

2238. Zhou, P. Y. *The murmuring flow of mountainous streams.* [Palo Alto, Calif.]: Harpress, 1985. 7 pp.

2239. Zimmerman, Harry, 1906–. *Descanso gardens: harp solo.* S.l.: Harry Zimmerman, c1978. 4 pp.

2240. ———. *Gigue: for harp.* S.l.: s.n., c1980. 6 pp.

2241. ———. *Shadows: harp solo.* S.l.: s.n., c1978. 6 pp.

2242. ———. *Toccata: for harp.* S.l.: Harry Zimmerman, c1979. 10 pp.

2243. Zingel, Hans Joachim, 1904–1978, ed. *Leipziger Studentenmusik: für Harfe: nach der "Musikalischen Rüstkammer auf der Harfe, 1719."* Hrsg. von Hans Joachim Zingel. Mainz: B. Schott's Söhne, c1956. 3 pp. CONTENTS: Menuet; L'aimable vainquer; Bourrée.

2244. Zingel, Hans Joachim, 1904–1978, and Haag, Gudrun, eds. *Kleine Werke alter Meister: für die Harfe.* Ausgewähle und eingerichtet von Gudrun Haag, Hans J. Zingel. Munich: Musikverlag Josef Preissler, c1968–1978. 2 v. CONTENTS: Vol.1. Partita: preludio harpeggiato by Joh. Kaspar Ferd. Fischer. Pavane: alt venezianischer Tanz. Minuet by Carlos Seixas. Menuett (um 1760/70). Preludio by Johann Kuhnau. Minuet by Carlos Seixas. Aus "Recueil de Walses" (Paris um 1800) by Corsin. Trinklied (um 1800). Allegretto; Menuett by Ign. Pleyel. Zweimal Schottisch (um 1800). Menuett by G. Ph. Telemann. Contratanz by W. A. Mozart. Thème varié by Joh. G. H. Backofen. Menuett (um 1761) by W. A. Mozart. Drachenflug by Carl Reinecke. Deutscher Tanz. Deutscher Tanz by Jos. Küffner.

Mineth aus dem Dorf Chrobold/Böhmerwald; Deutsches Menuett; Salzburger Tänzchen by Tobi Reiser. Serenade no. 4 by Jos. Haydn. Sarabande: andante con moto by G. F. Handel. Romanze by Bochsa. Menuett aus Sachrang by Peter Huber. Menuett aus Salzburg by Tobi Reiser. Vol.2. Zwei kleine Sätze: Andante; Allegretto by N. Ch. Bochsa. Studie by J. G. Backofen. Irisches Volkslied by Sheila Larchet-Cuthbert. Zwei Menuette by J. G. Cousineau. Studie by Viner. Scherzo by J. Haydn. Valse by Corsin. Wiegenliedchen by R. Schumann. Menuett by Leopold Mozart. Toccata by Carlos Seixas. Ländler by W. A. Mozart. Menuett by Pietro Locatelli. Präludium by Joh. Seb. Bach. Corranto. Irische Weise by Carrol O'Daly. Ein kleines Lächeln by J. Ph. Rameau. Der gälische Bauer by Mercedes McGrath. Studie by nach R. Schumann. Prélude by Henri Bertini. Toccatina by Joh. K. F. Fischer. Englisher Tanz by K. D. von Dittersdorf. Präludium by Carl Reinecke. Deutscher Tanz by Joseph Haydn. Menuett by Leopold Mozart. Bassa imperiale. Sonatine by Domenico Cimarosa. Prélude by François Joseph Nadermann. Ein Strauss Rosmarin by N. Charles Bochsa. Sonatina by Jan Ladislaus Dussek. Menuett by W. A. Mozart. Passacaglia by G. F. Handel. Rondo by N. Ch. Bochsa. Präludium by J. S. Bach.

2245. Zingel, Rudolf Ewald, 1876–1944. *Hymne.* Leipzig: J.H. Zimmermann, [19—?]. 7 pp.

Arranged Works for Solo Harp

2246. Abreu, Zequinha de, 1880–1935. *Tico-tico: for pedal or troubadour harp.* Arranged by Reinhardt Elster. New York: Peer International, [1980], c1943. 3 pp. [NP]

2247. ———. *Tico-tico.* Arranged by Lynne Wainwright Palmer. [San Mateo, Calif.]: F.C. Publishing Co., [1988], c1943. 5 pp. (Popcycle series)

2248. Abt, Franz, 1819–1885. [Wenn die Schwalben heimwharts zieh'n; arr.] *When the swallows fly towards home.* [Arr. by C. Oberthür]. London: Edwin Ashdown, n.d. 5 pp. (Gems of German song, no. 11) Originally for voice and piano.

2249. Adam, Adolphe, 1803–1856. [Cantique de Noël; arr.] *O holy night.* Arr. by William Truesdale Cameron. Washington, D.C.: William Truesdale Cameron, n.d. 2 pp. [NP]

2250. ———. [Cantique de Noel; arr.] *O holy night: for harp.* Arranged by Ruth Berman and Sydney Harris. White Plains, N.Y.: Sumark Press, c1981. 2 pp.

2251. Adams, A. Emmett. *The bells of St. Mary's: for harp solo, with adaptation for Irish or Troubadour harp.* Arranged by Dewey Owens. New York: Chappell & Co., Inc.; Ascherberg, Hopwood & Crew, Ltd., c1917. 4 pp. Includes versions for pedal and non-pedal harp. [NP]

2252. Albéniz, Isaac, 1860–1909. [España. Malagueña; arr.] *Malagueña: from España.* Arr. Nicanor Zabaleta. Madrid: Union Musical Española, 1989. 8 pp. Originally for piano.

2253. ———. [Pièces, piano. Automne; arr.] *L'automne.* Transcrit pour harpe par H. Renié. Paris: A. Leduc, c1922. 3 pp. No. 2 from *Dix pièces for piano.*

2254. ———. *Le printemps.* Transcrit pour harpe par H. Renié. Paris: A. Leduc, c1922. 3 pp. Originally for piano.

2255. ———. [Recuerdos de viaje. Rumores de caleta; arr.] *Recuerdos de viaje no. 6: Rumores de la caleta: malagueña.* Transcripción para arpa por Ginevra Bruno. Madrid: Union Musical Española, c1928. 5 pp. Originally for piano.

2256. ———. [Suite española, no. 1. Granada; arr] *Granada.* Trans. Nicanor Zabaleta. Madrid: Union Musical Española, 1990. 8 pp. Originally for piano.

2257. Albéniz, Mateo, d. 1831. [Sonata, piano, D major; arr.] *Sonata.* Trans. Susanna Mildonian. New York: Lyra Music Co., 1976. 4 pp.

2258. ———. [Sonata, piano, D major; arr.] *Sonata.* Trans. Nicanor Zabaleta. New York: Lyra Music Co., 1978. 5 pp. In E♭ major; original is in D major.

2259. Albert, Morris, 1951–. *Feelings.* Arranged for harp solo by Eleanor Fell. [Santa Monica, Calif.]: Salvi Publications, c1978. 3 pp. (Salvi pop series)

2260. Alessandrini, Roberta, arr. *10 pezzi clavicembalistici.* Revisionati e diteggiati par arpa da Roberta Alessandrini. Mantua: Edizioni Eridania, c1985. 24 pp. Originally for harpsichord. CONTENTS: Soeur Monique (Rondo) by F. Couperin. Minuetto (dalla Suite francese n. 6 in Mi magg.) by J. S. Bach. Sonata in Mi♭ maggiore; Sonata in Sol maggiore by D. Cimarosa. Aria in Re minore by D. Scarlatti. Giga; Sonata in Sol minore by D. Cimarosa. Allegro in La maggiore by B. Galuppi. Largo in Do minore by M. Vento. Allegro giusto in Do maggiore by B. Galuppi.

2261. Alfano, Franco, 1875–1954. *Quatre danses roumaines.* Transcription pour la harpe de Amedea Tapella. Paris: R. Deiss, c1939. 15 pp.

2262. Allen, Mimi, 1926–, arr. *Concert variations on four Christmas carols.* Arranged by Mimi Allen. [Santa Monica, Calif.]: Salvi Publications, c1979. 14 pp. CONTENTS: Jesu, joy of man's desiring by J. S. Bach. Greensleeves. Silent night by F. Gruber. Carol of the bells.

2263. Andreozzi, Gaetano, 1755–1826. [Vergine del sole. Ah, tu sei che stringo al seno; arr.] *Ah, tu sei che stringo al seno: a duett in the opera of La vergine del sole: arranged for the harp or piano forte.* London: Faulkner, [18—]. 6 pp.

2264. ———. [Vergine del sole. Ah, tu sei che stringo al seno; arr.] *Ah tu sei che stringo al seno: a favorite duett in the opera of La vergine del sole: arranged for the harp or piano forte.* London: Printed by Birchall, [180–?]. 7 pp.

2265. Arditi, Luigi, 1822–1903. *L'ardita: valse brillante.* [Arr. for harp by C. Oberthür]. London: Edwin Ashdown, n.d. 7 pp. (Popular melodies, no. 12) Originally for voice and piano.

2266. Ascher, Joseph, 1831–1869. *Les gouttes d'eau: caprice-etude, [op. 17].* Transcrite pour la harpe par Charles Oberthür, op. 126. Milan: G. Ricordi, [18—]. 11 pp. Originally for piano.

2267. Attl, Kajetan A., arr. *Longing = Ach neni tu neni: for harp.* Arr. by Kajetan Attl. Ross, Calif.: Harp Publications, [197–?]. 5 pp. Czech folk song.

2268. Bach, Carl Philipp Emanuel, 1714–1788. [Solfeggios, harpsichord, H. 220, C minor; arr.] *Solfeggietto.* Transcribed for harp by Marie Miller. New York: Composers' Music Corp., c1924. 5 pp.

2269. ———. [Solfeggios, harpsichord, H. 220, C minor; arr.] *Solfeggietto.* Transcribed for harp by Marie Miller. New York: Carl Fischer, Inc., c1924. 5 pp.

2270. ———. [Solfeggios, harpsichord, H. 220, C minor; arr.] *Solfeggietto: harp duet.* Transcribed by Clifford Wooldridge. Chicago, Ill.: Lyon & Healy, c1987. 2 parts. (Lyon & Healy treasury of harp music) The 2nd harp part is optional.

2271. ———. [Sonatas, keyboard instrument, H. 28, C major; arr.] *Prussian sonata no. 5: in C.* Trans. Mary Ann Froehlich. Ellensburg, Wash.: F.C. Publishing Co., 1989. 20 pp.

2272. ———. [Stücke, musical clock, H. 635. Selections; arr.] *Zwölf Stücke: für Flöten- und Harfenuhren, aus Wotquenne-Verzeichnis 193: für Orgel (Klavier, Cembalo, Harfe).* Herausgegeben von Kurt Walther. Frankfurt: Zimmermann, c1980. 19 pp. Originally for musical clock. CONTENTS: W. 193, nos. 2, 4, 6, 8–12, 15, 17, 23, 28, and 29.

2273. Bach, Johann Christian, 1735–1782. [Concertos, harpsichord, string orchestra, op. 1, no. 6; arr.] *Concerto: in D major.* Transcribed for harp solo or with strings. London: Salvi Publications, c1984. 4 parts.

2274. ———. [Sonatas, piano, op. 17, no. 5; arr.] *Sonata, op. 17, no. 5.* Transcribed by Ruth Inglefield. London: Salvi Publications, c1984. 10 pp.

2275. Bach, Johann Sebastian, 1685–1750. [Also hat Gott die Welt geliebt. Mein gläubiges Herze, frohlokke, sing', scherze; arr.] *Air de la cantate la pentecôte.* [Arr. by Tiny Béon]. Paris: Louis Rouhier, n.d. 3 pp.

2276. ———. [Chorales. Selections; arr.] *Six chorales.* Arranged for harp by Lucien Thomson. [Santa Monica, Calif.]: Salvi Publications, c1980. 7 pp.

2277. ———. [Choräle von verschiedener Art, S. 645–650. Wachet auf, ruft uns die Stimme; arr.] *Theme from Chorale prelude: Sleepers, wake = Wachet auf, ruft uns die Stimme.* Edited by Robert Barclay for harp. [S.l.]: Barger & Barclay, c1964. 4 pp. Originally for organ.

2278. ———. [Englische Suiten. Nr. 5. Passepied, no. 1; arr.] *Passepied I (en rondeau): dalla V suite inglese.* Trascrizione per arpa di Alba Novella Schirinzi. Milano: Carisch, c1962. 2 pp. Originally for harpsichord.

2279. ———. [Französische Suiten. Nr. 6; arr.] *Allemande [no. 3].* Leipzig: Jul. Heinr. Zimmermann, c1914. 3 pp. (Des Harfenisten Konzert-Programm) BWV 817; originally for harpsichord.

2280. ———. [Harpsichord music. Selections; arr.] *Bach album: twenty pieces for the harp.* Arr. by Annie Louise David. New York: G. Schirmer, c1936. 2 v. (Schirmer's library of musical classics, v. 1566–1567) Originally for harpsichord or flute and harpsichord. Mainly from *Das Wohltemperierte Clavier*, includes Siciliano, from the Sonata in E for flute and harpsichord.

2281. ———. [Harpsichord music. Selections; arr.] *Twenty pieces from The well-tempered clavier.* Arr. Annie Louise David. Marina del Rey, Calif.: Safari Publications, 1991. 58 pp. Reprint of 2280.

2282. ———. [Herz und Mund und Tat und Leben. Jesus bleibet meine Freude; arr.] *Jesu, joy of man's desiring: from Cantata 147: for harp.* Arr. by May Hogan Cambern. S.l.: Michael Cambern, c1964. 4 pp.

2283. ———. [Herz und Mund und Tat und Leben. Jesu bleibet meine Freude; arr.] *Jesu, joy of man's desiring.* Arr. Darhon Rees-Rohrbacher. Buffalo, N.Y.: Dragonflower Music, 1990. 3 pp. [NP]

2284. ———. [Instrumental music. Selections; arr.] *Junior Bach collection.* Adapted for harp by Pearl Chertok. [Santa Monica, Calif.]: Salvi Publications, c1974. 9 pp. [NP] CONTENTS: First prelude in C; Minuet in G; Gavotte; Chorale: Jesu, joy of man's desiring; Prelude in F; Prelude in D minor; Prelude in C: from *The well-tempered clavichord.*

2285. ———. [Instrumental music. Selections; arr.] *Junior Bach: for troubadour or pedal harp.* Adapted for harp by Pearl Chertok. New York: Interstate Music, [1975?]. 11 pp. [NP] CONTENTS: See 2284.

2286. ———. [Instrumental music. Selections; arr.] *Quatre petites pièces: pour harpe ou harpe celtique = Four short pieces for harp or Celtic harp.* Transcription and fingering by Maïté Etcheverry. Paris: Editions Choudens, c1976. 6 pp. (Les classiques transcrits pour la harpe) [NP] CONTENTS: Menuet no. 2 (from the Little book of music for Anna Magdalena Bach); Menuet (from the Suite in G minor); Little prelude in F major; Minuet no. 4 (from the Little book of music for Anna Magdalena Bach).

2287. ———. [Instrumental music. Selections; arr.] *Raccolta: scelta dalle Suites francesi, inglesi, dalle Sonate per violino, dalle cantate, dai Preludi e Fughe del Clavicembalo ben temperato.* Trascritte e diteggiate per arpa da Gabriella Consolini. Milan, New York: G. Ricordi & Co., c1916. 4 v. CONTENTS: Pt. 1. Raccolta dalle Suites francesi; Pt. 2. Raccolta dalle Suites ingles; Pt. 3. Raccolta dalle Sonate per violino e cantate; Pt. 4. Raccolta fra i Preludi e Fughe.

2288. ———. [Instrumental music. Selections; arr.] *Suite: für Harp: E dur.* Arr. by M. Yamahata. Tokyo?: Amada Harp Studio, 1977. 20 pp. CON-

TENTS: Prelude; Loure; Gavott en rondeau; Menuet I; Menuet II; Bourre; Gigue.

2289. ———. [Instrumental music. Selections; arr.] *Ten pieces: arranged for the harp.* Melville, N.Y.: Belwin Mills, [19—]. 28 pp. CONTENTS: Prelude; Prelude; Organ prelude; Prelude; Prelude; Allemande; Largo; Sarabande; Gavotte; Fantasia.

2290. ———. [Instrumental music. Selections; arr.] *Two J. S. Bach arrangements: harp solo.* [Arranged by] Daniel Burton. San Diego, Calif.: Jubal Press, c1986. 7 pp. (Jubal harp series) CONTENTS: God's time is best (Sonatina from Cantata no. 109); Jesu, joy of man's desiring.

2291. ———. [Komm, süsser Tod; arr.] *Come, sweet death.* Transcribed by Marjorie Tyre. [San Mateo, Calif.]: F.C. Publishing Co., c1987. 5 pp. (Solo series: harp) Originally for voice and continuo.

2292. ———. [Notenbuch der Anna Magdalena Bach (1725); arr.] *Cuaderno Ana Magdalena Bach.* Transcripcion para arpa por Ma. Rosa Calvo-Manzano. Madrid: Real Musical Editores, c1983. 26 pp. Originally for harpsichord. Textual notes on the music in English, Spanish, French, and German.

2293. ———. [Notenbuch der Anna Magdalena Bach (1725). Selections; arr.] *Pezzi: per arpa: tratti dal Piccolo libro di Magdalena Bach.* Trascritti e diteggiati da Irene Rossi. Milan: Edizioni Curci, c1972. 4 pp. Originally for harpsichord. CONTENTS: Minuetto in sol-bemolle maggiore [Anh. 114]; Minuetto in re minore [Anh. 132]; Musette [Anh. 126]; Minuetto in sol minore [Anh. 115].

2294. ———. [Partita, harpsichord, BWV 825. Giga; arr.] *Gigue.* [Arr. for harp by Tiny Béon]. Paris: Louis Rouhier, n.d. 3 pp.

2295. ———. [Partita, harpsichord, BWV 829, G major. Praeambulum; arr.] *Pièce: in sol.* Transcrite pour harpe par H. Renié. Paris: Durand; Philadelphia: Elkan-Vogel, c1910. 5 pp. Originally for harpsichord.

2296. ———. *Prelude: in C minor.* Adapted for harp by Pearl Chertok. Santa Monica, Calif.: Salvi Publications, [197–?]. 3 pp.

2297. ———. [Selections; arr.] *Bach for the harp.* Transcribed by Marjorie Tyre. Philadelphia: Elkan-Vogel, c1942. 11 pp. CONTENTS: Come, sweet death; Prelude in D♭ major; Prelude in E♭ minor; Fugue in C minor.

2298. ———. [Sonatas, organ, BWV 529, C major. Largo; arr.] *Largo: de la 5ème sonate de violon.* Adapté à la harpe d'après la transcription pour piano de C Saint-Saëns par Marcel Grandjany. Paris: Durand & Cie., c1931. 2 pp. (Six pièces classiques transcrites pour harpe, no. 1)

2299. ———. [Sonaten und Partiten, violin, BWV 1001–1006. Selections; arr.] *Twelve etudes: for harp: selected from Bach sonatas and partitas for unaccompanied violin, op. 45.* Transcribed by Marcel Grandjany. New York: Carl Fischer, Inc., c1970. 63 pp. CONTENTS: Presto from Violin sonata no. 1; Fugue from Violin sonata no. 1; Sarabande from Violin partita no. 1; Sarabande's double from Violin partita no. 1; Corrente's double (variation) from Violin partita no. 1; Andante from Violin sonata no. 2; Allemande from Violin partita no. 2; Bourrée from Violin partita no. 1; Bourrée's double from Violin partita no. 1; Giga from Violin partita no. 2; Allegro assai from Violin sonata no. 3; Prelude from Violin partita no. 3.

2300. ———. [Sonaten und Partiten, violin, BWV 1001–1006. Partita, no. 1. Allemande; arr.] *Allemande: de la 1ère partita en si-bémol.* Transcrit pour harpe par Marcel Grandjany. Paris: Durand & Cie., c1931. 3 pp. (Six pièces classiques transcrites pour harpe, no. 2)

2301. ———. [Sonaten und Partiten, violin, BWV 1001–1006. Partita, no. 1. Tempo di bourrée; arr.] *Gavotte.* [Arranged by] L. M. Magistretti. Frankfurt: Zimmermann, c1914. 5 pp. (Des Harfenisten Konzert-Programm, Nr. 4)

2302. ———. [Sonaten und Partiten, violin, BWV 1001–1006. Partita, no. 1. Tempo di bourrée; arr.] *Bourée: from the Partita I.* Transcribed for harp by Carlos Salzedo. New York: G. Schirmer, c1923. 5 pp. (Transcriptions for harp)

2303. ———. [Sonaten und Partiten, violin, BWV 1001–1006. Partita, no. 1. Tempo di bourrée; arr.] *Bourrée: from the Partita I.* Transcribed for harp by Carlos Salzedo. New York: Lyra Music, c1973. 5 pp.

2304. ———. [Sonaten und Partiten, violin, BWV 1001–1006. Partita, no. 3; arr.] *Partita III: (BWV 1006).* Redaction pour la harpe Liana Pasquali. London: Salvi Publications, c1984. 22 pp.

2305. ———. [Sonaten und Partiten, violin, BWV 1001–1006. Partita, no. 3; arr.] *Suite: BWV 1006a.* Edited for the harp by Sioned Williams. Oxford: Music Dept., Oxford University Press, c1986. vii, 23 pp. (Oxford music for harp)

2306. ———. [Sonaten und Partiten, violin, BWV 1001–1006. Sonata, no. 4. Chaconne; arr.] *Chaconne: from sonata IV for unaccompanied violin.* Transcribed for harp by Dewey Owens. New York: Lyra Music, c1975. 16 pp.

2307. ———. [Suites, lute, BWV 996, E minor; arr.] *Suite no. 1: BWV 996: pour le luth.* Adaptation en mi-bémol mineur pour la harpe par Marie-Claire Jamet. Paris: Alphonse Leduc, c1984. 9 pp. CONTENTS: Prélude; Allemande; Courante; Sarabande; Bourrée; Gigue.

2308. ———. [Suites, orchestra, BWV 1068, D major. Air; arr.] *Air on the G string.* Arr. Darhon Rees-Rohrbacher. Buffalo, N.Y.: Dragonflower Music, 1992. 2 pp. Originally for orchestra.

2309. ———. [Suites, violoncello, BWV 1012, D major. Sarabande; arr.] *Sarabande: from Cello suite no. 6.* Transcribed by Betty Paret. New York, N.Y.: Lyra Music Co., c1967. 3 pp.

2310. ———. [Wachet auf, ruft uns die Stimme (Cantata). Zion hört die Wächter singen; arr.] *Theme from chorale prelude Sleepers, wake (Wachet auf, ruft uns die Stimme).* Edited by Robert Barclay for harp. London: Salvi Publications, c1964. 4 pp.

2311. Bacharach, Burt, 1928–. *The look of love.* Arranged for harp solo by Stella Castellucci. [Santa Monica, Calif.]: Salvi Publications, c1978. 2 pp. (Salvi pop series)

2312. ———. *This guy's in love with you.* Arranged by Penny Howk Beavers. [San Mateo, Calif.]: F.C. Publishing Co., c1989. 3 pp. (Popcycle series)

2313. Balfe, M. W. (Michael William), 1808–1870. [Maid of Artois. Selections; arr.] *Three favorite melodies from Balfe's grand opera, The maid of Artois: Yon moon o'er the mountain; The rapture dwelling; and Come follow with us.* Arranged for the harp by N. C. Bochsa. London: Cramer, Addison & Beale, [1836?]. 9 pp.

2314. Barber, Gail, 1939–, arr. *Greensleeves; The minstrel boy.* Arranged for solo harp with or without pedals by Gail Barber. Lubbock, Texas: Gail Barber, c1989. 4 pp. [NP]

2315. Barry, John, 1933–. [Somewhere in time. Somewhere in time] *Somewhere in time: theme from the film Somewhere in time: a solo for folk harp.* Arranged by Louise Trotter. Edmonds, Wash.: Paradise Music, c1980. 3 pp. [NP]

2316. ———. [Somewhere in time. Somewhere in time] *Somewhere in time.* Arranged by Penny Howk Beavers. San Mateo, Calif.: F.C. Publishing Co., [1989], c1980. 3 pp. (Popcycle series)

2317. Bart, Lionel, 1930–. [Oliver! Where is love] *Where is love.* Arranged by Ray Pool. San Mateo, Calif.: F.C. Publishing Co., [1988], c1960. 2 pp. (Popcycle series)

2318. Bartók, Béla, 1881–1945. [Könnyű zongoradarab. Este a székelyeknél; arr.] *Este a székelyeknél = Ein Abend am Lande = An evening in the village.* Hárfára átírta Járdányi Pál. Budapest: Editio Musica, c1965. 4 pp. Originally for piano.

2319. ———. [Mikrokosmos. Selections; arr.] *Mikrokosmos: for harp: 20 intermediate solos and ensembles for harps with and without pedals.* Edited and arranged by Marilyn S. Marzuki. [New York]: Boosey and Hawkes, c1979. 35 pp. Originally for piano. [NP] CONTENTS: Solos: With alternate hands; In Phrygian mode; In Yugoslav mode; Melody with accompaniment; Méditation; Increasing-diminishing; Waves; Unison divided; In oriental style; Buzzing; Triplets; Five-tone scale; Merriment. Ensembles:

Triplets in Lydian mode; Melody divided; Two major pentachords; Play-song; Melody in the mist; Melody with interruptions; Whole tone scale.

2320. ———. [Piano music. Selections; arr.] *Eleven pieces: for harp: second selection.* Arranged by A. Von Würtzler. London: Salvi Publications, c1983. 14 pp. CONTENTS: Allegro; Andante; Poco allegretto; Andante grazioso; Allegretto; Allegro; Allegro; Allegro robusto; Andante; Andante sostenuto; Allegro moderato; Minuet andante.

2321. ———. [Piano music. Selections; arr.] *Seven pieces: for harp.* New York: Lyra Music Co., c1966. 9 pp. CONTENTS: From For children: nos. 14, 24, 37, Round dance, Sorrow; From First term at the piano: Waltz; From Ten easy pieces: Evening in the country.

2322. Beaujoyeulx, Baltasar de, d. ca. 1587. *Amaryllis: (air of King Louis XIII).* [Arr. by] Henri Ghys; edited and fingered for harp by Nina S. Miller. New York: Belwin, [194–?]. 5 pp.

2323. Beethoven, Ludwig van, 1770–1827. [Bagatelles, piano, WoO 59, A minor; arr.] *Für Elise.* Arr. Deborah Henson-Conant. San Mateo, Calif.: F.C. Publishing Co., c1988. 4 pp.

2324. ———. [Sonatas, piano, no. 5, op. 10, no. 1, C minor. Adagio; arr.] *Adagio (As dur): aus der Sonate in C moll, op. 10, no. 1.* Arr. by Johannes Snoer. Offenbach am Main: Johann André, n.d. 7 pp.

2325. ———. [Sonatas, piano, no. 14, op. 27, no. 2, C# minor. Adagio sostenuto; arr.] *Adagio: from Beethoven's Sonata quasi fantasia (known as the Moonlight sonata.* Transcribed for the harp by John Thomas. London: Leonard, Gould & Bolttler, [n.d.]. 19 pp.

2326. ———. [Sonatas, piano, no. 14, op. 27, no. 2, C# minor. Adagio sostenuto; arr.] *Adagio: from the Moonlight sonata, op. 27, no. 2.* Transcribed for harp by Carlos Salzedo. New York: G. Schirmer, c1952. 7 pp.

2327. ———. [Sonatas, piano, no. 14, op. 27, no. 2, C# minor. Adagio sostenuto; arr.] *Adagio: from the Moonlight sonata, op. 27, no. 2.* Transcribed for harp by Carlos Salzedo. New York, N.Y.: Lyra Music Co., c1975. 7 pp.

2328. ———. [Waltzes, piano, Ahn. 14. No. 6; arr.] *Cinquième valse.* Adapted by Patricia John. Houston, Texas: Pantile Press, [198–?]. 3 pp.

2329. Bellini, Vincenzo, 1801–1835. [Pirata. Tu vedrai la sventurata; arr.] *Cavatina: Tu vedrai la sventurata: de l'opera Il pirata.* Arr. pour la harpe par N. Ch. Bochsa. Milan: Ricordi, [1836]. 11 pp. "Opera 314."

2330. Benjamin, Arthur, 1893–1960. [Jamaican pieces. Jamaican rumba; arr.] *Jamaican rumba.* Arranged by Louise Trotter. San Mateo, Calif.: F.C. Publishing Co., c1989. 2 pp. (Popcycle series) Originally for orchestra.

2331. Bennett, Nicholas, ed. *Alawon fy Ngwlad = The lays of my land.* Collected by Nicholas Bennett of Glanyrafon; arranged for the harp or pianoforte by D. Emlyn Evans. London; Glasgow: Bayley and Ferguson, [1896]. xviii, 165 pp.

2332. Bennett, Richard Rodney, 1936–. [Nicholas and Alexandra. Theme] *Nicholas and Alexandra*. Arr. Dewayne Fulton. [Santa Monica, Calif.]: Salvi Publications, 1983. 3 pp. (Salvi pop series)

2333. Bird, Chuck, 1925–, and Peters, Susan, arr. *The heavenly harp*. Arranged by Chuck Bird and Susan Peters. Hollywood, Calif.: Katbird, c1988. 5 v. CONTENTS: *Traditional Christmas*, vol.1: Hark the herald angels sing; Deck the halls; The first noel; Joy to the world; God rest you merry gentlemen; Silent night. *Traditional Christmas*, vol.2: Jingle bells; Away in a manger; O Christmas tree; March of the toys; O little town of Bethlehem; We wish you a merry Christmas.

Weddings, vol.1: Hawaiian wedding song; Close to you; You light up my life; Get me to the church on time; Ice castles (Through the eyes of love); A man and a woman. *Weddings*, vol.2: Bridal chorus; I love you truly; The bells of St. Mary's; Because; The man I love; Wedding march.

Hymns, vol.1: I love to tell the story; Jesus loves me; In the garden; Since Jesus came into my heart; Softly and tenderly; What a friend we have in Jesus.

2334. ———, arr. *The pedal free harp*. Arranged by Chuck Bird and Susan Peters. Hollywood, Calif.: Katbird, c1988. 10 v. [NP] CONTENTS: *Irish*, vol.1. A little bit of heaven; Irish washerwoman; Dear old Donegal; Danny boy; My wild Irish rose; Endearing young charms. *Irish*, vol.2: Stack of barley; Galway bay; The Kerry dance; Mother Machree; Where the River Shannon flows; The wearing of the green. *Irish*, vol.3: Mickey; Garry Owen (The daughters of Erin); Saint Patrick's day; When Irish eyes are smiling; Macnamara's band; Roamin' in the gloamin'.

Pops, vol.1: Happy days are here again; Teddy bear's picnic; Paper moon; Deep night; Mountain greenery; Chinatown my Chinatown. *Pops*, vol.2: Chicago; Singin' in the rain; The peanut vendor; Mack the knife; I love a parade; By the light of the silvery moon.

Pops olé, vol.1: Lady of Spain; Te quiero dijeste (Magic is the moonlight); Amapola; Adios mariquita linda; Valencia; Adios.

Classic miniatures, vol.1: Can can; Wine women and song; Reverie; Dance of the buffoons; Finlandia; Russian sailor's dance. *Classic miniatures*, vol.2: Amaryllis; Merry widow waltz; Gavotte; Humoresque; Norwegian dance; Carnival of Venice. *Classic miniatures*, vol.3: Nocturne; To a wild rose; The skater's waltz; Emperor waltz; Brahms' lullaby; Light cavalry overture.

Party songs, vol.1: Bill Bailey; In the good old summertime; For he's a jolly good fellow; A bicycle built for two; When the saints go marching in; Auld lang syne; Goodnight ladies; Hail hail the gang's all here; Dixieland; Give my regards to Broadway.

2335. ———, arr. *Swingin' harp*. Arranged by Chuck Bird and Susan Peters. Hollywood, Calif.: Katbird, c1985. 12 v. CONTENTS: *Standards*, vol.1: Before the parade passes by; One; Seventy-six trombones; Sentimental journey; Hello Dolly; Witchcraft; Tenderly; It's a big wide wonderful world. *Standards*, vol.2: Tuxedo junction; What I did for love; Tomorrow; Autumn leaves; Mame; I'll remember April; A lot of livin' to do; There will never be another you. *Standards*, vol.3: Are you lonesome tonight?; September song; Oh look at me now; It's a most unusual day; What kind of fool am I; Speak low; The coffee song; Ballerina. *Standards*, vol.4: As long as he needs me; A wonderful day like today; Who can I turn to; Fly me to the moon; Twilight time; Those were the days; Early autumn; The gypsy in my soul.

   Duke Ellington, vol.1: Sophisticated lady; Prelude to a kiss; Caravan; Mood indigo. *Duke Ellington*, vol.2: Satin doll; I got it bad and that ain't good; Don't get around much anymore; Do nothin' 'til you hear from me.

   Bossa novas, vol.1: A man and a woman; Wave; Recado bossa nova; Desafinado; Meditation; Summer samba.

   Oldie goldies, vol.1: Peg o' my heart; Put your arms around me honey; Ja da; Oh you beautiful doll; Chinatown my Chinatown; In the good old summertime; You made me love you; After you've gone.

   Country western, vol.1: Don't it make my brown eyes blue; Snowbird; Behind closed doors; The most beautiful girl; Rhinestone cowboy; Always on my mind.

   Blues, vol.1: St. Louis blues; Basin Street blues; Birth of the blues; Blues in the night; Bye bye blues; Sugar blues; I get the blues when it rains.

   Pop Christmas, vol.1: Sleigh ride; The Christmas song; Rudolph the red-nosed reindeer; Winter wonderland; Jingle bell rock; Little drummer boy.

   Chuck Bird originals, vol.1: Harpanova; Harporientale; Harpsville U.S.A.; The haunted harp; La harpe affaire; Harpop-a-rebop.

2336. Bishop, Henry R. (Henry Rowley), 1786–1855. [Guy Mannering. Irish air; arr.] *A celebrated Irish air: sung by Mr. Braham in the opera of Guy Mannering with an introduction & variations*. London: Printed & sold by F. T. Latour, [1826?]. 9 pp. For harp.

2337. Bizet, Georges, 1838–1875. [Arlesienne. Intermezzo; arr.] *Agnus Dei*. Transcribed by Aristid von Würtzler. San Mateo, Calif.: F.C. Publishing Co., c1989. 5 pp. (Solo series: harp)

2338. ———. [Pêcheurs de perles. Je crois entendre encore; arr.] *Les pêcheurs de perles: opera en 3 actes de G. Bizet: Romance*. Paris: Choudens, n.d. 4 pp.

2339. Bochsa, Robert Nicolas Charles, 1789–1856, arr. *Les derniers adieux de Sontag: Sontag's mélange: introducing a Polish air, a Krakowiack and a mazurka*. London: Goulding & D'Almaine, [183–?]. 8 pp. "Performed by that celebrated vocalist [Mme. Sontag] at her last professional concert, St. Petersburg."

2340. ———, arr. *Duetti: Mille sospiri e lagrime [e] Questo cor ti giura amore; e cavatina, Sorgete miei cari eseguiti da Mad. Pasta e dal Sig. Velluti.* Ridotti per arpa sola da N. C. Bochsa. Milan: Ricordi, [1830 or 1831]. 13 pp. The two duets are from Rossini's *Aureliano in Palmira* and *Demetrio e Polibio* respectively.

2341. ———. [Morceau ossianique. March; arr.] *Grand Ossianic march: for the harp: introducing a favourite Irish melody, extracted from the admired Morceau ossianique for eight harps.* London: Mori & Lavenu, [1834?]. 5 pp.

2342. ———, arr. *Quatre fugues de Bach et de Haendel: pour harpe.* [Doigtés de] R. N. Ch. Bochsa. Paris: G. Billaudot, c1977. 12 pp. (La harpe)

2343. ———. *Scots wha hae; Gin a boddie.* Edited by Patricia John for the small harp fitted with levers. Houston, Tex.: Pantile Press, [198–?]. 5 pp. Reprint of: New York: J.F. Browne, 1860. [NP]

2344. ———. *Soirees dramatiques: select airs from the latest and most admired Italian, French and German operas and ballets arranged as solos for the harp, with accompt. of flute ad libitum by the most celebrated composers for that instrument.* London: Boosey, [183–?]. Score.

2345. Bock, Jerry, 1928–. [Fiddler on the roof. Sunrise, sunset] *Sunrise, sunset.* Arranged by Lynne Wainwright Palmer. San Mateo, Calif.: F.C. Publishing Co., c1989. 4 pp. (Popcycle series)

2346. Boieldieu, François Adrien, 1775–1834. [Béniowsky. Krakoviak; arr.] *The admired Krakoviak: as danced by Mlle. St. Romain in M. Deshayes grand Russian ballet or [sic] Beniowsky, or The exiles of Kamschatka, now performing at the King's Theatre.* Composed & arranged for the harp by N. C. Bochsa. London: D'Almaine, [183–]. 5 pp.

2347. ———. [Béniowsky. Mazurka; arr.] *The favorite Mazurka (originally composed for 16 horns): in M. Deshayes' grand Russian ballet of Beniowsky, or The exiles of Kamschatka, performing at the King's Theatre.* Composed & arranged for the harp by N. C. Bochsa. London: D'Almaine, [183–]. 5 pp.

2348. ———. [Béniowsky. Pas galop; arr.] *The admired Pas galop: as danced by Carlotta Grisi & M. Perrot in M. Deshayes's grand Russian ballet of Beniowsky, or The exiles of Kamschatka, now performing at the King's Theatre.* Composed and arranged for the harp by N. C. Bochsa. London: D'Almaine, [183–]. 5 pp.

2349. Borisovskii, Vadim Vasil'evich, 1900–1972, arr. *Chetyre p'esy kompozitorov xvi-xviii veka.* Svobodnaia obrabotka dlia arfy V. Borisovskogo. Moscow: Gos. muzykal'noe izd-vo, 1962. 11 pp. CONTENTS: Parisian bells by Anon., 16th cent. Scherzo by Anon., 16th cent. Trauer allemande by Robert de Visée. Prelude by S. L. Weiss.

2350. Bosch, Jacques. [Serenade, guitar; arr.] *Passacaille: sérénade pour guitare.* Transcrit pour la harpe par H. Renié. Paris: Henry Lemoine & Cie., n.d. 7 pp. Originally for guitar.

2351. Bouchaud, Dominig, arr. *Pièces classiques: pour harpe celtique ou la harpe à simple mouvement: cahier no. 5 (moyen).* Paris: Gérard Billaudot, c1987. 20 pp. (La harpe) [NP] CONTENTS: Sonate en do by D. Scarlatti. Sonate en sol majeur by D. Scarlatti. Presto by J. C. Bach. Presto by T. Arne. Rondoletto (extrait de la 1re sonate) by F. J. Naderman. Rondo by N. Ch. Bochsa. 2e mazurka by F. Chopin. Etude by F. Godefroid.

2352. Boyce, William, 1711–1779. *Canon.* Arr. for non-pedal harp by Darhon Rees-Rohrbacher. Buffalo, N.Y.: Dragonflower Music, 1992. 4 pp. [NP]

2353. Bradbury, William Batchelder, 1816–1868. *Jesus loves me: solo for harp.* Arr. by Joy Hujsak. La Jolla, Calif.: Mina-Helwig Publishing Co., c1982. 3 pp. [NP]

2354. Braga, Gaetano, 1829–1907. *La serenata.* Transcription pour la harpe [par] A. Hasselmans. Paris: Durand, [19—]. 5 pp. Originally for voice and violoncello.

2355. Brahms, Johannes, 1833–1897. [Lieder, op. 49. Wiegenlied; arr.] *Lullaby.* Transcribed for harp by Carlos Salzedo. Philadelphia: Elkan-Vogel, c1935. 3 pp. Originally for voice and piano.

2356. ———. [Symphonies, no. 3, op. 90, F major. Allegro un poco sostenuto; arr.] *Symphony no. 3: third movement.* Transcribed for harp by Clifford Wooldridge. Chicago, Ill.: Lyon & Healy Harps, c1983. 5 pp.

2357. ———. [Waltzes, piano, 4 hands, op. 39. Selections; arr.] *Valses: pour harpe.* Transcrite par Alys Lautemann. Paris: H. Lemoine, c1934. 8 pp. CONTENTS: Op. 39, nos. 3, 4, 8, 9, 15.

2358. ———. [Waltzes, piano, 4 hands, op. 39, no. 15; arr.] *Waltz: in A flat.* Transcribed for harp by Carlos Salzedo. New York: Carl Fischer, Inc., c1925. 3 pp.

2359. Bull, John, d. 1628. *The king's hunt: from the Fitzwilliam virginal book.* Harp adaptation by Marcel Grandjany. New York: Associated Music Publishers, Inc., c1949. 7 pp. Originally for virginal.

2360. Burke, Johnny, 1908–1964, and Van Heusen, Jimmy, 1913–1990. [Belle of the Yukon. Like someone in love] *Like someone in love.* Arranged by Stella Castellucci. Ellensburg, Wash.: F.C. Publishing Co., [1989], c1944. 2 pp. (Popcycle series)

2361. Burton, Daniel, arr. *Two folk songs.* Arranged by Daniel Burton. San Diego, Calif.: Jubal Press, c1986. 8 pp. (Jubal harp series) CONTENTS: Londonderry air; All through the night.

2362. Byman, Lorraine, arr. *Away in a manger with He is sleeping.* Arranged for non-pedal harp by Lorraine Byman. S.l.: Lorraine Byman, c1972. 3 pp. [NP]

2363. ———, arr. *Gärdeby gånglåt: for non-pedal harp.* Arranged for harp by Lorraine Byman. S.l.: Lorraine Byman, c1973. 3 pp. [NP]

2364. ———, arr. *Welsh folk song: All through the night = Ar hyd y nos.* Arranged for pedal and non-pedal harp by Lorraine Byman. S.l.: Lorraine Byman, c1972. 2 pp. [NP]

2365. Cabezón, Antonio de, 1510–1566. [Obras de musica. Qui en te me enojó, Ysabel?] *Diferencias: sobre el villancico Qui en te me enojó, Ysabel?: para tecla, arpa o vihuela.* Transcripcion e introduccion: Macario Santiago Kastner. Madrid: Union Musical Espanola, 1981. 10 pp.

2366. Cadman, Charles Wakefield, 1881–1946. [American Indian songs. From the land of sky-blue water; arr.] *From the land of sky-blue water.* Transcribed for harp solo by Zhay Clark. Boston: White-Smith Music Publishing Co., c1933. 5 pp.

2367. Calthorpe, Nancy, arr. *The Calthorpe collection: songs and airs: arranged for the voice and Irish harp.* Edited and arranged by Nancy Calthorpe. Dublin, Ireland: Waltons Piano & Musical Instrument Galleries, c1974. Score (95 pp.). In part for solo harp. Irish or English words. [NP] CONTENTS: A chuaichín bhinn dílis; Ancient Irish lullaby; Anonn's anall; Báidín fheidhilmidh; Bainis pheigí ní eadhra; The Bard of Armagh; The blue handkerchief; An caitín bán; Clare's dragoons; The coulin (An chuilfhoinn); Dé luain, dé máirt; Déirín dé; Domhnall bán; Famine song; An fhidil; The Gartan mother's lullaby; The grey man; Haigh didil dum; The heather glen; I won't marry at all; In old Donegal; Jimmy mo mhíle stór; The leprechaun; The mitcher; Mo theaghlach; My land; O'Donnell abu; Oró mo leanbh beag féin; Péarla an bhrollaigh bháin; The quiet land of Erin; Rory óg Mac Rory; Seoithín mo leinbhín; The snowy breasted pearl; A soldiers song (Irish national anthem); Suantraí bhair-bre; Tiocfaidh mo mhaimí; Túirne mháire.

2368. ———, arr. *A Celtic bouquet for the harp: a selection of favourite songs, airs, and a harp-violin duet.* Arranged for the harp by Nancy Calthorpe. Dublin: Walton's Piano and Musical Instrument Galleries, c1977. Score 30 pp. [NP] CONTENTS: The Spanish lady: song; The spinning wheel: song; Cockles and mussels: song; Eileen Aroon: air-song; A Celtic bouquet: a selection of airs; Bonaparte's advance: air; Marbhna na luimneach: air; Carolan's concerto: duet for violin and harp (or violin and piano).

2369. ———, arr. *A tribute to O'Carolan: music for the Irish harp.* Edited and arranged by Nancy Calthorpe. [S.l.: Nancy Calthorpe], 1976. 12 pp. [NP] CONTENTS: Miss MacDermot, or The princess royal; Constantine Ma-guire; Lament for Owen Roe; Planxty Drury; Lord Inchiquin (Dromoland

Castle); Mrs. Maxwell; Betty O'Brien; Father Brian MacDermot Roe; John O'Connor; Bumper Squire Jones; Bridget Cruise.

2370. Calvo-Manzano, María Rosa, 1943–, arr. *Repertorio instrumental ingles: musica para arpa.* Transcripción para arpa por Maria Rosa Calvo-Manzano. Madrid: Union Musical Española, c1983. 66 pp. CONTENTS: The kings morisco. The Irish march; The marche of the footmen; Ye souldiers dance; The buriing of the dead; La volta; The battell; The souldiers sommons; Wolseys wilde; The galliard to the fifth pavian; The galliard to the sixth pavian; The gaillarde for the victoire by William Byrd. The galliard dolorosa by Peter Philips. Doctor Bulls juell; A gigge: Doctor Bulls myselfe; The kings hunt by John Bull. Farnabys dreame by Giles Farnaby. Pavana: Lord Salisbury by Orlando Gibbons. Almand by John Blow. Suite: Prelude; Almand; Corant; Minuet by Henry Purcell. King William's marche by Jeremiah Clarke.

2371. ———, arr. *Sonatas españolas: del siglo XVIII.* Transcripción para arpa de Ma. Rosa Calvo-Manzano. Valencia: Piles, 1985. 77 pp. Originally for keyboard instrument. CONTENTS: Sonate en fa mayor by P. Vicente Rodríguez. Rondo en si bemol mayor by P. Felipe Rodríguez. Sonata en do menor by Cantallos. Sonata en re mayor by Mateo Albéniz. Sonata en do menor; Sonata en fa menor by P. José Gallés.

2372. Cambern, May Hogan, 1901–1988, arr. *Carol of the shepherds.* Arranged for harp by May Hogan Cambern. New York: Michael Cambern, c1963. 2 pp. (From the notebook of May Hogan Cambern)

2373. ———, arr. *Un flambeau, Jeanette, Isabelle: from an old French carol: for harp.* [Arranged by] May Hogan Cambern. New York: Michael Cambern, c1966. 2 pp. (From the notebook of May Hogan Cambern)

2374. ———, arr. *God rest you merry gentlemen; Lo, how a rose e'er blooming: Christmas music for harp.* Arranged for harp by May Hogan Cambern. New York: Michael Cambern, c1963. 3 pp. (From the notebook of May Hogan Cambern)

2375. ———, arr. *Greensleeves (What Child is this): Christmas music for harp.* Arranged by May Hogan Cambern. [New York]: Michael Cambern, c1963. 2 pp. (From the notebook of May Hogan Cambern) [NP]

2376. ———, arr. *Let all mortal flesh keep silence: old French carol: Picardy.* Arranged by May Hogan Cambern. [New York]: Michael Cambern, c1964. 2 pp. (From the notebook of May Hogan Cambern) [NP]

2377. ———, arr. *Londonderry air: Irish folk melody: for harp.* Arranged for harp by May Hogan Cambern. New York: Michael Cambern, c1963. 3 pp. (From the notebook of May Hogan Cambern)

2378. ———, arr. *O come, o come, Emmanuel: Christmas music for harp.* Arranged by May Hogan Cambern. [New York]: Michael Cambern, c1963. 3 pp. (From the notebook of May Hogan Cambern)

2379. ———, arr. *Sing noël: French carol, 15th century: for harp.* Arranged for harp by May Hogan Cambern. New York: Michael Cambern, c1966. 3 pp. (From the notebook of May Hogan Cambern)

2380. Cameron, William Truesdale, d. 1977, arr. [Adestes fideles] *O come all ye faithful.* Arr. Wm. T. Cameron. Washington, D.C.: William Truesdale Cameron, n.d. 1 p. [NP]

2381. Campen, Ank van, 1932–, arr. *Classical tunes for the Irish harp.* Compiled [and arr.] by Ank van Campen. Amsterdam: Broekmans & Van Poppel, c1972–1983. 2 v. [NP] CONTENTS: Vol.1. Prelude by Henry Purcell. Menuet: Noch dag noch nacht is mijne rust by J. Krieger. Napolitaine by G. Ph. Telemann. Rigaudon by L. C. Daquin. Menuet by J. B. Lully. Gavotte by G. F. Handel. Variations on a Welsh carol by Ank van Campen. The bard's love. David on the white rock. Now strike the harp gladly. The blackbird. Hunting the hare. The dove. All through the night. Let now the harp. Black Sir Harry. Why lingers my gaze? An Irish lullaby. Open the door softly. Dennis don't be threat'ning. If the cat had gold. Young Bridget. The butterfly. Irish lullaby. Baltighoran. Irish jigg. The blossom of raspberry. The bonny cuckoo. Castle O'Neil.

Vol.2. Corranto. Dance. The fall of the leafe by Martin Pierson. A toye. The minstrelsy of Chirk Castle. Margaret that lost her garter. Lament for Gerald. Plearaca (Planxty) by Turloch O'Carolan. Brian Boru's march. Dreams to sell (Dream Angus). Princess Augusta. Spinning song from Lewis. Strathpey. Lady Sutherland's reel.

2382. ———, arr. *My harp's delight: music of four centuries: for celtic harp.* Arranged by Ank van Campen. London: Salvi Publications, c1983. 13 pp. "Vol. 1." CONTENTS: Tiento II; Tiento VIII from Tres libros de musica en cifra para vihuela by Alonso Mudarra. My Lady Carey's dompe by Hugh Aston. Volte by Jan Pieterszoon Sweelinck. Purth clarseach = A lesson for the harp. Carolan's concerto by Turlough O'Carolan. Andante by Fernando Sor. Pavane by Ank van Campen.

2383. Carman, Faith, arr. *Folk songs.* Arranged by Faith Carman. San Mateo, Calif.: F.C. Publishing Co., c1986. 2 v. (Solo series: harp) CONTENTS: Vol.1. Shule aroon (Come oh love); Galileo's dance; Shenandoah; Scarborough fair.

Vol.2. Black is the color; Foggy, foggy dew; All through the night; Cockles and mussels; Greensleeves.

2384. Carmichael, Hoagy, 1899–1981. *Stardust.* Arranged by Lynne Wainwright Palmer. [San Mateo, Calif.]: F.C. Publishing Co., [1988], c1929. 3 pp. (Popcycle series)

2385. Carolan, Turlough, 1670–1738. *Carolan's concerto: homage to Geminiani.* Rev. and ed. for all harps by Ellis Schuman. Ellensburg, Wash.: F. C. Publishing Co., 1992. 3 pp. [NP]

2386. ———. [Harp music. Selections; arr.] *Forty O'Carolan tunes: for all harps.* Each arranged for beginning and advanced harpers by Sylvia Woods. Los Angeles, Calif.: Woods Music and Books Publishing, c1985. 112 pp. (A Sylvia Woods multi-level harp book) [NP] CONTENTS: Lady Athenry; George Brabazon no. 1; George Brabazon no. 2; Planxty Burke; Carolan's cap; Carolan's concerto; Carolan's dowry; Carolan's draught; Carolan's fancy; Carolan's farewell to music; Carolan's quarrel with the landlady; Carolan's receipt; Carolan's welcome; The clergy's lamentation; Sir Charles Coote; Planxty Crilly; Bridget Cruise no. 1; Bridget Cruise no. 2; Planxty Drew; John Drury; Lord Galway's lamentation; Lady Gethin; Hewlett; Lord Inchiquin; Baptist Johnston; Bumper Squire Jones; Thomas Morres Jones; Morgan Magan; Blind Mary; Mrs. Maxwell; John O'Connor; Charles O'Conor; Hugh O'Donnell; O'Flinn; Kean O'Hara; The O'Rourke's feast; Eleanor Plunkett; Fanny Power; Mrs. Power; Planxty Safaigh; Sheebeg and Sheemore; Dr. John Stafford; Captain Sudley; Planxty Sweeny.

2387. ———. [Harp music. Selections] *A patchwork suite.* Arranged for solo harp by Danielle Perrett. Yarnfield, Eng.: Piper Publications, c1984. 8 pp. Arr. from piano transcriptions by Edward Bunting of harp compositions by Carolan. CONTENTS: Carolan's concerto; Grace Nugent; Planxty Drury; Mrs. Crofton; Bumper Squire Jones; Mrs. Maxwell.

2388. ———. [Harp music. Selections; arr.] *Sette pezzi: per arpa.* Revisione di M. Vita. Milan: Edizioni Suvini Zerboni, c1970. 11 pp. CONTENTS: Planxty drury; The lamentation of Owen O'Neil; Nanny Mc. Dermontroe; Abigail Judge; Fairy queen; Madam Cole; Carolan's Concerto.

2389. ———. [Harp music. Selections; arr.] *A tribute to O'Carolan: music for the Irish harp.* Edited and arranged by Nancy Calthorpe. [Cork, Ireland: Ossian Publications, 1976?], c1970. 12 pp. [NP]

2390. Chaloupka, Stanley, 1922–, arr. *Christmas time: songs, hymns, carols.* Arranged for harp solo by Stanley Chaloupka. Glendale, Calif.: Glendale Printing Center, c1990. 3 v. CONTENTS: Vol.1. Adeste fideles; Away in a manger (Mueller); Carol of the bells; Coventry carol; Good King Wenceslas; Joy to the world; Lo, how a rose e'er blooming; We three kings of orient are; What child is this?; Winds through the olive trees.
    Vol.2. Angels from the realms of glory; Away in a manger (Luther); Christmas has come again; Deck the halls; The first Noël; Hark! the herald angels sing; O holy night; O Tannenbaum; Silent night.
    Vol.3. Angels we have heard on high; Bring a torch, Jeannette, Isabella; Carol of the bagpipers; God rest ye merry, gentlemen; It came upon a midnight clear; Jingle bells; O little town of Bethlehem; Rocking carol; The twelve days of Christmas.

2391. Charpentier, Louise. *Dix pièces variées: arrangées pour la harpe celtique.* Arr. O. Le Dentu. Paris: Gérard Billaudot, 1983. 13 pp. [NP]

2392. Chatton, Monique, arr. *Anthologie de musique des 16e, 17e et 18e siècles: pour le luth (ou clavecin, orgue, harpe).* Transcriptions et doigté: Denise Perret, Ricardo Correa, Monique Chatton. Ed. pratique. Bern: Mueller und Schade, c1983–1984.

2393. Chauvel, Marjorie, 1922–. *So they want a harp at the wedding.* [Palo Alto, Calif.: Encore Harp Service], c1982. 55 pp. Cover title: A harp at the wedding. CONTENTS: Love theme from Romeo & Juliet by Tchaikovsky. Andante maestoso by Biehl. Gott lebet noch; Prelude no. 1 by J. S. Bach. Eighteenth century march. Air. Renaissance march by P. Wachs. The little shepherd by Debussy. The Lord's prayer by Albert Hay Malotte. Reverie by Debussy. Trumpet voluntary by Purcell. Festival serenade. Ke kali nei au by Charles E. King. If I loved you by Richard Rodgers. September song by Kurt Weill. Misty by Erroll Garner.

2394. ———, arr. *Tunes I love to play.* [Arr. Marjorie Chauvel]. [S.l.]: Marjorie Chauvel, 1981. 32 pp. CONTENTS: Burlesca by Wilhelm Friede-mann Bach. Six German dances by Ludwig van Beethoven. King William's march by Jeremiah Clarke. Sailor's hornpipe. In church by Peter Ilyich Tchaikovsky. Bicycle ride by Alexander Gretchaninoff. Austrian folk tune by Louis Kohler. The little music box; The shepherd's flute by Samuel Maykapar. Fly little bird by Heitor Villa-Lobos. Llanover Welsh reel. Over the rainbow by Harold Arlen. Turkey in the straw. Rudolph, the red-nosed reindeer by Johnny Marks. Jingle bells by James Pierpont.

2395. Chertok, Pearl, 1918–1980, arr. *Classics for troubadour.* Adapted for harp by Pearl Chertok. New York: Interstate Music; Salvi Publications, [196–?]. 4 pp. [NP] CONTENTS: March (Allemande) by G. F. Handel. Sonata in C major (Longo 217). Minuetto by Domenico Scarlatti. Polon-aise in G minor by J. S. Bach. Les vieleux et les gueux (no. 2 from Les fastes de la grande et ancienne Mxnxstrxndxsx) by François Couperin.

2396. ———, arr. *Prelude by Henry Purcell. Gavotte by Joseph Exaudet.* Adapted for harp by Pearl Chertok. Santa Monica, Calif.: Salvi Publications, [197–?]. 4 pp.

2397. Cheshire, John, 1839–1910. *Home sweet home.* London: J.B. Cramer & Co., Ltd., n.d. 7 pp. For harp.

2398. Chipp, Thomas Paul, 1793–1870, arr. *A favorite Irish melody: with an introduction and variations for the harp.* London: F. T. Latour, [1826?]. 11 pp. An arrangement of the air, The moreen, later known as The minstrel boy, with words by Thomas Moore.

2399. ———, arr. *A selection of national and popular melodies: book 10.* Arr. in a familiar style for the harp by T. P. Chipp. London: J. Power, [183–?]. 8 pp. CONTENTS: Prelude; Love's young dream; Di tanti palpiti by Rossini; Le petit tambour.

2400. ———, arr. *Where the bee sucks: a favorite air.* Arr. for the harp by T. P. Chipp. London: Chappell, [182–?]. 7 pp.

2401. Chopin, Frédéric, 1810–1849. [Etudes, piano. Selections; arr.] *Drei Etüden:* op. 10, nos. 11 and 5; op. 25, no. 1. [Arr. by] Wilhelm Posse. Frankfurt: Zimmermann, c1919. 11 pp.

2402. ———. [Etudes, piano, op. 25, no. 1; arr.] *Etude in A♭: for harp.* [Arr.] by Samuel O. Pratt. New York: Colin, c1966. 4 pp. (Pratt Music Library series of masterworks transcribed for harp)

2403. ———. [Etudes, piano, op. 25, no. 1; arr.] *Etude in A♭ major, op. 25, no. 1.* Arr. and ed. Paul Hurst. Marina Del Rey, Calif.: Safari Publications, 1993. 6 pp. Originally for piano.

2404. ———. [Impromptus, piano, no. 4, op. 66, C♯ minor; arr.] *Fantaisie-impromptu.* Transcribed for harp by De Wayne Fulton. Chicago, Ill.: Lyon & Healy, c1987. 12 pp. (The Lyon & Healy treasury of harp music)

2405. ———. [Impromptus, piano, no. 4, op. 66, C# minor; arr.] *I'm always chasing rainbows: from the Fantasia impromptu.* Arranged by Penny Howk Beavers. San Mateo, Calif.: F.C. Publishing Co., c1989. 2 pp. (Popcycle series)

2406. ———. [Mazurkas, piano, op. 17, no. 4, A minor; arr.] *Mazurka, op. 17/4.* Trans. Clifford Wooldridge. Chicago: Lyon & Healy, 1985. 7 pp.

2407. ———. [Mazurkas, piano, op. 24, no. 1; arr.] *Mazurka, op. 24, Nr. 1: für Harfe solo.* Für Harfe eingerichtet von Wilhelm Posse. Frankfurt: Jul. Heinr. Zimmermann, [1987], c1919. 3 pp.

2408. ———. [Nocturnes, piano, B. 49, C♯ minor; arr.] *Nocturne: harp solo.* Transcribed by S. Mario de Stefano. [New York]: Lyra Music Co., c1964. 4 pp. Transposed from original key of C♯ minor to C minor.

2409. ———. [Preludes, piano, op. 28, no. 2; arr.] *Prelude no. 2.* Transcribed for harp by H. Renié. Paris: Gay & Tenton, c1928. 3 pp. Originally for piano.

2410. ———. [Preludes, piano, op. 28, no. 20; arr.] *Prelude: in C minor.* Transcribed for harp by Marie Miller. New York: Carl Fischer, Inc., c1925. 1 p. (Popular classics transcribed for harp, Series 2)

2411. Clarke, Jeremiah, 1669?–1707. *Trumpet voluntary.* Arranged by Deborah Henson-Conant. [San Mateo, Calif.]: F.C. Publishing Co., c1989. 2 pp. (Popcycle series) Erroneously attributed to Henry Purcell.

2412. Clementi, Muzio, 1752–1832. [Sonatas, piano, op. 12, no. 1. Allegretto; arr.] *Andante con variazioni: per arpa.* Rev. Mirella Vita. Milan: Edizioni Suvini Zerboni, 1968. 8 pp.

2413. Cola, Giulia, arr. *Trascrizioni per arpa: tre pezzi facili di autori classici.* [Arr. by] Giulia Cola. Ancona, Italy: Edizioni musicali Bèrben, c1976. 7 pp.

CONTENTS: Minuetto by J. S. Bach. Gavotta by G. F. Haendel. Danza tedesca by W. A. Mozart.

2414. Constant, Marius, 1925–. *Harpalycé: pour harpe solo et quintette à cordes (ou orchestre à cordes)*. Paris: Ricordi, c1980. 11 pp. Harp solo version (omitting accompaniment and measures of silence).

2415. Corelli, Arcangelo, 1653–1713. [Sonatas, violin, continuo, op. 5, no. 7; arr.] *Sonata VII, op. 5*. Trascrizione per arpa di Silvana Figlios. London: Salvi Publications, c1983. 7 pp.

2416. ———. [Sonatas, violin, continuo, op. 5, no. 9. Giga; arr.] *Giga*. [Arr. by Carlos Salzedo]. New York: G. Schirmer, c1923. 5 pp. Excerpt from Corelli's sonata no. 9, op. 5.

2417. Coulman, John, arr. *The Favourite air in The wood daemon*. Arranged for the harp or piano forte by John Coulman. London: G. Walker, [181–?]. 3 pp. Music possibly by Michael Kelly.

2418. Couperin, François, 1668–1733. [Concerts royaux. No. 4. Sarabande; arr.] *Sarabande: from the Quatrième concert royal*. Transcribed for harp by Carlos Salzedo. New York, N.Y.: G. Schirmer, c1923. 3 pp.

2419. ———. [Concerts royaux. No. 4. Sarabande; arr.] *Sarabande: from the Quatrième concert royal*. Transcribed for harp by Carlos Salzedo. Paris: Heugel, c1923. 3 pp.

2420. ———. [Instrumental music. Selections; arr.] *Six pièces: adaptées pour la harpe celtique ou la harpe à pédales*. Transcription and fingering by Maïté Etcheverry. Paris: Editions Choudens, c1978. 10 pp. (Les classiques transcrits pour la harpe) [NP] CONTENTS: La bourbonnaise; Le petit rien; Air tendre; Les moissonneurs; Les barricades mystérieuses; Soeur Monique.

2421. ———. [Pièces de clavecin, 3e livre. No 18. Tic-toc-choc; arr.] *Tic-toc-choc, ou, Les maillotins*. Transcribed for harp by H. Renié. Paris: Gay & Tenton, c1928. 3 pp. Originally for harpsichord.

2422. Cramer, Johann Baptist, 1771–1858. *Air with variations: Rousseau's dream*. Arranged for harp by John Balsir Chatterton; edited by Alice Lawson Aber. Ross, Calif.: Harp Publications, c1974. iv, 7 pp. Originally for piano.

2423. Cummings, William Hayman, 1831–1915. *Hark the herald angels sing*. Arr. Cameron. Washington, D.C.: William Truesdale Cameron, n.d. 1 p. Adapted by Cummings from a work by Mendelssohn. [NP]

2424. Daquin, Louis Claude, 1694–1772. [Pièces de clavecin. Coucou; arr.] *Le coucou*. [Bearbeitet von L. M. Magistretti]. Frankfurt: Zimmermann, c1914. 5 pp. (Des Harfenisten Konzert-Programm, Nr. 8)

2425. ———. [Pièces de clavecin. Coucou; arr.] *Le coucou*. Transcribed for harp by Henriette Renié. Paris: Gay & Tenton, [1928]. Score 3 pp. Originally for harpsichord.

2426. ———. [Pièces de clavecin. Hirondelle; arr.] *L'hirondelle.* Transcribed for harp by H. Renié. Paris: Gay & Tenton, c1928. 3 pp. Originally for harpsichord.

2427. ———. [Pièces de clavecin. Mélodieuse; arr.] *La mélodieuse.* Transcribed for harp by H. Renié. Paris: Gay & Tenton, c1928. 2 pp. Originally for harpsichord.

2428. Datshkovsky, Yasha, 1931–. [Cancion de cuna de Alejandra; arr.] *Lullaby for Alexandra.* Arranged for harp solo by Jean Altshuler. San Antonio, Tex.: Southern Music Co., c1990. 2 pp. Originally for piano.

2429. Davies, Reuben. *Remembrance.* Arranged for harp by Maudetta Martin Joseph. Boston, Mass.: Boston Music Co., c1925. 5 pp. Originally for piano.

2430. Davis, Katherine, 1892–; Onorati, Henry, and Simeone, Harry, 1911–. [Little drummer boy; arr.] *Little drummer boy.* Arr. Mimi Allen for solo harp, duo, or multiple harps. Ellensburg, Wash.: F C Publishing Co., [1992?]. Score 10 pp.

2431. Debussy, Claude, 1862–1918. [Arabesques, piano. No. 1; arr.] *Première arabesque.* Transcription pour harpe par H. Renié. Paris: A. Durand, c1906. 7 pp. Originally for piano.

2432. ———. [Arabesques, piano. No. 2; arr.] *Deuxième arabesque.* Transcription pour harpe par H. Renié. Paris: A. Durand, c1906. 7 pp. Originally for piano.

2433. ———. [Children's corner. Doctor Gradus ad Parnassum; arr.] *Doctor Gradus ad Parnassum.* Transcribed by Carl Swanson. Boston, Mass.: Boston Editions, c1984. 5 pp. Originally for piano.

2434. ———. [Children's corner. Little shepherd; arr.] *The little shepherd.* Transcribed by Carl Swanson. Boston, Mass.: Boston Editions, c1984. 2 pp. Originally for piano.

2435. ———. [Children's corner. Little shepherd; arr.] *The little shepherd.* Transcribed by Mimi Allen. Ellensburg, Wash.: F.C. Publishing Co., 1990. 3 pp. Originally for piano.

2436. ———. [Children's corner. Serenade of the doll; arr.] *Serenade of the doll.* Transcribed by Carl Swanson. Boston, Mass.: Boston Editions, c1984. 6 pp. Originally for piano.

2437. ———. [Estampes. Jardins sous la pluie; arr.] *Jardins sous la pluie: extrait des Estampes: pour le piano.* Transcrit pour harpe par Alys Lautemann. Paris: Durand, c1928. 11 pp. Originally for piano.

2438. ———. [Nocturnes, piano, D♭ major; arr.] *Nocturne: en ré bémol.*

Transcription pour harpe par H. Maurice Jacquet. Paris: La Sirène Musicale, c1907. 7 pp.

2439. ———. [Petite suite. En bateau; arr.] *En bateau: extrait de la Petite suite.* [Transcription pour harpe par H. Renié]. New York: Lyra Music, n.d. 7 pp. Originally for piano, 4 hands.

2440. ———. [Petite suite. En bateau; arr.] *En bateau: extrait de Petite suite.* Transcription pour harpe par H. Renié. Paris: Durand et Cie., c1908. 7 pp. Originally for piano, 4 hands.

2441. ———. [Piano music. Selections; arr.] *Pour la harpe.* Clair de lune trans. Victor Coeur. Rêverie trans. Frédérique Cambreling. Valse romantique trans. Lily Laskine. Paris: Editions Jobert, 1988. 18 pp.

2442. ———. [Piano music. Selections; arr.] *Three pieces.* Arr. by Samuel O. Pratt. New York: C. Colin, c1966. 11 pp. Originally for piano. CONTENTS: Prelude: Le soleil se lève, le calme regne sur la campagne; Sarabande; Doctor Gradus ad Parnassum.

2443. ———. [Pour le piano. Sarabande; arr.] *Sarabande.* Arranged by Faith Carman. San Mateo, Calif.: F.C. Publishing Co., c1986. 7 pp. (Solo series: harp) Originally for piano.

2444. ———. [Preludes, piano, book 1. Des pas sur la neige; arr.] *Des pas sur la neige; Danseuses de Delphes.* Trans. Ruth K. Inglefield. [Santa Monica, Calif.]: Salvi, 1977. 6 pp.

2445. ———. [Preludes, piano, book 1. Fille aux cheveux de lin; arr.] *La fille aux cheveux de lin.* Transcrit pour harpe par Marcel Grandjany. Paris: Durand, c1931. 3 pp.

2446. ———. [Preludes, piano, book 1. Fille aux cheveux de lin; arr.] *La fille aux cheveux de lin.* Transcribed for harp by Carlos Salzedo. New York: Lyra Music, c1974. 2 pp.

2447. ———. [Preludes, piano, book 1. Fille aux cheveux de lin; arr.] *The maid with the flaxen hair.* [Arranged] for harp solo; edited by Susann McDonald. Bloomington, Ind.: Musicworks-Harp Editions, c1982. 2 pp.

2448. ———. [Preludes, piano, book 1. Fille aux cheveux de lin; arr.] *La fille aux cheveux de lin.* [Arranged by] Schlomovitz. Palo Alto, Calif.: Harpress of California, c1983. 2 pp.

2449. ———. [Rêverie; arr.] *Reverie.* Arranged for harp by Joy Hujsak. [La Jolla, Calif.: Mina-Helwig Publishing Co.], [197–?]. 5 pp. Originally for piano.

2450. ———. [Suite bergamasque. Clair de lune; arr.] *Clair de lune: extrait de la Suite bergamasque.* Transcription pour harpe par Victor Coeur. Paris: Editions Jobert, c1929. 7 pp. Originally for piano.

2451. ———. [Suite bergamasque. Clair de lune; arr.] *Clair de lune.* Transcribed for harp by Carlos Salzedo. New York: Southern Music Pub. Co., c1962. 8 pp. Originally for piano.

2452. ———. [Suite bergamasque. Clair de lune; arr.] *Clair de lune.* Simplified harp arrangement by Phyllis Schlomovitz. Palo Alto, Calif.: Harpress of California, c1978. 5 pp. (Phyllis Schlomovitz harp transcriptions) Originally for piano.

2453. ———. [Suite bergamasque. Clair de lune; arr.] *Clair de lune: harp solo.* [Arr.] by Marcel Grandjany. [New York]: Lyra Music Co., c1963. 7 pp. Originally for piano.

2454. ———. [Valse romantique; arr.] *Valse romantique: pour harpe.* Adaptation de Lily Laskine. Paris: J. Jobert, c1924. 7 pp. Originally for piano.

2455. Delibes, Léo, 1836–1891. [Sylvia. Pizzicati; arr.] *Pizzicati.* Arranged for harp by Inez Carusi. Chicago: Lyon & Healy, c1905. 5 pp.

2456. DeVorzon, Barry, and Botkin, Perry, 1933–. *Nadia's theme.* Arranged by Lynne Wainwright Palmer. San Mateo, Calif.: F.C. Publishing Co., c1988. 3 pp. (Popcycle series)

2457. Dilling, Mildred, arr. [Little classics] *Thirty little classics: for the harp.* Compiled and arranged by Mildred Dilling. Bryn Mawr, Pa.: Oliver Ditson Co., c1938. 39 pp. CONTENTS: Gavotte from Iphegenia in Aulis by Christoph W. von Gluck. Minuet in G minor by Jean Jacques Rousseau. Dragonfly in the sunshine by Carl Reinecke. Strolling musicians (Musiciens ambulants), op. 31, no. 2 by Vladimir Rebikov. Pavane (Style renaissance) by Paul Wachs. Minuet in F by Wolfgang Amadeus Mozart. Gavotte gracieuse by Franz Joseph Haydn. Adeste fideles by John Reading. Minuet in G by Johann Sebastian Bach. Soldiers' march (Soldatenmarsch), op. 68, no. 2 by Robert Schumann. Menuet d'Exaudet by Joseph Exaudet. Allegro. Glissando waltz (La tartine de beurre). Such chiming, melodious from The magic flute by Wolfgang Amadeus Mozart. Allegretto from the Seventh symphony by Ludwig van Beethoven. Dance of the blessed spirits from Orpheus by Christoph W. von Gluck. Waltz, op. 9, no. 33 by Franz Schubert. Allegretto by Franz Joseph Haydn. 2 country dances by Ludwig van Beethoven. Les coucous benevoles by François Couperin. Prelude in A major, op. 28, no. 7 by Frédéric Chopin. Minuet in G; Musette by Johann Sebastian Bach. Chorus from Alceste by Christoph W. von Gluck. Little prelude, no. 1 by Johann Sebastian Bach. Waltz, op. 39, no. 2 by Johannes Brahms. Corrente by George Frederic Handel. Bridal chorus from Lohengrin; Song to the evening star from Tannhäuser by Richard Wagner. Wedding march from the music to Midsummer night's dream by Felix Mendelssohn.

2458. ———, arr. *Old tunes for new harpists: a collection of folktunes progressively arranged: with an introduction to harp technic, and illustrations.* Compiled and arranged by Mildred Dilling. Bryn Mawr, Penn.: Oliver Ditson Co., c1934.

xii, 48 pp. CONTENTS: Hot cross buns; Do, do, l'enfant do; Buzz, buzz, buzz; Song of the river; Lavender's blue; Good King John; Westminster chimes; Frère Jacques; If I were a nightingale; Hop, hop, hop; London Bridge; Green gravel; Pussy cat; Bugle call; The chimes of St. Paul's; Breton dancing tune; Evening song; Swedish dance; Goodbye to winter; Cuckoo, cuckoo; The King of France; Little waltz; Au clair de la lune; Holy night; Yellow bird; Spring song; Elfin dance; Country dance; Shepherd's carol; Sleep, baby, sleep; The bagpipes; Fais dôdô; The little goose girl's song; Sur le pont d'Avignon; Cradle song; Meunier, tu dors; Blow away the morning dew; Going to the fair; Gentil Coquelicot; Old English country dance; When I was a young girl; Early one morning; Il était une bergère; Fairest Lord Jesus; Oh, dear! what can the matter be?; Ah! vous dirai-je, maman; Cornish dance; Go down, Moses; The first Noël; Old Christmas carol; Flow gently, sweet Afton; Reaping song; Savez-vous planter les choux?; Song of the watch; As I went a-walking one morning in spring; The wraggle taggle gypsies, o!; Sedlak; Robin Adair; King David and his harp; Polish dance; The Christ Child's lullaby; Nous n'irons plus au bois; Spinning song; Amaryllis by Henry Ghys; Lullaby; I hear the mill; Spinning tune; The Campbells are comin'; Gaily the troubadour; How many miles to London town?; Two bagpipe tunes; The minstrel boy; Swing low, sweet chariot; March of the kings; John Anderson, my Jo; The soldier's joy; Noël de Cluny; Dance song; Song of the Volga boatmen; Santa Lucia; Il pleut, il pleut, bergère (harp duet); Die Henne; The jasmine flower; Bring a torch, Jeannette, Isabella; Cuckoo; Aloha oe; The harp that once through Tara's halls; Old folks at home by Stephen C. Foster; Londonderry air; Deep river; Theme from the Surprise symphony by Franz Josef Haydn; David of the white rock.

2459. Długoraj, Wojciech, 1557 or 8–ca. 1619, and Polak, Jakub, d. ca. 1605. [Lute music. Selections; arr.] *Utwory z tabulatur lutniowych na harfe.* [By] W. Dlugoraj, J. Polak, Anonim (XVI/XVII w.) Z pierwodrukøw podali Zofia Steszewska i Piotr Poźniak. Wyboru dokonała i opracowała na harfe Urszula Mazurek. [Krakow]: Polskie Wydawn. Muzyczne, [1969]. Score 14 pp. (Florilegium musicae antiquae, 41)

2460. Dominguez, Alberto. *Perfidia: for pedal or troubadour harp.* [Arranged by Reinhardt Elster]. New York: Peer International, c1939. 2 pp. [NP]

2461. Donizetti, Gaetano, 1797–1848. [Linda di Chamounix. A consolarmi affrettati; arr.] *A consolarmi affrettisi: scena del delirio nell'opera Linda di Chamounix di Donizetti.* Ridotta per arpa nello stile brillante da N. C. Bochsa. Milan: Ricordi, [1845?]. 7 pp. For harp.

2462. ———. [Lucia di Lammermoor. Chi mi frena; arr.] *Chi mi frena: Lucia.* [Arr. by J. Cheshire]. London: J.B. Cramer & Co., 18—? 7 pp.

2463. ———. [Lucrezia Borgia. Segreto; arr] *Ballade favorite, Il segreto per esser felice du celebre opera Lucrezia Borgia.* Arrangé pour la harpe par N. C. Bochsa. London: Boosey, [183–?]. 7 pp. For harp.

2464. ———. [Marino Faliero. Or che in cielo alta è la notte; arr.] *Or che in ciel alto è la notte: barcarola nell'opera Marino Falliero.* Ridotta per arpa sola da Tiberio Natalucci. Milan: Ricordi, [1836 or 1837]. 7 pp. For harp.

2465. ———. [Roberto Devereux. A te diro; arr.] *The favorite cavatina "A te diro": from Donizetti's opera Roberto Devereux.* Arranged for the harp by N. C. Bochsa. London: E. Ashdown [& Parry, 19—?]. 6 pp.

2466. Dubin, Al, 1891–1945, and Franklin, Dave, 1895–1970. *Anniversary waltz.* Arranged by Deborah Henson-Conant. San Mateo, Calif.: F.C. Publishing Co., [1989], c1941. 3 pp. (Popcycle series)

2467. Dubois, Theodore, 1837–1924. *Sorrente.* [Arr. by H. Renié]. Paris: Alphonse Leduc, n.d. 5 pp.

2468. Dulova, Vera, 1910–, ed. *Sbornik p'es.* Obrab. dlia arfy i red. V. Dylovoi. Moscow: Gos. myz. izd-vo, 1954. 31 pp. Originally for harpsichord. CONTENTS: Suite: Allemande, Sarabanda, Gigue by John Loeillet [erroneously attributed to Lully]. Coucou by C. Daquin. Little hammers; Soeur Monique by F. Couperin.

2469. Durand, Auguste, 1830–1909. [Chaconne, piano, op. 62, A minor; arr.] *Chaconne.* Transcribed for harp by Carlos Salzedo. New York: G. Schirmer, c1923. 9 pp.

2470. ———. [Chaconne, piano, op. 62, A minor; arr.] *Chacone: pour le piano, op. 62.* Arr. for harp by Alphonse Hasselmans. Paris: Durand; Philadelphia, Pa.: Elkan-Vogel, 1951. 5 pp.

2471. ———. [Waltzes, piano, no. 1, op. 83, E♭ major; arr.] *Première valse, op. 83.* [Transcription pour harpe par H. Renié]. Paris: Durand, c1908. 7 pp.

2472. ———. [Waltzes, piano, no. 1, op. 83, E♭ major; arr.] *First waltz = Première valse.* Arr. by Schlomovitz. [Palo Alto, Calif.]: Harpress of California, [198–?]. 12 pp.

2473. Dussek, Johann Ladislaus, 1760–1812. [Concertos, harp, orchestra, op. 15, E♭ major] *Concerto: for the harp, or piano-forte with the additional keys and accompaniments, op. 15.* London: Goulding & Co., [1814]. 1 part (25 pp.). Keyboard or harp part, including reduction of orchestral tuttis that enable the soloist to perform the piece alone.

2474. ———. [Concertos, harp, orchestra, op. 15, E♭ major; arr.] *Concerto: in E♭ for harp and orchestra, op. 15.* Ed. by Catherine Michel. Santa Monica, Calif.: Salvi Publications, c1977. 39 pp. Arranged for harp unacc.

2475. Dussek, Olivia B., arr. *The harpist's friend: a series of popular melodies.* Arranged for the harp by O. B. Dussek. Boston: Edwin Ashdown, n.d. 24 v. CONTENTS: March Megan; The rising of the lark; March of the men of

Harlech; Lilla's a lady; Savourneen deelish; La rosa valse; She wore a wreath of roses; The last rose of summer; Home sweet home; The heart bow'd down; What are the wild waves saying; Within a mile of Edinboro' town; By the sad sea waves; The harp that once through Tara's halls; Isle of beauty; The lass of Richmond Hill; The maid of Llangollen; My lodging is on the cold ground; Oft in the stilly night; Robin Adair; Rose softly blooming; The wearing of the green; O dear what can the matter be; I dreamt that I dwelt in marble halls.

2476. ———, arr. *Merch Megan.* Tr. Olivia B. Dussek. Abergavenny, Gwent, Wales: Adlais, n.d. 5 pp.

2477. Dvořák, Antonín, 1841–1904. [Humoresky, op. 101, no. 7, G♭ major; arr.] *Humoreske.* Transcribed for harp by Carlos Salzedo. [New York]: Carl Fischer, Inc., c1925. 5 pp. Originally for piano.

2478. ———. [Symphonies, no. 9, op. 95, E minor. Largo; arr.] *Aus dem Largo des 5. Symphonie, op. 95: Aus der neuen Welt.* Arr. by Marie Zunová. London: N. Simrock, c1926. 5 pp.

2479. Eberl, Anton, 1765–1807. [Variations, harpsichord, op. 6, D major. Selections; arr.] *Air with variations; and, Rondo pastoral.* [Arr. by Samuel O. Pratt]. New York: Lyon & Healy, n.d. 11 pp. Originally for harpsichord (1st work) or string trio (2nd work). The 1st work, once attributed to Mozart, is actually by Eberl, based on Dittersdorf's aria "Freundin sanfter Herzenstreibe" from *Der Gutsherr*; the 2nd work, by Mozart, arranged from the 6th movement of his Divertimento, K. 563.

2480. ———. [Variations, harpsichord, op. 6, D major. Selections; arr.] *Air with variations, and, Rondo pastorale: for solo harp.* From the original edition as arranged by John Thomas; present edition edited by Beverly Fitts. Bryn Mawr, Pa.: Theodore Presser, c1981. 12 pp. For description, see 2479.

2481. Elgar, Edward, 1857–1934. *Salut d'amour by Elgar. Minuet: Grandmother by Grieg. Musical moment [no. 3] by Schubert.* Transcribed for harp by A. Francis Pinto. New York: International Music, 1919. 7 pp. Originally for piano.

2482. Ellington, Duke, 1899–1974. *Satin doll.* Arranged by Eleanor Fell. San Mateo, Calif.: F.C. Publishing Co., c1988. 6 pp. (Popcycle series)

2483. Erb, Laura, arr. *Pop goes the harp.* Arranged by Laura Erb. New York: Charles Hansen, c1974. 40 pp. CONTENTS: Sunrise, sunset from Fiddler on the roof by Sheldon Harnick and Jerry Bock. Day by day from Godspell by Stephen Schwartz. Kum by ya. Love is blue = L'amour est bleu by André Pop. My love, forgive me = Amore, scusami by Gino Mescoli. Fascination by F. D. Marchetti. Satin doll by Duke Ellington. Colour my world by James Pankow. Sweet is my ladye love by Valerie von Pechy. Alley cat and Frankie and Johnny by Frank Bjorn. Havah nagila. Black is the color of my true love's hair. Amazing grace.

2484. ———, arr. *Pops for harp.* Arranged by Laura Erb. New York: C. Hansen Educational Sheet Music & Books, c1972. 40 pp. CONTENTS: Love theme from The godfather by Nino Rota. Theme from Love story by Francis Lai. Moon river from Breakfast at Tiffany's by Henry Mancini. (They long to be) Close to you by Burt Bacharach. Christmas medley: Silver bells from The lemon drop kid by Jay Livingston and Ray Evans; The Christmas song (Chestnuts roasting on an open fire) by Mel Torme and Robert Wells; What Child is this? Love said goodbye from The godfather, part II by Nino Rota. Supercalifragilisticexpialidocious from Mary Poppins by Richard M. Sherman and Robert B. Sherman. Louise from Innocents of Paris by Richard A. Whiting. Mona Lisa from After midnight by Jay Livingston and Ray Evans. Raindrops keep fallin' on my head from Butch Cassidy and the Sundance Kid by Burt Bacharach. Midnight cowboy from Midnight cowboy by John Barry. Basin Street blues by Spencer Williams.

2485. Erdeli, K. A. (Kseniia Aleksandrovna), 1878–1971, arr. *Russkaia muzyka: proizvedeniia russkikh kompozitorov v obrabotke i perelozhenii K. Erdeli: dlia arfy.* Moscow: Muzyka, 1967. 64 pp. For for harp solo. CONTENTS: Zhavoronok by Glinka-Balakirev. Chustvo; Val's; Mazurka by M. Glinka. Fantaziia na temy opery P. Chaikovskogo Evgenii Onegin by E. Val'ter-Kiune. Serenada; Kolybel'naia pesn' v buriu; Noktiurn, op. 19, no. 4; Val's, op. 40, no. 9 by P. Tchaikovsky. O, ne grusti = [Oh, do not grieve]; U moego okna = Dans mon jardin je vois] by S. Rachmaninoff. Preliudiia, op. 9, no. 1; Preliudiia, op. 15, no. 3; Preliudiia, op. 11, no. 13 by A. Scriabin. Preliudiia, op. 31, no. 2; Bagatel', op. 30 by A. Liadov.

2486. Escosa, John B., 1928–1991, arr. *Good King Wenceslas.* Arranged by John B. Escosa. San Mateo, Calif.: F.C. Publishing Co., c1988. 3 pp. (Popcycle series)

2487. ———, arr. *Greensleeves.* Arranged by John B. Escosa. San Mateo, Calif.: F.C. Publishing Co., c1988. 3 pp. (Popcycle series)

2488. Falla, Manuel de, 1876–1946. [Selections; arr.] *Three pieces: for harp.* Arr. by David Watkins. London: Chester Music, c1976. 11 pp. 1st and 3rd movements originally for orchestra; the 2nd originally for guitar. CONTENTS: I. Danse du corregidor, from The three-cornered hat; II. Homenaje, pièce écrite pour Le tombeau de Claude Debussy; III. Dance [sic] du meunier, from The three-cornered hat.

2489. ———. *Serenata andaluza.* Arr. Nicanor Zabaleta. Madrid: Union Musical Española, 1989. 11 pp. Originally for piano.

2490. ———. [Vida breve. Danza, no. 1; arr.] *Spanish dance no. 1: from the opera La vida breve.* Transcribed for harp by Marcel Grandjany. New York: Associated Music Publishers, Inc., c1943. 11 pp. Originally for orchestra.

2491. Farkas, Ferenc, 1905–. *Rége magyar táncok a XVII. századból = Danses hongroises du 17ème siècle.* Hárfára átírta = rédigées pour la harpe par Lian Pasquali. Budapest: Editio Musica, c1979. 12 pp. CONTENTS: Erdélyi fejedelem tánca = Danse du Prince de Transylvanie; Magyar tánc = Danse hongroise; Chorea; Lapockás tánc = Danse "Lapockás"; Chorea; Apor Lázár tánca = Danse de Lázár Apor.

2492. Farolfi, Giovanna, arr. *Trascrizioni: per arpa.* Di Giovanna Farolfi. Florence: Edizioni R. Maurri, c1972. 7 pp. CONTENTS: Sarabanda dalla Partita in si minore per violino solo by J. S. Bach. 2 Allegros by G. F. Händel.

2493. Fauré, Gabriel, 1845–1924. [Cantique de Racine; arr.] *Cantique de Racine: [pour] harp ou piano.* Trans. par Omer Letorey. Paris: J. Hamelle, n.d. 4 pp. Originally for mixed chorus and orchestra.

2494. ———. [Dolly. Selections; arr.] *Trois morceaux.* Arr. by M. Kahn. Paris: J. Hamelle, n.d. 3 v. 1st and 2nd works originally for piano, 4 hands. 3rd work originally for violoncello and piano. CONTENTS: Berceuse de Dolly; Jardin de Dolly; Sicilienne.

2495. Fell, Arthur. *Teri's theme.* Arranged by Eleanor Fell. San Mateo, Calif.: F.C. Publishing Co., c1988. 3 pp. (Popcycle series)

2496. Fell, Eleanor, arr. *Children's favorites: for non-pedal or pedal harp.* Ed. Linda Wood Rollo. Bloomington, Ind.: Vanderbilt Music Co., 1993. 22 pp. [NP] CONTENTS: Over the rainbow; Chopsticks; Happy hornpiper; The muffin man; Babes in toyland; Nursery rhyme medley: Skip to my lou, I'm a little teapot, Twinkle twinkle little star; Turkey in the straw.

2497. ———, arr. *Opera themes: a medley of famous arias.* Boston, Mass.: Boston Editions, c1985. 11 pp. CONTENTS: E lucevan le stelle from Tosca by Puccini. Là ci darem la mano from Don Giovanni; Voi, che sapete from The marriage of Figaro by Mozart. Un bel di from Madama Butterfly; Musetta's waltz (Quando m'en vo) from La bohème by Puccini. La donna è mobile from Rigoletto by Verdi.

2498. ———, arr. *Popular classic collection.* Arranged by Eleanor Fell; edited by Linda Wood Rollo for non-pedal or pedal harp. Bloomington, Ind.: Vanderbilt Music Co., Inc., 1992. 24 pp. (Pop 'n easy) [NP] CONTENTS: Introduction. Glossary. La donna e mobile by Verdi. Lullaby by Brahms. Melody by Mozart. Minuet in G by Paderewski. Ode to joy by Beethoven. Skaters waltz by Waldteufel. Valse brillante by Chopin. Strauss waltz medley by Strauss.

2499. ———, arr. *Popular holiday music collection.* Arranged by Eleanor Fell; edited by Linda Wood Rollo for non-pedal or pedal harp. Bloomington, Ind.: Vanderbilt Music Co., Inc., 1992. 27 pp. (Pop 'n easy) [NP] CONTENTS: Introduction; Glossary; Frosty the snowman; He is born, this child divine; Jolly old Saint Nicholas; Patapan; Jingle bells; What child

is this?; We wish you a merry Christmas; Chanukah o Chanukah; My
dreydl; Chanukah, Chanukah; Menorah memories; Auld lang syne.

2500. ———, arr. *Symphony themes: a medley of famous orchestra music by
Tchaikovsky, Brahms, Beethoven: for harp.* Arranged by Eleanor Fell. Boston,
Mass.: Boston Editions, c1986. 10 pp. CONTENTS: Excerpts from: Symphony no. 6 in B minor, op. 74, first movement by Tchaikovsky; Symphony
no. 1 in C minor, op. 68, fourth movement by Brahms; Symphony no. 3 in
F major, op. 90, third movement by Brahms; Symphony no. 9 in D minor,
op. 125, fourth movement (Ode to joy) by Beethoven.

2501. ———, arr. *Viennese waltzes: for harp: a medley of music by Lehar &
Strauss.* Arranged by Eleanor Fell. Boston, Mass.: Boston Editions, c1987.
12 pp. CONTENTS: Excerpts from: The merry widow (Vilia; The merry
widow waltz) by Franz Lehar; Tales from the Vienna Woods by Johann
Strauss; The blue Danube waltz by Johann Strauss.

2502. Fellows, Sylvia, arr. [American folk songs] *Four American folk songs.*
Arranged for folk harp by Sylvia Fellows. Anaheim, Calif.: Quicksilver
Music, c1988. 8 pp. [NP] CONTENTS: Wayfaring stranger; Blow the
candles out; Soldier, soldier; When Johnny comes marching home.

2503. ———, arr. [American folk tunes] *Four American folk tunes.* Arranged
for folk harp by Sylvia Fellows. Anaheim, Calif.: Quicksilver Music, c1988.
8 pp. [NP] CONTENTS: Dona dona; Cindy; The frog and the mouse;
Four in a boat.

2504. Ferrai, Louis. *Domino.* Arranged for harp solo by Eleanor Fell. [Santa
Monica, Calif.]: Salvi Publications, c1980. 4 pp. (Salvi pop series)

2505. Fibich, Zdeněk, 1850–1900. [At twilight. Andante placido; arr.]
Poeme: fantaisie. Arr. M. Zunová. Prague: Urbánek, c1927. 7 pp. Consists of
2 sections taken from composer's symphonic poem *V poovecer* (At twilight).

2506. Foster, Stephen Collins, 1826–1864. *I dream of Jeannie: paraphrase for
solo harp.* Arr. Michael Amorosi. [Santa Monica, Calif.]: Salvi Publications,
1977. 2 pp.

2507. ———. *My old Kentucky home.* Transcribed for harp by Carlos Salzedo.
New York: Composers' Music Corp., c1925. 3, [1] pp. (Favorite melodies
transcribed for the harp, Series I)

2508. ———. [Songs. Selections; arr.] *Famous melodies of Stephen Foster.*
Arranged for the harp by Joseph Riley. Los Angeles: Wilshire Publishers,
c1940. 13 pp. CONTENTS: Massa's in de cold ground; Jeanie with the
light brown hair; Old black Joe; Old folks at home; Beautiful dreamer; My
old Kentucky home.

2509. ———. [Songs. Selections; arr.] *Famous melodies of Stephen Foster.*
Arranged for the harp by Joseph Riley. [Boston: Boston Music Company,
c1956]. 12 pp.

2510. ———. [Songs. Selections; arr.] *A Stephen Foster medley.* Arranged by John B. Escosa. San Mateo, Calif.: F.C. Publishing Co., c1986. 8 pp. (Solo series: harp) CONTENTS: I dream of Jeanie; Beautiful dreamer; De Camptown races.

2511. Fowle, Julia, arr. *Ye banks and braes o' Bonnie Doon.* Arranged for the harp by Julia Fowle. Baltimore: H. McCaffrey; Washington, D.C.: John E. Ellis, c1847. 5 pp.

2512. Fox, Charlotte Milligan, 1864–1916, arr. *Songs of the Irish harpers: collected and arranged for harp or piano.* London: Bayley & Ferguson; New York: Schirmer, c1910. 57 pp. CONTENTS: My thousand times beloved; Golden locks are my delight; The parting of friends; Men of Connaught; Moorlough Mary; Sorrow of sorrows; The red haired girl; The gates of dreamland; The foggy dew; The thresher; Dear dark head; Pastheen Fionn; Farewell, my gentle harp.

2513. Francisque, Anthoine, ca. 1575–1605. [Trésor d'Orphée. Courante; arr.] *Courante from Le trésor d'Orphée.* Free transcription for harp by Jane B. Weidensaul. Teaneck, N.J.: Willow Hall Press, c1990. 5 pp. Originally for lute.

2514. ———. [Trésor d'Orphée. Pavane et bransles; arr.] *Pavane et bransles: from Le trésor d'Orphée.* Free transcription for harp by Marcel Grandjany. New York, N.Y.: Associated Music Publishers, Inc., c1949. 11 pp. (Music for the harp) Originally for lute.

2515. Franck, César, 1822–1890. [Panis angelicus; arr.] *Panis angelicus: for harp.* Arranged by May Hogan Cambern. [New York]: Michael Cambern, c1964. 3 pp. (From the notebook of May Hogan Cambern) Originally for voice, organ, harp, violoncello, and double bass.

2516. Franco, José María, 1894–, arr. *Tres piezas: para arpa, op. 62, 63 y 64.* Version para arpa por Jose Ma. Franco. Madrid: Union Musical Española, c1963. 11 pp. CONTENTS: Gallarda by A. Mudarra. O guardame las vaca: diferencias sobre la version de Narváez by José Ma. Franco. Villancico variado: sobre un tema de Luis Milán by José Ma. Franco.

2517. Freeburg, Janie, arr. *Folk dance tunes: for folk harp.* Arranged and transcribed by Janie Freeburg. Santa Barbara, Calif.: Nirilamba Music Productions, c1986. 16 pp. [NP] CONTENTS: Ma navu; Erev ba; Makedonsko devocje; Vari hasapikos; Kol dodi; Hava nagila; Doublebska polka; Humours of Westport; Westphalia waltz; I stand on the road alone; Korobushka.

2518. Freire, Osman Perez, 1878–1930. *Ay, ay, ay.* Freely transcribed by Robert Maxwell. New York: American Academy of Music, c1948. 4 pp.

2519. Friou, Deborah, 1951–, arr. *Danny boy.* Arranged by Deborah Friou for non-pedal and pedal harp. Montrose, Calif.: Woods Music & Books Publishing, c1990. 2 pp. [NP]

2520. ———, arr. *Early music: for the harp: for non-pedal and pedal harp*. [Arr. by Deborah Friou]. Los Angeles, Calif.: Woods Music and Books Publishing, c1988. 79 pp. [NP] CONTENTS: Au renouvel du tens; Hec dies; Chanson; Lai; Winder wie ist; Reis glorios; Alle, psallite cum luya-Alleluya; Nobilis humilis; Las, las, las, las par grand delit; Dehors lonc pre; Edi beo thu, hevene Quene; Chanson; 7 cantigas; Second estampie royal; Fourth estampie royal; Fifth estampie royal; Seventh estampie royal; English estampie; Dance royal; 2 ductias; Chansonnette; La rotta; Lament of Tristan; Douce dame jolie; Trotto; Chanconeta tedesca; Estampie; Ingrata; Not wolde y fayne summer this mak; My Lady Carey's dompe; Branle; The Kings's dance; Passamezzo antico; Pavanne d'Angleterre; Galliarde; Camen vernale; The western wynde.

2521. ———, arr. *Renaissance music: for the harp: for pedal and non-pedal harp*. Los Angeles, Calif.: Woods Music and Books Publishing, c1985. 32 pp. [NP] CONTENTS: Lord Willoughby's welcome home by John Dowland. Corranto. Toy by Francis Cutting. Bransle by Pierre Attaignant. Corranto. All in a garden green by John Playford. Nachtanz by Tielman Susato. Alman by Thomas Morley. Robin by John Munday. Fortune by William Byrd. It was a lover and his lass by Thomas Morley. Alman. Corranto. Nobody's gigge by Giles Farnaby. Lady Riche. Wolseys wilde; La volta; Variation of La volta by William Byrd. Greensleeves by Francis Cutting. The carman's whistle; Variation of The carman's whistle by William Byrd. Hartes ease by Anthony Holborne. Alman. The Earl of Essex galliard by John Dowland.

2522. ———, arr. *Scarborough Fair*. Arranged by Deborah Friou for non-pedal and pedal harp. Montrose, Calif.: Woods Music & Books Publishing, c1990. 2 pp. [NP]

2523. Froberger, Johann Jacob, 1616–1667. [Keyboard music. Selections; arr.] *Dances and toccata: for harp solo*. Arranged by Ze'ev W. Steinberg. Kiryat-Ono, Israel: Z. W. Steinberg, c1980. 7 pp. "Plainte . . . appears as the first movement of Suite XXX of the complete edition. Courante and Sarabande are taken from Suite XV. The Toccata is from 'Libro secondo di Toccate, Canzone, Ricercari. . . .'" CONTENTS: Plainte; Courante; Sarabande; Toccata.

2524. Froehlich, Mary Ann, 1955–, arr. *Celebration*. Arr. Mary Ann Froehlich. Ellensburg, Wash.: F.C. Publishing Co., 1990. 6 pp. "Inspired by 'Chant arabe' and 'Christmas day secrets,' Suzuki volume 1."

2525. ———, arr. *Collage for childhood*. Arr. Mary Ann Froehlich. Ellensburg, Wash.: F.C. Publishing Co., 1990. 9 pp.

2526. ———, arr. *Collage for Christmas*. Arr. Mary Ann Froehlich. Ellensburg, Wash.: F.C. Publishing Co., 1989–90. 2 v. (12, 10 pp.).

2527. ———, arr. *Collage for worship*. Ellensburg, Wash.: F.C. Publishing Co., 1989. 8 pp.

2528. ———, arr. *Collage for worship, vol.* 2. Ellensburg, Wash.: F.C. Publishing Co., 1991. 9 pp.

2529. Fulton, DeWayne, 1932–, arr. *Scarborough Fair.* Arranged for harp solo by De Wayne Fulton. [Santa Monica, Calif.]: Salvi Publications, c1980. 11 pp. (Salvi pop series)

2530. Gallenberg, Robert, Graf von, 1783–1839. *A favorite waltz by Count Gallenburg.* Arranged by Robert Nicholas Charles Bochsa for the harp. [Edited by Alice Lawson Aber]. San Anselmo, Calif.: A. Lawson, c1970. 3 pp.

2531. Gallès, José, 1761–1836. [Sonatas, piano, C minor; arr.] *Sonata: in c minor.* Trans. Nicanor Zabaleta. New York: Lyra Music Co., 1978. 6 pp.

2532. Galuppi, Baldassare, 1706–1785. [Sonatas, harpsichord, B♭ major. Allegro; arr.] *Presto.* Trascrizione per arpa di Alba Novella Schirinzi. Bologna: Edizioni Bongiovanni, 1960. 6 pp.

2533. ———. [Sonatas, harpsichord, B♭ major. Allegro; arr.] *Scherzo.* Adaptation for harp by Pearl Chertok. New York: Interstate Music, [197–?]. 5 pp.

2534. ———. [Sonatas, harpsichord, C minor. Larghetto e Allegro; arr.] *Larghetto (quasi fantasia) e Allegro della Sonata in do minore per cembalo.* Arr. per arpa da Mariagiulia Scimeca. Milan: G. Ricordi & Co., c1940. 7 pp.

2535. ———. [Sonatas, harpsichord, D major; arr.] *Sonata: in D.* Transcribed for harp by Lynne W. Palmer. Santa Monica, Calif.: Salvi Publications, c1981. 11 pp.

2536. Ganz, Wilhelm, 1833–1914. *Forget me not: song.* [Arr. by C. Oberthür]. London: Edwin Ashdown, n.d. 5 pp. Originally for voice and piano.

2537. Garner, Erroll, 1921–1977. *Misty.* Arranged for harp solo by Michael Amorosi. [Santa Monica, Calif.]: Salvi Harps, c1978. 3 pp. (Salvi pop series)

2538. ———. *Misty.* Arr. Penny Howk Beavers. Ellensburg, Wash.: F.C. Publishing Co., 1993. 4 pp.

2539. Gates, David. *If.* Arr. Stella Castellucci. [Santa Monica, Calif.]: Salvi Publications, 1978. 3 pp. (Salvi pop series)

2540. Gershwin, George, 1898–1937. *An American in Paris; and, Rhapsody in blue.* Arranged for harp solo by Eleanor Fell. [Santa Monica, Calif.]: Salvi Publications, c1978. 4 pp. (Salvi pop series) First work originally for orchestra; second originally for piano and orchestra.

2541. ———. [Girl crazy. Bidin' my time] *Bidin' my time: a study in jazz pedals.* Arranged for harp solo by Mimi Allen. [Santa Monica, Calif.]: Salvi Harps, [1980], c1930. 3 pp. (Salvi pop series)

2542. ———. [Girl crazy. Bidin' my time] *Bidin' my time.* Arranged by Ray Pool. San Mateo, Calif.: F.C. Publishing Co., c1988. 4 pp. (Popcycle series)

2543. ———. [Girl crazy. But not for me] *But not for me.* Arranged by Stella Castellucci. [Santa Monica, Calif.]: Salvi, c1978. 3 pp. (Salvi pop series)

2544. ———. [Girl crazy. But not for me] *But not for me.* Arranged by John B. Escosa. San Mateo, Calif.: F.C. Publishing Co., c1988. 2 pp. (Popcycle series)

2545. ———. [Girl crazy. Embraceable you] *Embraceable you.* Arranged for harp by Verlye Mills. [Santa Monica, Calif.]: Salvi Harps, c1978. 3 pp. (Salvi pop series)

2546. ———. [Girl crazy. Embraceable you] *Embraceable you.* Arranged by Michael Rado. San Mateo, Calif.: F.C. Publishing Co., c1988. 2 pp. (Popcycle series)

2547. ———. [Goldwyn follies. Our love is here to stay; arr.] *Our love is here to stay.* Arr. Paul Baker. Ellensburg, Wash.: F. C. Publishing Co., 1992. 3 pp.

2548. ———. [Lady, be good! Fascinatin' rhythm] *Fascinatin' rhythm.* Arranged by Ray Pool. San Mateo, Calif.: F.C. Publishing Co., c1988. 2 pp. (Popcycle series)

2549. ———. [Lady, be good! Man I love] *The man I love.* Arranged for harp solo by John Escosa. [Santa Monica, Calif.]: Salvi Publications, c1978. 3 pp. (Salvi pop series)

2550. ———. [Lady, be good! Oh, lady be good] *Lady be good.* Arranged for harp solo by Mimi Allen. [Santa Monica, Calif.]: Salvi Publications, [1980?], c1924. 4 pp. (Salvi pop series)

2551. ———. [Oh, Kay! Someone to watch over me] *Someone to watch over me.* Arr. Stella Castellucci. [Santa Monica, Calif.]: Salvi Publications, 1978. 2 pp. (Salvi pop series)

2552. ———. [Oh, Kay! Someone to watch over me] *Someone to watch over me.* Arranged by John B. Escosa. San Mateo, Calif.: F.C. Publishing Co., [1989], c1988. 2 pp. (Popcycle series)

2553. ———. [Porgy and Bess. Summertime] *Summertime.* Arranged for harp solo by Mimi Allen. [Santa Monica, Calif.]: Salvi Harps, c1981. 4 pp. (Salvi pop series)

2554. ———. [Porgy and Bess. Summertime] *Summertime.* Arr. Paul Baker. Ellensburg, Wash.: F.C. Publishing Co., 1993. 3 pp.

2555. ———. [Preludes, piano, no. 2, C# minor; arr.] *Prelude no. 2.* Arranged for harp solo by Mimi Allen. [Santa Monica, Calif.]: Salvi Publications, c1978. 3 pp. (Salvi pop series)

2556. ———. [Shall we dance? They can't take that away from me; arr.] *They can't take that away from me.* Arr. Paul Baker. Ellensburg, Wash.: F.C. Publishing Co., 1992. 3 pp.

2557. Gillmann, Kurt, 1889–1975, arr. [Stücke alterer Meister] *Zehn Stücke, alterer Meister.* Nach den Klavier-Originalen frei übertragen für die Harfe von Kurt Gillmann. Hannover: A. Nagel, 1932. 23 pp. Originally for keyboard instrument. CONTENTS: Allemande: erster Satz einer Suite by Gottfried Kirchhoff. Gigue: aus einer Suite in F-dur by Anon. Allemande und Menuett: aus einer Suite by Anon. Air und Double: aus einer Suite in C-moll by Joh. Mattheson. Allegro di molto; Solfeggietto by C.P.E. Bach. Aria: I. Satz einer Suite in B-dur by Anon. Gavotte: aus einer Suite; Gigue by Domenico Zipoli. Andantino by W.A. Mozart.

2558. ———, arr. [Stücke alterer Meister] *Ten pieces from the masters.* [Arr. by Kurt Gillmann]. New York: Lyra Music Co., 1992. 23 pp. Originally for keyboard instrument. CONTENTS: Allemande: erster Satz einer Suite by Gottfried Kirchhoff. Gigue: aus einer Suite in F-dur by Anon. Allemande und Menuett: aus einer Suite by Anon. Air und Double: aus einer Suite in C-moll by Joh. Mattheson. Allegro di molto; Solfeggietto by C.P.E. Bach. Aria: I. Satz einer Suite in B-dur by Anon. Gavotte: aus einer Suite; Gigue by Domenico Zipoli. Andantino by W.A. Mozart.

2559. Giornovichi, Giovanni Mane, 1745–1804. [Concertos, violin, orchestra, F major; arr.] *Sonata za harfu: [the celebrated concerto composed and performed by Mr. Giornovichi, arranged for the harp or piano forte with an accompaniment for the violin and violoncello ad libitum by S. Dussek (Sophia Corri Dussek)].* Preface by Rajka Dobronić-Mazzoni. S.l.: Azur Journal, 1993. 14 pp. For harp solo.

2560. Giovaninetti, Frank, 1958–, arr. [Chansons populaires françaises] *Vingt-deux chansons populaires françaises d'auteurs anonymes.* Harmonisées pour harpe celtique par Frank Giovaninetti. Paris: Gérard Billaudot, c1982. 12 pp. [NP] CONTENTS: Ne pleure pas Jeannette; J'ai descendu dans mon jardin; Je vais . . . où va la route; Miren a dit à son berger; Les gars de locminé; Partons tous deux; La laine des moutons; Les trois marins de Groix; Les scieurs de long; Vive la rose; Eh, qui marierons-nous?; C'n'est pas l'état des filles; Qu'il fait chaud; Cherchons une promise; Ah! que les femmes sont bêtes; Quand trois poules; Chant des corsaires; Que venez-vois chercher; Moi j'ai cinq sous; C'orphéoniste; Plainte des papetiers; A la claire fontaine.

2561. Glazunov, Aleksandr Konstantinovich, 1865–1936. [Raimonda. Selections; arr.] *Prelude et variation.* Arranged by Faith Carman. San Mateo, Calif.: F.C. Publishing Co., c1987. 4 pp. (Solo series: harp) Originally for orchestra.

2562. Gluck, Christoph Willibald, Ritter von, 1714–1787. [Armide. Gavotte;

arr.] *Gavotte: from Armide.* Arr. by Carlos Salzedo. New York: New Sounds in Modern Music, c1965. 5 pp.

2563. ———. [Iphigénie en Aulide. Gavotte; arr.] *Gavotte: from Iphigenia in Aulis.* Transcribed for harp from the original orchestra score by Carlos Salzedo. New York: Composer's Music, c1925. 5 pp.

2564. Godard, Benjamin, 1849–1895. [Jocelyn. Berceuse; arr.] *Jocelyn: célèbre berceuse.* [Arr. by G. Verdalle]. Paris: Choudens, n.d. 4 pp.

2565. Goldhar, Jeanette Pass, 1921–, arr. [Israeli love songs] *Three Israeli love songs.* [Arr. Jeanette Pass Goldhar]. [S.l.]: Edition Negen, 1982. 7 pp. CONTENTS: Erev ba = Evening is approaching; Dodi li = My beloved is mine; Erev shel shoshanim = Evening of scented roses.

2566. Goossens, Marie, 1894–1991, arr. [Folk tunes] *Eight folk tunes.* Arranged for harp by Marie Goossens. London: Chandos Music, c1981. 8 pp. CONTENTS: Swiss melody (Musical box); Over the sea to skye; Snowy breasted pearl; The lark in the clear air; David of the white rock; Japanese lullaby; Wiegenlied (Cradle song); Bourée by Henry Purcell.

2567. ———, arr. *Kaleidoscope: folk tune from many lands.* Arranged for harp by Marie Goossens. London: Chandos Music, c1981. 2 v. CONTENTS: Vol.1. Evening song; Helena; Make a bargain pretty sweetheart; Swiss melody (Musical box); Little Katie; Madame Wang.
Vol.2. The minstrel of Sorrento; A Spanish dance; The ash grove; Finnish song; Farewell, darling Maggie; The lark in the clear air.

2568. ———, arr. [Tunes for celtic harp] *Fourteen tunes for celtic harp.* Arranged by Marie Goossens. London: Chandos Music, c1969. 2 v. [NP] CONTENTS: Bk.1. Adieu, fair love; Begone, dull care; Mme. Wang; A Basque lullaby; Greece; When the little children sleep by Carl Reinecke; Spring song.
Bk.2. Fais do do; Swabian song; Believe me if all those endearing young charms; Cradle song by Brahms; Old Dutch ballad; Minuet, My lady's garland; O, give me a cot.

2569. Gore, Michael, 1951–. [Fame. Fame] *Fame.* Arranged by Katherine Honey. San Mateo, Calif.: F.C. Publishing Co., [1988], c1980. 3 pp. (Popcycle series)

2570. Gounod, Charles, 1818–1893. *Au printemps: mélodie de Charles Gounod.* Transcription pour harpe par Gabriel Verdalle. Paris: Choudens, n.d. 3 pp. Originally for voice and piano.

2571. ———. [Au printemps; arr.] *Spring song.* Trans. by H. Trneček; edited by De Wayne Fulton. Marina Del Rey, Calif.: Safari, c1989. 11 pp. Originally for voice and piano.

2572. ———. [Ave Maria (Instrumental version); arr.] *Ave Maria: méditation sur le premier prelude de J. S. Bach.* [Arr. by C. Oberthür]. London: Schott & Co., n.d. 5 pp.

2573. ———. [Ave Maria (Instrumental version); arr.] *Méditation: sur le premier prélude de S. Bach.* [Arr. by C. Oberthür]. Mainz: B. Schott's Söhne, n.d. 5 pp.

2574. ———. [Ave Maria (Instrumental version); arr.] *Ave Maria: meditation on the First prelude of J. S. Bach.* Arr. for harp by P. Schlomovitz. [Palo Alto, Calif.]: Harpress of California, c1989. 3 pp.

2575. ———. [Ave Maria (Instrumental version); arr.] *Ave Maria.* Arr. Aristid von Würtzler. Ellensburg, Wash.: F.C. Publishing Co., 1990. 5 pp.

2576. ———. [Ciel a visité la terre; arr.] *Le ciel a visité la terre: cantique.* [Arr. by G. Verdalle]. Paris: Choudens, n.d. 3 pp. Originally for voice and piano.

2577. ———. [Philémon et Baucis. Introduction pastorale; arr.] *Philémon et Baucis: opéra-comique en 3 actes de Ch. Gounod: Introduction pastorale.* Transcription pour harpe par Gabriel Verdalle. Paris: Choudens, [19—]. 4 pp. (Nouvelle collection pour harpe seule par Gabriel Verdalle, 12)

2578. ———. [Roméo et Juliette. Selections; arr.] *Roméo et Juliette: opéra en 5 actes.* Transcription pour harpe par Gabriel Verdalle. Paris: Choudens, [19—]. 4 pp. CONTENTS: A. Entr'acte (2e acte); B. Le sommeil de Juliette (5e acte).

2579. Govea, Wenonah M., 1924–. *Harp and holly: ancient carols in modern dress.* Arranged by W. M. Govea. Mission San Jose, Calif.: Coach Publications, 1988–. Chiefly medleys. CONTENTS: Vol.1. Carols for Christmas; Christmas bells; Noel française; O come little children; Shepherd carols.

2580. ———. [Modern meditation, no. 1] *Modern meditation.* Arranged by W. M. Govea. [Mission San José, Calif.: Coach Publications], c1987. 3 pp. (Sacred harp, MM 1)

2581. ———. [Modern meditation, no. 2] *Modern meditation 2.* Arranged by W. M. Govea. Mission San Jose, Calif.: Coach Publications, 1987. 3 pp. (Sacred harp) Medley on children's hymns, arr. for harp. Based on Jesus loves me and Jesus loves the little children.

2582. ———. [Modern meditation, no. 3] *Modern meditation 3.* Arranged by W. M. Govea. Mission San Jose, Calif.: Coach Publications, 1991. 3 pp. (Sacred harp)

2583. ———. [Modern meditation, no. 4] *Modern meditation 4.* Arranged by W. M. Govea. Mission San Jose, Calif.: Coach Publications, 1991. 4 pp. (Sacred harp)

2584. ———. *Sacred harp.* Arranged by W. M. Govea. Mission San Jose, Calif.: Coach Publications, c1987. 3 v. CONTENTS: Vol.1. Balm in Gilead;

Amazing grace; How firm a foundation.

Vol.2. Jesus thou divine companion; Hamburg; Nettleton.

Vol.3. Can you count the stars; Wayfaring stranger; Every time I feel the spirit.

Vol.4. There is a happy land; Jesus walked the lonesome valley; Jerusalem, my happy home; Let us break bread together; What wondrous love is this.

2585. Granados, Enrique, 1867–1916. [Danzas españolas. No. 2; arr.] *Danza española no. 2.* Arr. Nicanor Zabaleta. Madrid: Union Musical Española, 1989. 8 pp. Originally for piano.

2586. ———. [Danzas españolas. No. 4; arr.] *Danza española no. 4: Villanesca.* Adaptacion para arpa: Nicanor Zabaleta. Madrid: Union Musical Española, c1989. 9 pp.

2587. ———. [Danzas españolas. No. 5; arr.] *Danza española no. 5.* Arr. Nicanor Zabaleta. Madrid: Union Musical Española, 1989. 7 pp. Originally for piano.

2588. ———. [Danzas españolas. No. 7; arr.] *Danza española no. 7.* Transcripcion para arpa por Ginevra Bruno. Madrid: Union Musical Española, c1927. 5 pp. Originally for piano.

2589. ———. *Valses poeticos.* Arreglo para arpa: Nicanor Zabaleta. Madrid: Union Musical Ediciones, 1990. 27 pp. Originally for piano.

2590. Grandjany, Marcel, 1891–1975, arr. *Chanson de Guillot Martin: air de Clément Marot (1495–1544).* Harmonisation de A. Périlhou. Paris: Heugel, c1958. 4 pp.

2591. ———, arr. *The Kerry dance.* Arranged for harp by Marcel Grandjany. [Santa Monica, Calif.]: Salvi Publications, c1967. 6 pp.

2592. ———, arr. *Music for the harp.* [Free transcription for harp by] Marcel Grandjany. New York: Associated Music Publishers, Inc., c1949. 5 v. CONTENTS: Pavane et bransles from Le trésor d'Orphée by Anthoine Francisque. Aria and rigaudon by Gottfried Kirchoff. Prelude and toccata. Saraband by Handel. The king's hunt by John Bull.

2593. ———, arr. [Pièces classiques] *Six pièces classiques.* Transcrites pour harpe par Marcel Grandjany. Paris: Durand; Bryn Mawr, Pa.: T. Presser, c1931. 6 v. CONTENTS: Largo: de la 5e sonate de violon by J.S. Bach. Allemande: [de] Partita en si bémol by J. S. Bach. Rondeau: [de] Partita en ut mineur by J. S. Bach. Tempo di minuetto: [de] Partita en sol by J. S. Bach. Les tourbillons: rondeau by J.-Ph. Rameau. Le moucheron: gigue by F. Couperin.

2594. ———. [Pièces, piano. No. 1; arr.] *Arabesque: pour harpe: no. 1 des Trois pièces pour le piano.* Paris: A. Durand, c1912. 4 pp.

2595. ———, arr. *Short pieces from the masters: easy arrangements for harp without pedals.* [Arr. by Marcel Grandjany]. New York: Carl Fischer, Inc., 1969. 7 pp. [NP] CONTENTS: Lullaby by Franz Schubert. Dance from Alceste by C. W. Gluck. Rondo by E. Pässler.

2596. ———, arr. *Transcriptions classiques: for harp.* New York: E. B. Marks Music Corp., c1943. 13 pp. CONTENTS: Toccata by J. B. Loeillet. Allemande by J. S. Bach. Allegretto by J. B. Sammartini. La commère by François Couperin.

2597. ———, arr. *Transcriptions classiques: for harp.* New York: Lyra Music Co., [197-?]. 13 pp. CONTENTS: See 2596.

2598. ———, arr. [Transcriptions classiques. Selections] *Transcriptions classiques: pour harpe: 1er recueil.* [Arr.] Marcel Grandjany. Paris: Salabert, 1942. 8 pp. CONTENTS: Toccata by J. B. Loeillet. Allemande by J. S. Bach.

Grandjany, Marcel, 1891–1975, and Weidensaul, Jane B., 1935–. *First-grade pieces for harp: 18 solos for harp (or harp without pedals).* See 36.

2599. Graziani, Maria Pia, arr. *Trascrizioni classiche: per arpa.* [Arr. by] M. Pia Graziani. Milan: Carisch, c1978. 9 pp. CONTENTS: Minuet (from the VI French suite, BWV 817) by J. S. Bach. Gavotte (from the V French suite, BWV 816) by J. S. Bach. Allegro (from the "collection" of pieces for keyboard) by B. Galuppi. Scherzo (Songs, no. 19, K. 598) by W. A. Mozart. Little rondo (from small practical course for piano).

2600. Grazioli, Giovanni Battista, 1755–ca. 1820. *Moderato.* Leipzig: Jul. Heinr. Zimmermann, c1914. 5 pp.

2601. *Great harp standards.* Secaucus, N.J.: Warner Brothers Publications, c1988. 40 pp. CONTENTS: Princess Leia's theme by John Williams, arr. Katherine Honey. Fascinating rhythm by George Gershwin, arr. Ray Pool. Lullaby of birdland by George Shearing, arr. Ray Pool. But not for me by George Gershwin, arr. John B. Escosa. Satin doll by Duke Ellington, arr. Eleanor Fell. Embraceable you by George Gershwin, arr. Michael Rado. Bidin' my time by George Gershwin, arr. Ray Pool. Nadia's theme (The young and the restless) by Barry DeVorzon and Perry Botkin, Jr., arr. Lynne Wainwright Palmer. I get a kick out of you by Cole Porter, arr. Ray Pool. Night and day by Cole Porter, arr. Lynne Wainwright Palmer. You're gonna hear from me by André Previn, arr. Jack Nebergall.

2602. Grechaninov, Aleksandr Tikhonovich, 1864–1956. [Stücke, harp, op. 168. No. 5] *Remembrance of the ball = Souvenir du ball, op. 168, no. 5: for harp solo or duet.* Edited and arr. by Marcel Grandjany. New York: Piedmont Music, 1963. 2 parts.

2603. Green, Ray, 1908–. [Sonatinas, piano. Cowboy sonatina; arr.] *Cowboy sonatina: for harp solo.* Arr. for harp solo by Edward Vito. New York:

American Music Edition, c1956. 4 pp. (Harp teacher's series) Originally for piano.

2604. ———. [Sonatinas, piano. March sonatina, no. 1; arr.] *March sonatina no. 1: for harp solo.* Arr. for harp solo by Edward Vito. New York: American Music Edition, c1956. 2 pp. (Harp teacher's series) Originally for piano.

2605. ———. [Sonatinas, piano. Square dance sonatina; arr.] *Square dance sonatina: for harp solo.* Arr. for harp solo by Edward Vito. New York: American Music Edition, c1956. 3 pp. (Harp teacher's series) Originally for piano.

2606. Greselin, Caterina, arr. [Pezzi clavicembalistici] *12 pezzi clavicembalistici: trascritti per arpa e disposti in ordine progressivo di difficolta ad uso dei conservatori.* [Padua: G. Zanibon, c1970]. 32 pp. CONTENTS: Minuetto in sol magg.; Minuetto in sol magg.; Minuetto in sol min. by J. S. Bach. Sonata n. 18 in si-bemolle magg.; Sonata n. 17 in re min.; Sonata n. 62 in si-bemolle magg.; Sonata n. 53 in sol magg.; Sonata n. 27 in si-bemolle magg. by D. Cimarosa. Sonata in fa min. by Jose Galles. Sonata in la magg. by Giuseppe de Rossi. Corrente (dalla Va suite francese) by J. S. Bach. Giga by Karl Heinrich Graun.

2607. Gretry, André Ernest Modeste, 1741–1813. [Richard Coeur-de-Lion. Selections; arr.] *Airs favoris de Richard Coeur de Lion: extrait simplifié de la fantaisie, oeuvre 39.* Arr. pour la harpe par Vernier. Paris: Naderman, [181–?]. 9 pp.

2608. Grieg, Edvard, 1843–1907. [Concerto, piano, orchestra, op. 16, A minor. Selections; arr.] *Grieg concerto theme.* Arranged by Katherine Honey. San Mateo, Calif.: F.C. Publishing Co., c1989. 4 pp. (Popcycle series)

2609. Groot, Cor de, 1914–. *Cloches dan le matin: pour harpe (1972).* Amsterdam: Donemus, c1974. 3 pp. Originally for piano solo.

2610. Gross, Walter, 1909–1967. *Tenderly.* Arranged by Jack Nebergall. San Mateo, Calif.: F.C. Publishing Co., [1989], c1946. 3 pp. (Popcycle series)

2611. Grosso, Emma Gramaglia, arr. *Dal liuto all'arpa: nove pezzi: per arpa.* Elaborazione di Emma Gramaglia Grosso. Milan: G. Ricordi, c1958. 12 pp. CONTENTS: O bella più che viola; Galliarda Vulgo dolorata by Pomponii Bononiensis; Ricercare (15) by Francesco da Milano. Tanto zentil me mostri tua figura; Napolitana by Giulio Abondante. Brando gentile by Cesare Negri. La sola grazia che 'l mio cor desia; Campanae parisienses by G. B. Besard. Tant que vivrai by D. Bianchini.

2612. Gruber, Franz Xaver, 1787–1863. [Stille Nacht, heilige Nacht; arr.] *Silent night.* Washington, D.C.: William Truesdale Cameron, n.d. 1 p. Includes version for non-pedal harp (2 p.) [NP]

2613. ———. [Stille Nacht, heilige Nacht; arr.] *Silent night, holy night.* Arranged by Maudetta Martin Joseph. Boston, Mass.: Boston Music Co., c1925. 3 pp.

2614. ———. [Stille Nacht, heilige Nacht; arr.] *Silent night, holy night.* Free transcription for harp by Marcel Grandjany. Philadelphia: Elkan-Vogel, c1930. 5 pp.

2615. ———. [Stille Nacht, heilige Nacht; arr.] *Silent night.* [Arr.] for harp [by] May Hogan Cambern. [New York]: Michael Cambern, c1966. 2 pp. (From the notebook of May Hogan Cambern)

2616. ———. [Stille Nacht, heilige Nacht; arr.] *Silent night.* Arranged for pedal or non-pedal harp by Lorraine Byman. New York: Lorraine Byman, c1972. 4 pp. [NP]

2617. ———. [Stille Nacht, heilige Nacht; arr.] *Silent night: folk harp solo or duet.* Arranged by Maryjean Z. Lucchetti. Edmonds, Wash.: Paradise Music, c1987. Score 2 pp. and 2 parts. [NP]

2618. ———. [Stille Nacht, heilige Nacht; arr.] *Silent night.* Arranged by John B. Escosa. San Mateo, Calif.: F.C. Publishing Co., c1988. 2 pp. (Popcycle series)

2619. Guglielmo, Pasquale D., 1810–1872. *The lover and the bird: ballad.* [Arr. by C. Oberthür]. London: Edwin Ashdown, n.d. 7 pp.

2620. Gwynn Williams, W. S. (William Sidney), 1896–, arr. *Ceinciau telyn cymru: Harp tunes of Wales.* Selected, edited and arranged by W. S. Gwynn Williams. Penygroes, Gwynedd: Cwmni Cyhoeddi Gwynn, 1962. 50 pp.

2621. Haag, Gudrun, 1935–, arr. *Lieder und Spielmusik zur Weihnacht: für die Volksharfe.* Gesetzt von Gudrun Haag, mit Beiträgen von Berta Höller, Maria Willroider-Müller und Herbert Baumann. Munich: Musikverlag Josef Preissler, c1980. 25 pp. CONTENTS: Wachet auf, ihr Menschenkinder; Menuett; Stader Ländler; Leise rieselt der Schnee; Stille Nacht; Heiligste Nacht; Schneeflöckchen; Es ist ein Ros' entsprungen; Mariä Wiegenlied; Wiegenlied der Fischbachauerinnen; Dort oben auf dem Berge; Ihr Kinderlein, kommet; Orgellandler; Süsser die Glocken nie klingen; Präludium; Auf dem Berge, da wehet der Wind; Still, still, still; Was tut denn der Ochs im Krippei drin; Wiegenlied; Deine Wangerln san rosenrot; Präludium; Es wird scho glei dumpa; O du fröhliche.

2622. Hackh, Otto, 1852–1917. *Rose d'automne: romance.* [Arr. by J. Snoer]. Leipzig: Aug. Cranz, n.d. 3 pp. Originally for piano.

2623. Halffter, Rodolfo, 1900–1987. [Piezas breves; arr.] *Tres piezas breves, op. 13a.* Rev. y dig. Ma. Rosa Calvo-Manzano. Madrid: Union Musical Española, c1973. 12 pp. Pieces from composer's piano work *Homenaje a Antonio Machado,* op. 13.

2624. Hamlisch, Marvin, 1944–. [Ice castles. Through the eyes of love] *Through the eyes of love: from the film Ice castles.* Arranged by Penny Howk Beavers. [San Mateo, Calif.]: F.C. Publishing Co., [1988], c1978. 4 pp. (Popcycle series)

2625. Handel, George Frideric, 1685–1759. [Allegro, il Penseroso ed il Moderato. Let me wander not unseen; arr.] *Siciliana from L'Allegro (1740)*. Arr. Ellis Schuman. Ellensburg, Wash.: F.C. Publishing Co., 1992. 2 pp.

2626. ———. [Berenice. Minuet; arr.] *Minuet: from Berenice (1737)*. Arranged for harp solo by Ellis Schuman. New York: Lyra Music Co., c1981. 2 pp.

2627. ———. [Chaconnes, harpsichord, C major. Selections; arr.] *Chaconne with variations*. Adapted for harp by Pearl Chertok. New York: Interstate Music, n.d. 4 pp.

2628. ———. [Chaconnes, harpsichord, C major. Selections; arr.] *Chaconne: en ut majeur*. Transcrit pour la harpe par Henrik Boye. Paris: H. Lemoine, c1950. 8 pp. Harp transcription of excerpts from a harpsichord piece originally with 49 variations. Cf. A. Craig Bell,*Chronological catalogue of Handel's works* (Greenock [Renfrewshire]: Grain-Aig Press, 1969), 175, no. 67.

2629. ———. [Concertos, organ, orchestra, op. 4. No. 5; arr.] *Concerto: in F major, op. 4, no. 5*. Transcribed for harp, with original cadenza by Aristid von Wurtzler. Dobbs Ferry, N.Y.: General Music Pub. Co., c1968. 11 pp.

2630. ———. [Concertos, organ, orchestra, op. 4. No. 6; arr.] *Concerto: en si bémol*. Transcription pour harpe seule et cadence originale de Marcel Grandjany. Paris: Durand, c1933. 16 pp. For harp unaccompanied.

2631. ———. [Concertos, organ, orchestra, op. 4. No. 6; arr.] *Concerto: in B♭*. Transcribed for harp solo or to be played with orchestral acc., with an original cadenza by Carlos Salzedo. New York: G. Schirmer, 1966. 19 pp. For harp solo or with orchestra.

2632. ———. [Concertos, organ, orchestra, op. 4. No. 6; arr.] *Concerto: B-Dur, op. 4, Nr. 6*. [Realisation von] Paul Angerer. Wien: Doblinger, c1980. 1 part (11 pp.). (Diletto musicale, 839) For harp; originally for harp with orchestra.

2633. ———. [Concertos, organ, orchestra, op. 4. No. 6; arr.] *Concerto: en si bémol: pour harpe celtique et orchestre*. Arrangement Odette Le Dentu. Paris: Gérard Billaudot, c1982. 8 pp. For harp solo or with orchestra. [NP]

2634. ———. [Concertos, organ, orchestra, op. 4. No. 6; arr.] *Concerto, op. 4/6*. Arr. for harp solo by Pierre Augé. [Bonn]: Simrock, 1986. 11 pp. For harp unaccompanied.

2635. ———. *Joy to the world*. Arr. Wm. T. Cameron. Washington, D.C.: William Truesdale Cameron, n.d. 1 p. [NP]

2636. ———. [Musical clock music. Selections; arr.] *Little suite for a musical clock*. Arranged for non-pedal or pedal harp by Ellis Schuman. Ellensburg, Wash.: F.C. Publishing Co., c1990. 9 pp. (Solo series: harp) [NP] CONTENTS: Prelude; Menuet; Air; Gigue.

2637. ———. [Musical clock music. Selections; arr.] *Second little suite for a musical clock*. Arr. Ellis Schuman. Ellensburg, Wash.: F.C. Publishing Co., 1993. 13 pp.

2638. ———. [Saul. Act 1. Symphony; arr.] *David's harp solo: from Handel's oratorio Saul.* Realized by John Marson. London: Salvi International, n.d. 2 pp.

2639. ———. [Saul. Sinfonie pour les carillons; arr.] *Two sinfonias from Saul (1738).* Arranged and realized by Ellis Schuman. Ellensburg, Wash.: F.C. Publishing Co., c1990. 9 pp. (Solo series: harp) CONTENTS: Carillon sinfonia; David's harp interlude (on the aria Oh Lord whose mercies numberless).

2640. ———. [Scipione. Marche; arr.] *Triumphal march from Scipione.* Arr. Ellis Schuman. Ellensburg, Wash.: F.C. Publishing Co., 1991. 2 pp.

2641. ———. [Selections; arr.] *Colección de obras para arpa de G. F. Haendel (1685–1759).* Revisión, transcripción, y realización de los ornamentos: María Rosa Calvo-Manzano. Madrid: Editorial Apuerto, 1986. 72 pp. CONTENTS: El herrero armonioso: tema con variaciones; Allegro; Preludio: allegro; Arpegio: preludio; Preludio en re menor; Tema con variaciones; Chacona en do mayor: con XVII variaciones; Chacona en sol mayor: con XXI variaciones; Pasacalle.

2642. ———. [Semele. Ouverture. Gavotte; arr.] *Gavotte from Semele.* Arr. Ellis Schuman. Ellensburg, Wash.: F.C. Publishing Co., 1991. 5 pp. Originally for string orchestra.

2643. ———. [Semele. Where'er you walk; arr.] *Where'er you walk from Semele.* Arr. Darhon Rees-Rohrbacher. Buffalo, N.Y.: Dragonflower Music, 1990. 3 pp. [NP]

2644. ———. [Serse. Ombra mai fù; arr.] *Largo.* Transcribed for harp by Carlos Salzedo. New York: Carl Fischer, Inc., c1923. 3 pp.

2645. ———. [Serse. Ombra mai fù; arr.] *Largo: from the opera Xerxes.* Transcribed by Daniel Burton. San Diego, Calif.: Jubal Press, c1986. 4 pp. (Jubal harp series)

2646. ———. [Serse. Ombra mai fù; arr.] *Ombra mai fu (Largo) from Serse.* Arr. Darhon Rees-Rohrbacher. Buffalo, N.Y.: Dragonflower Music, 1990. 3 pp. [NP]

2647. ———. [Suites, harpsichord, HWV 430, E major. Air con variazioni; arr.] *The harmonious blacksmith.* [Arr. by J. Thomas]. London: Edwin Ashdown, n.d. 7 pp.

2648. ———. [Suites, harpsichord, HWV 430, E major. Air con variazioni; arr.] *The harmonious blacksmith: harp solo.* Transcribed by Carlos Salzedo. New York: Lyra Music Co., [19—]. 7 pp.

2649. ———. [Suites, harpsichord, HWV 430, E major. Air con variazioni; arr.] *The harmonious blacksmith: air with variations.* Transcribed for harp by Carlos Salzedo (1931). Philadelphia, Pa.: Elkan-Vogel, c1936. 7 pp.

2650. ———. [Suites, harpsichord, HWV 430, E major. Air con variazioni; arr.] *The harmonious blacksmith: air with variations.* Transcribed for harp by Carlos Salzedo (1931) (rev. 1960). New York: C. Colin, c1965. 7 pp.

2651. ———. [Suites, harpsichord, HWV 430, E major. Passacaille; arr.] *Passacaille: pour la harpe.* [Arr.] par Tiny Béon. Paris: Editions Musicales Alphonse Leduc, c1951. 4 pp.

2652. ———. [Suites, harpsichord, HWV 431, F# minor. Gigue; arr.] *Gigue.* Arranged for the harp by John Thomas. Abergavenny, Gwent, Wales: Adlais, c1979. 5 pp.

2653. ———. [Suites, harpsichord, HWV 432, G minor. Passacaille; arr.] *Passacaglia.* Bearbeitet von L. M. Magistretti. Frankfurt: Zimmermann, c1914. 5 pp. (Des Harfenisten Konzert-Programm, Nr. 6)

2654. ———. [Suites, harpsichord, HWV 437, D minor. Sarabande; arr.] *Sarabande: with variations.* Adapted for harp by Pearl Chertok. New York: Interstate Music, n.d. 3 pp.

2655. ———. [Suites, harpsichord, HWV 441, G major. Corante; arr.] *Courante.* Bearbeitet von L. M. Magistretti. Frankfurt: Zimmermann, c1914. 5 pp. (Des Harfenisten Konzert-Programm, Nr. 5)

2656. ———. [Suites, harpsichord, HWV 445, C minor. Prelude; arr.] *Prelude and Toccata.* Free transcription for harp; "Arpeggiando" ad libitum written by Marcel Grandjany. New York: Associated Music Publishers, Inc., c1949. Score 11 pp. Both works originally for harpsichord.

2657. Hardy, Hagood, 1937–. *The homecoming.* Arranged by Penny Howk Beavers. Ellensburg, Wash.: F.C. Publishing Co., c1975. 4 pp. (Popcycle series)

2658. Harline, Leigh, 1907–1969. [Pinocchio. When you wish upon a star] *When you wish upon a star.* Arranged by Michael Rado. Ellensburg, Wash.: F.C. Publishing Co., [1988], c1938. 3 pp. (Popcycle series)

Harris, Ruth Berman, 1916–. *Miniatures.* See 929.

2659. Hass, Adolf, arr. *Russian folk melody: song of the boatmen of Volga.* [Transcription for harp solo by Adolf Hass]. New York, N.Y.: International Music, c1922. 7 pp.

2660. Haydn, Joseph, 1732–1809. [Musical clock music. Selections; arr.] *Twelve musical clock pieces: for the non-pedal harp.* [Arr. by] Wendel Diebel. New York: Lyra Music Co., 1974. 14 pp. Originally for mechanical flute-clock. [NP]

2661. ———. [Sonatas, piano, H. XVI, 33, D major. Menuet; arr.] *Minuetto*

(Sonate en sol maj. no. 33). [Arr. by H. Renié]. Paris: Gay & Tenton, c1928. 3 pp. Originally for piano.

2662. ———. [Sonatas, piano, H. XVI, 34, E minor; arr.] *Sonate: for harp.* New York: C. Colin, c1966. 10 pp.

2663. ———. [Sonatas, piano, H. XVI, 34, E minor; arr.] *Sonata: en mi menor: para arpa.* Transcripción de Ma. Rosa Calvo-Manzano. Madrid: Unión Musical Española, 1985. 21 pp.

2664. ———. [Variations, piano, H. XVII, 5, C major; arr.] *Theme and variations.* Transcribed for the harp by Carlos Salzedo. [New York]: Composers' Music Corp., c1923. 7 pp.

2665. ———. [Variations, piano, H. XVII, 5, C major; arr.] *Theme and variations.* Arranged by Carlos Salzedo. New York: Carl Fischer, Inc., c1924. Score 7 pp. (Original solos and arrangements for harp)

2666. Haymes, Bob, 1924–. *That's all.* Arranged by Penny Howk Beavers. San Mateo, Calif.: F.C. Publishing Co., c1988. 4 pp. (Popcycle series)

2667. Heller, Stephen, 1813–1888. [Etudes, piano. Selections; arr.] *Six etudes.* Transcrites pour la harpe par Alph. Hasselmans. Paris: Henry Lemoine et Cie., n.d. 13 pp. Originally for piano. CONTENTS: No. 1, op. 45, no. 1; No. 2: Feuillet d'album, op. 16, no. 15; No. 3, op. 46, no. 12; No. 4, op. 46, no. 18; No. 5, op. 47, no. 16; No. 6, op. 45, no. 2.

2668. Henderson, Ray, 1896–1971. *Bye, bye blackbird.* Arranged by Eleanor Fell. San Mateo, Calif.: F.C. Publishing Co., c1989. 4 pp. (Popcycle series)

2669. Henson-Conant, Deborah, 1953–, arr. *Danny boy.* Arranged by Deborah Henson-Conant. San Mateo, Calif.: F.C. Publishing Co., c1988. 3 pp. (Popcycle series)

2670. Hill, Mildred J., 1859–1916. *Happy birthday.* Arr. Deborah Henson-Conant. [Ellensburg, Wash.]: F.C. Publishing Co., 1988. 1 p.

2671. Hochbrucker, Christian, 1733–ca. 1799. [Sonatas, harp, op. 1, no. 6, G major. Allegro; arr.] *Allegro: extrait de la Sonate no. 6.* Adaptation et doigtés pour la harpe celtique par Annie Challan. Paris: Editions Aug. Zurfluh, c1989. 4 pp. [NP]

2672. Hopkins, John Henry, 1820–1891. *We three kings of orient are.* Arr. by Wm. T. Cameron. Washington, D.C.: William Truesdale Cameron, n.d. 1 p. [NP]

2673. Hujsak, Joy, 1924–, arr. [Communion hymns] *Four communion hymns.* Arranged for harp by Joy Hujsak. La Jolla, Calif.: Mina-Helwig Publishing Co., c1981. 11 pp. CONTENTS: When I survey the wondrous cross; Break thou the bread of life; Beneath the cross of Jesus; Jesus, thou joy of loving hearts.

2674. ———, arr. *Fairest Lord Jesus: Silesian folk melody*. Arr. by Joy Hujsak. [La Jolla, Calif.: Mina-Helwig Pub. Co.], c1990. 9 pp.

2675. Hummel, Johann Nepomuk, 1778–1837. *Selections: from the works of Hummel*. Arr. for the harp by N. C. Bochsa. London: Chappell, [182–?]. v.

2676. Humperdinck, Engelbert, 1854–1921. [Hansel und Gretel. Abends will ich schlafen gehn; arr.] *Evening prayer: from the opera Hansel und Gretel*. Arranged by Daniel Burton. San Diego, Calif.: Jubal Press, c1986. 4 pp. (Jubal harp series)

2677. Hupfeld, Herman, 1894–1951. [Casablanca. As time goes by; arr.] *As time goes by*. Arr. Stella Castellucci. [Santa Monica, Calif.]: Salvi Publications, 1978. 3 pp. (Salvi pop series) Used in the film Casablanca; previously an additional song from the musical Everybody's welcome.

2678. Inglefield, Ruth K., arr. *Branle et galliarde*. Trans. from the Jobin lutebook, 1573. S.l.: Ruth K. Inglefield, c1973. 2 pp.

2679. ———, arr. *Danz proficiat*. Trans. from the Jobin lutebook, 1573 [by Ruth K. Inglefield]. [Santa Monica, Calif.]: Salvi Publications, c1972. 3 pp. Originally for lute.

2680. ———, arr. *Suite brunette*. Transcribed from the Jobin lutebook of 1573 by Ruth K. Inglefield. Santa Monica, Calif.: Salvi Publications, c1972. 4 pp. For troubadour or pedal harp. [NP] CONTENTS: Galliarde brunette; Branle; Galliarde.

2681. Inglefield, Ruth K., and Roush, Dean K., eds. *Plaisir d'amour: a wedding album: for harp*. Editors, Ruth K. Inglefield, Dean K. Roush. [Santa Monica, Calif.]: Salvi Publications, c1978. 29 pp. CONTENTS: Plaisir d'amour by Giovanni Martini. Träumerei by Robert Schumann. Liebestraum by Franz Liszt. Because by Guy d'Hardelot. Ich liebe dich by Edvard Grieg. My heart at thy sweet voice by C. Saint-Saens. I love you truly by Carrie Jacobs Bond. Meditation from Thaïs by Jules Massenet. O promise me by R. de Koven. Bridal chorus from Lohengrin by Richard Wagner.

2682. Jacobs-Bond, Carrie, 1862–1946. [Songs as unpretentious as the wild rose. I love you truly; arr.] *I love you truly: harp solo*. Chicago, Ill.: Lyon & Healy Harps, n.d. 3 pp. Originally for voice and piano.

2683. Jaeger, Patricia, arr. *Baroque sampler: for folk harp*. Arranged by Patricia Jaeger. Edmonds, Wash.: Paradise Music, c1988. 8 pp. [NP] CONTENTS: Sheep may safely graze (Theme from Birthday cantata) by J. S. Bach. Allegretto by C.P.E. Bach. Rondeau (Theme from Masterpiece theater) by Mouret. Rigaudon by Daquin. Trumpet tune by Purcell [i.e., J. Clarke].

2684. ———, arr. *Maid from the parish of Penderyn: a Welsh tune*. Arranged by Patricia Jaeger for folk harp & melody instrument [or] folk harp solo [or] folk harp duet. Edmonds, Wash.: Paradise Music, c1987. Score 2 pp. and 2 parts. [NP]

2685. Jarre, Maurice, 1924–. [Dead poets society. Main theme] *Theme from Dead poets society.* Arranged for harp by Sylvia Woods. Montrose, Calif.: Woods Music & Books, Inc., c1991. 4 pp.

2686. ———. [Doctor Zhivago. Lara's theme] *Lara's theme.* Arranged by Katherine Honey. Ellensburg, Wash.: F.C. Publishing Co., c1965. 3 pp. (Popcycle series)

2687. Jensen, Adolf, 1837–1879. [Gesänge aus dem Spanischen Lieder-buch. Murmelndes Luftchen; arr.] *Murmelndes Luftchen = Venticico murmur-ador = Murmuring breezes = Air murmurante, op. 21, no. 4.* [Arr. by E. Schuëcker]. Leipzig: F. Schuberth, c1895. 7 pp. Originally for voice and piano.

2688. John, Patricia, 1916–, arr. *For the troubadour: 16th century dances.* Adapted for the non-pedal harp by Patricia John. Houston, Tex.: Pantile Press, c1986. 16 leaves. [NP] CONTENTS: Branle, l'espoir que j'ay; Branle (gay); Branle; Gaillarde; Branle (gay): Mari je songeois l'autre jour; 3 branles; 2 tourdions.

2689. ———, arr. *For the troubadour: (the classics).* Adapted for the non-pedal harp by Patricia John. [Houston, Tex.]: The Pantile Press, [198–?]. 10 pp. (Notebook series) Originally for keyboard instrument? [NP] CON-TENTS: Carnival (no. 3 from Les fastes de la grande et ancienne Mxnxstrxndxsx) by François Couperin. Prelude; Trumpet piece; Song tune by Henry Purcell. Fanfare minuet by William Duncombe. Country waltz by Joseph Haydn. Minuet by Leopold Mozart. Austrian folk theme; Etude; Austrian folk theme by Carl Czerny.

2690. Joplin, Scott, 1868–1917. [Entertainer; arr.] *The entertainer.* Arranged by Schlomovitz. [Palo Alto, Calif.]: Harpress of California, c1981. 3 pp. (Phyllis Schlomovitz harp transcriptions) Originally for piano.

2691. ———. [Entertainer; arr.] *The entertainer: ragtime for folkharp.* Adapted by Maryjean Z. Lucchetti. Edmonds, Wash.: Paradise Music, c1987. 3 pp. Originally for piano. [NP]

2692. ———. [Maple leaf rag; arr.] *Maple leaf rag.* Arr. by De Wayne Fulton. [Marina Del Rey, Calif.]: Safari, c1989. 4 pp. Originally for piano.

2693. Kahn, Gus, 1886–1941; King, Wayne, and Bivens, Burke. *Josephine.* Arranged by Lynne Wainwright Palmer. San Mateo, Calif.: F.C. Publishing Co., c1936. 3 pp. (Popcycle series)

2694. Kaper, Bronislaw, 1902–1983. [Green Dolphin Street. On Green Dolphin Street] *Green Dolphin Street.* Arranged by Michael Rado. San Mateo, Calif.: F.C. Publishing Co., [1989], c1947. 4 pp.

2695. Kern, Jerome, 1885–1945. [Cover girl. Long ago] *Long ago and far away.* Arranged for harp solo by Michael Amorosi. [Santa Monica, Calif.]: Salvi Publications, c1978. 3 pp. (Salvi pop series)

2696. ———. [Roberta. Smoke gets in your eyes] *Smoke gets in your eyes.* Arr. Alberto Salvi. [Santa Monica, Calif.]: Salvi, 1978. 5 pp. (Salvi pop series)

2697. ———. [Roberta. Yesterdays] *Yesterdays.* Arranged for harp solo by Stella Castellucci. [Santa Monica, Calif.]: Salvi Publications, c1978. 3 pp. (Salvi pop series)

2698. ———. [Showboat. Can't help lovin' dat man] *Can't help lovin' dat man.* Arranged for harp solo by John Escosa. [Santa Monica, Calif.]: Salvi Publications, c1978. 3 pp. (Salvi pop series)

2699. ———. [Swing time. Way you look tonight] *The way you look tonight.* Arranged for harp solo by John Escosa. [Santa Monica, Calif.]: Salvi Publications, c1978. 3 pp. (Salvi pop series)

2700. ———. [Very warm for May. All the things you are] *All the things you are.* Arranged by Paul Baker. Ellensburg, Wash.: F.C. Publishing Co., c1990. 4 pp. (Popcycle series)

2701. Khachaturian, Aram Ilich, 1903–1978. [Quartet, strings, C minor. Andantino; arr.] *Andantino.* Adapted for harp by Pearl Chertok. Santa Monica, Calif.: Salvi Publications, [197–?]. 2 pp. Originally for 2 violins, viola, and violoncello.

2702. Kinnaird, Alison, arr. *The harp key: music for the Scottish harp.* Arranged by Alison Kinnaird. Shillinghill, Temple, Midlothian, Scotland: Kinmor Music, c1986. 94 pp. [NP] CONTENTS: McLoud's salute; Ge do theid mi do m'leabaidh (Though I go to my bed); Cumh Easbig Earraghaal (Lament for the Bishop of Argyle); Bas Alastruim (The death of Alasdair); MacDonnell's march; Killiekrankie; Caoineadh rioghail (Royal lament); Carrill's lament; Port Patrick; Hi ri ri ri ho (The harper's land); The battle of Sheriff Moor; Blar sliabh an t-Siorradh (2 versions); Rory Dall's port; Port Atholl; Ruairidh dall; Suipeir tighearna Leoid (Lude's supper); Fuath nam fidhleirean (Contempt for fiddle players); Cumha peathar Ruaidhri (Lament for Rory's sister); Far-fuadach a' chlarsair (The harper's dismissal); The lament for the harp key (Cumha crann nan teud); Ellen's dreams; The Braidwood waits; Sheuglie's contest betwixt his harp, fiddle and pipes; The Keiking glasse.

2703. Kirchhoff, Gottfried, 1685–1746. *Aria and rigaudon: harp.* Adaptation by Marcel Grandjany. New York: Associated Music Publishers, Inc., c1949. 4 pp.

2704. Klein, Virginia, ed. *Playing the masters: for the troubadour or pedal harp.* Edited by Virginia Klein. Dallas, Tex.: Little Pub. House, c1974. 4 v. [NP] CONTENTS: Vol. 1. Capriccio by F. J. Haydn. A dance by G. P. Telemann. Bourrée by L. Mozart. On the green by L. Streabbog. Minuet by A. Scarlatti. Allemande by L. van Beethoven. Little piece by R. Schumann.

2705. Kodály, Zoltán, 1882–1967. *Children's dances.* Edited by Aristid Von Würtzler. Santa Monica, Calif.: Salvi Publications, c1983. 8 pp.

2706. ———. [Háry János. Intermezzo; arr.] *Intermezzo: from Háry János.* Edited by Aristid Von Würtzler. Santa Monica, Calif.: Salvi Publications, c1983. 4 pp.

2707. ———. *Hungarian folk-songs.* Edited by Aristid Von Würtzler. Santa Monica, Calif.: Salvi Publications, c1983. 4 pp. CONTENTS: Azért hogy én huszár vagyok; A nád jancsi csárdában; Genercséri utca; Láttad-e te babám; Isten hozzád szülöttem föld.

2708. ———. *Székler folk-songs.* Edited by Aristid Von Würtzler. Santa Monica, Calif.: Salvi Publications, c1983. 5 pp.

2709. Koffman, Moe. *Swingin' shepherd blues.* Arranged by Deborah Henson-Conant. San Mateo, Calif.: F.C. Publishing Co., [1987], c1958. 8 pp. (Solo series: harp)

2710. Kosma, Joseph, 1905–1969, and Prévert, Jacques, 1900–1977. [Feuilles mortes] *Autumn leaves.* Arranged by Eleanor Fell. San Mateo, Calif.: F.C. Publishing Co., [1989], c1947. 3 pp. (Popcycle series)

2711. Kreiss, Adolf G. *Pushkin's love song.* Arranged for harp by Hulda E. Kreiss. West Babylon, N.Y.: Harold Branch Publishing, c1978. 3 pp.

Kreiss, Hulda E., 1924–, ed. *Compositions of David Loeb, Hulda E. Kreiss, Rudolf Forst.* See 1152.

2712. Kreutzer, Rodolphe, 1766–1831. [Astianax. Selections; arr.] *Marche et air de ballet d'Astianax.* Arr. pour la harpe ou piano par M. P. Dalvimare. Paris: Naderman, 18—. 9 pp.

2713. Lai, Francis, 1932–. [Homme et une femme. Homme et une femme] *A man and a woman.* Arranged for harp solo by Eleanor Fell. [Santa Monica, Calif.]: Salvi Publications, c1980. 3 pp. (Salvi pop series)

2714. ———. [Love story. Main theme] *Theme from Love story.* Arranged for harp by Verlye Mills. [Santa Monica, Calif.: Salvi Harps, c1970. 4 pp. (Salvi pop series)

2715. ———. [Love story. Main theme] *Theme from the movie Love story: folk harp solo.* Arranged by Louise Trotter. Edmonds, Wash.: Paradise Music, c1970. 3 pp. [NP]

2716. Lane, Burton, 1912–. [On a clear day you can see forever. On a clear day] *On a clear day.* Arranged by Michelle Sell. Ellensburg, Wash.: F.C. Publishing Co., c1990. 3 pp. (Popcycle series)

2717. Lanjean, Marc. *Forbidden games = Jeux interdits.* Arranged for harp solo by Eleanor Fell. [Santa Monica, Calif.]: Salvi Publications, c1978. 3 pp. (Salvi pop series)

2718. Lantz, Oren L. *Song of the coqui: harp solo.* Arranged by Louise Trotter. Houston, Texas: Louise Trotter, n.d. Score 2 pp. and 2 parts. For harp or for 2 flutes and harp.

2719. Lara, Agustín, 1900–1970. *Granada: concert fantasy*. [Arranged] by Carlos Salzedo for harp. New York: Peer International; Southern Music Pub. Co., c1932. 9 pp. Originally for voice and piano.

2720. ———. *Granada: for pedal or troubadour harp*. Arranged by Reinhardt Elster. New York: Peer International, [1980], c1932. 5 pp. Originally for voice and piano. [NP]

2721. ———. *Granada: rhapsody*. Arranged for harp by Mimi Allen. Chicago, Ill.: Lyon & Healy, c1988. 9 pp. (Lyon & Healy treasury of harp music) Originally for voice and piano.

2722. Latimer, Jack, 1918–. *Chinese rock*. Arranged for harp by Verlye Mills. Santa Monica, Calif.: Salvi Publications, c1982. 4 pp. (Salvi pop series)

2723. Lawrence, Lucile, 1907–, ed. *Early English pieces for the beginner: for troubadour and (or) pedal harp*. Edited by Lucile Lawrence. New York, N.Y.: Lyra Music Co., c1972. 9 pp. [NP] CONTENTS: Variations by Peter Lee of Putney. King William's march by Jeremiah Clarke. Prelude by Henry Purcell. Trumpet piece by Henry Purcell. Fanfare minuet by William Duncombe. Christ-Church bells by M. Camidge. The prince's march by Anthony Young.

2724. ———, ed. *Early French pieces: for the beginner: for troubadour and (or) pedal harp*. Edited by Lucile Lawrence. New York, N.Y.: Lyra Music Co., c1973. 14 pp. Originally for keyboard instrument. [NP] CONTENTS: Les fifres = The fifes by Jean François Dandrieu. Musette by Felix Le Couppey. Le colin maillard = Blind man's bluff by François d'Agincourt. Minuet by J. B. Lully. Carnival (no. 3 from Les fastes de la grande et ancienne Mxnxstrxndxsx) by François Couperin. Les moissonneurs = The reapers by François Couperin. Tambourin by Louis-Claude Daquin. Dance by J. Ph. Rameau. Gavotte in rondo form by Jean François Dandrieu. La confession by Michel Corrette.

2725. ———, ed. *Early German pieces: for the beginner: for troubadour and (or) pedal harp*. Edited by Lucile Lawrence. New York, N.Y.: Lyra Music Co., c1973. 9 pp. [NP] CONTENTS: Allegro; Country waltz by Haydn. Song by C. P. E. Bach. German dance in F; German dance in D by Beethoven. Passepied by Handel. Minuet by L. Mozart. Musette by J. S. Bach.

———, ed. *Solos: for the harp player*. See 1221.

2726. Lecuona, Ernesto, 1896–1963. [Andalucía. Malagueña; arr.] *Malagueña*. Arranged for harp by Dewayne Fulton. [Santa Monica, Calif.]: Salvi Publications, [197–?]. 8 pp. (Salvi pop series) Originally for piano.

2727. ———. [Andalucía. Malagueña; arr.] *Malagueña*. Trans. Arabella Sparnon for 23–string lap harp. [S.l.]: Arabella Sparnon, 1988. 6 pp. Originally for piano. [NP]

2728. Le Dentu, Odette, 1900–, arr. [Pièces classiques. Cahier no. 1] *Pièces classiques: pour la harpe celtique: cahier no. 1 (débutant 1)*. Révision et adaptation, Odette Le Dentu. Paris: Gérard Billaudot, c1980. 16 pp. (La harpe) [NP] CONTENTS: Tanto zentil me mostri tua figura. Coucou dans la forêt. Chanson de la petite gardeuse d'oies. Promenades by Felix Le Coupey. Berceuse by Albeniz. Rigaudon by Rameau. Berceuse irlandaise. Petite marche by Bertini. Rigaudon 1; Rigaudon 2 by Daquin. Passacaille by Lalande. Valse allemande by Kohler. Danse rustique by Gurlitt. Andante by Bertini. Menuet tranquille by W. A. Mozart. Menuet by Chambonnières. Menuet du Bourgeois gentilhomme by Lully. Rouet 1; Rouet 2 by Gurlitt. Mélodie by Kohler. Rigaudon; Menuet by Purcell. Mouvement de valse; Allegretto by Bochsa. Lamentation de Xerxès by Huete. Canzion flamenca by Huete. Ronde by Bochsa. Kol slaven by Bortniansky.

2729. ———, arr. [Pièces classiques. Cahier no. 2] *Pièces classiques: pour la harpe celtique: cahier no. 2 (débutant 2)*. Révision et adaptation, Odette Le Dentu. Paris: Gérard Billaudot, c1978. 12 pp. (La harpe) [NP] CONTENTS: Menuet by J. Krieger. Gavote (extrait d'Iphigénie en Aulide) by Christoph W. von Gluck. Menuet en sol mineur by Jean Jacques Rousseau. Gavotte by Franz Joseph Haydn. Fileuse by Jean-Louis Adam. Thème de la sonatine no. 2 by Latour. Valse en mi-bémol by W. A. Mozart. Les chasseurs by Cornélien Gurlitt. Menuet by Georg-Philipp Telemann. Valse en sol majeur; Valse en fa majeur by W. A. Mozart.

2730. ———, arr. [Pièces classiques. Cahier no. 3] *Pièces classiques: pour la harpe celtique: cahier no. 3 (préparatoire)*. Révision et adaptation, Odette Le Dentu. Paris: Gérard Billaudot, c1978. 11 pp. (La harpe) [NP] CONTENTS: Valse en fa by W. A. Mozart. Romance; Sicilienne by Kotzeluch. Sonatine by L. van Beethoven. Menuet en rondo by J. Ph. Rameau. Le garçon courageux by Cornélius Gurlitt. Rondo by Karl Czerny. Divertissement by Nicolas-Joseph Hullmandel. Allegro sonatine no. 1 by T. Latour. Valse russe by Joseph Léon Gatayes.

2731. ———, arr. [Pièces classiques. Cahier no. 4] *Pièces classiques: pour la harpe celtique: cahier no. 4 (élémentaire)*. Révision et adaptation, Odette Le Dentu. Paris: Gérard Billaudot, c1979. 14 pp. (La harpe) [NP] CONTENTS: Chanson des moissonneurs by R. Schumann. Rondo de la sonatine op. 36, no. 1 by Muzio Clémenti. Air tendre by François Couperin. Final de la sonate no. 8 by Joseph Haydn. L'écossaise by T. Latour. Air suisse by Muzio Clémenti. Le petit cavalier by Robert Schumann. Danse villageoise by L. van Beethoven. Marche militaire by Robert Schumann. Sonatine by Jean Latour. Ländler by Daniel Steibelt.

2732. Legrand, Michel, 1932–. [Happy end. What are you doing the rest of your life?] *What are you doing the rest of your life*. Arranged by Stella Castellucci. San Mateo, Calif.: F.C. Publishing Co., [1989], c1969. 4 pp. (Popcycle series)

2733. ————. [Parapluies de Cherbourg. Watch what happens] *Watch what happens.* Arranged for harp solo by Stella Castellucci. [Santa Monica, Calif.]: Salvi Publications, c1978. 4 pp. (Salvi pop series)

2734. ————. [Parapluies de Cherbourg. Watch what happens] *Watch what happens.* Arranged by Michelle Sell. San Mateo, Calif.: F.C. Publishing Co., [1989], c1964. 2 pp. (Popcycle series)

2735. ————. [Summer of '42. Summer knows] *Summer of '42.* Arranged for harp solo by Michael Amorosi. [Santa Monica, Calif.]: Salvi Publications, c1978. 3 pp. (Salvi pop series)

2736. Lennon, John, 1940–1980, and McCartney, Paul, 1942–. *Eleanor Rigby.* Arranged for harp solo by Eleanor Fell. [Santa Monica, Calif.]: Salvi Publications, c1978. 3 pp. (Salvi pop series)

2737. ————. *Here, there and everywhere.* Arranged by William Lovelace. San Mateo, Calif.: F.C. Publishing Co., [1989], c1969. 2 pp. (Popcycle series)

2738. ————. *Yesterday.* Arr. Verlye Mills. [Santa Monica, Calif.]: Salvi, 1978. 3 pp. (Salvi pop series)

2739. Leoncavallo, Ruggiero, 1858–1919. [Bohème. Valse de musette; arr.] *La bohème: comédie lyrique en 4 actes de Leoncavallo: valse de musette.* [Arr. by G. Verdalle]. Paris: Choudens, n.d. 4 pp.

2740. Leybach, Ignace Xavier Joseph, 1817–1891. *Fantasia brillante per pianoforte sull'opera La sonnambula di Bellini, op. 27.* Trascritta e variata per arpa da Ferdinando Marcucci. Milan: Lucca, [186–?]. 15 pp. Originally for piano.

2741. Liszt, Franz, 1811–1886. *Consolations: für Harfe.* [Arr. by E. Schuëcker]. Leipzig: Breitkopf & Härtel, n.d. 21 pp. Originally for piano.

2742. ————. [Grandes etudes de Paganini. No. 5. Caccia; arr.] *La caccia: capriccio per violino solo.* Riduzione per arpa di L. M. Magistretti. Milan: G. Ricordi, c1916. 6 pp. From Liszt's piano arrangement of no. 5 of Paganini's 6 *grand studi* for violin.

2743. ————. [Kleine Klavierstücke. Sospiri; arr.] *Un sospiro: caprice poétique.* Transcrit pour harpe par Henriette Renié. Nice, France: Delrieu Frères, c1934. 11 pp. Originally for piano.

2744. ————. [Kleine Klavierstücke. Sospiri; arr.] *Un sospiro: caprice poétique.* Transcrit pour harp par H. Renié. London: Salvi Publications, [198–?]. 11 pp. Originally for piano.

2745. ————. [Liebesträume; arr.] *Liebesträume: drei Notturnos: für Harfe.* Übertragen von Wilh. Posse. Leipzig: Wilhelm Zimmermann, c1917. 24 pp. Originally for piano.

2746. ————. [Liebesträume. Nos. 1–2; arr.] *Zwei Notturnos aus den*

Liebesträumen von Franz Liszt. Für Harfe übertragen von Edmund Schuëcker. Leipzig: Fr. Kistner, [189–?]. 19 pp. Originally for piano.

2747. ———. [Mélodies russes. Rossignol; arr.] *Le rossignol: d'après la mélodie russe d'Alabieff.* Transcribed for harp by Henriette Renié; extract from Book no. 9, Les classiques de la harpe. [London]: Salvi Publications, [1980?]. 5 pp. Originally for piano.

2748. Lloyd Webber, Andrew, 1948–. *Andrew Lloyd Webber.* Arranged for the harp by Sylvia Woods. Montrose, Calif.: Woods Music and Books, c1991. 36 pp. CONTENTS: The phantom of the opera: Angel of music; Think of me; The music of the night (excerpt); The phantom of the opera; All I ask of you. Cats: Memory. Evita: Don't cry for me, Argentina. Tell me on a Sunday: Tell me on a Sunday. Requiem: Pie Jesu. Starlight Express: Starlight Express. Jesus Christ Superstar: I don't know how to love him.

2749. ———. [Cats. Memory] *Memory.* Arr. Penny Howk Beavers. Ellensburg, Wash.: F. C. Publishing Co., 1992. 5 pp.

2750. ———. [Evita. Don't cry for me, Argentina] *Don't cry for me, Argentina: folk harp solo.* Arranged by Julia Sanders. Edmonds, Wash.: Paradise Music, c1976. 3 pp. [NP]

2751. ———. [Evita. Don't cry for me, Argentina] *Don't cry for me, Argentina.* Arranged by Katherine Honey. Ellensburg, Wash.: F.C. Publishing Co., [1989], c1976. 4 pp. (Popcycle series)

2752. ———. [Phantom of the opera. All I ask of you] *All I ask of you.* Arr. William Lovelace. Ellensburg, Wash.: F. C. Publishing Co., 1991. 5 pp.

2753. Loesberg, John, 1947–. *The Celtic harp: a hand-picked collection of the finest old airs & dance tunes from Ireland, Scotland, Brittany, England, Wales, Cornwall & The Isle of Man.* Arrangements by Christine Martin & Siobhán Bhreathnach. Cork, Ireland: Ossian Publications, c1988. 36 pp. [NP] CONTENTS: John O'Connor; The rising of the lark; An alarc'h; Sally gardens; Me a gar eur goulmik; Morfa'r frenhines; Oíche nollage; Dydd trwy'r dellt; Ar serjant-major; Buain na rainich; Come under my plaidie; Kemp's jig; Hela'r 'sgyfarnog; Carval ny drogh vraane; Miss Loudon; Rhiwabon; There was a lad; The siege of St. Malo; Miss Sally Hunter; The banks of the Suir; Santez mari, mamm doue; The miller's dance; Difyrrwch arglwyddes owain; Doue lan a vadeleh; Windsor Terrace; Putney Ferry; Mairi bhan og; Ma fransez; Lord Willoughby; Sir Festus Burke; Follow me down to Carlow.

2754. ———. *More musical reflections of Ireland: 25 of the very best of Irish airs & dance tunes.* Arranged for easy piano, keyboards, harp, accordion & melody instruments. Cork, Ireland: Ossian Publications, c1988. 34 pp. CONTENTS: Spancil Hill; In Dublin's fair city; Blind Mary; 'Tis pretty to be in Ballinderry; The salamanca; Spinningwheel song; She moved through the fair; A Kerry polka; Eireóidh mé amáireach; Come back Paddy Reilly; The rose of Mooncoin; Fanny Power; Mary from Dungloe; The king of the fairies; The wild colonial boy; Colonel John Irwin; A bunch of thyme; Wellington's advance; The mountains of Mourne; The Wexford carol; Suí síos fá mo dhídean; Nora; Connemara cradle song; The meeting of the waters; Oíche nollag.

2755. ————. *Musical reflections of Ireland: 25 of the very best of Irish airs & dance tunes, arranged for easy piano, keyboards, harp, accordion & melody instruments.* Selected by John Loesberg. Cork, Ireland: Ossian, 1988. 32 pp. [NP]

2756. Loesser, Frank, 1910–1969, and McHugh, Jimmy, 1894–1969. *Spring is here.* Arranged by Jack Nebergall. San Mateo, Calif.: F.C. Publishing Co., [1989], c1938. 3 pp. (Popcycle series)

2757. Lovelace, William, 1960–, arr. *The gypsy rover.* Ellensburg, Wash.: F.C. Publishing Co., 1993. 5 pp.

2758. Lucchetti, Maryjean Z., arr. *The ash grove: a Welsh tune.* Arranged by Maryjean Z. Lucchetti for folk harp and voice [or] folk harp solo [or] folk harp duet. Edmonds, Wash.: Paradise Music, c1987. Score 4 pp. and 2 parts. [NP]

2759. ————, ed. *The lap harp companion: a collection of 50 arrangements for small harp.* Edited by Mary-jean Z. Lucchetti. Edmonds, Wash.: Paradise Music, c1989. 75 pp. [NP] CONTENTS: Blue Danube waltz; Waves of the blue Danube; Merry widow waltz; The green hills of Tyrol; Waltz; Emmett's lullaby; Lullaby by Brahms; Come live with me; Three ravens; Music box dancer; Take me home country roads; Annie's song; The sound of music; Edelweiss; Lara's theme; I don't know how to love him; King of the road; Never on a Sunday; It's a small world; Blue eyes cryin' in the rain; Your cheatin' heart; Arkansas traveler; Turkey in the straw; Amazing grace; When the saints go marchin' in; Black is the color; Swing low sweet chariot; El condor pasa; Sambalele; Oft in the stilly night; O Danny boy; Open the door softly; The man from Dunmoore; Ryan's rant; Maires wedding; Rise, rise thou merry lark; Rhisart Annwyl (Sweet Richard); Bwlch Llanberis (Llanberis Pass); Whistling gypsy rover; Hole in the wall; English dance; The black nag; Trunkles; The Upton-on-Severn stick dance; The maroon bells; Ode to joy; A little scherzo; Siciliana by Bach; Bridal chorus (from Lohengrin); Wedding march (from A midsummer night's dream); Happy birthday; Away in the manger; Deck the halls.

2760. Lyadov, Anatoly Konstantinovich, 1855–1914. *The musical snuff-box, op. 32.* Transcribed for harp by Lucile Lawrence. New York: G. Schirmer, c1959. 7 pp. Originally for piano.

2761. Lyons, George, and Yosco, Bob. *Spaghetti rag.* Harp arrangement by Robert Maxwell. New York: Maxwell Music Corp., c1990. 7 pp.

2762. Macdearmid, Anne, arr. *Celtic garland: a collection of traditional Scottish and Gaelic airs.* Arranged for Celtic harp by Anne Macdearmid. [Great Britain]: A. Macdearmid, c1985. 18 pp. [NP] CONTENTS: Macintosh's lament; In yon garden fine and gay; Glen Ogle; Hush-a-bye birdie; Ae fond kiss; Afton water; The queen's maries; Buain nan dearcan (Plucking berries); Fairy lullaby; Glen lyon lament; Hug o' laithill o horo; O luaidh (O dearest); Tail toddle; My Jo, Janet.

2763. ———, arr. *Ceol na clarsaich: arrangements and compositions for Celtic harp by Anne Macdearmid.* [Great Britain]: A. Macdearmid, c1987. 44 pp. [NP] CONTENTS: Caidil gu lo; St. Columba's hymn (Caol muile); Bhanarach dhonn a' chruaidh (The dairymaid); Cumha peathar ruaidhri (Rory Dall's sister's lament); Bi falbh o'n uinneig (Go away from my window); Och nan och, 'smi fo leireadh (Sad am I); Bo lurach thu (Sweet dun cow); Gu ma mear a charaid (Merry may the pair be); A' bhanais irteach (St. Kilda wedding); Snaim a' phosaidh (The nuptial knot); An long reubaidh (The reiving ship); Deoch slainte do'n Armailt (Round with a health to glorious Wellington); Creag Ghuanach; Cumha MhicCriomainn (MacCrimmon's lament); Aye waukin' o; Niel Gow's lamentation for James Moray of Abercarney; The May of the glen; When ye cold winter nights were frozen (Braes o' Yarrow); Bobbin John; The road to Ford; Lasswade hornpipe; Merry boys o' Greenland; Sleep soond in da morning; Willa fiord.

2764. ———, arr. *Ceol na clarsaich: book 2: arrangements and compositions for Celtic harp by Anne Macdearmid.* [Great Britain]: A. Macdearmid, c1990. 36 pp. [NP] CONTENTS: Air Eilean Mhara nach Triagh; The lure of the sea maiden; Lasses o' Lasswade; An gille ban; Crò chinn t-sàile; The burning of the piper's hut; Mr. Sharpe of Hoddam; Roslin castle; The dusty miller; Geld him, lassies, geld him; Wee totum fogg; Lumps o' pudding; Mnathan a ghlinne Sèo; 'Sa choill ud thall; The silver moon my mistress is; The rowan tree; Morag nighean domhnuill duinn; Coilsfield house; Lady Charlotte Campbell; Loch Earn; Mo nighean chruinn donn; Queen Mary's lament; The lea rig; My Lady Heron's dompe.

2765. ———, arr. *Christmas garland: a collection of carols for Celtic harp.* Arranged by Anne Macdearmid. S.l.: A. Macdearmid, c1984. 24 pp. [NP] CONTENTS: O little One sweet; I saw three ships; Sans day carol; Away in a manger (solo); Away in a manger (acc.); A maiden most gentle; Coventry carol; Sussex carol; Still in the night; Deck the hall; Down in yon forest.

2766. MacDowell, Edward, 1860–1908. *Forgotten fairy tales.* Adapted for the concert harp by Patricia John. Houston, Tex.: Pantile Press, [198–?]. 3 pp. Originally for piano.

2767. Malotte, Albert Hay, 1895–1964. *The Lord's prayer.* Transcribed for harp by Carlos Salzedo. New York: G. Schirmer, c1935. 5 pp. Originally for voice and piano.

2768. ———. *The Lord's prayer.* Arranged by William Lovelace. San Mateo, Calif.: F.C. Publishing Co., [1989] c1935. 3 pp. (Popcycle series) Originally for voice and piano.

2769. Mancini, Henry, 1924–1994. [Breakfast at Tiffany's. Moon river] *Moon River.* Arranged by Paul Baker. San Mateo, Calif.: F.C. Publishing Co., [1989], c1961. 3 pp. (Popcycle series)

2770. ———. [Charade. Charade] *Charade.* Arranged by Arabella Sparnon. Ellensburg, Wash.: F.C. Publishing Co., [1989], c1963. 3 pp. (Popcycle series)

2771. ———. [Days of wine and roses. Days of wine and roses] *Days of wine and roses.* Arranged by Arabella Sparnon. San Mateo, Calif.: F.C. Publishing Co., c1989. 2 pp. (Popcycle series)

2772. ———. [Mr. Lucky. Mr. Lucky] *Mr. Lucky.* Arranged by Arabella Sparnon. San Mateo, Calif.: F.C. Publishing Co., [1989], c1959. 2 pp. (Popcycle series)

2773. ———. [Pink panther. Pink panther] *The pink panther.* Arr. Mavis Cauffman. Ellensburg, Wash.: F. C. Publishing Co., [1991?]. 2 pp.

2774. Mandel, Johnny, 1935–. [Americanization of Emily. Emily] *Emily.* Arranged by Jack Nebergall. San Mateo, Calif.: F.C. Publishing Co., [1988], c1964. 3 pp. (Popcycle series)

2775. ———. [Sandpiper. Shadow of your smile] *The shadow of your smile.* Arranged by Jack Nebergall. San Mateo, Calif.: F.C. Publishing Co., [1989], c1965. 3 pp. (Popcycle series)

2776. ———. *A time for love.* Arranged by Jack Nebergall. San Mateo, Calif.: F.C. Publishing Co., c1989. 3 pp. (Popcycle series)

2777. Marcello, Benedetto, 1686–1739. [Estro poetico-armonico. 18; arr.] *Psalm XIX.* Arr. Darhon Rees-Rohrbacher. Buffalo, N.Y.: Dragonflower Music, 1990. 3 pp. Originally for 4 voices and continuo. [NP]

2778. Maria, Domenico della, 1768–1800. [Prisonnier. Selections; arr.] *Ouverture, airs, rondeau & duo du Prisonnie ou la Ressemblance.* Arrangés et variés pour la harpe par F. J. Naderman, fils. 2d recueil. Oeuvre 3. Paris: Chez Lobry Chez H. Naderman, [180–?]. 27 pp.

2779. Marot, Clément, 1495?-1544. *Chanson de Guillot Martin.* Harmonisation de A. Périlhou. Transcrite pour harpe de Marcel Grandjany. Paris: Heugel et Cie., c1958. 4 pp.

2780. Martin, Christine, arr. *Taigh na teud = Harpstring house: traditional tunes arranged for the clarsach.* [Ireland?]: Taigh Na Teud; Cork, Ireland: Ossian Publications [distributor], [198–?]. 20 pp. [NP] CONTENTS: Kinloch of

Kinloch; Temple house; Balconie house; The spell; Archibald McDonald of Keppoch; O'Chiadainn an Là; Highland widow's lament; Stu mo run; Highland solo; Lochaber no More; Wexford hornpipe; Captain O'Kean; Neil Gow's farewell to whisky; Highland pibroch; Angus Cameron's compliments to Alex Webster; Miss Gordon of Gight; Logan water; Dunkeld hermitage bridge; Huntingtone Castle; Fairy dance; Bothan an Easan.

2781. Martin, Hugh, 1914–, and Blane, Ralph, 1914–. [Meet me in St. Louis. Boy next door] *The boy next door.* Arranged by Jack Nebergall. San Mateo, Calif.: F.C. Publishing Co., [1988], c1943. 4 pp. (Popcycle series)

2782. ———. [Meet me in St. Louis. Have yourself a merry little Christmas] *Have yourself a merry little Christmas.* Arranged by Eleanor Fell. San Mateo, Calif.: F.C. Publishing Co., [1989], c1943. 4 pp. (Popcycle series)

2783. Martini, Giovanni Battista, 1706–1784. *Aria con variazioni.* Trascrizione per arpa do Gabriella Elsa Consolini. Bologna: U. Pizzi, 1928. 4 pp. Originally for keyboard instrument.

2784. ———. *Guardami un poco: air.* Composed by Martini; arr. with variations for the harp by N. C. Bochsa. London: Birchall, [183– ?]. 10 pp.

2785. Mary Charles, Sister, 1893–1990, arr. *The G. Schirmer harp album for beginners: twelve pieces.* Selected and transcribed for the harp by Sister M. Charles, O.S.F. New York: G. Schirmer, 1941. 27 pp. Originally for piano. CONTENTS: Wee folks' march by Cora Mae Raezer. Playing with kitty by Cedric W. Lemont. Three- and-twenty pirates, op. 21, no. 5 by Marie Suel-Holst. On stilts by Marie F. Hall. The woodcutters by Mathilde Bilbro. From a birch canoe by Richard Bender. Veil dance by N. Louise Wright. Wood magic by Bernice Cougill. Celestial voices, op. 45, no. 9 by Stephen Heller. Little prelude in C, [BWV 939] by Johann Sebastian Bach. Minuet in E♭, [WoO 82] by Ludwig van Beethoven. In a dream, op. 81, no. 7 by Theodor Kullak.

2786. Marzuki, Marilyn S., 1942–, arr. *The Christmas harpist: early to intermediate solos for harps with and without pedals.* Annotations by Judith M. Costello. New York: Carl Fischer, Inc., c1976. 24 pp. CONTENTS: God rest ye merry, gentlemen; Silent night; It came upon a midnight clear; O little town of Bethlehem; Good King Wenceslas; Away in the manger (Flow gently, sweet Afton); The march of kings; The first Noel; As lately we watched; Journey to the manger: a fantasy on We three kings; O Christmas tree; O holy night.

2787. ———, arr. *The sacred harpist.* [Arr. by Marilyn S. Marzuki]. Chapel Hill, N.C.: Hinshaw Music, 1980. 48 pp. CONTENTS: God is good; Kum ba yah; We are climbing Jacob's ladder; Amazing grace; Abide with me by W. H. Monk; Jesus, lover of my soul by Simeon B. Marsh; O for a thousand tongues to sing by Carl G. Glaser; Rock of ages by Thomas Hastings; Rock of ages (Mo'oz tsur); Just as I am, without one plea by William Bradbury; Kadosh by Solomon Sulzer; Sh'ma yisroeyl; Sweet hour of prayer by William B. Bradbury; Fairest Lord Jesus; Jesus saves by William J. Kirkpatrick; Oseh shalom; Nothing but the blood by Robert Lowry; 'Mid all the traffic of the ways by John B. Dykes; Old hundred arr. Thomas Aptommas; Do-di li-nira chen; He's got the whole world in His hands; Jesu, joy of man's desiring by J. S. Bach; A love medley; The bridal ring by Robert Nicolas Charles Bochsa; Ode to joy by Ludwig van Beethoven; Trumpet tune by Henry Purcell [i.e., J. Clarke]; Trumpet voluntary by Jeremiah Clarke; Variations on a theme by Haydn, op. 56b by Johannes Brahms; March pontifical by Charles Gounod; Bridal chorus by Richard Wagner; March napolitaine by Robert Nicolas Charles Bochsa.

Marzuki, Marilyn S., 1942–, and Kaplan, Barbara, eds. *Harp album: repertoire primer.* See 1331.

2788. Massenet, Jules, 1842–1912. [Therèse. Menuet d'amour; arr.] *Menuet d'amour: extrait de Therèse = from the music drama Therèse.* Transcribed for harp by Carlos Salzedo. New York: Lyra Music Co., n.d. 4 pp.

2789. ———. [Thérèse. Menuet d'amour; arr.] *Menuet d'amour: extrait de Thérèse = from the music drama Thérèse.* Transcrit pour harpe par Carlos Salzedo. Paris: Heugel & Cie., c1956. 4 pp.

2790. Mayer, Carl. [Shadow pictures. No. 4. Scherzino; arr] *Scherzino.* Arranged for the harp by John Thomas. London: Edwin Ashdown, n.d. 7 pp.

2791. Mayr, Giovanni Simone, 1763–1845. [Medea in Corinto. Selections; arr.] *A selection of airs from: Meyer's celebrated opera of Medea in Corinto.* Arr. for the harp by N. C. Bochsa. London: Goulding & D'Almaine, [182–?]. "In three books."

2792. Mazurek, Urszula, comp. *Utwory z tabulatur lutniowych: na harfe.* Z pierwodruków podali Zofia Steszewska i Piotr Pozniak; wyboru dokanala i opracowala na harfe Urszula Mazurek. Kraków: Polskie Wydawn. Muzyczne, 1970. 14 pp. (Florilegium musicae antiquae, 32) Transcriptions of lute music by Wojciech Długoraj and Jakub Polak.

2793. McDonald, Susann, 1935–, arr. *Greensleeves: harp solo.* Arranged by Susann McDonald. [Bloomington, Ind.]: Musicworks-Harp Editions, c1982. 4 pp.

2794. McDonald, Susann, 1935–, and Wood, Linda, 1945–, arr. *Christmas music.* Arranged for harp by Susann McDonald and Linda Wood. Bloomington, Ind.: Musicworks-Harp Editions, c1982. 3 v. CONTENTS: Vol.1. O holy night; Away in a manger; Adeste fideles; The first noel; O little town of Bethlehem; Joy to the world; Lo, how a rose e'er blooming; Winds through the olive trees.

Vol.2. Silent night; Away in a manger (Kirkpatrick); We three kings; It came upon a midnight clear; Hark the herald angels sing; Coventry carol; Come thou long expected Jesus; Petite litanies de Jesus.

Vol.3. Sleigh ride; Jingle bells; Bring a torch Jeannette Isabella; Rudolph the red-nosed reindeer; We wish you a merry Christmas; O Christmas tree; Deck the halls; The twelve days of Christmas.

2795. ———, arr. *Music for worship and weddings.* Arranged for harp by Susann McDonald and Linda Wood. Bloomington, Ind.: Musicworks-Harp Editions, c1983. 3 v. CONTENTS: Vol.1. Meditation from Thaïs by Jules Massenet. Trumpet tune by Henry Purcell [i.e., J. Clarke]. Trumpet voluntary by Jeremiah Clarke. Ode to joy by Ludwig van Beethoven. Bist du bei mir by Johann Sebastian Bach. To a wild rose by Edward MacDowell. Andantino by Edwin Lemare. Havah nagila. O perfect love by Joseph Barnby. I love you truly by Carrie Jacobs Bond. Because by Guy d'Hardelot. Blest be the tie that binds by Johann G. Naegeli.

Vol.2. O God our help in ages past by William Croft. Amazing grace. Fairest Lord Jesus. All creatures of our God and King. Kol nidre. Adon olom. Praise to the Lord. All through the night. We gather together. Abide with me by William Monk. Parting hymn of praise (Ellers) by Edward Hopkins. Consolation by Felix Mendelssohn. The Lord bless and keep you by Peter Lutkin.

Vol.3. Spirit of God, descend upon my heart by Frederick Atkinson. Let us break bread together. Jesus, the very thought of Thee by John B. Dykes. When I survey the wond'rous Cross by Lowell Mason. Were you there? Just as I am by William B. Bradbury. Breathe on me, breath of God by Robert Jackson. Jesus loves me by William B. Bradbury. Children of the heavenly Father. In the garden by C. Austin Miles. Beneath the Cross of Jesus by Frederick Maker. Kum-by-yah. What a friend by Charles Converse.

2796. ———, arr. *Spanish music: for the harp.* Transcribed by Susann McDonald and Linda Wood. [Bloomington, Ind.]: Musicworks-Harp Editions, c1984. 3 v. CONTENTS: Vol.1. Suite espagnole: No. 1, Granada (Serenata); Malagueña; Torre bermeja (Serenata) by Isaac Albeniz.

Vol.2. Zaragoza from Second suite espagnole; Malagueña, Recuerdos de viaje; Prelude (Asturias) from Cantos de España by Isaac Albeniz.

Vol.3. Spanish dance no. 1 (Oriental); Spanish dance no. 5 (Andaluza (Playera)); Spanish dance no. 6 (Jota (Rondalla argonesa)); Escenas romanticas no. 6 (Epilogo) by Enrique Granados.

2797. McHugh, Jimmy, 1894–1969. [Blackbirds of 1928. I can't give you anything but love] *I can't give you anything but love, baby.* Arranged by John Escosa. San Mateo, Calif.: F.C. Publishing Co., 1988. 4 pp. (Popcycle series)

2798. ———. [Every night at eight. I'm in the mood for love] *I'm in the mood for love.* Arranged by Arabella Sparnon. Ellensburg, Wash.: F.C. Publishing Co., c1935. 3 pp. (Popcycle series)

2799. McLean, Don, 1945–. [Vincent] *Starry, starry night.* Arranged by William Lovelace. San Mateo, Calif.: F.C. Publishing Co., [1989], c1971. 3 pp. (Popcycle series)

2800. McMichael, Leslie, arr. *The holly and the ivy.* Arr. by Leslie McMichael. Ellensburg, Wash.: F.C. Publishing Co., 1992. 2 pp.

2801. Mégevand, Denise, 1947–, arr. *Marv Pontkalleg (Mort de Pontcalek).* Arrangement de Denise Mégevand. Paris: Editions Musicales Intersong Tutti, c1973. 3 pp.

2802. ———, arr. [Morceaux sur des thèmes du Moyen Age (10)] *Dix morceaux: sur des thèmes du moyen age et des airs du folklore breton.* Adaptation et harmonisation, Denise Mégevand. Paris: Editions Choudens, c1973. Score 19 pp. plus 1 part. (Oeuvres pour harpe celtique) [NP] CONTENTS: Pastourelle; Ce fut en mai; Organum I; Organum II; Estampie (harp and recorder); Vadurie (harp and recorder); Berceuse; Fantaisie sur An hini a garan; Variations sur un chant de noël; Variations sur Les trois rubans; Deux danses.

2803. ———, arr. [Morceaux sur des thèmes du Moyen Age (12)] *Douze morceaux: sur des thèmes du moyen age et des airs du folklore breton.* Adaptation et harmonisation, Denise Mégevand. Paris: Editions Choudens, c1972. Score 10 pp. and 1 part. (Oeuvres pour harpe celtique) [NP] CONTENTS: Le lai d'Iseut; Chanson de trouvère; Rondel (harp and drum); Estampie (harp and recorder); Rondel (Harp, recorder and drum); Chanson de croisade; L'héritière de kéroulaz; L'hermine; Mariez-moi ma mère; Merlin au berceau; Angélus; Chanson à danser.

2804. Mendelssohn-Bartholdy, Felix, 1809–1847. [Lieder ohne Worte, piano. Selections; arr.] *Three songs without words: for harp.* Arr. by Samuel O. Pratt. New York: C. Colin, c1966. 11 pp.

2805. ———. [Lieder ohne Worte, piano, op. 19, no. 1. Andante con moto; arr.] *Sweet remembrance: first Song without words, op. 19, no. 1.* [Rev. and] transcr. for harp by Carlos Salzedo. New York: G. Schirmer, c1957. 5 pp.

2806. ———. [Lieder ohne Worte, piano, op. 30, no. 3; arr.] *Consolation from Songs without words.* Harp solo arranged by Lewis G. Hunter. New York: Belwin, n.d. 3 pp.

2807. ———. [Lieder ohne Worte, piano, op. 62, no. 6, Frühlingslied; arr.] *Spring-song.* [Transcribed] for harp by Carlos Salzedo. New York: G. Schirmer, c1923. 5 pp.

2808. ———. [Lieder ohne Worte, piano, op. 62, no. 6, Frühlingslied; arr.] *Spring-song = Chanson de printemps.* Transcribed for harp by Carlos Salzedo. Paris: Heugel, c1923. 5 pp.

2809. ———. [Lieder, op. 34. Auf Flügeln des Gesanges; arr.] *On wings of song*. [Arr. by Nina S. Miller]. New York: Belwin, n.d. 5 pp. Originally for voice and piano.

2810. ———. [Sommernachtstraum. Hochzeitsmarsch; arr.] *Hochzeitsmarsch aus dem Sommernachtstraum: für Harfe, op. 61, no. 4.* [Arr. by E. Parish-Alvars]. Leipzig: Breitkopf & Härtel, n.d. 5 pp.

2811. ———. [Sommernachtstraum. Hochzeitsmarsch; arr.] *Wedding march: harp solo.* Arr. by Wm. T. Cameron. Washington, D.C.: William Truesdale Cameron, n.d. 2 pp.

2812. ———. [Sommernachtstraum. Hochzeitsmarsch; arr.] *Wedding march.* Arr. Darhon Rees-Rohrbacher. Buffalo, N.Y.: Dragonflower Music, 1989. 2 pp. [NP]

2813. ———. [Sommernachtstraum. Hochzeitsmarsch; arr.] *Wedding recessional: from A midsummer night's dream.* Arranged by Deborah Henson-Conant. San Mateo, Calif.: F.C. Publishing Co., c1989. 2 pp. (Popcycle series)

2814. Menken, Alan, 1949–. [Aladdin. Whole new world] *A whole new world (Aladdin's theme).* Ellensburg, Wash.: F.C. Publishing Co., 1993. 4 pp.

2815. ———. [Beauty and the beast. Beauty and the beast] *Beauty and the beast.* Arr. by Penny Howk Beavers. Ellensburg, Wash.: F.C. Publishing Co., 1991. 4 pp.

2816. ———. [Beauty and the beast. Beauty and the beast] *Beauty and the beast.* Arr. by Kathy Bundock Moore. Ellensburg, Wash.: F.C. Publishing Co., 1991. 3 pp.

2817. Meyer, Friedrich Karl, arr. *Gramachree: a favorite Irish air: arranged for the harp.* London: Printed for the author, [18—?]. 9 pp. (Porte-feuille de pièces legères et amusantes pour la harpe, no. 7)

2818. Meyer, Philippe-Jacques, 1737–1819. *Sonata in G minor: for harp, op. 3, no. 6.* Arr. by Samuel O. Pratt. New York: C. Colin, c1966. 8 pp.

2819. Meyerbeer, Giacomo, 1791–1864. [Robert le diable. Jadis regnait en Normandie; arr.] *Jadis regnait en Normandie: the favorite ballad from Meyerbeer's celebrated opera Robert le diable.* Arr. for the harp by N. C. Bochsa. London: Mori & Lavenu, [183–?]. 5 pp.

2820. ———. [Robert le diable. Quand je quittais la Normandie; arr.] *Two favorite melodies from Meyerbeer's celebrated opera Robert le diable: no. 1, Quand je quittais la Normandie; no. 2, La trompette guerrière.* Arr. for the harp by N. C. Bochsa. London: Mori & Lavenu, [183–?]. 9 pp.

2821. ———. [Robert le Diable. Sicilienne; arr.] *The celebrated Sicilienne from Meyerbeer's grand opera Robert le diable.* Arr. for the harp by N. C. Bochsa. London: Mori & Lavenu, [183–?]. 7 pp.

2822. ———. [Robert le Diable. Sonnez clairons; arr.] *The admired quatuor da tournois Sonnez clairons: from Meyerbeer's celebrated opera Robert le diable.* Arr. as a quick march for the harp by N. C. Bochsa. London: Mori & Lavenu, [183–?]. 5 pp.

2823. Miaskovskii, N. (Nikolai), 1881–1950. *Yellowed leaves: 7 bagatelles, op. 31.* Trans. and ed. Tatiana Tauer. New York: Lyra Music Co., 1992. 15 pp. Originally for piano.

2824. Miles, C. Austin (Charles Austin), 1868–1946. *In the garden.* Arr. J. Wade. Choctaw, Ok.: Harp Celebration Corp., c1990. 10 pp. (Awake the harp)

2825. Miller, Marie, ca. 1898–ca. 1985, arr. *Chanson de Guillot-Martin.* Transcribed by Marie Miller; harmonized by A. Périlhou. New York: Carl Fischer, Inc., c1925. 5 pp. (Popular classics transcribed for harp. Series 2)

2826. Miller, Nina S., arr. *Santa Lucia.* [Arr. by Nina S. Miller]. New York: Belwin, n.d. 3 pp.

Milligan, Samuel, ed. *Fun from the first!: with the Lyon-Healy troubadour harp.* See 1368.

———, ed. *Medieval to modern: repertoire for the Lyon-Healy troubadour harp.* See 1369.

2827. Mills, Frank. *Music box dancer and Peter Piper.* Harp arr. by Renée Quinn. Palo Alto, Calif.: Harpress of California, [1986?], c1974. 6 pp.

2828. Molnar, Josef, 1929–, arr. *Great melodies: for small harp.* [Japan]: s.n., n.d. 8 pp. [NP] CONTENTS: Includes works by Dvořák, Werner, Handel, Weber, and T. Narita.

———. *Itsuki no komori uta by Molnar. Der Lindenbaum by Schubert.* See 1377.

2829. Moore, Thomas, 1779–1852. [Last rose of summer; arr.] *A favorite Irish air: on which is founded Moore's ballad The last rose of summer.* London: Edwin Ashdown, n.d. 5 pp.

2830. ———. *Last rose of summer.* [Arr. by J. Cheshire]. London: J.B. Cramer & Co., n.d. 5 pp.

2831. ———. [Last rose of summer; arr.] *The last rose of summer.* Arranged for the harp by O. B. Dussek. London: Edwin Ashdown, 18—? 3 pp. (Harpist's friend, no. 8)

2832. ———. [Last rose of summer; arr.] *Groves of blarney (Last rose of summer).* [Arr. by G.I. Robinson]. New York: Carl Fischer, c1912. 5 pp.

2833. ———. [Last rose of summer; arr.] *Petite paraphrase (The last rose of summer): harp solo.* [Arr. A. F. Pinto]. New York: International Music, n.d. 5 pp.

2834. ———. [Last rose of summer; arr.] *The last rose of summer.* Transcribed for harp by Carlos Salzedo. [New York]: Carl Fischer, Inc., c1925. 3 pp. (Archive series)

2835. Moret, Neil, 1878–1943. [I got a woman crazy for me] *She's funny that way*. Arranged by Jack Nebergall. San Mateo, Calif.: F.C. Publishing Co., [1989], c1928. 2 pp. (Popcycle series)

2836. Moszkowski, Moritz, 1854–1925. [Stücke, piano, op. 15. Serenata; arr.] *Serenata: für die Harfe, op. 15*. Arr. for harp by E. Schuëcker. Breslau: Julius Hainauer, n.d. 5 pp.

2837. Mouret, Jean-Joseph, 1682–1738. [Fanfares avec une suitte de simphonies. No. 1. Rondeau; arr.] *Rondeau*. Arr. for pedal or non-pedal harp by Darhon Rees-Rohrbacher. Buffalo, N.Y.: Dragonflower Music, 1993. 2 pp. [NP]

2838. Mozart, Wolfgang Amadeus, 1756–1791. [Don Giovanni. Menuetto; arr.] *Menuet from Don Giovanni = Don Juan*. Edited and fingered for harp by Nina S. Miller. New York: Belwin, [19—]. 5 pp.

2839. ———. [Nozze de Figaro. Selections; arr.] *Twenty two pieces: selected from the celebrated opera of Le nozze di Figaro*. Adapted for the piano forte or harp with an accompaniment for the flute by F. Fiorillo. London: Printed & sold by Birchall, [181–?]. Parts 3 v.

2840. ———. [Selections; arr.] *Six pièces de Wolfgang Amadeus Mozart*. Adaptées pour la harpe celtique ou la harpe à pédales par Maïté Etcheverry. Paris: Éditions Choudens, c1981. 9 pp. CONTENTS: Menuet; Menuet; Menuet; Allegro; La tartine de beurre; Valse favorite.

2841. ———. [Sonatas, piano, K. 331, A major; arr.] *Sonate avec variations: la majeur*. [Arr. by A. Kastner]. Berlin: Carl Simon, c1913. 19 pp.

2842. ———. [Symphonies, K. 543, E♭ major. Minuet; arr.] *Menuet: extrait de la symphonie en mi flat*. [Arr. by Tiny Béon]. Paris: Louis Rouhier, n.d. 4 pp.

2843. Mudarra, Alonso, 1506 (ca.)-1580. *Fantasia: en la manera de Ludovico*. Trasladada de la tablatura antigua por A. Griffiths para arpa de una orden. Abergavenny, Gwent, Wales: Adlais, c1983. 13 pp. Originally for vihuela.

2844. Mussorgsky, Modest Petrovich, 1839–1881. [Fair at Sorochinsk. Gopak; arr.] *Hopak: aus der Oper Der Jahrmarkt von Sorotschintsi: für Harfe*. Übertragen von Kira Saradschew. Moscow: Edition de Musique de l'État, 1931. 5 pp.

2845. ———. [Shveya; arr.] *La couturière: pour la harpe*. Arrangée par K. Ssaradgeff. Moscow: Edition de Musique de l'État, 1931. 7 pp. Originally for piano.

2846. Naderman, François Joseph, 1773 (ca.)-1835, and Schuëcker, Edmund, 1860–1911. [Harp music. Selections; arr.] *Études et préludes*.

Revision de Odette Le Dentu. Paris: Gérard Billaudot, c1980. 3 v. (La harpe) CONTENTS: Vol.1. 30 études progressives.
Vol.2. 24 préludes.
Vol.3. Études de haut niveau.

2847. Narváez, Luis de, 16th cent. *Theme and variations on a popular air.* Version for harp by Aida Salvi Perkins. London: Salvi Publications, c1989. 5 pp. Originally for vihuela.

2848. Nevin, Ethelbert Woodbridge, 1862–1901. [Rosary; arr.] *The rosary: paraphrase: harp solo with organ accompaniment ad libitum.* Arranged by A. F. Pinto. Boston: G. Schirmer, c1900. Score 3 pp. and 1 part. Originally for piano and voice. "Can be played as a harp solo without organ accompaniment."

2849. ———. [Water scenes. Narcissus; arr.] *Narcissus, op. 13, no. 4.* Transcribed for harp by A. F. Pinto. Boston: Boston Music Co.; New York: G. Schirmer, 1914, c1891. Score 7 pp. and 1 part. For harp solo or for harp and organ (or piano); originally for piano solo.

2850. Niles, John Jacob, 1892–1980. *I wonder as I wander: Appalachian carol.* Collected & adapted by John Jacob Niles; harmonized for harp by Carlos Salzedo. New York: G. Schirmer, c1957. 2 pp.

2851. ———. *I wonder as I wander: Appalachian carol.* Collected and adapted by John Jacob Niles; harmonized for harp by Carlos Salzedo. New York, N.Y.: Lyra Music Co., c1975. 3 pp.

2852. Offenbach, Jacques, 1819–1880. [Contes d'Hoffmann. Belle nuit; arr.] *Les contes d'Hoffmann: [Barcarolle].* Transcription pour harpe par Gabriel Verdalle. Paris: Choudens, [19—]. 3 pp.

2853. ———. [Contes d'Hoffmann. Belle nuit; arr.] *Barcarolle: from the opera Les contes d'Hoffmann, op. 6.* [Arr. by Max Schuster-Seydel]. New York: International Music Pub., c1915. 4 pp.

2854. ———. [Contes d'Hoffmann. Belle nuit; arr.] *Barcarolle: from The tales of Hoffmann.* Transcribed for harp by Carlos Salzedo. New York: Composers' Music Corp., c1925. 5 pp. (Popular classics transcribed for harp)

2855. ———. [Contes d'Hoffmann. Belle nuit; arr.] *Barcarolle.* Arranged by Patricia Jaeger. Seattle, Wash.: Patricia Jaeger, c1979. 2 pp.

2856. Ó Gallchobhair, Éamonn, arr. *Irish airs for the harp.* Arrangements and introduction by Éamonn Ó Gallagher; historical notes by Leo Maguire. Dublin: Walton's Musical Instrument Galleries, c1968. 48 pp. CONTENTS: The mellow drop; Carrigdown; Ballinderry; Eileen my love; Double jig; Snowy breasted pearl; Lullaby; The lark in the clear air; Youghal; Three sea captains; The fiann mount; Open the door; The itinerant labourer; Reel; Christmas carol; A hymn from Tyrconnell; Kelly from Killann; Hop jig; Kilcash; Jimmy, my thousand loves; Mountains of

Pomeroy; Chorus jig; The red haired girl; Kathleen the daughter of Houlihan; Single jig; I once loved a boy; The peacock.

2857. O'Hara, Kane, 1714?-1782. [Midas. Pray Goody; arr.] *Pray goody: the favorite air from the opera of Midas.* [Arr. by J.L. Dussek]. London: Chappel, n.d. 5 pp.

2858. Orth, Lizette Emma Blood, 1858–1913. *Bed time (1899).* Adapted by Patricia John. [Calif.]: Harpress of California, [198–?]. 3 pp.

2859. Owens, Dewey, arr. *Air from county Antrim: I know where I'm goin'.* Arr. by Dewey Owens. New York: Lyra Music Co., c1971. 2 pp.

2860. ———, ed. *An anthology of music for the harp: from the Elizabethan, baroque, classical, romantic, and modern periods, easy to medium difficulty.* Compiled and edited by Dewey Owens. New York: Lyra Music Co., c1977. 31 pp. Originally for keyboard instrument. CONTENTS: Pavane by William Byrd. Loth to depart by Giles Farnaby. Bourrée; Minuet in G minor by J. S. Bach. Minuet by Domenico Zipoli. Chaconne; Little fugue by G. F. Handel. The juggler; Minuet by J. P. Kirnberger. Un poco adagio (Sonatino, op. 36, no. 3) by Muzio Clementi. About strange lands and people; First loss, op. 68, no. 16 by Robert Schumann. Ave Maria, op. 107, no. 24 by Carl Reinecke. Waltz (G# minor) by Johannes Brahms. Elegie, op. 10, no. 5 by Jules Massenet. Chanson français by P. I. Tchaikovsky. To a wild rose, op. 51, no. 1 by E. A. Macdowell. Cradle song by Hugo Wolf. Dance (from Children's pieces) by Béla Bartók. Shepherd playing his pipe, op. 31, no. 8 by Vladimir Rebikoff. Galop (Children's pieces, op. 39); March (Children's pieces, op. 39) by Dmitri Kabalevsky. Prelude symphonique, op. 2, no. 5; Prelude symphonique, op. 2, no. 10 by John Haussermann.

2861. ———, arr. *The foggy dew: an Irish folk melody.* Arranged for harp by Dewey Owens. New York: Charles Colin, c1964. 2 pp.

2862. ———, arr. [Folk melodies] *9 folk melodies.* Arr. by Dewey Owens. New York: C. Colin, c1962. 12 pp. CONTENTS: Steal away; Drink to me only; Song of Alsace; Londonderry air; My love Nell; Greensleeves; All through the night; Come, my love; The voice of my beloved.

2863. ———, arr. [Folk melodies] *Nine folk melodies: for the troubadour and (or) pedal harp.* Rev. ed. Arr. by Dewey Owens. New York: Lyra Music Co., c1972. 12 pp. [NP] CONTENTS: See 2862.

2864. ———, arr. *Hymns: for the harp: twenty-eight familiar hymns.* Compiled and arranged by Dewey Owens. New York: Lyra Music Co., c1977. 27 pp. CONTENTS: A mighty fortress is our God; Abide with me; Angels from the realms of glory; Christ the Lord is risen today; Come thou almighty King; Come ye thankful people, come; Fairest Lord Jesus; Faith of our fathers; For the beauty of the earth; Holy, holy, holy! Lord God almighty;

Jesus shall reign; Lead on, o King eternal; My country 'tis of thee; My faith looks up to Thee; Now thank we all our God; O beautiful for spacious skies; O come all ye faithful; O God our help in ages past; O sacred Head now wounded; O worship the King; Praise God from whom all blessings; Ride on! Ride on in majesty; Sun of my soul; The Church's one foundation; The strife is o'er; When morning gilds the skies; When I survey the wondrous Cross; Ye servants of God.

2865. Pachelbel, Johann, 1653–1706. [Canon, violins (3), continuo, D major; arr.] *Canon in D.* Arranged for harp solo by Susann McDonald and Linda Wood. Bloomington, Ind.: Musicworks-Harp Editions, c1982. 5 pp.

2866. ———. [Canon, violins (3), continuo, D major; arr.] *The celebrated canon.* Harp transcription, Beyer and Schlomovitz. Palo Alto, Calif.: Harpress of California, c1985. 5 pp.

2867. ———. [Canon, violins (3), continuo, D major; arr.] *Pachelbel's canon.* Arranged for harp solo, harp duet, and harp and flute or violin by Sylvia Woods. Los Angeles, Calif.: Woods Music and Books Publishing, c1986. Score 26 pp.

2868. ———. [Canon, violins (3), continuo, D major; arr.] *Canon in D.* Trans. for pedal or non-pedal harp by Darhon Rees-Rohrbacher. Buffalo, N.Y.: Dragonflower Music, 1993. 4 pp. [NP]

2869. Paganini, Nicolò, 1782–1840. [Caprices, violin, op. 1. No. 24; arr.] *Tema e variazioni: dai Capricci per violino solo di Nicolò Paganini.* Trascritti per arpa da L. M. Magistretti. Milan; New York: Ricordi, c1922. 12 pp.

2870. Paisiello, Giovanni, 1740–1816. [Re Teodoro. Selections; arr.] *Sonate: Ouverture et Entr'actes de "Théodore": für Harfe = pour harpe = for harp: mit Violine ad lib = with accompaniment of violin ad lib.* Herausgegeben von Frédérique Cambreling. Mainz, New York: Schott, c1981. Score 19 pp. and 1 part 6 pp. For harp solo or for harp and violin.

2871. Palmer, Lynne Wainwright, 1919–, arr. *Baby pictures: You must have been a beautiful baby; You oughta be in pictures.* Arranged for harp by Lynne Wainwright Palmer. San Mateo, Calif.: F.C. Publishing Co., c1989. 4 pp. (Popcycle series)

2872. Palmgren, Selim, 1878–1951. [Toukokuun yö; arr.] *May night.* Transcribed for harp by Florence Wightman. New York: G. Schirmer, c1934. 5 pp. Originally for piano.

2873. ———. [Toukokuun yö; arr.] *May night.* Arr. by Florence Wightman. New York: Lyra Music Co., c1966. 4 pp. Originally for piano.

2874. Paradies, Pietro Domenico, 1707–1791. [Sonatas, harpsichord, no. 4. Toccata; arr.] *Toccata.* Ed. M. Magistretti. Frankfurt: Zimmermann, 1988. 5 pp. (Des Harfenisten Konzert-Programm, Nr. 10) Reprint; originally pub. ca. 1914.

2875. ———. [Sonatas, harpsichord, no. 6. Allegro; arr.] *Toccata.* Leipzig: Jul. Heinr. Zimmermann, c1914. 5 pp. Originally for harpsichord.

Paret, Betty, arr. [Harp book, no. 1] *First harp book.* See 1525 and 1526.

———, arr. [Harp book, no. 2] *Second harp book.* See 1527.

2876. ———, arr. *The harpist's book of Christmas music.* [Arr. by] Betty Paret. New York: Lyra Music Co., c1965. 25 pp. CONTENTS: Carols: Angels from the realms of glory; God rest ye merry gentlemen; Good King Wenceslas; Hark! the herald angels sing; It came upon a midnight clear; Joy to the world; O come all ye faithful; O little town of Bethlehem; Silent night, holy night; The first Nowell; We three kings of orient; What child is this?. Harp solos: Chorale Ah! dearest Jesus by Bach. Chorale How shall I fitly meet Thee? by Bach. Children's Christmas march; Christmas bells; Christmas fantasy on I saw three ships by Paret. He shall feed His flock from the Messiah by Handel. Silent night, holy night by Gruber. The legend of the rose by Paret.

2877. Pasquini, Bernardo, 1637–1710. *Il cuculo: scherzo.* Trascrizione per arpa di Alba Novella Schirinzi. Bologna: Edizioni Bongiovanni, 1960. 3 pp. Originally for harpsichord.

2878. Pescetti, Giovanni Battista, 1704 (ca.)-1766. [Sonatas, harpsichord. Selections; arr.] *Due sonate: per arpa: dal gravicembalo.* Trascrizione Giuliana Stecchina Pittaro. Udine, Italy: Pizzicato Edizioni Musicali, c1990. 15 pp. Originally for harpsichord. CONTENTS: Sonata III in sol minore; Sonata V in do minore.

2879. ———. [Sonatas, harpsichord, C minor; arr.] *Sonata in C minor.* Transcribed for harp by Carlos Salzedo. New York: G. Schirmer, c1937. 11 pp.

2880. ———. [Sonatas, harpsichord, C minor; arr.] *Sonata in C minor.* Transcribed for harp by Carlos Salzedo. New York: Charles Colin, c1965. 11 pp.

2881. ———. [Sonatas, harpsichord, C minor; arr.] *Sonata in C minor: for harp.* Transcribed for harp by Carlos Salzedo (1931). New York: Lyra Music, c1970. 11 pp.

2882. ———. [Sonatas, harpsichord, no. 8, C major. Allegro; arr.] *Allegretto: per arpa.* Trascrizione di Mariagiulia Scimeca. Milan: G. Ricordi, c1954. 3 pp. Originally for harpsichord.

2883. Pieczonka, Albert. *The angel of peace: nocturne.* [Arr. by C. Oberthür.] London: Edwin Ashdown, n.d. 5 pp. Originally for piano (?)

2884. Pierné, Gabriel, 1863–1937. [Album pour mes petits amis. Marche des petits soldats de plomb; arr.] *March of the little tin soldiers.* Trans. Mimi Allen. [Santa Monica, Calif.]: Salvi, 1978. 4 pp. Originally for piano.

2885. Pierpont, James, 1822–1893. *Jingle bells.* Transcribed for harp by Carlos Salzedo (revised 1956). Philadelphia: Elkan-Vogel, 1956, c1945. 3 pp.

2886. Pinto, Angelo Francis, d. 1948, arr. [Popular hymns] *Six popular hymns.* New York: International Music Pub. Co., c1923. 5 pp. CONTENTS: Lead, kindly light by John B. Dykes. Jesus, lover of my soul by S. B. Marsh. Rock of ages by Thomas Hastings. Holy, holy, holy by J. B. Dykes. Abide with me by W. H. Monk. Onward, Christian soldiers by Arthur Sullivan.

2887. Pitfield, Thomas, 1903–, arr. *Folk songs from near & far: for clarsach or harp.* Arranged by Thomas Pitfield. Abergavenny: Adlais, c1982. 21 pp. [NP] CONTENTS: The blackbird (Y fwyalchen); Mowing the barley; The keys of Canterbury; So far from my country; Carrion crow; Ballad of Jesus Christ; The bells of Aberdovey; Robin Adair; Herefordshire carol; The hobby horse; Jenny pluck pears; Russian vesper; The gentle dove (Y deryn pur); Greensleeves; Faithful Johnny; Do, do, l'enfant do; Bonny sweet Robin; Cossack lullaby; The billy goat; The Volga boatmen.

2888. Polonska, Elena, 1922–, arr. *Airs et danses de la renaissance: pour harpe celtique.* [Réalisation de] Elena Polonska. Paris: Editions musicales transatlantiques, c1986. 26 pp. [NP] CONTENTS: Pavane et galliarde d'Angleterre; Galliarde (dansée par la Reine Elisabeth I d'Angleterre; Bransle de Bourgogne by Claude Gervaise. Pavane. Bransle de Champagne by Claude Gervaise. Der Hupff auff by Hans Neusidler. A jig by R. Askue. The sick tune (joue dans le Much ado about nothing de Shakespeare). Donna leggiadra; Chiara stella; Pungente dardo by Fabritio Caroso. Calliope; Polinnia; Villanella by Vincenzo Galilei. Tiento IX; Fantasia X by Alonso Mudarra.

2889. ——, arr. *Airs et danses du Moyen Age: pour harpe celtique.* [Réalisation de] Elena Polonska. Paris: Editions musicales transatlantiques, c1982. 32 pp. [NP] CONTENTS: En Mai la rousee by Thibault de Champagne. Palestinalied by Walter von der Vogelweide. Trop penser me font amours. Ma viele by Gautier de Coincy. A l'entree de l'este by Blondel de Nesle. Domino; Domino clausola; Clausulae Haec dies from Ecole de Notre-Dame. Can vei l'alauzeta by Bernard de Ventadour. La septime estampie royale. Ballata Angelica belta by Francesco Landino. Lochamer Liederbuch: Deutsches Lied; Danse; Lamento di Tristano; Danse royale; Trotto; Saltarello.

2890. Ponce, Manuel M. (Manuel María), 1882–1948. *Estrellita.* Transcribed for harp by Joseph Vito. New York: Belwin, c1942. 7 pp. (Classics for concert harp) Originally for voice.

2891. ——. *Estrellita.* Arranged by May Hogan Cambern. [New York]: Michael Cambern, c1964. 2 pp. (From the notebook of May Hogan Cambern) Originally for voice.

2892. ———. *Estrellita.* Arranged for harp by Anna B. Stuckey. S.l.: Anna B. Stuckey, c1979. 3 pp. Originally for voice.

2893. Pool, Ray, 1947–, ed. *The harpist's fake book.* Chicago: Lyon & Healy, c1991. 56 pp. Includes lyrics. CONTENTS: About a quarter to nine; Ain't misbehavin'; All the way; Am I blue?; Anniversary song; April showers; As long as he needs me; Bidin' my time; Body and soul; Bye bye blackbird; Chances are; Days of wine and roses; Don't get around much anymore; Dream; Embraceable you; Everybody loves somebody; Fascination; Feelings; Fools rush in; Go away little girl; I left my heart in San Francisco; I want to be happy; I'll see you again; If you were the only girl in the world; Imagination; It's all in the game; It's been a long, long time; Jean; Killing me softly; La vie en rose; Les bicyclettes de Belsize; Lover come back to me; M*A*S*H (song from); Misty; Moonglow; Mountain greenery; My heart stood still; Rhythm of the rain; Secret love; September in the rain; Softly, as in a morning sunrise; Somebody loves me; Someone to watch over me; Stardust; Stranger on the shore; Tea for two; Three coins in the fountain; Time after time; Where is love?; Wonderful! Wonderful!

2894. Porter, Cole, 1891–1964. [Anything goes. I get a kick out of you] *I get a kick out of you.* Arranged by Ray Pool. San Mateo, Calif.: F.C. Publishing Co., c1988. 3 pp. (Popcycle series)

2895. ———. [Gay divorcée. Night and day] *Night and day.* Arranged by Lynne Wainwright Palmer. San Mateo, Calif.: F.C. Publishing Co., c1988. 4 pp. (Popcycle series)

2896. ———. [Jubilee. Begin the beguine] *Begin the beguine.* Arranged by Mimi Allen. Ellensburg, Wash.: F.C. Publishing Co., c1990. 3 pp. (Popcycle series)

2897. Post, Mike, 1944–. *Hill Street blues.* Arranged by Katherine Honey. San Mateo, Calif.: F.C. Publishing Co., [1988], c1980. 2 pp. (Popcycle series)

2898. Powell, Christopher, comp. *Y telynor clasurol = The classical harpist.* [Compiled by] Christopher Powell. Y Fenni, Gwent, Wales: Adlais, [198–?]. 13 pp. CONTENTS: Hornpipe by Purcell. Passacaille: suite no. 7 in G minor by Handel. Adagio by Croft. Chaconne by Clarke. Allegro: suite no. 8 in G major; Sonatina by Handel. Carillon attr. Handel.

2899. Pradher, Louis Barthélemy, 1781–1843. [Rondo alla polacca; arr.] *Rondo alla polacca.* Arrangé pour la harpe par N. Charles Bochsa. Bordeaux: Filliatre et Neveu, [181–?]. 11 pp.

2900. Pratt, Rosalie Rebollo, 1933–, and Pratt, Samuel O., 1925–1985, eds. *Baroque and classic pieces: for harp.* [Compiled and edited by Rosalie and Samuel Pratt]. Orem, Utah: SARO Publishing Co., 1966. 24 pp. CONTENTS: Gaillarde. Saltarello. Prélude; Menuet; Sarabande by Johann Kuhnau. Fantasie by Georg Philipp Telemann. Menuet. Der Wildfang by Johann Philipp Kirnberger. Menuet. The little rope dancer by Friedrich

Wilhelm Marpurg. Ricercata by Georg Christoph Wagenseil. Galliard; Pavan by Don Luis Milan. Andante by Luis de Narvaéz. Sonata in re maggiore by Mateo Albeniz. Forlana. Pavana (The Earle of Salisbury) by William Byrd. Irisches Lied; Rigadoon; Minuet; Chanson by Henry Purcell. Siciliana by Jean Christophe Smith. Awakening of the lilies = [Lis naissans] by François Couperin. German waltz; Geister Walzer by L. van Beethoven.

2901. ———, eds. *Bon bons: for harp.* Compiled and edited by Rosalie and Samuel Pratt. Upper Montclair, N.J.: SARO Publishing Co., n.d. 37 pp. CONTENTS: Russian impressions: Idyle: On the steppes by Sascha Frieberg; Idyll: moment musical, op. 26 by Woldemar Loukine; At the brook: Prélude no. 2 in F minor by W. Loukine. Two minuets: Minuet danced before General Washington; Minuet danced before Mrs. Washington by Pierre Landrin Duport. An evening at home: four easy pieces for the harp, op. 24: Children's thoughts = Pensées enfantines; At the fireside = Au coin du feu; Youngsters at play = Marche enfantine; A little dance = Valse petite by Alfred Holy. 4 Tyrolean waltzes by Ludwig van Beethoven. A spring thought by Charles Schuetze. First arabesque; Second arabesque by Claude Debussy. The Czarina's music box by Drozdoff. The fall of Paris.

2902. ———, eds. *Petit fours: a delightful confection of harp music for special occasions.* Compiled and edited by Rosalie and Samuel Pratt. Upper Montclair, N.J.: SARO Publishing Co., n.d. 37 pp. CONTENTS: Gagliarda in G minor by Girolamo Frescobaldi, arr. Pinto. Nocturne by M. Ippolitov-Ivanov. Vision by Gabriel Verdalle. Sonata in la minore by Padre Antonio Soler. Log cabin sketches (Winter): Snowdrifts; Moonlight; The ring of the axe; The hunter; The awakening of the maples. Three sketches, op. 25 by Alfred Holy. A remembrance (Pagina d'album) by Domenico Sodero. Tenerezza by Salvatore Mario de Stefano. Colonial days by Johanes Snoer.

2903. Previn, André, 1929–. [Inside Daisy Clover. You're gonna hear from me] *You're gonna hear from me.* Arranged by Jack Nebergall. San Mateo, Calif.: F.C. Publishing Co., c1988. 3 pp. (Popcycle series)

2904. Price-Glynn, Cynthia, 1946–, arr. *Seventeenth and eighteenth century music: for harp.* Arranged by Cynthia Price-Glynn. Boston, Mass.: Boston Editions, c1988. 26 pp. CONTENTS: March from Suite no. 5; Air; Sarabande from Suite no. 2; Hornpipe from The old bachelor (theatre music) by Henry Purcell. Jigg by Jeremiah Clark. Fughetta by Domenico Zipoli. Aria by Johann Kuhnau. Toccata by Leonardo Leo. La florentine; La Diane by François Couperin. Courante by George Frideric Handel. Bourrée II from the French overture by Johann Sebastian Bach. Passepied by George Phillip Telemann. Allemande; Menuett in E flat by Ludwig van Beethoven. Scherzo by Johann Nepomuk Hummel. Alla polacca by Carl Philipp Emanuel Bach.

Prokofiev, Sergey, 1891–1953. [Piece, harp] *Piece: for harp; Prelude, op. 12, no. 7: for harp or piano.* See 1666.

2905. Prokofiev, Sergey, 1891–1953. [Pieces, piano, op. 12. Prelude; arr.] *Prélude, op. 12, no. 7.* Specially edited by the composer. New York: G. Schirmer, c1919. 7 pp.

2906. ———. [Pieces, piano, op. 12. Prelude; arr.] *Prelude in C: for harp.* Edited by Carlos Salzedo. New York: Leeds Music Corp., c1949. 7 pp.

2907. ———. [Pieces, piano, op. 12. Prelude; arr.] *Prélude in C, op. 12, no. 7.* Specially edited by the composer. New York: G. Schirmer, c1947. 7 pp. (Piano compositions by Russian composers. Series one)

2908. ———. [Pieces, piano, op. 12. Prelude; arr.] *Prelude in C, op. 12, no. 7 (1913).* Edited by Lucile Lawrence. New York, N.Y.: Lyra Music Co., c1974. 7 pp.

2909. ———. [Pieces, piano, op. 12. Prelude; arr.] *Pièce: pour harpe.* [Transcription de V. Dulova]. [Paris]: Le Chant du Monde, c1975. 7 pp.

2910. ———. [Pieces, piano, op. 12. Prelude; arr.] *Prélude, op. 12, nr. 7: piano ou harpe.* [East Germany]: Rob. Forberg; P. Jurgenson, [198–]. 7 pp.

2911. ———. [Romeo and Juliet (Ballet). Utrenniaia serenada; arr.] *Utrenniaia serenada: iz baleta Romeo i Dzhul'etta.* Obrabotka dlia arfy V. Dulovoi. Moscow: Gos. muz. izd-vo, 1960. 7 pp. Originally for orchestra.

2912. Provost, Heinz, b. 1891. [Souvenir de Vienne. Intermezzo; arr.] *Intermezzo: a love story.* Transcription for harp solo by A. Francis Pinto. New York: Edward Schuberth, c1941. 6 pp. Originally for orchestra; from the motion picture Souvenir de Vienne.

2913. Prume, François, 1816–1849. *La mélancolie: pour la harpe, op. 29.* London: Edwin Ashdown, n.d. 5 pp. Originally for piano.

2914. Purcell, Henry, 1659–1695. *Purcell for the harp.* Transcribed for harp by Dewey Owens. New York: G. Schirmer, c1975. 24 pp. Originally for keyboard instrument. CONTENTS: Two song tunes: Ah how pleasant 'tis to love; Sylvia, now your scorn give over. Minuet, G major; Aire (Minuet), D minor. Rigadoon (Suite V). Hornpipe (E minor). Almand (Suite I). Minuet, A minor. Air, F major. Air, G minor. Rondo (Round o, rondeau). Air, G major. Prelude (Suite V). Minuet (Suite I). Rigaudon, D minor. A new Irish tune (Lilliburlero). Minuet, A minor. Sefauchi's farewell. Hornpipe in B♭. Ground in G.

2915. ———. [Suite, harpsichord, no. 1, G major; arr.] *Suite.* Adapted for harp by Pearl Chertok. New York: Interstate Music, [1975?]. 3 pp. Prelude; Almand; Courante; Menuet. [NP]

2916. ———. [Suite, harpsichord, no. 1, G major; arr.] *Suite.* Adapted for harp by Pearl Chertok. Santa Monica, Calif.: Salvi Publications, [197–?]. 3 pp. CONTENTS: Prelude; Almand; Courante; Minuet.

2917. Quintile, Joseph, arr. *Chicken reel: transcribed for harp.* Hollywood, Calif.: La Brea Music Publishers, c1942. 5 pp.

2918. Rachmaninoff, Sergei, 1873–1943. [Concertos, piano, orchestra, no. 2, op. 18, C minor. Selections; arr.] *Themes from the second piano concerto: for harp.* Arranged by Eleanor Fell. Boston, Mass.: Boston Editions, c1986. 9 pp.

2919. ———. [Morceaux de fantaisie, op. 3. Prélude; arr.] *Prelude: for harp.* Arr. by Samuel O. Pratt. New York: C. Colin, c1966. 4 pp. Originally for piano.

2920. ———. [Preludes, piano, op. 23. No. 4; arr.] *Prelude, op. 23, no. 4.* Arr. by Samuel O. Pratt. New York: C. Colin, c1966. 4 pp. Originally for piano.

2921. ———. [Rapsodie sur un thème de Paganini, piano, orchestra. Selections; arr.] *Rhapsody on a theme by Paganini: 18th variation.* Trans. Clifford Wooldridge. Chicago: Lyon & Healy, 1985. 5 pp.

2922. ———. [Rapsodie sur un thème de Paganini, piano, orchestra. Selections; arr.] *Eighteenth variation: rhapsody on a theme by Paganini: from the movie Somewhere in time.* Arranged by Penny Howk Beavers. San Mateo, Calif.: F.C. Publishing Co., c1988. 3 pp. (Popcycle series)

2923. Rameau, Jean Philippe, 1683–1764. [Boréades. Gavotte; arr.] *Gavotte: Boréales [sic].* [Transcribed for the harp by] Henriette Renié. Paris: Leduc, c1957. 19 pp. Originally for orchestra.

2924. ———. [Dardanus. Rigaudon; arr.] *Rigaudon de Dardanus.* Libera trascrizione per harpa di Giulia Principe. Milan, New York: G. Ricordi & Co., [19—]. 4 pp.

2925. ———. [Dardanus. Sommeil; arr.] *Rondeau des songes.* Transcribed for harp by H. Renié. Paris: Gay & Tenton, c1928. 3 pp. Originally for orchestra.

2926. ———. [Harpsichord music. Selections; arr.] *Six pieces de Jean-Philippe Rameau.* Adaptées pour la harpe celtique ou la harpe à pédales par Maïté Etcheverry. Paris: Editions Choudens, c1979. 13 pp. (Les classiques transcrits pour la harpe) Originally for harpsichord. [NP] CONTENTS: Musette en rondeau; Gigue; Tambourin; Rigaudon; La follette; Les sauvages.

2927. ———. [Pièces de clavecin (1724). Rigaudon; arr.] *Rigaudon.* Trans. for harp by Carlos Salzedo. New York: G. Schirmer, c1934. 6 pp.

2928. ———. [Pièces de clavecin (1724). Tambourin; arr.] *Tambourin.* Transcribed for the harp by Carlos Salzedo. New York: G. Schirmer, c1924. 5 pp. Originally for harpsichord.

2929. ———. [Pièces de clavecin (1724). Tambourin; arr.] *Tambourin.* Transcribed for the harp by Carlos Salzedo. Paris: Heugel, c1924. 5 pp. Originally for harpsichord.

2930. ———. [Pièces de clavecin (ca. 1728). Egiptienne; arr.] *L'Égyptienne: extrait du 2e livre de Pièces de clavecin.* Transcription pour la harpe par H. Renié. Paris: Durand, 1959. 5 pp. Originally for harpsichord.

2931. ———. [Temple de la gloire. Gavotte; arr.] *Gavotte: from Le temple de la gloire.* [Transcribed for harp by Carlos Salzedo]. New York: G. Schirmer, c1923. 5 pp. Originally for orchestra.

2932. ———. [Temple de la gloire. Gavotte; arr.] *Gavotte: from Le temple de la gloire.* Transcribed for harp by Carlos Salzedo. New York: Lyra Music Co., c1966. 5 pp. Originally for orchestra.

2933. Rathgeber, Valentin, 1682–1750. [Selections; arr.] *Aria; Pastorella.* Arranged for folk harp by Sylvia Fellows. Anaheim, Calif.: Quicksilver Music, 1988. 2 pp. Originally for keyboard instrument. [NP]

2934. Ravel, Maurice, 1875–1937. [Ma mère l'oye (Piano duet). Laideronette, impératrice des pagodes; arr.] *Dance: from the Mother Goose suite.* [Transcribed by Vera Dulova]. New York, N.Y.: Lyra Music Co., c1967. 10 pp.

2935. ———. [Prelude, piano; arr.] *Prélude: pour le piano.* Transcrit pour harpe par Carlos Salzedo. Paris: Durand, c1952. 3 pp.

2936. ———. [Sonatina, piano. Mouvt. de menuet; arr.] *Menuet from Sonatine.* Adapted for harp by Pearl Chertok. Santa Monica, Calif.: Salvi Publications, n.d. 3 pp.

2937. Redner, Lewis H., 1831–1908. *O little town of Bethlehem.* Arr. by Wm. T. Cameron. Washington, D.C.: William Truesdale Cameron, n.d. 1 p. [NP]

2938. Rees-Rohrbacher, Darhon, 1952–, arr. *Folk harp preludes for the liturgical church. Set. 2: American folk hymns.* Buffalo, N.Y.: Dragonflower Music, 1990. 9 pp. [NP]

2939. ———, arr. *Folk harp preludes for the liturgical church. Set. 3: Spirituals.* Buffalo, N.Y.: Dragonflower Music, 1990. 5 pp. [NP]

2940. ———, arr. *Folk harp preludes for the liturgical church. Set. 4: Six variations on Brother James' air.* Buffalo, N.Y.: Dragonflower Music, 1992. 7 pp.

2941. ———, arr. *The minstrel boy.* Arr. Darhon Rees-Rohrbacher. Buffalo, N.Y.: Dragonflower Music, 1989. 2 pp. [NP]

2942. ———, arr. *Spanish songs of the Renaissance.* Buffalo, N.Y.: Dragonflower Music, 1990. 2 pp. [NP] CONTENTS: Triste estaba el Rey David; La manana de San Juan.

2943. ———, arr. *Tomorrow shall be my dancing day.* Arr. Darhon Rees-Rohrbacher. Buffalo, N.Y.: Dragonflower Music, 1990. 3 pp. [NP]

2944. ———, arr. [Welsh folk tunes] *Three Welsh folk tunes.* Buffalo, N.Y.: Dragonflower Music, 1990. 4 pp. [NP] CONTENTS: The maid of Penderyn; The slender lad; The red-headed cobbler.

2945. Reinecke, Carl, 1824–1910. [Kinderlieder. Selections; arr.] *Five children's songs.* Arranged for harp solo or harp and children's voices by Marie Goossens. London: Chandos Music, c1981. 6 pp. CONTENTS: The rain song; When the little children sleep; A carriage to ride in; Doll's cradle song; Barcarole.

2946. Reissiger, Carl Gottlieb, 1798–1859. [Danses brillantes, piano, op. 26. No. 5; arr.] *Weber's last waltz.* Arranged for the harp by Robert Nicholas Charles Bochsa. Edited by Alice Lawson. San Anselmo, Calif.: A. Lawson, c1970. 3 pp. Originally attributed to Weber, though actually composed by Reissiger.

2947. Renié, Henriette, 1875–1956, arr. [Classiques de la harpe, book 1] *Les classiques de la harpe: collection de transcriptions classiques pour harpe à pédales: recueil no. 1.* [Transcrit par] Henriette Renié. Paris: Alphonse Leduc, c1950. 15 pp. CONTENTS: Musette (Les indes galantes); Menuet (Castor et Pollux); Menuets (Platée) by Rameau. Romance; Rondeau by Marin Marais. La mélodieuse by Daquin. Andante (Sonate en sol majeur) by Beethoven. Menuet (33me sonate) by Haydn.

2948. ———, arr. [Classiques de la harpe, book 2] *Les classiques de la harpe: collection de transcriptions classiques pour harpe à pédales: recueil no. 2.* [Transcrit par] Henriette Renié. Paris: Alphonse Leduc, c1951. 15 pp. CONTENTS: L'hirondelle by Daquin. Sarabande; Gigue by Zipoli. Pièce en ré by Scarlatti. Célèbre gavotte en rondeau (Ballets du roy) by Lully. Barcarolle (Romances sans paroles no. 6) by Mendelssohn. Préludes, nos. 20 et 23 by Chopin.

2949. ———, arr. [Classiques de la harpe, book 3] *Les classiques de la harpe: collection de transcriptions classiques pour harpe à pédales: recueil no. 3.* [Transcrit par] Henriette Renié. Paris: Alphonse Leduc, c1950. 19 pp. CONTENTS: Tambourin (Les fêtes d'Hébé); Rondeau des songes by Rameau. Le coucou by Daquin. Adagio (Sonate au clair de lune) by Beethoven. Bourrée (Suite en ut pour violoncelle) by J. S. Bach. Moment musical no. 3 by Schubert.

2950. ———, arr. [Classiques de la harpe, book 4] *Les classiques de la harpe: collection de transcriptions classiques pour harpe à pédales: recueil no. 4.* [Transcrit par] Henriette Renié. Paris: Alphonse Leduc, c1954. 15 pp. CONTENTS: Toccata (4me sonate pour clavecin) by Paradisi. Sonate facile en ut by Mozart.

2951. ———, arr. [Classiques de la harpe, book 5] *Les classiques de la harpe: collection de transcriptions classiques pour harpe à pédales: recueil no. 5.* [Transcrit par] Henriette Renié. Paris: Leduc, c1940. 19 pp. CONTENTS: v. 5. L'harmonieux forgeron by Handel. Les fifres; Les tourbillons by Dandrieu. Consolations no. 3 by Liszt.

2952. ———, arr. [Classiques de la harpe, book 6] *Les classiques de la harpe:*

Vol. 6. [Transcrit par] Henriette Renié. New York: Lyra Music Co., 1980. 15 pp. Originally for harpsichord or piano. CONTENTS: Tic-toc-choc ou Les maillotins by Couperin. Gavotte variée by Handel. Adagio from Sonate pathétique by Beethoven. Prelude no. 2 [i.e., no. 3] by Chopin.

2953. ———, arr. [Classiques de la harpe, book 7] *Les classiques de la harpe: collection de transcriptions classiques pour harpe à pédales: recueil no. 7.* [Transcrit par] Henriette Renié. Paris: Alphonse Leduc, c1957. 19 pp. Originally for orchestra or harpsichord or piano. CONTENTS: Gavotte [from] Boréales [sic] by Rameau. Presto [from] 20me sonate en sol majeur [K. 13] by Scarlatti. L'oiseau-prophète by Schumann. Célèbre valse dite du chat = [Minute waltz] by Chopin.

2954. ———, arr. [Classiques de la harpe, book 8] *Les classiques de la harpe: collection de transcriptions classiques pour harpe à pédales: recueil no. 8.* [Transcrit par] Henriette Renié. Paris: Alphonse Leduc, c1958. 15 pp. CONTENTS: Consolation no. 2 by Liszt. L'étourdie (Rondeau) by Dagincourt. Allegrissimo (4me sonate) by Scarlatti. Fileuse (Romances sans paroles no. 34) by Mendelssohn.

2955. ———, arr. [Classiques de la harpe, book 9] *Les classiques de la harpe: collection de transcriptions classiques pour harpe à pédales: recueil no. 9.* [Transcrit par] Henriette Renié. Paris: Alphonse Leduc, c1958. 14 pp. CONTENTS: Capriccio: sonata en mi majeur by Scarlatti. Consolation no. 5 by Liszt. Preludes, nos. 6 et 11 by Chopin. Le rossignol: d'après un mélodie d'Alabieff by Liszt.

2956. ———, arr. [Classiques de la harpe, book 10] *Les classiques de la harpe: collection de transcriptions classiques pour harpe à pédales: recueil no. 10.* [Transcrit par] Henriette Renié. Paris: Alphonse Leduc, c1956. 15 pp. CONTENTS: La victoire by Duphly. Pastorale by Scarlatti. Au soir by Schumann. Nocturne (No. 3 des rêves d'amour) by Liszt.

2957. ———, arr. [Classiques de la harpe, book 11] *Les classiques de la harpe: collection de transcriptions classiques pour harpe à pédales: recueil no. 11.* [Transcrit par] Henriette Renié. Paris: Alphonse Leduc, c1964. 21 pp. CONTENTS: Dix pièces by J. S. Bach.

2958. ———, arr. [Classiques de la harpe, book 12] *Les classiques de la harpe: collection de transcriptions classiques pour harpe à pédales: recueil no. 12.* [Transcrit par] Henriette Renié. Paris: Alphonse Leduc, c1964. 22 pp. CONTENTS: Dix préludes (Clavecin bien tempéré) by J. S. Bach.

2959. Rensch, Roslyn, arr. *Harp solos for joyous and solemn occasions.* Arranged by Roslyn Rensch. New York: Salvi Publications, c1981. 19 pp. CONTENTS: The guardian angel (based on H. F. Biber's Sonata for solo violin). The cat's bagpipe. Vermeland. Prelude in G♭ (excerpt from the first of Zwei Phantasiestücke by Schuëcker). The strife is o'er by G. P. Palestrina. Josephine impromptu by G. Navone.

2960. Respighi, Ottorino, 1879–1936. [Antiche arie e danze per liuto, no. 3. Siciliana; arr.] *Siciliana: da un pezzo di liuto del sec. XVI.* Trascrizione per arpa di M. Grandjany. Milan: G. Ricordi, 1955. 6 pp. Originally an anonymous work for lute.

2961. ———. [Antiche arie e danze per liuto, no. 3. Siciliana; arr.] *Siciliana: after the orchestration by Respighi.* Arranged for [solo] harp by Phyllis Schlomovitz. Palo Alto, Calif.: Harpress of California, c1988. 7 pp. Originally an anonymous work for lute.

2962. ———. [Boutique fantasque. Valse lente; arr.] *Valse: from La boutique fantasque.* Transcribed for harp by Clifford Wooldridge. Chicago: Lyon & Healy, c1987. 7 pp. (Lyon & Healy treasury of harp music) Originally for orchestra.

2963. ———. [Notturno, piano; arr.] *Notturno.* Trasc. per arpa di Maria-giulia Scimeca. Bologna: Bongiovanni, c1966. 5 pp.

2964. Rimsky-Korsakov, Nikolay, 1844–1908. [Sheherazade. Andantino quasi allegretto; arr.] *The love theme from Scheherezade.* Harp arrangement by Robert Maxwell. New York: Maxwell Music Corp., c1990. 9 pp.

2965. Ritchie, Lionel. [Endless love. Endless love] *Endless love.* Arranged by Penny Howk Beavers. San Mateo, Calif.: F.C. Publishing Co., c1989. 3 pp. (Popcycle series)

2966. Rivoal, Yvon, 1944–, and Garson, Catherine, arr. *Chansons et danses d'Amérique latine.* Paris: Henry Lemoine, 1993. 24 pp.

2967. Robertson, Kim, arr. *Celtic Christmas: folk harp.* Winona, Minn.: Hal Leonard Publishing Corp., c1987. 55 pp. [NP] CONTENTS: Christ Child's lullaby; Coventry carol; Divinum mysterium; Entre le boeuf; The first Nowell; God rest ye merry, gentlemen; Good King Wenceslas (medley); Greensleeves (What Child is this?); I wonder as I wander; Jesu, joy of man's desiring; Quand il bergiè; Rosa mystica (Lo how a rose); Saltarello; Sheep may safely graze; Veni Emmanuel; Venite adoremus.

2968. ———, arr. [Moonrise. Selections] *Selections from Moonrise.* Santa Barbara, Calif.: Folk Mote Music, c1986. 20 pp. [NP] CONTENTS: Paduana alla venetiana by Joanambrosio Dalza. Carolan's draught by Turlough O'Carolan. Som coïman. Moonrise by Kim Robertson. La rotta. Gratitude by Kim Robertson. Sonatina no. 3 by Johann L. Dussek. Rain; Bailey's fancy by Kim Robertson. Moon over the rising castle.

2969. ———, arr. [Water spirit. Selections] *The music from Water spirit: a collection of 10 pieces arranged for Celtic harp from Kim's recording Water spirit.* Santa Barbara, Calif.: Folk Mote Music, c1984. 20 pp. [NP] CONTENTS: Lauda to Sta. Maddalena. Separation of soul from the body by Carolan. Roving Galway boy. Water spirit by Kim Robertson. Chanter. Pavane by Fauré. Maids of Mourne Shore. The parting glass. Alfonso XII [i.e., X] el Sabio. Kalenda maya.

————, arr. [Wind shadows, no. 1] *The music from Wind shadows: a collection of traditional and original music for harp.* See 1721.

————, arr. [Wind shadows, no. 2] *The music from Wind shadows II.* See 1722.

Robinson, Gertrude Ina, b. 1868. *Original compositions & adaptations: for the harp.* See 1729.

2970. Rode, Pierre, 1774–1830. [Air varié, piano, violin, G major; arr.] *The celebrated air and variations.* Arr. for the harp with the addition of new variations composed by N. C. Bochsa. London: Printed & sold by Chappell, [between 1819 and 1826]. 9 pp. Originally for piano and violin.

2971. Rodgers, Richard, 1902–1979. [Babes in arms. My funny valentine] *My funny valentine.* Arranged for harp by Michael Amorosi. [Santa Monica, Calif.]: Salvi Harps, c1937. 3 pp. (Salvi pop series)

2972. ————. [Babes in arms. My funny valentine] *My funny valentine.* Arranged by Paul Baker. Ellensburg, Wash.: F.C. Publishing Co., c1990. 6 pp. (Popcycle series)

2973. ————. [Babes in arms. Where or when] *Where or when.* Arranged for harp by Michael Amorosi. Santa Monica, Calif.: Salvi Publications, c1937. 2 pp. (Salvi pop series)

2974. ————. [Musical comedies. Selections] *Rodgers & Hammerstein for the harp.* [Arr. by Deborah Friou]. Glendale, Calif.: Friou Music, c1990. 48 pp. For pedal or non-pedal harp. [NP] CONTENTS: The sound of music: The sound of music; Edelweiss; My favorite things; Morning hymn; Alleluia. Carousel: If I loved you; You'll never walk alone. South Pacific: Some enchanted evening; Dîtes-moi; A wonderful guy. Flower drum song: Love, look away; You are beautiful. Oklahoma: Oklahoma; Oh, what a beautiful mornin'; The surrey with the fringe on top. The king and I: Getting to know you; We kiss in a shadow; Dance of Anna and Sir Edward; Hello, young lovers.

2975. ————. [On your toes. There's a small hotel] *There's a small hotel.* Arranged by Lynne Wainwright Palmer. San Mateo, Calif.: F.C. Publishing Co., [1989], c1948. 3 pp. (Popcycle series)

2976. ————. [Sound of music. Edelweiss] *Edelweiss.* Arranged by Louise Trotter. Ellensburg, Wash.: F.C. Publishing Co., c1990. 4 pp. (Popcycle series)

2977. ————. [South Pacific. Some enchanted evening] *Some enchanted evening.* Arr. Victoria Hughes. New York: Williamson Music, 1993. 3 pp.

2978. ————. [State Fair. It might as well be spring] *It might as well be spring.* Arranged by John B. Escosa. San Mateo, Calif.: F.C. Publishing Co., c1989. 3 pp. (Popcycle series)

2979. Rodrigo, Joaquín, 1901–. *Concerto de Aranjuez.* Transcripción para arpa. Digitación de = fingering by Nicanor Zabaleta. [New York]: Schott, c1959. 1 part (35 pp.). For harp unacc.; originally for guitar and orchestra.

2980. ———. [Concierto de Aranjuez. Adagio; arr.] *Concerto de Aranjuez: second movement: solo harp.* Transcribed by Paul Hurst from the celebrated guitar concerto. Marina Del Rey, Calif.: Safari, c1989. 11 pp. "The full orchestra accompaniment is integrated into this solo harp arrangement."

2981. Rollin, Monique, 1927–, arr. *Pièces anciennes: pour harpe celtique.* Recueillies par Monique Rollin. Paris: Alphonse Leduc, c1986. 19 pp. [NP] CONTENTS: Courante italienne. Greensleeves. Bourrée by Robert de Visée. The squirrel's toy by Francis Cutting. Willson's wilde. Aria autrichien. Grisse his delight by Thomas Robinson. Chaconne autrichienne. The queen's gigue by Thomas Robinson. Courante anglaise. Les cloches de Paris. Row well, you mariners by Thomas Robinson. Romance. Melancholy gaillarde by John Dowland. Fantasia by Alonso Mudarra.

2982. Rosati, Luigi. *Preludio.* Trascrizione per arpa di Alba Novella Schirinzi. Milan: Carisch, c1960. 7 pp.

2983. Rose, David, 1910–1990. *Our waltz.* Arr. Louise Trotter. Ellensburg, Wash.: F.C. Publishing Co., 1992. 2 pp.

2984. Rossi, Irene, arr. *Raccolta di clavicembalisti italiani.* Trascritti e diteggiati per arpa da Irene Rossi. Milan: Edizioni Curci, c1972. 9 pp. CONTENTS: Corrente by G. Frescobaldi. Aria di ballo by Grieco. Pastorale by D. Scarlatti. Gavotta by D. Zipoli. Allegretto by G. B. Pescetti.

2985. Rossi, Michelangelo, 17th cent. *Andantino.* Trascrizione per arpa di Alba Novella Schirinzi. Milan: Carisch, c1965. 3 pp.

2986. ———. *Andantino ed Allegro.* [Arr. by] L. M. Magistretti. Frankfurt: Zimmermann, n.d. 5 pp. (Des Harfenisten Konzert-Programm, Nr. 1)

2987. Rossini, Gioacchino, 1792–1868. [Guillaume Tell. Selections; arr.] *The most admired airs: from G. Rossini's celebrated opera Guillaume Tell.* Arr. for the harp by N. C. Bochsa. London: Goulding & D'Almaine, [183–?]. 2 v.

2988. ———. [Guillaume Tell. Petit souvenir; arr.] *Petit souvenir: the celebrated air Tyrolien in Rossini's opera Guillaume Tell.* Arr. in an easy & effective manner for the harp by N. C. Bochsa. London: Goulding & D'Almaine, [183–?]. 6 pp.

2989. ———. [Guillaume Tell. Toi que l'oiseau; arr.] *Petit souvenir: the celebrated Air tyrolien in Rossini's opera Guillaume Tell.* Arranged in an easy & effective manner for the harp by N. C. Bochsa. London: Goulding & D'Almaine, [183–?]. 6 pp.

2990. ———. [Soirées musicales. Selections; arr.] *La partenza; La promessa; et, L'orgia: trois airs des Soirées musicales de Rossini.* Arr. d'une manière facile pour la harpe par E. Parish-Alvars. Milan: Ricordi, [1837? or 1838?]. 12 pp. Originally for 1 or 2 voices and piano.

2991. ———. [Zelmira. Cara deh attendimi; arr.] *Cara deh attendimi: a favorite air from the opera of Zelmira.* Arr. for the harp by Gustavus Holst. London: Lavenu, [between 1821? and 1827?]. 5 pp.

2992. Rota, Nino, 1911–1979. [Romeo and Juliet. Love theme] *A time for us: love theme from the movie Romeo and Juliet.* Arranged for folk harp by Louise Trotter. Edmonds, Wash.: Paradise Music, c1968. 2 pp. [NP]

2993. ———. [Romeo and Juliet. Love theme] *A time for us.* Arranged by Penny Howk Beavers. San Mateo, Calif.: F.C. Publishing Co., [1988], c1968. 4 pp. (Popcycle series)

2994. Rouget de Lisle, Claude Joseph, 1760–1836. [Marseillaise; arr.] *27th, 28th & 29th of July in Paris: The French national air of liberty (The Marseillaise hymn).* Arranged for the harp by N. Bochsa. London: Bochsa, [184–?]. 7 pp.

2995. Rubinstein, Anton, 1829–1894. [Melodies, piano, op. 3, no. 1; arr.] *Melody in F.* New York: International Music, n.d. 9 pp.

2996. ———. [Melodies, piano, op. 3, no. 1; arr.] *Melody in F.* Transcribed for harp by Carlos Salzedo. New York: Carl Fischer, Inc., c1925. 5 pp.

2997. ———. [Pieces, piano, op. 26. Romance; arr.] *Romance en fa (F-dur), op. 26, no. 1.* [Transciption] pour la harpe de J. Snoer. Leipzig: Aug. Cranz, ca. 1910? 2 pp.

2998. Saint-Saëns, Camille, 1835–1921. [Carnaval des animaux. Cygne; arr.] *Le cygne = The swan.* Trancription pour la harpe par Alph. Hasselmans. Paris: Durand, 1888. 4 pp.

2999. ———. [Samson et Dalila. Mon coeur s'ouvre à ta voix; arr.] *Mon coeur s'ouvre à ta voix, op. 60 [in D♭ major].* Transcription pour harpe [par J. Snoer de] Samson et Delilah. Cantabile extrait du duo "Mon coeur s'ouvre à ta voix." Paris: Durand, n.d. 7 pp.

3000. ———. [Samson et Dalila. Mon coeur s'ouvre à ta voix; arr.] *My heart at thy sweet voice: aria from Samson and Delilah.* Transcr. and arr. for harp by Nina S. Miller. New York: Belwin, [19—?]. 7 pp. (Classics for concert harp, no. 5)

3001. ———. [Samson et Dalila. Mon coeur s'ouvre à ta voix; arr.] *My heart at thy sweet voice.* Arranged by Phyllis Schlomovitz. [Palo Alto, Calif.]: Harpress of California, [198–?]. 4 pp.

3002. ———. [Sérénade, organ, piano, violin, viola, op. 15; arr.] *Sérénade.* Transcrite pour harpe par Gabriel Verdalle. Paris: Choudens, [18—?]. 4 pp.

3003. Salzedo, Carlos, 1885–1961, arr. *Believe me, if all those endearing young charms.* Transcribed for harp by Carlos Salzedo. New York: Carl Fischer, c1925. 5 pp.

3004. ———, arr. *Deep River: old negro melody.* Transcribed for harp by Carlos Salzedo. New York: Carl Fischer, Inc., c1925. 5 pp.

3005. ———, arr. *Favorite melodies: transcribed for harp: series 1.* New York: Composers' Music Corp., c1925. 1 v. CONTENTS: Believe me, if all those endearing young charms. My old Kentucky home. The last rose of summer. Annie Laurie. Deep river. Song of the Volga boatmen. Theme and variations by Josef Haydn. Largo by G. F. Handel.

3006. ———, arr. *Londonderry air.* Transcribed for harp by Carlos Salzedo. Philadelphia: Elkan-Vogel, c1945. 3 pp.

3007. ———, arr. [New wedding marches] *Two new wedding marches.* Philadelphia: Elkan-Vogel, c1950. 7 pp. CONTENTS: March of the priests from Alceste by C. W. von Gluck. Coronation march from Le prophete by Giacomo Meyerbeer.

3008. ———, arr. [Popular classics, book 1] *Popular classics: transcribed for harp: series I.* New York: Composers' Music Corp., c1925. 1 v. CONTENTS: Waltz in A flat by Johannes Brahms. Humoreske by Anton Dvorak. Gavotte from Iphigenia in Aulis by C. W. von Gluck. Barcarolle from The tales of Hoffmann by Jacques Offenbach. Melody in F by Anton Rubinstein.

3009. ———, arr. *Song of the Volga boatmen.* Transcribed for harp by Carlos Salzedo. New York: Carl Fischer, c1923. 3 pp.

3010. ———, arr. [Wedding marches] *Two wedding marches.* Transcribed for harp [by Carlos Salzedo]. Philadelphia: Elkan-Vogel, c1942. 7 pp. CONTENTS: Lohengrin by Wagner. Midsummer night's dream by Mendelssohn.

3011. Samazeuilh, Gustave, 1877–1967. [Serenade, guitar; arr.] *Sérénade: pour guitare.* Version pour harpe à pédales par l'auteur. Paris: Durand, c1927. 5 pp.

3012. Satie, Erik, 1866–1925. [Gymnopédies. No. 1; arr.] *Gymnopédie no. 1.* Arr. Victoria Hughes. Ellensburg, Wash.: F.C. Publishing Co., 1993. 3 pp. Originally for piano.

3013. Scarlatti, Domenico, 1685–1757. [Sonatas, harpsichord. Selections; arr.] *Trois sonates de Domenico Scarlatti: pour la harpe à pédales.* [Arr. by] Maïté Etcheverry. Paris: Editions Choudens, c1984. 11 pp. (Les classiques transcrits pour la harpe)

3014. ———. [Sonatas, harpsichord. Selections; arr.] *Sonatas: para arpa.* Transcripción de Ma. Rosa Calvo-Manzano. Madrid: Unión Musical Española, 1985. 30 pp.

3015. ———. [Sonatas, harpsichord, K. 9, D minor; arr.] *Pastorale*. Transcrizione per arpa di Gabriella Elsa Consolini. Bologna: Umberto Pizzi, 1928. 4 pp.

3016. ———. [Sonatas, harpsichord, K. 14, G major; arr.] *Two sonatas.* Transcribed for the harp by Stephanie Curcio. Stratham, N.H.: Stephanie Curcio Publications, c1990. 7 pp.

3017. ———. [Sonatas, harpsichord, K. 113, A major; arr.] *Sonata: in A major.* Transcribed by Susanna Mildonian. New York, N.Y.: Lyra Music Co., c1972. 5 pp.

3018. ———. [Sonatas, harpsichord, K. 208, A major; arr.] *Two sonatas.* Transcribed for harp by Clifford Wooldridge. Chicago, Ill.: Lyon & Healy, c1987. 7 pp. (The Lyon & Healy treasury of harp music) CONTENTS: A major (K.208, Longo 238); F minor (K. 239, Longo 281).

3019. ———. [Sonatas, harpsichord, K. 377, B minor; arr.] *Bourrée.* [Arr. by] L. M. Magistretti. Frankfurt: Zimmerman, n.d. 5 pp. (Des Harfenisten Konzert-Programm, Nr. 2) Originally in B minor; transposed to B♭ minor.

3020. ———. [Sonatas, harpsichord, K. 380, E major. Capriccio; arr.] *Capriccio: sonata in mi majeur.* [Transcribed for harp by] H. Renié. Paris: Alphonse Leduc, c1958. 5 pp.

3021. ———. [Sonatas, harpsichord, K. 441, B♭ major; arr.] *Sonata: in B♭ minor* [*sic*]. Transcribed by Susanna Mildonian. New York, N.Y.: Lyra Music Co., c1974. 4 pp.

3022. Schlomovitz, Phyllis, arr. [Christmas carols] *Six Christmas carols: with interludes to be played as medleys or separately.* Arranged by Phyllis Schlomovitz. [Palo Alto, Calif.]: P. Schlomovitz, c1958. 12 pp. CONTENTS: Three medieval carols: The first Noel; God rest ye merry gentlemen; Wake now ye shepherds. Three favorite carols: Joy to the world; Oh little town of Bethlehem; Silent night.

3023. ———, arr. [Christmas carols for beginning harpists and improvisation] *Four Christmas carols for beginning harpists and improvisation.* Transcribed by Phyllis Schlomovitz. Sunnyvale, Calif.: Harpress, c1976. 2 pp. CONTENTS: Christ was born on Christmas day. Silent night by Gruber, arr. Schlomovitz. The first noel. Coventry carol.

3024. ———, arr. *Fascination: old Viennese melody.* Arranged by Phyllis Schlomovitz. Palo Alto, Calif.: Harpress of California, [1981?]. 2 pp. (Phyllis Schlomovitz harp transcriptions: popular series)

3025. ———, arr. [Medieval Christmas carols] *Four medieval Christmas carols.* Arranged by Phyllis Schlomovitz. [Palo Alto, Calif.]: Harpress of California, c1971. 7, [2] pp. (Phyllis Schlomovitz harp transcriptions) "for the intermediate player . . . . The carols may be played as a medley if a pedal harp is used. . . ." [NP] CONTENTS: The first Noel; Angels we have heard on high; Greensleeves; He is born.

3026. ———, arr. *More songs for special occasions*. Transcribed by Phyllis Schlomovitz. Palo Alto, Calif.: Harpress of California, c1980. 2, 2 pp. (Phyllis Schlomovitz harp transcriptions) CONTENTS: Trumpet voluntary by Purcell [i.e. Jeremiah Clarke]. Rigaudon (from Idominée-1712) by André Campra.

3027. ———, arr. *Songs for special occasions*. Arranged by Phyllis Schlomovitz. Palo Alto, Calif.: Harpress of California, c1977. 7 pp. (Phyllis Schlomovitz harp transcriptions) CONTENTS: Wedding march from Midsummer night's dream by Mendelssohn. Anniversary waltz. Bride's march from Lohengrin by R. Wagner. Happy birthday. Pomp and circumstance: for graduations by Elgar.

3028. ———, arr. *Variations on Sakura*. Arranged by Schlomovitz. Palo Alto, Calif.: Harpress of California, c1983. 9 pp. [NP]

3029. Schmidt, Harvey, 1929–. [Fantasticks. Soon it's gonna rain] *Soon it's gonna rain*. Arranged for harp by Verlye Mills. Santa Monica, Calif.: Salvi Harps, c1960. 4 pp. (Salvi pop series)

3030. ———. [Fantasticks. Try to remember] *Try to remember*. Arranged by Phyllis Schlomovitz. Palo Alto, Calif.: Harpress of California, [1981?], c1960. 2 pp. (Phyllis Schlomovitz harp transcriptions: popular series)

3031. ———. [Fantasticks. Try to remember] *Try to remember*. Arranged by Mimi Allen. Ellensburg, Wash.: F.C. Publishing Co., c1990. 4 pp. (Popcycle series)

3032. Schobert, Johann, 1720–1767. *Andante [in D minor]*. Trans. classique pour harpe par Marcel Grandjany. Paris: Senart, c1930. 3 pp. Originally for harpsichord?

3033. Schroeder, R., arr. *Favorite airs*. Arranged for the harp by R. Schroeder. [London: R. Schroeder, 182–]. 5 v. "Published by R. Schroeder, Professor of the Harp & pianoforte, 7 New Bridge Str. Vauxhall. . . ." CONTENTS: Ye banks and braes; Dunois the brave; Hungarian waltz; Miss Dennett's waltz; Flow on thou shining river; Depuis longtems [*sic*]; O! Nanny wilt thou gang wi' me?; Waters of Elle; Cease your funning; My lodging; The legacy; Gramachree; Sul margine; O pescator dell' onda; The carnival of Venice; Fly not yet!

3034. Schubert, Franz, 1797–1828. [Ellens Gesang, D. 839; arr.] *Meditation*. [Arr. by Tiny Béon]. Paris: Louis Rouhier, n.d. 3 pp. Originally for voice and piano.

3035. ———. [Ellens Gesang, D. 839; arr.] *Ave Maria*. Transcribed for harp by John Thomas. Abergavenny, Gwent, Wales: Adlais, n.d. 10 pp. Originally for voice with piano accompaniment.

3036. ———. [Ellens Gesang, D. 839; arr.] *Ave Maria*. [Arr. by Beatrix Fels]. Berlin: Bote & Bock, c1894. 7 pp. Originally for voice and piano.

3037. ———. [Ellens Gesang, D. 839; arr.] *Ave Maria: harp solo*. Transcribed by Marcel Grandjany. New York, N.Y.: Lyra Music Co., c1963. 8 pp. Originally for voice with piano accompaniment.

3038. ———. [Ellens Gesang, D. 839; arr.] *Ave Maria*. Harp arr. by Sharon Watson. West Palm Beach, Fla.: Sharon Watson, c1981. 4 pp. Originally for voice with piano accompaniment.

3039. ———. [Ellens Gesang, D. 839; arr.] *Ave Maria*. Arranged by Penny Howk Beavers. Ellensburg, Wash.: F.C. Publishing Co., c1990. 3 pp. Originally for voice with piano accompaniment.

3040. ———. [Originaltänze. No. 2. Trauerwalzer; arr.] *Waltz: no. 2: in A flat*. Transcribed for the harp by Félix Godefroid; edited by Alice Lawson Aber. Ross, Calif: Harp Publications; Bryn Mawr, Penn.: T. Presser, c1974. 4 pp. Originally for piano.

3041. ———. [Schwanengesang. Ständchen; arr.] *Schubert's Serenade*. Transcription by D. Alberti. New York: Carl Fischer, Inc., c1914. 9 pp. Originally for piano and voice.

3042. ———. [Schwanengesang. Ständchen; arr.] *Two Schubert songs*. Arranged by Daniel Burton. San Diego, Calif.: Jubal Press, c1986. 8 pp. (Jubal harp series) Originally for voice with piano acc. CONTENTS: Serenade; Ave Maria.

3043. ———. [Selections; arr.] *Schubert-Album: für Harfe*. Pedal- oder chromatische Harfe eingerichtet und progressive geordnet von Johannes Snoer. Leipzig: F. Leuckhart, c1908. 18 pp. CONTENTS: Der Tod und das Mädchen, op. 84; Moment musical, op. 94, no. 3; Lied der Mignon; Lob der Tränen; Sechsuchts-Walzer; Deutsche Tänze, op. 33; Häiden Röslein; Entre-Act aus Rosamunde; Aus der A-dur Sonate, op. 120.

3044. ———. [Songs. Selections; arr.] *Schubert's songs*. Transcribed for the harp by John Thomas. London: Hutchings & Romer, n.d. 1 v. Originally for piano and voice. CONTENTS: Ave Maria; The Erl king; Serenade; The praise of tears (Lob der Thränen); Marguerite (Gretchen at her spinning-wheel); The wanderer; Barcarolle; The maiden's lament (Das Mädchens Klage); The promise of spring (Frühlingsglaube); L'adieu.

3045. ———. [Waltzes, piano. Selections; arr.] *Waltzes: for harp*. Transcribed by Cynthia Price. Boston, Mass.: Boston Editions, c1984. 21 pp. Contains 26 waltzes, originally for piano.

3046. Schuman, Ellis, 1931–, arr. *The minstrel boy*. Arr. Ellis Schuman. Ellensburg, Wash.: F.C. Publishing Co., 1992. 4 pp. [NP]

3047. Schumann, Robert, 1810–1856. [Album für die Jugend. No. 1.

Melodie; arr.] *Melody.* Transcribed for harp by Marie Miller. New York: Carl Fischer, c1925. 3 pp. (Popular classics transcribed for harp: series 2) Originally for piano.

3048. ———. [Album für die Jugend. No. 14. Kleine Studie; arr.] *Petite etude.* Transcribed for harp by Marie Miller. New York: Carl Fischer, Inc., c1925. 5 pp. (Popular classics transcribed for harp. Series 2) Originally for piano.

3049. ———. [Album für die Jugend. No. 41. Nordisches Lied; arr.] *Norse song: theme and variations.* Transcription for harp by Hulda E. Kreiss. West Babylon, N.Y.: Harold Branch Publishing, c1967. 8 pp. Originally for piano.

3050. ———. [Albumblätter. Wiegenliedchen; arr.] *Cradle song, op. 124, no. 6.* Adapted for harp by Pearl Chertok. New York: Interstate Music, n.d. 2 pp. Originally for piano.

3051. ———. [Carnaval. Selections; arr.] *Eusebius; and, Chopin: from Carnaval.* Transcribed for harp by Clifford Wooldridge. Chicago, Ill.: Lyon & Healy, c1986. 5 pp. (The Lyon & Healy treasury of harp music) Originally for piano.

3052. ———. [Kinderscenen. Träumerei; arr.] *Träumerei.* [Arr. by D. Alberti]. New York: Carl Fischer, c1914. 5 pp. Originally for piano.

3053. ———. [Kinderscenen. Träumerei; arr.] *Traumerei.* Arranged for harp by Anna B. Stuckey. S.l.: s.n., c1979. 2 pp. Originally for piano.

3054. ———. [Waldscenen. Vogel als Prophet; arr.] *L'oiseau-prophète.* Transcribed for harp by H. Renié. Paris: Gay & Tenton, c1928. 3 pp. Originally for piano.

3055. Scott, Alicia Ann Spottiswoode, Lady John Montague-Douglas, 1810–1900. *Annie Laurie.* Transcription for harp by John Cheshire. Boston: O. Ditson, c1912. 5 pp. Originally a Scottish ballad.

3056. ———. *Annie Laurie.* Transcribed for harp by Carlos Salzedo. New York: Carl Fischer, c1925. 3 pp. Originally a Scottish ballad.

3057. Scriabin, Aleksandr Nikolayevich, 1872–1915. [Preludes, piano. Selections; arr.] *Trois préludes.* Adaptation pour harpe de Francis Pierre. Paris: Jobert, c1990. 7 pp. CONTENTS: Prélude, op. 51, no. 2; Prélude pour la main gauche, op. 9, no. 1; Prélude en si-bémol majeur (extrait des 7 préludes, op. 17).

3058. Segal, Jack, 1918–, and Danzig, Evelyn. *Scarlet ribbons.* Arranged by John B. Escosa. San Mateo, Calif.: F.C. Publishing Co., c1949. 3 pp. (Popcycle series)

3059. Séverac, Déodat de, 1872–1921. *En vacances = Holiday time = Ferien: petites pièces romantiques de moyenne difficulté pour piano.* Transcrit pour harpe par H. Renié. Paris: Rouart, c1929. 23 pp. Originally for piano. CONTENTS: Invocation à Schumann; Les caresses de grand'maman; Les petites voisines en visite; Toto déguise en Suisse d'église; Mimi se déguise en marquise; Ronde dans le parc; Où l'on entend une vieille boîte à musique; Valse romantique.

3060. ———. [En vacances. Selections; arr.] *En vacances = Holiday time = Ferien: petites pièces romantiques de moyen difficulté pour piano: 1er recueil.* Le recueil pour harpe H. Renié. Paris: Rouart, Lerolle, c1911. 23 pp. Originally for piano. CONTENTS: Au château et dans le parc, précédé de Invocation à Schumann.

3061. Shearing, George, 1919–. *Lullaby of birdland.* Arranged by Ray Pool. San Mateo, Calif.: F.C. Publishing Co., c1988. 4 pp. (Popcycle series)

3062. Sherman, Daryl, 1949–. *Cycling along with you.* Arranged by Eleanor Fell. San Mateo, Calif.: F.C. Publishing Co., c1988. 5 pp. (Popcycle series)

3063. Silésu, Lao. *Un peu d'amour: mélodie (paraphrased).* [Arr. by. A. Pinto]. New York: Chappell & Co., c1913. 8 pp.

3064. Smart, Henry Thomas, 1813–1879. *Angels from the realms of glory.* Arr. by Wm. T. Cameron. Washington, D.C.: William Truesdale Cameron, n.d. 1 p. [NP]

3065. Smetana, Bedřich, 1824–1884. [Má vlast. Vltava; arr.] *Moldau: symphonische Dichtung, op. 43.* Transcr. v. Hans Trneček. [New York, N.Y.?]: Lyra Music Co., [197–?]. 19 pp. Originally for orchestra.

3066. ———. [Má vlast. Vyšehrad; arr] *Vysehrad.* Arr. Hans Trneček; ed. Rajka Dobronić-Mazzoni. New York, N.Y.: Lyra Music Co., 1990. 19 pp. Originally for orchestra.

3067. Smith, John Stafford, 1750–1836. *The star-spangled banner: national American anthem.* Harmonized and transcribed for harp [by Carlos Salzedo]. New York: Composers' Music Corp., c1925. 3 pp.

3068. Smith, Wilfred, 1911–, arr. *Music for the harp and clarsach.* Selected and arranged by Wilfred Smith. London: Thames Publishing, c1979. 21 pp. [NP] CONTENTS: Music for the court of Henry VII. Menuet in the style of XVIIth century. Study. Tambourine by Jean Philippe Rameau. Andante; Menuet in F by Wolfgang Amadeus Mozart. The boatie rows: Scotch air with variations by Johann Ladislaus Dussek. Cradle song by Franz Schubert. The sheriff's fancy. Ferdinando. Eriskay love lilt. The delight of Merioneth. Greensleeves. David of the white rock.

3069. Snoer, Johannes, 1868–1936, arr. *Album für Harfe: ausgewahlte Melodien: progressiv geordnet und mit Fingersatz und Pedalbezeichnung versehen für angehende Harfenspieler.* Arr. by Johannes Snoer. Leipzig: Friedrich Hofmeister, n.d. 31 pp. CONTENTS: Letzte Rose. Sarabande; Largo by Handel. Arie aus Joseph in Egypten by Méhul. Arie aus Zar und

Zimmermann by Lortzing. Menuett aus Don Juan by Mozart. An Alexis send' ich dich by Himmel. Beigen seliger Geister by Gluck. Die Nachtigall by Alabieff. Meermädchen aus Oberon by Weber. Arie aus Die Zauberflöte by Mozart. Gute Nacht by Schubert. Im wunderschönen Monat Mai; Allnächtlich im Traume by Schumann. Lob der Thränen; Heidenröslein by Schubert. Abendlied by Schumann. Der Lindenbaum; Lied der Mignon by Schubert. 1. prelude by Bach. Frühlingsglaube; Ständchen by Schubert. Von fremden Ländern; Bittendes Kind; Glückes genug; Träumerei; Fast zu ernst; Der Dichter spricht by Schumann. Du bist die Ruh by Schubert. Melodie by Rubinstein.

3070. ———, arr. *Klassische Stücke, op. 58: Sammlung beliebter Melodien klassischer Komponisten für Harfe eingerichtet.* Leipzig: Breitkopf & Härtel, c1905. CONTENTS: Einsam bin ich nicht alleine: arie aus Preziosa by von Weber. Bei Männern, welche Liebe fühlen: Duett aus der Zauberflöte; O Isis und Osiris: Arie und Cor aus der Zauberflöte: K.620 by Mozart. Sarabande: [BWV 1012] by Bach. Durch die Wälder, durch die Auen: Arie aus dem Freischütz by von Weber. Andante by Gluck. Armes Waisenkind op. 68, no. 6; Fröhlicher Landmann op. 68, no. 10; Matrosenlied op. 68, no. 37 by Schumann. Larghetto aus dem Klarinetten-Quintett, K.581 by Mozart. Ernteliedchen op. 68, no. 24; Sylvesterlied op. 68, no. 43 by Schumann.

3071. Soler, Antonio, 1729–1783. [Sonatas, keyboard instrument. Selections; arr.] *Seis sonatas: para arpa.* Transcripción de Ma. Rosa Calvo-Manzano. Madrid: Unión Musical Española, c1975. xvi, 44 pp. Arr. from the ed. by S. Rubio. CONTENTS: No. 70, A minor; no. 77, F# minor; no. 78, F# minor; no. 73, D major; no. 76, F major; no. 72, Doric mode.

3072. ———. [Sonatas, keyboard instrument. Selections; arr.] *Seis sonatas: para arpa: volumen II.* Transcripción de Ma. Rosa Calvo-Manzano. Madrid: Unión Musical Española, c1980. xvi, 49 pp. Arr. from ed. by S. Rubio. CONTENTS: No. 84, D major; no. 45, G major; no. 53, A major; no. 54, C major; no. 22, D major; no. 38, C major.

3073. Sondheim, Stephen, 1930–. [Little night music. Send in the clowns] *Send in the clowns.* Arranged by Paul Baker. Ellensburg, Wash.: F.C. Publishing Co., [1989], c1973. 4 pp. (Popcycle series)

3074. ———. [Merrily we roll along. Not a day goes by] *Not a day goes by.* Arranged by Michael Rado. Ellensburg, Wash.: F.C. Publishing Co., c1981. 3 pp. (Popcycle series)

3075. Sor, Fernando, 1778–1839. [Introduction à l'étude de la guitare. Elegancia; arr.] *Elegancia, op. 60, no. 3.* [Arranged] for harp [by] May Hogan Cambern. [New York]: Michael Cambern, c1966. 2 pp. (From the notebook of May Hogan Cambern) For harp or troubadour harp; originally for guitar. [NP]

3076. Spiller, Henry, arr. *Three medieval songs and dances.* [Calif.]: Harpress of California, 1989. 6 pp.

3077. Sporck, Georges, 1870–1943. [Petites pièces, piano] *Deux petites pièces: de piano.* Transcrites pour harpe par Mlle. Lucile Delcourt. Paris: A. Quinzard & Cie., n.d. 2 v. CONTENTS: Pensée lointaine; Élégie.

3078. Stefano, Salvatore de, 1887–1981. *Variations on a theme by Corelli: from the Gavotte of the Sonata in F for violin, op. 5, no. 10: harp solo.* [New York]: Lyra Music Co., c1965. 12 pp.

3079. Steibelt, Daniel, 1765–1823. *Study: a study in pedalling.* Arr. by Marie Goossens. London: Salvi International, n.d. 3 pp. Originally for piano.

3080. Stevenson, Ronald, 1928–, arr. *Sounding strings: an album of Celtic music for clarsach, pedal harp or piano.* Arranged by Ronald Stevenson. London: United Music Publishers, Ltd., c1979. 16 pp. [NP] CONTENTS: Harp of gold (Y delyn aur); The ash grove (Llwyn on); Hal-an-tow; A fairy's love song; The sheep under the snow; Savourneen Deelish; The cockle-gatherer; Tune from County Derry; Eriskay love-lilt; Ben Dorain; La basse bretonne; The old woman's reel; L'angelus breton; The Christ Child's lullaby.

3081. Still, William Grant, 1895–1978. [Song for the lonely; arr.] *Song for the lonely.* Words by Verna Arvey; transcribed for solo harp by Mary Spalding Portanova. [S.l.: s.n.], 1972. 6 pp. Originally for piano and voice.

Stivell, Alan, 1944–, arr. *Renaissance de la harpe celtique.* See 1958.

3082. Strauss, Johann, 1825–1899. [An der schönen blauen Donau; arr.] *The blue Danube waltz.* Arranged by Louise Trotter. Ellensburg, Wash.: F.C. Publishing Co., c1989. 8 pp. (Popcycle series) Originally for orchestra.

3083. Streisand, Barbra, 1942–. [Star is born. Evergreen; arr.] *Evergreen.* Arr. Stella Castellucci. [Santa Monica, Calif.]: Salvi Publications, 1978. 5 pp. (Salvi pop series)

3084. Strick, Susan, arr. *A Christmas medley: folk harp solo.* Arranged by Susan Strick. Edmonds, Wash.: Paradise Music, c1987. 5 pp. [NP] CONTENTS: God rest ye merry, gentlemen; The holly and the ivy; In dulci jubilo; Silent night.

3085. ――――, arr. [Old English carols] *Three old English carols: for folk harp [and voice].* Arranged by Susan Strick. Edmonds, Wash.: Paradise Music, c1987. Score 6 pp. and 1 part. [NP] CONTENTS: When Christ was born of Mary free; Blessed be that maid Marie; Wassail song.

3086. Suessdorf, Karl, 1911–. *Moonlight in Vermont.* [Santa Monica, Calif.: Salvi Publications], c1978. 4 pp. (Salvi Pop series)

3087. Suriano, Alberta, arr. *Partita: da antiche danze ed arie per liuto di autori anonimi del Sec. XVII.* Elaborate e trascritte per arpa Alberta Suriani.

Bologna: Edizioni Bongiovanni, 1953. 8 pp. Originally for lute. CONTENTS: Preludio; Balletto; Pastorale; Gagliarda.

3088. Tchaikovsky, Peter Ilich, 1840–1893. [Morceaux, piano, op. 51. Valse sentimentale; arr.] *Valse sentimentale, op. 51, no. 6.* Moscow: P. Jurgenson, c1900. 9 pp. Originally for piano.

3089. ———. [Nutcracker. Selections; arr.] *The nutcracker suite.* Arranged by Chuck Bird and Susan Peters. Hollywood, Calif.: Katbird, n.d. 1 v. Originally for orchestra. CONTENTS: Overture; Marche; Dance of the sugar plum fairy; Russian dance (Trepak); Arabian dance; Chinese dance; Dance of the mirlitons; Waltz of the flowers.

3090. ———. [Nutcracker. Selections; arr.] *The nutcracker ballet selections.* Arranged by Eleanor Fell; edited by Linda Wood Rollo for non-pedal or pedal harp. Bloomington, Ind.: Vanderbilt Music Co., Inc., 1992. 16 pp. (Pop 'n easy) [NP] CONTENTS: Introduction; Glossary; March; Trepak; Arabian dance; Chinese dance; Dance of the reed pipes; Waltz of the flowers.

3091. ———. [Nutcracker. Selections; arr.] *Waltz of the flowers; and, Dance of the sugar plum fairy.* Arr. Katherine Honey. Ellensburg, Wash.: F. C. Publishing Co., 1992. 4 pp.

3092. ———. [Selections; arr.] *Twelve works for solo harp.* Marina del Rey, Calif.: Safari Publications, n.d. 84 pp. CONTENTS: Distant past; Natasha's waltz; Romance in F; Song of the lark; Waltz in F minor; White nights; Lullaby; Sentimental waltz; Barcarolle; Lyrical moment; Autumn song; The troika ride.

3093. ———. [Songs, op. 54. Legenda; arr] *Legend.* [Calif.]: Harpress of California, 1990. 8 pp.

3094. Telemann, Georg Philipp, 1681–1767. [Fantaisies, harpsichord. 1ere douzaine. No. 8; arr.] *Little fantaisie: harp solo.* Transcribed by Solange Renié. New York, N.Y.: Lyra Music Co., c1964. 4 pp.

3095. Thalberg, Sigismond, 1812–1871. *Home sweet home: fantaisie of S. Thalberg.* Transcribed for the harp by William Streather. London: Edwin Ashdown, n.d. 15 pp.

3096. Thomas, John, 1826–1913, arr. *Ar hyd y nos = All through the night.* Arranged by John Thomas. London; Boston: Ashdown, [1919?]. 7 pp. (Welsh melodies for the harp, no. 19)

3097. ———, arr. *Ar hyd nos = All through the night: harp.* Arranged by John Thomas. Santa Monica, Calif.: Salvi Publications, c1983. 7 pp.

3098. ———, arr. *Bugeilio'r gwenith gwyn = Watching the wheat.* [Arranged by] John Thomas. Abergavenny, Gwent: Adlais, [197–?]. 5 pp.

3099. ———, arr. *Bugeilio'r gwenith gwyn = Watching the wheat.* [Arranged by] John Thomas. New York: Lyra Music Co., [1980?]. 5 pp.

3100. ——, arr. *Codiad yr haul = The rising of the sun.* [Arranged by] John Thomas. [Abergavenny, Gwent]: Adlais, c1979. 5 pp.

3101. ——, arr. *Dafydd y garreg wen = David of the white rock.* [Arr. by] John Thomas. Abergavenny, Gwent: Adlais, c1976. 8 pp. [NP]

3102. ——, arr. *Llwyn onn = The ash grove.* [Arranged by] John Thomas. [Abergavenny, Gwent]: Adlais, n.d. 5 pp. (Traditional Welsh melodies)

3103. ——, arr. *Merch Megan = Megan's daughter.* [Arr. by] John Thomas. Abergavenny, Gwent, Wales: Adlais, n.d. 9 pp.

3104. ——, arr. *Nos galan = New Year's eve: for harp.* Arranged by John Thomas. Santa Monica, Calif.: Salvi Publications, c1983. 6 pp.

3105. ——, arr. *Per alaw = Sweet melody: Sweet Richard: for harp.* [Arr. by] John Thomas. Santa Monica, Calif.: Salvi Publications, c1983. 8 pp.

3106. ——, arr. *Torriad y dydd = The dawn of day: harp.* Arranged by John Thomas. Santa Monica, Calif.: Salvi Publications, c1983. 8 pp.

3107. ——, arr. *Transcriptions: for the harp.* Abergavenny: Adlais, [1983?]. 4 v. CONTENTS: 1. Una furtiva lagrima (L'elisir d'amore); 2. M'apparì tutt'amor (Martha); 3. Assisa a piè d'un salice (Otello); 4. Nocturne (Dreyschock).

3108. ——, arr. *Welsh melodies: for the harp.* [Arr. by] John Thomas. London: Edwin Ashdown Ltd., n.d. 2 v. CONTENTS: Vol.1. Llwyn on (The ash grove). Clychau aberdyfi (The bells of Aberdovey). Per alaw (Sweet melody sweet Richard). Codiad yr haul (The rising of the sun). Rhyfelgyrch gwyr Harlech (The march of the men of Harlech). Riding over the mountain (original melody by J. Thomas). Morva Rhuddlan (The plain of Rhuddlan). Serch hudol (Love's fascination). Codiad yr hedydd (The rising of the lark). Y gadlys (The camp of noble race was Shenken). Merch Megan (Megan's daughter). The minstrel's adieu to his native land (original melody by J. Thomas).

Vol.2. Bugeilior gwenith gwyn (Watching the wheat). Nos galan (New Year's Eve). Dafydd y garreg wen (David of the white rock or The dying Bard to his harp). Tros y garreg (Over the stone). Merch y melinydd (The miller's daughter). Dewch ir frwydyr (Come to battle). Ar hyd y nos (All through the night). Y fwyalchen (The blackbird). Torriad y dydd (The dawn of day). Cwynfan Prydain (Britain's lament). Syr Harri ddu (Black Sir Harry). Ymadawiad y brenin (The departure of the king).

3109. Thomé, Francis, 1850–1909. *Simple aveu: romance sans paroles.* Transcription pour la harpe, Alph. Hasselmans. Paris: Durand Schoenewerk, [19—?]. 5 pp. Originally for piano.

3110. ——. *Sous la feuillée.* Transcription pour la harpe par Alph. Hasselmans. Paris: Durand & Fils, n.d. 5 pp. Originally for piano.

3111. Thomson, Lucien, 1913–, arr. [Christmas carols] *Ten Christmas carols.*

Transcribed for the harp with or without pedals by Lucien Thomson. New York: O. Pagani & Bro., Inc., c1969. 24 pp. Includes an accompaniment for 2nd harp for Silent night. [NP] CONTENTS: Away in a manger by M. Luther; The first Noel; God rest ye merry gentlemen; Good King Wenceslas; In the bleak mid-winter by Gustav Holst; It came upon the midnight clear by Richard S. Willis; Joy to the world by Handel; O come all ye faithful; Silent night (2 versions) by Franz Gruber; We three kings of orient are by John S. Hopkins.

3112. ———, arr. *Eighteenth century music.* Transcribed for harp by Lucien Thomson. San Mateo, Calif.: F.C. Publishing Co., c1987. 10 pp. (Solo series: harp) CONTENTS: Piece in A by Wilhelm Friedman Bach. Minuet by Georg Böhm. Allegro by Giovanni Battista Sammartini.

3113. ———, arr. *Romantic music.* Transcribed for the harp with or without pedals by Lucien Thomson. New York: O. Pagani & Bro., c1970. 14 pp. [NP] CONTENTS: Beautiful dreamer by S. Foster. Cradle song by F. Schubert. I dream of Jeanie by S. Foster. Lullaby, op. 49, no. 4 by J. Brahms. Nadir's song from The pearl fishers by G. Bizet. Old French song by P. Tchaikovsky.

3114. Torovsky, A. *Softly the stars were shining.* Arr. Wm. T. Cameron. Washington, D.C.: William Truesdale Cameron, n.d. 1 p. [NP]

3115. Trotter, Louise, 1927–, arr. *American heritage harp: solos and duets for all harps: folksongs.* Arranged by Louise Trotter. Houston, Tex.: Louise Trotter, [198–?]. Score 16 pp. [NP] CONTENTS: Red River valley; Streets of Laredo; Shenandoah; Arkansas traveler-Turkey in the straw; Camptown races; Amazing grace.

3116. ———, arr. *Black is the color of my true love's hair: traditional American melody: solo for folk harp.* Arranged by Louise Trotter. Houston, Texas: Louise Trotter, c1990. 3 pp. [NP]

3117. ———, arr. *Old Joe Clark.* Arranged by Louis Trotter. Houston, Texas: Louis Trotter, n.d. 3 pp.

3118. Turina, Joaquín, 1882–1949. *Tocata y fuga.* Version para arpa: Nicanor Zabaleta. Madrid: Union Musical Ediciones, c1990. 24 pp.

3119. Ungar, Jay, 1946–. *Ashokan farewell.* Arranged for harp by Deborah Friou. Glendale, Calif.: Friou Music, c1991. 2 pp. Originally published for piano. [NP]

3120. Van Heusen, Jimmy, 1913–1990. *Here's that rainy day.* Arr. Verlye Mills. [Santa Monica, Calif.]: Salvi, 1978. 4 pp. (Salvi pop series)

3121. Verdi, Giuseppe, 1813–1901. [Rigoletto. Donna è mobile; arr.] *La donna è mobile: the celebrated barcarolle sung by Mario in Verdi's new and admired opera Rigoletto.* London: Schott & Co., n.d. 7 pp.

3122. Vidal, Paul, 1863–1931. [Burgonde. Legende du glaive; arr.] *La burgonde: Legende du glaive.* Paris: Choudens, n.d. 7 pp. (Nouvelle collection pour harpe seule)

3123. Vito, Edward, 1902–1990, arr. *Londonderry air: for harp.* Transcribed by Edward Vito. New York: Composers Press, c1954. 4 pp.

3124. Vito, Joseph, 1887–. *By the brook.* Transcribed for harp by Joseph Vito. New York: Belwin, [1942]. 7 pp. (Classics for concert harp, no. 16)

3125. Vivaldi, Antonio, 1678–1741. [Estro armonico. N. 5; arr.] *Concerto: from concerti grossi L'estro armonico, op. 3, no. 5.* Arr. for the harp by Alice Lawson. San Anselmo, Calif.: A. Lawson, c1970. 9 pp. Originally for 2 violins and string orchestra.

3126. Von Würtzler, Aristid, 1930–, arr. *Adagio by Benedetto Marcello. Largo by Antonio Vivaldi.* Transcribed by Aristid von Würtzler. San Mateo, Calif.: F.C. Publishing Co., c1989. 12 pp. (Solo series: harp) Marcello work originally for oboe and string orchestra; Vivaldi work originally for lute, 2 violins, and continuo.

3127. ———, arr. *Seventeenth century Hungarian dances.* Arranged by Aristid Von Würtzler. Santa Monica, Calif.: Salvi Publications, c1983. 5 pp.

3128. Wade, Jill, arr. *Christmas celebrations: for harp.* Arranged by Jill Wade. Choctaw, Ok.: Harp Celebration Corp., c1990. CONTENTS, Vol.1: I saw three ships; The holly and the ivy; Infant holy, Infant lowly.

3129. ———. *Crown him medley.* Arr. Jill Wade. Choctaw, Ok.: Harp Celebration Corp., c1990. 8 pp. (Awake the harp)

3130. ———, arr. *Favorite hymns for harp.* Arranged by Jill Wade. Choctaw, Ok.: Harp Celebration Corp., c1986–1990. 2 v. Vol.2 has imprint: Harp Music Publications. CONTENTS: Vol.1. I need Thee every hour; Love divine, all loves excelling; This is my Father's world-Fairest Lord Jesus; Praise the Lord (To God be the glory); Nearness medley.
    Vol.2. When I survey the wondrous Cross; Power in the blood; Saviour like a shepherd lead us; Sun of my soul; Amazing grace.

3131. ———, arr. *The old rugged Cross.* [Arranged by] Jill Wade. Choctaw, Ok.: Harp Celebration Corp., c1990. 8 pp. (Awake the harp)

3132. Wagner, Richard, 1813–1883. [Lohengrin. Treulich geführt; arr.] *The bridal chorus: from Richard Wagner's opera Lohengrin.* [Arr. by C. Oberthür]. London: Edwin Ashdown, n.d. 7 pp.

3133. ———. [Lohengrin. Treulich geführt; arr.] *Wedding march: from Lohengrin.* Arr. by Wm. T. Cameron. Washington, D.C.: William Truesdale Cameron, n.d. 2 pp.

3134. ———. [Lohengrin. Treulich geführt; arr.] *Wedding processional: bridal chorus from Lohengrin.* Arranged by Deborah Henson-Conant. San Mateo, Calif.: F.C. Publishing Co., c1989. 2 pp. (Popcycle series)

3135. ———. [Meistersinger von Nürnberg. Morgenlich leuchtend im rosigen Schein; arr.] *Die Meistersinger von Nürnberg: Walther's Preislied.* [Arr. by C. Oberthür]. Mainz: B. Schott's Söhne, n.d. 9 pp.

3136. ———. [Meistersinger von Nürnberg. Morgenlich leuchtend im rosigen Schein; arr.] *Die Meistersinger von Nürnberg: Walther's Preislied.* Transcr. by H. Trneček; edited by De Wayne Fulton. Marina Del Rey, Calif.: Safari, 1989. 11 pp.

3137. ———. [Ring des Nibelungen. Walküre. Selections; arr.] *Die Walküre: extrait du 3e acte.* Arr. pour une harpe seule par Carlos Salzedo. Paris: Alphonse Leduc, c1921. 5 pp.

3138. ———. [Ring des Nibelungen. Walküre. Siegmunds Liebesgesang; arr.] *Siegmunds Liebesgesang: aus dem Music Drama Die Walküre: für Harfe.* Übertragen von C. Oberthür. Mainz: B. Schott's Söhne, [1879]. 7 pp.

3139. Waller, Fats, 1904–1943. *Ain't misbehavin'.* Arranged for harp solo by John Escosa. [Santa Monica, Calif.]: Salvi Publications, [1980], c1929. 4 pp. (Salvi pop series)

3140. Walters, Gareth, 1928–. [Suites, flute, harp; arr.] *Little suite: for harp.* Chesham, Bucks, England: G. Ricordi & Co., c1969. 8 pp. "This is the composer's adaptation of his Little suite for flute and harp. . . ."

3141. Warren, Harry, 1893–. [Gold diggers of 1935. Lullaby of Broadway] *Lullaby of Broadway.* Arr. Jan Jennings. Ellensburg, Wash.: F.C. Publishing Co., 1993. 5 pp.

Watkins, David, 1938–, ed. *Anthology of English music: for the harp.* See 2173.

3142. Watson, Sharon, arr. *Christmas book.* Arr. Sharon Watson. Indianapolis, Ind.: Sharon Watson, n.d. 2 v. CONTENTS: Vol.1. Deck the halls; Let it snow; Rudolph; Sussex carol; We three kings; Gesu bambino; Drummer boy; Jingle bells; Sweet little Jesus boy.
    Vol.2. God rest ye merry, gentlemen; Sleighride; Three Christmas carols (He is born; I saw three ships; Shepherds); Santa Claus is comin' to town; I heard the bells; Patapan; Coventry carol; Carol of the bells; O holy night; In dulce jubilo; Silent night.

3143. Weber, Carl Maria von, 1786–1826. [Freischütz. Selections; arr.] *The celebrated march, waltz, and hunting chorus from Der Freischutz.* Arr. for the harp by G. Holst. London: G. Holst, [183–?]. 9 pp. "No. 6 of Popular airs for the harp."

Weidensaul, Jane B., 1935–. *Lessons for the Renaissance harp: a beginner's book.* See 96.

3144. Weill, Kurt, 1900–1950. [Lady in the dark. My ship] *My ship.* Arr. Tony Kaye. Ellensburg, Wash.: F.C. Publishing Co., 1993. 2 pp.

3145. Williams, John, 1932–. [Star wars. Cantina band] *Cantina band: from*

Star wars. Arranged for harp by Carrol McLaughlin. Santa Monica, Calif.: Salvi Publications, c1977. 4 pp. (Salvi pop series)

3146. ———. [Star wars. Princess Leia's theme] *Princess Leia's theme: from the films Star wars and Return of the Jedi.* Arranged by Katherine Honey. San Mateo, Calif.: F.C. Publishing Co., c1988. 3 pp. (Popcycle series)

3147. Williams, Langton. *The wood nymph's call: song.* [Arr. for harp by C. Oberthür]. London: Edwin Ashdown, n.d. 7 pp. (Popular melodies, no. 6)

3148. Winter, Peter von, 1754–1825. [Unterbrochene Opferfest. Selections; arr.] *A selection of the most admired melodies from Winter's opera The Oracle, or The interrupted sacrifice.* Arr. for the harp by N. Charles Bochsa. London: Welsh & Hawes, [183–?]. 7 pp.

3149. Woods, Sylvia, 1951–, arr. *Chanukah music: for all harps.* Each arranged for beginning and advanced harpers by Sylvia Woods. Los Angeles, Calif.: Woods Music and Books Publishing, c1990. 25 pp. (A Sylvia Woods multi-level harp book) [NP] CONTENTS: Blessings over the candles (Chanukah blessings); Chanukah, Chanukah; Chanukah, o Chanukah; Hanerot halalu; Hatikvah; I have a little dreydl; Ma'oz tsur; Mi y'malel; My dreydl; Ner li; Rock of ages; Sevivon; Yodim atem.

3150. ———, arr. [Christmas carols] *Fifty Christmas carols: for all harps: each arranged for beginning and advanced harpers.* Los Angeles, Calif.: Woods Music and Books Publishing, c1984. 96 pp. [NP] CONTENTS: The angels and the shepherds; Angels we have heard on high; Away in a manger (2 melodies); Blessed be that maid Marie; Boar's head carol; Bring a torch, Jeannette, Isabella; The cherry tree carol; Christ was born on Christmas day; The Coventry carol; Deck the halls; Ding dong merrily on high; The first Nowell; Entre le boeuf; The Gloucestershire wassail; Go, tell it on the mountains; God rest ye merry, gentlemen; Good Christian men, rejoice; Good King Wenceslas; Hark! the herald angels sing; Here we come a'wassailing; The holly and the ivy; I saw three ships; Il es né; Ihr Kinderlein, kommet; Infant holy; It came upon the midnight clear; Jingle bells; Joy to the world; Let all mortal flesh keep silence; Lo, how a rose e'er blooming; Masters in this hall; Noël nouvelet; O come all ye faithful; O come, o come Emmanuel; O holy night; O sanctissima; O Tannenbaum; Shepherds hurried to Bethlehem; Silent night; The snow lay on the ground; The twelve days of Christmas; What child is this?; Whence is that goodly fragrance?; While by my sheep; While shepherds watched their flocks; Willie, take your little drum.

3151. ———, arr. *Hymns and wedding music: for all harps.* Each arranged for beginning and advanced harpers by Sylvia Woods. Los Angeles, Calif.: Woods Music and Books Publishing, c1987. 96 pp. (A Sylvia Woods multi-level harp book) [NP] CONTENTS: Amens for key of C; Amens for key of

G; Abide with me; All glory, laud and honor; All hail the power of Jesus'
name; Amazing grace; Be thou my vision; Blest be the tie that binds;
Christ the Lord is risen today (Jesus Christ is risen today); The Church's
one foundation; Come, Christians, join to sing; Come, Thou almighty
King; Doxology; All people that on earth do dwell; Fairest Lord Jesus;
Faith of our fathers; For the beauty of the earth (As with gladness men of
old); I love Thy kingdom, Lord; Guide me, o Thou great Jehovah; Holy,
holy, holy; Jacob's ladder; Jesus loves me; Kum ba yah; A mighty fortress is
our God; Morning has broken; Nearer my God to Thee; Now the day is
over; O God, our help in ages past; O perfect love; Rock of ages; Stand up,
stand up for Jesus; This is my Father's world; We gather together (Prayer
of thanksgiving); What a friend we have in Jesus; When morning gilds the
skies; Bridal march from Lohengren (Here comes the bride); Trumpet
tune; Trumpet voluntary; Artsa alinu; Hava nagila; Hevenu shalom; Hine
ma tov no. 1; Hine ma tov no. 2; Kozatzke; L'cha dodi; Ave Maria
(Schubert) with voice or melody instrument.

3152. Woods, Sylvia, and Chathasaigh, Maire ni, eds. *Irish dance tunes: for all
harps: 50 jigs, reels, hornpipes, and airs*. Edited by Sylvia Woods and Maire ni
Chathasaigh. Los Angeles, Calif.: Woods Music and Books Publishing,
c1984. 54 pp. [NP] CONTENTS: Jigs: Blarney pilgrim; Garryowen; Geese
in the bog; Haste to the wedding; Maid at the spinning wheel; Merrily kiss
the quaker; Money in both pockets; Morrison's jig; Off she goes; Road to
Lisdoonvarna; Smash the windows; Tobin's favorite. Slip jigs: A fig for a
kiss; Boys of Ballysodare; Dublin streets; Give us a drink of water; Hard-
iman the fiddler; Kid on the mountain; Rocky road to Dublin. Hornpipes:
Boys of Blue Hill; Fisher's hornpipe; Ladies' hornpipe; Little beggarman;
O'Donnell's hornpipe; Off to California; Plains of Boyle; Rights of Man;
Soldier's joy. Reels: Earl's chair; Fairy dance reel; Green fields of America;
Leather buttons; Maid behind the bar; Mason's apron; Miss McLeod's
reel; Music in the glen; Musical priest; Tent at the fair; Thro' the field;
Waterfall; Who made your breeches?; Wind that shakes the barley; Wise
maid. Airs, marches, and other tunes: Battle of Aughrim; Brian Boru's
march; Pig Town fling; Carrickfergus; King of the fairies; March of the
King of Laois; Parting glass.

3153. Yarrow, Peter, 1938–, and Lipton, Lenny, 1940–. *Puff the magic dragon*.
Arr. Eleanor Fell. Ellensburg, Wash.: F.C. Publishing Co., 1993. 3 pp.

3154. Youmans, Vincent, 1898–1946. [No, no, Nanette. Tea for two] *Tea for
two*. Arr. Eleanor Fell. Ellensburg, Wash.: F. C. Publishing Co., 1992. 6 pp.

3155. Young, Victor, 1900–1956. [Stella by starlight] *Stella*. Arranged by
Michelle Sell. San Mateo, Calif.: F.C. Publishing Co., [1989], c1946. 3 pp.
(Popcycle series)

3156. Young, Victor, 1900–1956, and Heyman, Edward, 1907–. [One minute to zero. When I fall in love] *When I fall in love.* Arranged by Stella Castellucci. Ellensburg, Wash.: F.C. Publishing Co., [1989], c1952. 2 pp. (Popcycle series)

3157. Zabel, Albert, 1834–1910. *Concerto: in C minor.* First movement transcribed for harp solo by Paul Hurst. Marina Del Rey, Calif.: Safari Publications, 1992. 12 pp.

3158. Zaerr, Laura, 1960–, arr. *Aires of olde: a collection of medieval tunes.* Arranged for small harp by Laura Zaerr; text translation by Linda Zaerr. Edmonds, Wash.: Paradise Music, c1989. 18 pp. [NP] CONTENTS: Allepsalite; Stella splendens; The shepherd and the Lord (2 versions); Christo psallat; Hymn to St. Magnus; The leper's daughter; Pour mon cuer; Estampie; Ungaresca; Danza asturiana.

3159. Zimmerman, Harry, 1906–. *I saw the wild geese fly: harp solo.* North Hollywood, Calif.: J. Forrest Music Co., c1975. 3 pp. Originally for recorder and harp.

Zingel, Hans Joachim, 1904–1978, and Haag, Gudrun, eds. *Kleine Werke alter Meister: für die Harfe.* See 2244.

3160. Zipoli, Domenico, 1688–1726. [Suite, harpsichord, B minor; arr.] *Suite in B minor.* Edited by Dewey Owens. New York, N.Y.: Lyra Music Co., c1974. 8 pp. Originally for harpsichord. CONTENTS: Preludio; Corrente; Aria; Gavotta.

3161. ———. [Suite, harpsichord, B minor. Corrente; arr.] *Corrente.* Leipzig: Jul. Heinr. Zimmermann, c1914. 3 pp. Originally for harpsichord.

Original Works for Harp Duet and/or Ensemble

3162. Allen, Mimi, 1926–. *Shamrocks: for harp(s) with or without pedals*. [New York]: Salvi Publications, c1986. Score (13 pp.). For harp and voice; a second harp may play the vocal line instead of the voice. [NP] CONTENTS: Brite is the morn; Irish dance; Patrick's lullaby; Firefly; Nocturne; Little David play on your harp.

3163. Andrès, Bernard, 1941–. *A fresca: quatuor de harpes = harp quartet*. Paris: International Music Diffusion, c1988. Score 15 pp.

3164. ———. *Dyades: sept petits duos pour harpes celtiques*. Paris: G. Billaudot, c1991. Score 16 pp. For 2 harps. [NP]

3165. ———. *Parvis: cortège et danse*. Paris: Editions Musicales Hortensia, c1977. Score 14 pp. For 2 harps.

3166. ———. *La ragazza: suite pour 2 ou 4 petites ou grandes harpes*. Paris: Gérard Billaudot, c1988. 4 parts (9 pp. each). (La harpe) For 2 or 4 harps. [NP]

3167. Andriessen, Jurriaan, 1925–. *Sonate voor twee harpen*. Amsterdam: Donemus, c1991. 2 scores. For 2 harps.

3168. Barber, Gail, 1939–. *Duets for harps: for two (or more) harps with or without pedals*. [New York]: Salvi Publications, c1986. 2 parts. [NP] CONTENTS: Dusk in the Sandias; Mexican serenade.

3169. ———. *Duets for harps*. Lubbock, Tex.: Gail Barber, c1988. 2 parts. CONTENTS: Dusk in the Sandias; Mexican serenade.

3170. Barclay, Robert, 1918–1980. *The mission at Santa Fe: for two harps*. Great Neck, N.Y.: Barger & Barclay, c1960. 2 parts (7 pp. each).

3171. Beauchant, Pierre. *Triptic dance: for two (or three) harps*. New York: Lyra Music Co., c1967. 2 parts (3 pp. each). "When played by a large ensemble of harps, the majority of the harpists should play Harp I. Harp II needs very few players."

3172. Bertouille, Gérard, 1898–1981. *Prelude: pour quatuor de harpes.* Brussels: CeBeDeM, c1957. Score 24 pp. and 4 parts. For 4 harps.

Braal, Andries de, 1909–. *Drie-in-één: muziek voor 4 kleine harpen, kleine harpsolo, cello en kleine harp.* See 434.

———. [Kleine harp als solo-en begeleidings instrument] *De kleine harp als solo-en begeleidings instrument.* See 435.

3173. ———. *Samenspel: 5 stukken voor drie kleine harpen; 4 stukken voor vier kleine harpen.* Amsterdam: Donemus, c1979. Score 25 pp. First works for 3 harps; remaining works for 4 harps. [NP] CONTENTS: Plechtige mars; Rondo; Berceuse; Eenmaal-andermaal; Allegro con brio; Klein koraal; Echo-fantasie (hommage à J. P. Sweelinck); Serenade; Nocturne.

3174. ———. *Sonata: per due arpe.* Amsterdam: Donemus, c1968. Score 30 pp. For 2 harps.

3175. ———. [Sonatinas, harps (2)] *Twee sonatines; Twee stukken: voor drie kleine harpen.* Amsterdam: Donemus, 1979. Score 17 pp. For 3 harps. [NP] CONTENTS: Sonatine no. 1; Sonatine no. 2; Intermezzo; Elegie.

3176. ———. [Variaties zonder thema] *Zes variaties zonder thema: voor 4 kleine harpen.* Amsterdam: Donemus, c1979. Score 15 pp. For 4 harps. [NP]

3177. Bunge, Sas, 1924–1980. *Snaren-spel: 21 stukken voor twee kleine harpen (1979).* Amsterdam: Donemus, c1979. 2 scores. For 2 harps.

Bussotti, Sylvano, 1931–. *Fragmentations: pour en jouer de harpes.* See 464.

3178. Butterfield, David. *Fantasy: for three harps, op. 2, no. 1.* Santa Monica, Calif.: Salvi, c1978. 3 parts.

3179. Cady, Harriette. *Oriental dance: for two harps.* New York: Lyra Music Co., 1989. 2 parts.

Cage, John, 1912–1992. *Postcard from heaven: for 1–20 harps.* See 470.

3180. Calvo-Manzano, María Rosa, 1943–. *Una noche en New York: para quinteto de arpas.* Madrid: Editorial Alpuerto, c1988. Score 72 pp.

3181. ———. *Tríptico de Navidad: para seis arpas.* Madrid: Union Musical Española, c1983. Score 44 pp.

3182. Cameron, William Truesdale, d. 1977. *Duet: music to dream by.* Chicago: Lyon & Healy, n.d. Score 3 pp. For 2 harps.

3183. ———. *Miniature suite: for harps.* Chicago: Lyon & Healy, n.d. Score 6 pp.

3184. ———. *Premier melodie: harp duet.* Washington, D.C.: William Truesdale Cameron, n.d. Score 4 pp.

3185. Capelletti, Daniel. *Suite: pour deux harpes, opus 19.* Paris: Jobert, c1984. Score 29 pp. For 2 harps.

3186. Challan, Annie, 1940–. *Cache-cache: pour deux harpes.* Paris: Leduc, 1984. Score 4 pp. For 2 harps.

3187. ———. *Pour bercer Laura: pour 2 harpes celtiques.* Paris: Harposphère, c1988. Score 3 pp. For 2 harps. [NP]

3188. ———. *Le roy fait battre tambour: pour harpe celtique et harpe ou 2 harpes ou harpe celtique et piano.* Harmonisation, Annie Challan. Paris: A. Leduc, c1988. Score 3 pp. (Collection de pièces instrumentales destinées aux examens et concours des conservatoires et écoles de musique) For 2 harps or harp and piano. [NP]

3189. ———. *Sardane à Lully: pour 6 harpes celtiques et une harpe ou un piano (et un tambourin).* Paris: Editions Aug. Zurfluh, 1986. 7 parts. For 6 non-pedal harps and 1 pedal harp (or piano) and tambourine. [NP]

3190. ———. *Variations pour morphée: pour 2 harpes celtiques.* Paris: Editions Aug Zurfluh, c1989. Score 8 pp.

3191. Charpentier, Jacques, 1933–. *Pour une apsara: pour deux harpes.* Paris: A. Leduc, c1972. Score 10 pp. For 2 harps.

3192. Chiti, Gian Paolo, 1939–. *Breakers: for 4 harps.* New York: Chappell Music Co., c1976. Score 23 pp.

Damase, Jean Michel, 1928–. *Pieces pour 1, 2 et 3 harpes celtiques (ou grande harpe).* See 636.

3193. ———. *Sonatine: pour deux harpes (ou deux pianos).* Paris: Éditions Salabert, c1966. Score 39 pp. For 2 harps.

3194. Delden, Lex van, 1919–1988. *Concertino: per due arpe, opus 76.* Amsterdam: Donemus, c1962. Score 18 pp. For 2 harps.

3195. ———. *Intrada e danza: per 6 arpe, op. 70.* Amsterdam: Donemus, c1961. Score 25 pp. and 6 parts. For 6 harps.

3196. Delden, Lex van, 1919–1988, and Flothuis, Marius, 1914–. *Kleine Suite: voor 12 harpen.* Amsterdam: Donemus, c1951. 12 parts. For 12 harps.

3197. Durkó, Zsolt, 1934–. *Serenata: per quattro arpe.* Budapest: Editio Musica, c1975. Score 14 pp. For 4 harps.

3198. Ellis, Osian, 1928–. *Diversions: for two harps.* S.l.: Ossianic Music, c1990. 2 parts, 10 pp. each. CONTENTS: Chasing; Descanting; Gossiping.

3199. Escosa, John B., 1928–1991. [Dances, harps (2)] *Three dances: for two harps.* Santa Monica, Calif.: Salvi, c1977. Score 14 pp. CONTENTS: Gavotte; Minuet; Gigue.

3200. ———. *Diddling with Yankee doodle.* Ellensburg, Wash.: F.C. Publishing Co., 1991. Score 8 pp. For 2 harps.

3201. Flothuis, Marius, 1914–. *Allegro vivace, op. 75, no. 2: per due arpe.* Amsterdam: Donemus, c1972. Score 4 pp. For 2 harps.

3202. Frid, Géza, 1904–. *Fuga: voor harpen, op. 62.* Amsterdam: Donemus, 1961. Score 9 pp. and 3 parts. For 3 harps.

3203. Giner, Bruno, 1960–. *Distortions: pour deux harpes.* Paris: Billaudot, 1986. Score 18 pp. For 2 harps.

3204. Grandjany, Marcel, 1891–1975. *Les agneaux dansent = Dancing lambs: for harp with or without pedals.* [Harp ensemble]. New York, N.Y.: O. Pagani & Bro., c1971. 3 parts. For 3 harps. [NP]

3205. ———. [Duets, harps (2), op. 26] *Two duets for harps.* New York: M. Baron, c1947. Score 2 v. CONTENTS: Sally and Dinny duet; Eleanor and Marcia duet.

3206. Graziani, V. M., 1825–1889. *Grand duo: pour deux harpes ou harpe et piano [in F major], op. 20.* Milan: Ricordi, n.d. Score. For 2 harps or for harp and piano.

3207. Groot, Cor de, 1914–. *Le chat rouge: pour deux harpes.* Amsterdam: Donemus, c1983. Score 7 pp. For 2 harps.

3208. ———. *Music for the party's* [*sic*]: *for two harps.* Amsterdam: Donemus, c1983. Score 43 pp. CONTENTS: Entrée; Cortège; Polka; Ballade; Tango-satire; Valse pour le foyer.

3209. Hanus, Jan, 1915–. *Introduzione e toccata: Ninfa e Pan: for four harps.* Hastings-on-Hudson, N.Y.: General Music Publishing Co., c1976. Score 35 pp. and 4 parts.

3210. Harrington. *There's a song in the air: harp ensemble.* Washington, D.C.: William Truesdale Cameron, n.d. Score 1 p.

Haubenstock-Ramati, Roman, 1919–. *Cathedrale: für Harfe.* See 996.

3211. Hermans, Niko, 1919–. *Sonantia: quatre pièces pour deux harpes (1984).* Amsterdam: Donemus, c1985. Score 17 pp. For 2 harps.

3212. Holy, Alfred, 1866–1948. *Festmusik: [für zwei Harfen], op. 13.* Leipzig: J.H. Zimmermann, c1901. 2 parts. For 2 harps.

3213. ———. *Festmusik: for two harps, op. 13.* [New York]: Lyra Music Co., [198–?]. 2 parts.

3214. Hujsak, Joy, 1924–. *God be with you this Christmastide: duo for harp.* La Jolla, Calif.: Mina-Helwig Publishing Co., c1971. Score 2 pp.

3215. ———. [Short preludes, harp] *Four short preludes for early harpists.* La Jolla, Calif.: Mina-Helwig Publishing Co., c1972. 2 parts. For 2 harps. CONTENTS: When I daydream; Cottage; Through the mist; Lullaby.

3216. Jersild, Jorgen, 1913–. [Impromptus, harps (2)] *Two impromptus: for two harps: für gefühlvolle Spieler.* Copenhagen: Edition W. Hansen, c1984. Score 20 pp.

John, Patricia, 1916–. *Tachystos = Swift: music for one or several harps.* See 1110.

3217. Krumpholz, Jan Křtitel, 1742–1790. [Duets, harps, op. 5] *Two duetts: for two harps or two piano fortes, op. 5.* London: Rt. Birchall, [between 1789 and 1819]. 2 parts.

3218. ———. [Duets, harps, op. 5] *Première duo: pour deux harpes, op. 5.* Ed. Suzanne Balderston. [Santa Monica, Calif.]: Salvi, 1977. 2 parts (15 pp. each). For 2 harps.

3219. Lancen, Serge, 1922–. *Crépuscule: pièce pour 2 harpes ou 2 pianos, ou 1 harpe et 1 piano.* Paris: Harposphere, c1989. Score 9 pp.

3220. Lo Vetere, Italo, 1940–. *Preludietto diatonico: per due arpe.* Milan: Edizioni Curci, c1980. 2 parts. For 2 harps.

3221. Malec, Ivo, 1925–. *Pieris: pour 2 harpes.* Paris: Ed. Salabert, c1985. Score 18 pp.

3222. Margoni, Alain, 1934–. *Danse ancienne et danse moderne: duo de harpes.* Paris: Hortensia, c1985. Score 11 pp. For 2 harps.

3223. Marischal, Louis, 1928–. [Esquisses] *Quatre esquisses: pour cinq harpes.* Paris: E.F.M. Technisonor, c1970. Score 19 pp. For 5 harps.

3224. ———. *Harpophonie en quarte: pour 3 harpes.* Paris: Editions françaises de musique, c1969. Score 27 pp.

3225. Marson, John, 1932–. *Waltzes and promenades: for two harps.* [Santa Monica, Calif.]: Salvi, 1978. Score 35 pp.

3226. Matsumoto, Hinoharu. *Hana-Tsutae-no-tabi: for 4 kotos or 4 harps.* Tokyo, Japan: Japan Federation of Composers, 1986. Score 14 pp.

Molnar, Josef, 1929–. *Colors: suite for solo or multiple harps.* See 1376.

3227. ———. *Humoreske: for 2 harps.* [Japan]: s.n., n.d. Score 6 pp.

———. *Itsuki no komori uta by Molnar. Der Lindenbaum by Schubert.* See 1377.

3228. ———. *Spring rain: sketch for grand harp and 2 Irish harp.* [Japan]: s.n., n.d. Score 8 pp. [NP]

3229. Montori, Sergio, 1916–. *Iron garden: for 4 harps.* New York: Chappell & Co., Inc., c1976. Score 28 pp.

3230. Osieck, Hans, 1910–. *Berceuse antique: voor 3 harpen.* Amsterdam: Donemus, c1954. Score 6 pp. For 3 harps.

3231. Otten, Ludwig, 1924–. *Duo: voor twee harpen.* Amsterdam: Donemus, c1960. Score 31 pp. For 2 harps.

3232. Paulus, Stephen, 1949–. *Inscriptions: for two harps.* St. Paul, Minn.: Composers' Union Press, c1976. Score 29 pp.

3233. Poenitz, Franz, 1850–1913. *Fantasie in Ges dur: für zwei Harfen, op. 65.* Leipzig: J. H. Zimmermann, c1902. 2 parts.

3234. ———. *Spukhafte Gavotte: für zwei Harfen, op. 75.* Leipzig: J.H. Zimmermann, c1907. 2 parts. For 2 harps.

3235. ———. *Wikingerfahrt: Fantasie in As moll: [für zwei Harfen].* [Leipzig: W. Zimmermann, c1913]. 2 parts. For 2 harps.

3236. Praag, Henri C. van, 1894–1968. *Duettino: per due arpe.* Amsterdam: Donemus, c1960. 2 scores. For 2 harps.

3237. Press, Jacques, 1903–. *Polka in C: for two harps.* New York, N.Y.: Lyra Music Co., c1970. Score 2 leaves and 1 part.

3238. Quinn, Renée. *At the Tori gate: for junior harp ensemble.* Palo Alto, Calif.: Harpress of California, c1986. 3 parts. For 3 harps. [NP]

3239. Ragué, Louis-Charles, 1760 (ca.)-after 1793. [Sonatas, harpsichord, harp, no. 1] *Trois sonates: pour la harpe avec accompagnement de clavecin ou de violon obligé, ouvre 1er.* Paris: Cousineau, [180–?]. 3 parts. For harp and harpsichord (or 2nd harp or violin).

3240. Renié, Henriette, 1875–1956. [Pins de Charlannes] *Les pins de Charlannes: petite pièce très facile pour la harpe, sans pédales, avec piano ou seconde harpe.* Paris: Leduc, c1940. Score 5 pp. For 2 harps or for harp and piano. [NP]

3241. Rogers, Van Veachton, 1864–1937. *In Spainland.* Washington, D.C.: William Truesdale Cameron, c1916. 2 parts. For 2 harps or for harp and piano.

Rose, Beatrice Schroeder. *The enchanted harp: 10 easy descriptive pieces for the non-pedal or pedal harp with a supplement for a second harp.* See 1750.

Salzedo, Carlos, 1885–1961. *Fraicheur = Zephyrs: for harp alone, or several harps in unison.* See 1788.

3242. ———. *Pentacle: suite for two harps.* [S.l.]: Salzedo Centennial Fund, 1990. Score 39 pp. CONTENTS: Steel; Serenade; Felines; Catacombs; Pantomime.

———. *Prelude for a drama: for one or several harps.* See 1804.

3243. ———. *Second harp parts for three famous compositions.* New York, N.Y.: Lyra Music Co., c1973. 13 pp. (part for 2nd harp only). CONTENTS: Chanson dans la nuit = Song in the night; Tango; Rumba.

Schubert, Erich, 1913–. *Harfen-Duos: spielbar für 2 Harfen, auch für 1 Harfe und ein anderes Instrument, 1. Stimme auch für Solo-Harfe.* See 1854.

———. *Harfenmusik aus Tirol: acht neue Tänze für ein und zwei Harfen.* See 1855.

3244. Šerly, Tibor, 1901–1978. *Chorale in 3 harps.* New York, N.Y.: Lyra Music Co., c1967. 3 parts. For 3 harps.

3245. ———. *Fantasy on a double quodlibet: for three harps or groups.* New York: Southern Music Publishing Co.; Hamburg: Peer Musikverlag, c1972. Score 12 pp.

3246. Smith, Larry Alan, 1955–. *Poems: for two harps (or two-part harp ensemble).* Bryn Mawr, Pa.: Merion Music, c1986. Score 8 pp.

3247. Snyder, Randall, 1944–. *Ennead: a set of nine fantasy-soundpieces for 3 harps.* [S.l: s.n.], 1981. Score 18 pp. CONTENTS: Phosphenes; Alembic fantasy; Corona; Palimpsest; Homage a Harpo; Homeostasis; Tropes; Phlogisticated homophones; Sesquiltera games.

3248. Soulage, Marcelle, 1894–. *Pièce: pour deux harpes à pédales.* Paris: Rouart, Lerolle & Cie., c1917. Score 12 pp. For 2 harps.

3249. Tenney, James, 1934–. *Harmonium no. 3: for 3 harps.* S.l.: Smith Publications, 1990. Score 4 leaves.

3250. Thomas, John, 1826–1913. *Cambria: two harps.* Abergavenny, Gwent: Adlais, c1984. 2 parts.

3251. ———. *Duet: for two harps, or harp and piano on melodies from La sonnambula.* London: Hutchings & Romer, [19—?]. 2 parts.

3252. ———. *Duet: for two harps or harp & piano on themes from Norma.* London: Hutchings & Romer, [19—?]. 2 parts.

3253. ———. [Duets, piano, harp. Selections] *Welsh duets: for two harps or harp and piano.* London: Hutchings & Romer, [19—?]. 2 parts.

3254. ———. *Grand duet: in E♭ minor: for two harps or harp and piano.* London: Hutchings & Romer, [18—?]. 3 parts.

3255. ———. *March of the Welsh Fusiliers: for two harps or harp & piano.* London: Hutchings & Romer, [1900?]. 2 parts.

3256. ———. *Souvenir du nord: duo for two harps or harp and piano on Russian melodies.* London: Cannon, [19—?]. 2 parts.

3257. Tocchi, Gianluca, 1901–. *Ritratto di Händel: per quartette d'arpe.* Diteggiatura de Elena Zaniboni. Roma: Edi-Pan, c1982. Score 64 pp. For 4 harps.

3258. Tôn-Thât, Tiêt, 1933–. *Tranh: pour harpe celtique et harpe.* Paris: Editions Musicales Transatlantiques, c1980. Score 7 pp. For 2 harps. [NP]

3259. Trneček, Hanuš, 1858–1914. *Duo, op. 23: [für zwei Harfen].* Leipzig: J.H. Zimmermann, c1922. 2 parts. For 2 harps.

3260. Vishkarev, Leonid Vasilevich, 1907–. *Partita: dlia dvukh arf.* Leningrad: Izdatelstvo "Sovetskii Kompozitor," 1978. Score 39 pp. For 2 harps.

Voirpy, Alain, 1955–. [Pièces, harp] *Cinq pièces: pour harpe(s).* See 2145.

3261. Vries, Klaas de, 1944–. *Drie harpisten: 3 stukjes voor 3 kleine harpen.*

Amsterdam: Donemus, c1979. Score 16 pp. For 3 harps. [NP] CON-
TENTS: Orpheus' harp; David's harp; De harp van Thimoteus.

3262. Weippert, John M. [Divertimenti, harps (2)] *Twelve divertimentos: for
two pedal harps or a pedal harp and piano forte.* Edited by David Watkins.
Filkins, Nr Lechlade, Glos., England: The Clive Morley Collection,
[198–?]. Score 13 pp.

Arranged Works for Harp
Duet and/or Ensemble

3263. Albéniz, Isaac, 1860–1909. [Chants d'Espagne. Córdoba; arr.] *Cordova: [for] two harps.* [New York]: Michael Cambern, c1965. 2 parts. Originally for piano solo.

3264. Albéniz, Mateo, d. 1831. [Sonata, piano, D major; arr.] *Sonata in ré: for three harps.* Arr. Whit Dudley. S.l.: Barrington Music Publications, 1992. Score 3 pp. Originally for piano solo.

Bach, Carl Philipp Emanuel, 1714–1788. [Solfeggios, harpsichord, H. 220, C minor; arr.] *Solfeggietto: harp duet.* See 2270.

3265. Bach, Johann Christian, 1735–1782. [Sonatas and duetts, op. 15. No. 6; arr.] *Sonata in Do maggiore (da due clavicembali).* Trascrizione per arpa di Giuliana Stecchina Pittaro (anch per arpa e arpa celtica opp. arpa e clavicembalo). Udine, Italy: Pizzicato Edizioni Musicali, c1990. Score 26 pp. Originally for 2 harpsichords; arr. for harp and non-pedal harp or harp and harpsichord. [NP]

3266. Bach, Johann Sebastian, 1685–1750. [Englische Suiten. No. 3. Gavotte, no. 1; arr.] *Gavotte in G minor.* Arranged by Lynne W. Palmer [for harp duet]. Ellensburg, Wash.: F. C. Publishing Co., 1992. Score 5 pp. Originally for harpsichord solo (English suite BWV 808, no. 5).

3267. ———. [Herz und Mund und Tat und Leben. Jesu bleibet meine Freude; arr.] *Jesu, joy of man's desiring.* As arranged for two harps by Dewey Owens. New York: Lyra Music, c1967. 2 parts.

3268. ———. [Herz und Mund und Tat und Leben. Jesus bleibet meine Freude; arr.] *Jesu, joy of man's desiring.* Arr. John B. Escosa. Ellensburg, Wash.: F. C. Publishing Co., 1992. Score 10 pp. For harp ensemble.

3269. ———. [Instrumental music. Selections; arr.] *Two pieces.* Arranged for two harps or harp and organ with or without pedals [by Gail Barber]. Lubbock, Texas: Gail Barber, c1988. 2 parts. The first work originally for organ (Kleine Präludien und Fugen, no. 3, BWV 555); 2nd work originally for flute and harpsichord (Sonata, BWV 1031). CONTENTS: Prelude in E minor; Siciliano.

3270. ———. [Sonaten und Partiten, violin, BWV 1001–1006. Partita, no. 3. Preludio; arr.] *Prelude: from Partita no. 3: for two harps.* Transcribed by M. Mchedelov. [New York, N.Y.]: Lyra Music Co., [197–?]. Score 17 pp.

———. [Sonaten und Partiten, violin, BWV 1001–1006. Partita, no. 3. Preludio; arr.] *Preliudiia iz partity no. 3: obrabotka dlia dueta arf by I. S. Bakh. Tema s variatsiami: dlia arfy by F. Dizi.* See 247.

3271. Barber, Gail, 1939–, arr. *Duet album # 1.* Lubbock, Tex.: Gail Barber, c1990. 2 parts. For 2 harps. CONTENTS: Scarborough fair; Brahms' lullaby; A Chinese tale.

3272. ———, arr. *Duet album # 2: Scotch-Irish suite.* Arranged for two (or more) harps with or without pedals. Lubbock, Tex.: Gail Barber, c1990. 2 parts. [NP] CONTENTS: O'Carolan's air; Minstrel boy; Brian Boru's march.

Bartók, Béla, 1881–1945. [Mikrokosmos. Selections; arr.] *Mikrokosmos: for harp: 20 intermediate solos and ensembles for harps with and without pedals.* See 2319.

3273. Beaujoyeulx, Baltasar de, d. ca. 1587. [Amaryllis; arr.] *Gavotte di Luigi XIII.* Riduzione per 2 o 4 arpe di Riccardo Ruta. Naples: R. Izzo, c1924. 2 parts. Trad. attibuted to Louis XIII; current attribution to Baltasar de Beaujoyeulx by Louis C. Elson.

3274. Berlioz, Hector, 1803–1869. [Damnation de Faust. Marche hongroise; arr.] *Rákóczy induló: the celebrated Hungarian march.* Arranged for two harps or harp and piano by John Thomas. London: Gould & Bolttler, [19—?]. 2 parts. Originally for orchestra.

3275. Biggs, Bonnie, arr. *Christmas favorites: for troubadour harps duet or ensemble.* Arranged by Bonnie Biggs. Chicago: Lyon & Healy Harps, c1983. 2 parts. [NP] CONTENTS: Jolly old St. Nicholas; The little drummer boy; Neapolitan carol; What child is this; O holy night; Up on the roof top; Jingle bells; Deck the halls; Angels we have heard on high; O Christmas tree.

3276. ———, arr. *Light classics: for troubadour harps: duet or ensemble.* Arranged by Bonnie Biggs. Chicago, Ill.: Lyon & Healy Harps, c1984. 2 scores. [NP] CONTENTS: The cuckoo and the wanderer; The little music box; Peasant dance; The reaper's song; Russian folk song; Für Elise; Spanish dance; The wild horseman; Triptic dance; The little huntsman.

3277. Bizet, Georges, 1838–1875. [Symphonies, C major. Adagio; arr.]

Symphony in C: second movement. Transcribed for three harps by Clifford Wooldridge. Chicago: Lyon & Healy Harps, 1987. 3 parts (7 pp. each). (Lyon & Healy treasury of harp music)

3278. Blanco, Pedro José, 1750–1811. [Concertos, keyboard instruments (2), unacc. No. 1, G major] *I concierto de dos organos oder für zwei Harfen, zwei Tasteninstrumente (Cembali, Clavichorde, Klaviere), eine Harfe und ein Tasteninstrument.* Hrsg. von Macario Santiago Kastner. Fingersätze und Bezeichnungen für Harfe von Mario Falcao. Mainz: Schott, c1965. Score 16 pp. For 2 harps or for harp and keyboard instrument.

3279. Campen, Ank van, 1932–, arr. *La harpe de melodies: music for two harps.* [Arranged by] Ank van Campen. Amsterdam: Broekmans & Van Poppel, c1987. 2 parts. CONTENTS: Rondeau. Danse royale. Stantipes. Cornetto. La barcha del mio amore. Ungaresca; Saltarello by Pierre Phalèse. Saltarello. The last gallant. Prince Rupert's march. Menuet by Jean Philippe Rameau. Air by Georg Friedrich Handel. Musette by Johann Sebastian Bach. Menuet by Wolfgang Amadeus Mozart. Waltz of the triads by Ank van Campen. Northumbrian pipe tunes: Blancland races; Water of tyne; Random. Songs from Czecho-Slovakia: The dove; I have a little garden; We are all musicians. The clock-shop by Hans Kox and Ank van Campen.

3280. Carolan, Turlough, 1670–1738. *Brigid Cruis: a duet for two harps.* Arranged by Leone Paulson. Edmonds, Wash.: Paradise Music, c1989. 2 parts. [NP]

3281. ———. *O'Carolan's concerto: for two harps.* Arranged by Leone Paulson. Edmonds, Wash.: Paradise Music, c1988. 2 parts. [NP]

3282. Challan, Annie, 1940–, arr. *Au clair de la lune: pour harpe celtique et harpe ou 2 harpes ou harpe celtique et piano.* Harmonisation, Annie Challan. Paris: A. Leduc, c1988. Score 3 pp. (Collection de pièces instrumentales destinées aux examens et concours des conservatoires et écoles de musique) For 2 harps or for harp and piano. [NP]

3283. ———, arr. *Fais dodo: pour harpe celtique et harpe ou 2 harpes ou harpe celtique et piano.* Harmonisation: Annie Challan. Paris: Alphonse Leduc, c1987. Score 2 pp. (Collection de pièces instrumentales destinées aux examens et concours des conservatoires et ecoles de musique) For 2 harps. [NP]

3284. ———, arr. *Frère Jacques: pour harpe celtique et harpe ou 2 harpes ou harpe celtique et piano.* Harmonisation: Annie Challan. Paris: Alphonse Leduc, c1987. Score 3 pp. (Collection de pièces instrumentales destinées aux examens et concours des conservatoires et ecoles de musique) For 2 harps. [NP]

3285. ———, arr. *J'ai du bon tabac: pour harpe celtique et harpe ou 2 harpes ou harpe celtique et piano*. Harmonisation: Annie Challan. Paris: Alphonse Leduc, c1987. Score 2 pp. (Collection de pièces instrumentales destinées aux examens et concours des conservatoires et ecoles de musique) For 2 harps. [NP]

3286. Dandrieu, Jean François, 1682–1738. [Pièces de clavecin. Tourbillons; arr.] *Les tou[r]billons = Play of the winds*. Arr. for two harps by Carlos Salzedo. New York: Lyra Music Co., c1970. 2 parts. Originally for harpsichord solo.

Davis, Katherine, 1892–; Onorati, Henry, and Simeone, Harry. *Little drummer boy*. See 2430.

3287. Debussy, Claude, 1862–1918. [Preludes, piano, book 1. Cathédrale engloutie; arr.] *La cathédrale engloutie*. Arranged for 7 harps by Carlos Salzedo. [S.l.]: Salzedo Centennial Fund, 1990. 2 v. (Salzedo centennial edition) Four copies of Harp I and three copies of Harp II are needed for performance.

3288. ———. [Preludes, piano, book 1. Fille aux cheveux de lin; arr.] *Maid with the flaxen hair*. Arranged by John Escosa. Ellensburg, Wash.: F.C. Publishing Co., 1991. Score 6 pp. For 2 harps.

3289. ———. [Suite bergamasque. Clair de lune; arr.] *Clair de lune*. Transcribed for two or multiple harps by Carlos Salzedo (1927). New York: Southern Music Pub. Co.; Hamburg: Peer Musikverlag, 1966. Score 14 pp. Originally for piano solo.

3290. ———. [Suite bergamasque. Clair de lune; arr.] *Clair de lune*. Arr. John B. Escosa. Ellensburg, Wash.: F. C. Publishing Co., 1992. Score 11 pp. For harp ensemble; originally for piano solo.

3291. Dudley, Whit, 1957–1992, arr. *Greensleeves: for four harps*. Arr. Whit Dudley. S.l.: Barrington Music Publications, 1992. Score 3 pp.

3292. Escosa, John B., 1928–1991, arr. *Music for two harps*. Arranged by John Escosa. Boston, Mass.: Boston Editions, c1985. Score 22 pp. CONTENTS: Vol. 1. Rigaudon from Idoménée by André Campra. Largo from Sonata no. 3 for solo violin, BWV 1005; Come, sweet death, BWV 478; Bourrée from Partita no. 1 for solo violin, BWV 1002 by J. S. Bach.

3293. ———, arr. *Sakura*. Arranged by John Escosa. San Mateo, Calif.: F.C. Publishing Co., c1989. Score 3 pp. For 2 harps.

3294. Fibich, Zdeněk, 1850–1900. [At twilight. Lento; arr.] *Poeme: two harps*. Arranged by May Hogan Cambern. [New York]: Michael Cambern, c1965. 2 parts (3 pp. each). Originally for orchestra.

3295. Foster, Stephen Collins, 1826–1864. *Beautiful dreamer: a folk harp duet*. Arranged by Patricia Jaeger. Edmonds, Wash.: Paradise Music, c1987. Score 2 pp. and 1 part. For 2 harps. [NP]

3296. Franck, César, 1822–1890. [Pièces, organ (1860–62). Prélude, fugue et variation; arr.] *Prelude, fugue, variation, op. 18.* Transcribed for two harps by Dewey Owens. New York, N.Y.: Lyra Music Co., c1978. 2 parts.

3297. Galuppi, Baldassare, 1706–1785. [Sonatas, harpsichord, op. 1. No. 4, D major. Andante maestoso et gigue; arr.] *Andante maestoso et gigue: de la Sonata pour clavecin en re majeur.* [New York]: Lyra Music Co., [197–?]. 2 parts (4 pp.). (Transcriptions classiques pour 2 harpes) For 2 harps.

3298. Gluck, Christoph Willibald, Ritter von, 1714–1787. [Alceste. Caprice; arr.] *Caprice from Alceste.* Transcribed for two harps by Carlos Salzedo. New York: Lyra Music Co., c1986. 2 parts (3 pp. each).

3299. ———. [Armide. Gavotte; arr.] *Gavotte: (Armide).* [New York]: Lyra Music Co., [197–?]. 2 parts (2 pp.). (Transcriptions classiques pour 2 harpes) For 2 harps.

3300. Gounod, Charles, 1818–1893. *Marche solennelle.* Arr. for two harps or harp & piano by John Thomas. London: Hutchings & Romer, [188–?]. 2 parts. Originally for piano.

3301. ———. *Marche solennelle.* Arr. for two harps or harp & piano by John Thomas. London: Novello, [19—]. Score 7 pp. and 2 parts. Originally for piano.

3302. Granados, Enrique, 1867–1916. [Danzas españolas. No. 5; arr.] *Spanish dance no. 5.* Transcribed for two or multiple harps by Carlo Salzedo. [New York]: Southern Music Pub. Co., c1966. Score 12 pp. Originally for piano solo.

3303. Grandjany, Marcel, 1891–1975. [Agneaux dansent; arr.] *Les agneaux dansent = Dancing lambs: for harp with or without pedals: harp ensemble.* New York: O. Pagani & Bro., c1971. 3 parts. For 3 harps. [NP]

Grechaninov, Aleksandr Tikhonovich, 1864–1956. [Stücke, harp, op. 168. No. 5] *Remembrance of the ball = Souvenir du ball, op. 168, no. 5: for harp solo or duet.* See 2602.

3304. Grétry, André Ernest Modeste, 1741–1813. [Caravane du Caire. Danse des femmes; arr.] *Danse des femmes: pour trois harpes.* Arr. by H. J. Zingel. New York: Lyra Music Co., c1965. 3 parts. Originally for orchestra.

Gruber, Franz Xaver, 1787–1863. [Stille Nacht, heilige Nacht; arr.] *Silent night: folk harp solo or duet.* See 2617.

3305. Handel, George Frideric, 1685–1759. *Sarabande and Allegro.* Arranged for two harps by Linda Booth. Ellensburg, Wash.: F.C. Publishing Co., c1991. Score 11 pp. Originally for harpsichord; Sarabande from Suite, HWV 437; Allegro from Suite HWV 432.

3306. ———. [Suites, harpsichord, HWV 432, G minor. Passacaille; arr.] *Passacaglia in G minor: for three harps.* Arr. Whit Dudley. S.l.: Barrington Music Publications, 1992. Score 6 pp.

3307. Haydn, Joseph, 1732–1809. [Symphonies, H. I, 6, D major. Minuet, G major; arr.] *Menuet en sol: de la 6e. Symphonie.* New York: Lyra Music Co., [197–?]. 2 parts (2 pp.). (Transcriptions classiques pour 2 harpes) For 2 harps.

3308. ———. [Symphonies, H. I, 14, A major. Minuet, D major; arr.] *Menuet en ré: de la 14e. Symphonie.* New York: Lyra Music Co., [197–?]. 2 parts (2 pp.). (Transcriptions classiques pour 2 harpes) For 2 harps.

3309. Humperdinck, Engelbert, 1854–1921. [Hänsel und Gretel. Abends will ich schlafe gehn; arr.] *Evening prayer.* Transcribed for two (or three) harps by Dewey Owens. New York: Lyra Music Co., c1966. 2 parts.

3310. Hutchison, William M. (William Marshall), 1854–. *Carillons blancs et carillons noirs, [op. 53].* Transcrit [pour 4 harpes] par l'auteur. Paris: A. Leduc, [188–?]. 2 parts. For 4 harps; first part is for Harps I & III, second part is for Harps II & IV. CONTENTS: Cloches matinales; Cloches mélancoliques; Air de carillon.

3311. Inglefield, Ruth K., arr. *Trio: Les quatre branles.* Transcribed from the Jobin lutebook, 1573; arr. for harp trio by Ruth K. Inglefield. Santa Monica, Calif.: Salvi Publications, c1972. 2 pp. For troubadour or pedal harps. [NP]

Jaeger, Patricia, arr. *Maid from the parish of Penderyn: a Welsh tune.* See 2684.

3312. Lecuona, Ernesto, 1896–1963. [Andalucía. Malagueña; arr.] *Malagueña.* Arranged for 4 harps, pedal and/or non-pedal [by Arabella Sparnon]. [New York]: Edward B. Marks Music Co., c1928. Score 12 pp. and 4 parts. Originally for piano solo. [NP]

3313. ———. [Andalucía. Malagueña; arr.] *Malagueña.* Arranged for four harps, pedal or non-pedal by Arabella Sparnon. [S.l.]: Arabella Sparnon, 1987. Score 9 pp. and 4 parts. Originally for piano solo. [NP]

3314. Leontovych, Mykola Dmytrovych, 1877–1921. *Carol of the bells: four harps.* Arr. Whit Dudley. S.l.: Barrington Music Publications, 1992. Score 3 pp.

Lucchetti, Maryjean Z., arr. *The ash grove: a Welsh tune.* See 2758.

3315. Macdearmid, Anne, arr. *Duets: for clarsach.* Arranged by Anne Macdearmid. S.l.: A. Macdearmid, c1991. [NP] CONTENTS: Vol.1. Oran Nan Eilean.
  Vol.3. Ceol Measgadh.

3316. MacDowell, Edward, 1860–1908. [Woodland sketches. To a water-lily; arr.] *To a water-lily: two harps.* [Arranged by] May Hogan Cambern. New York: Carl Fischer, Inc., c1963. 2 parts. For 2 harps; originally for piano solo.

3317. Marson, John, 1932–, arr. *Santa Lucia.* Arr. John Marson. Santa

Monica, Calif.: Salvi Publications, c1979. Score 4 pp. and 4 parts. (Harp quartets series) For 4 harps.

3318. Martini, Giovanni Battista, 1706–1784. [Sonatas (1742). No. 12. Gavotte; arr.] *Gavotta.* Arranged for two harps by Carlos Salzedo. New York: Lyra, c1969. 2 parts (4 pp. each). Originally for organ or harpsichord.

3319. Massenet, Jules, 1842–1912. [Cid. Aragonaise; arr.] *Aragonaise: from the ballet Le Cid: harp duet.* Transcribed by Clifford Wooldridge. Chicago, Ill.: Lyon & Healy, c1986. 2 parts. (Lyon & Healy treasury of harp music) For 2 harps; originally for orchestra.

3320. Mégevand, Denise, 1947–, arr. [Musique du Barzaz Breiz] *La musique du Barzaz Breiz: chants populaires de la Bretagne.* Harmonisation de Denise Mégevand. Paris: G. Billaudot, c1986–1990. Score 2 v. and 1 part. (La harpe) Vol.1 for flute (or oboe or violin) and celtic harp; vol. 2 for 2 celtic or concert harps. [NP] CONTENTS: Vol.1. Les séries; La prophétie de Gwenc'hlan; Le seigneur Nann et la fée; L'enfant supposé; Les nains; Submersion de la ville d'Is; Le vin des Gaulois; La marche d'Arthur; La peste d'Elliant; Merlin au berceau; Merlin devin, Merlin barde; Conversion de Merlin; Lez-Breiz; Le tribu de Noménoé; Alain le renard; Bran; Le faucon; Héloïse et Abaillard.

Vol.2. Le retour d'Angleterre; L'epouse du croisé; Le rossignol; La fiancée de Satan; Le frère de lait; Le clerc de Rohan; Les trois moines rouges; Le combat des trente; L'Hermine; Le baron de Jauioz; La filleule de Duguesclin; Le vassal de Duguesclin; Le cygne; La ceinture de noces; Azenor-la-Pâle; Les jeunes hommes de Plouyé; Le siège de Guingamp; Le carnaval de Rosporden; Geneviève de Rustéfan.

3321. Mendelssohn-Bartholdy, Felix, 1809–1847. [Lieder ohne Worte, piano, op. 19, no. 3, Jägerlied; arr.] *La chasse.* Transcription pour 2 harpes, Gérard Auffray. Paris: Harposphère; Distribué par le Magasin de la harpe, c1987. 2 parts. For 2 harps.

3322. ———. [Lieder ohne Worte, piano, op. 62, no. 1; arr.] *Romance sans paroles, no. 25.* Transcription pour 2 harpes, Gérard Auffray. Paris: Harposphère, c1987. 2 parts. For 2 harps.

3323. ———. [Lieder ohne Worte, piano, op. 85, no. 6; arr.] *Romance sans paroles, no. 42.* Transcription pour 2 harpes, Gérard Auffray. Paris: Harposphère, c1987. 2 parts. For 2 harps.

3324. ———. [Lieder, op. 34. Auf Flügeln des Gesanges; arr.] *On wings of song.* Arranged for two harps by Carlos Salzedo. New York: Lyra Music, c1970. 2 parts. Originally for voice and piano.

3325. Molnar, Josef, 1929–. *Album for Irish harps ensemble.* [Composed or arranged] by J. Molnar. Tokyo: Tokyo Irish Harp Ensemble, 1967. Score 51 pp. Primarily arrangements for 2 or 3 harps. [NP]

3326. ———. *Medley on Irish folk songs.* Arr. J. Molnar. New York: Lyra Music Co., c1981. 2 parts (8 pp. each). For harp ensemble. [NP] CONTENTS: The lone rock; As I went a-walking; The minstrel boy; Now strike the harp gladly; Last rose of summer; The harp that once through Tara's hall.

3327. Mozart, Wolfgang Amadeus, 1756–1791. [Minuets, piano, K. 2, F major; arr.] *Menuet.* Transcription pour 3 harpes, Frédérique Garnier. Paris: Harposphère, c1989. Score 3 pp.

3328. ———. [Sonatas, piano, K. 545, C major; arr.] *Sonata in C: for two harps.* Arranged for 2 harps by Schlomovitz. Palo Alto, Calif.: Harpress of California, c1988. 2 parts.

3329. ———. [Symphonies, K. 550, G minor. Selections; arr.] *Theme from symphony no. 40: arranged for two harps.* New York: Lyra Music Co., 1981. 2 parts (4 pp. each).

3330. Owens, Dewey, arr. [Christmas carols] *Two Christmas carols: for two harps.* New York: Lyra Music Co., c1956. Score 2 pp. CONTENTS: The first Noel; Deck the hall.

3331. Pachelbel, Johann, 1653–1706. [Canon, violins (3), continuo, D major; arr.] *Canon in D.* Arranged for multiple harps by Susann McDonald and Linda Wood. Bloomington, Ind.: Musicworks- Harp Editions, c1984. 1 part (4 pp.). Part for Harp II; intended to be used with the arrangers' version for harp solo as Harp I.

———. [Canon, violins (3), continuo, D major; arr.] *Pachelbel's canon.* See 2867.

3332. Palmer, Lynne Wainwright, 1919–, arr. *Carol of the bells.* Arr. Lynne W. Palmer. Ellensburg, Wash.: F. C. Publishing Co., 1992. Score 3 pp. For harp ensemble.

3333. Pierné, Gabriel, 1863–1937. [Album pour mes petits amis. Marche des petits soldats de plomb; arr.] *March of the lead soldiers, op. 14, no. 6.* [Arr. by] Pearl Chertok. New York: Interstate Music, n.d. 3 parts. For 3 harps; originally for piano solo.

3334. ———. [Album pour mes petits amis. Marche des petits soldats de plomb; arr.] *March of the lead soldiers, op. 14, no 6.* [Arranged for harp trio by] Pearl Chertok. Santa Monica, Calif.: Salvi Publications, [197–?]. 3 parts. Originally for piano solo.

3335. Prokofiev, Sergey, 1891–1953. [Love for three oranges. Suite. March; arr.] *March from The love of three oranges.* Trans. for three harps by Clifford Wooldridge. Chicago: Lyon & Healy, 1987. 3 parts (3 pp. each). Originally for orchestra.

3336. Rameau, Jean Philippe, 1683–1764. [Joyeuse, harpsichord; arr.] *La joyeuse: rondeau.* Transcribed for two harps by Carlos Salzedo. New York: Lyra Music, c1969. 2 parts.

3337. Ravel, Maurice, 1875–1937. [Introduction et allegro, harp, wood-winds, strings; arr.] *Introduction and allegro: for two harps.* Edited and second harp accompaniment arranged by Clifford Wooldridge. Chicago, Ill.: Lyon & Healy, c1989. 2 parts. (Lyon & Healy treasury of harp music)

3338. Respighi, Ottorino, 1879–1936. [Antiche arie e danze per liuto, no. 3. Siciliana; arr.] *Siciliana: [after the orchestration by] Respighi.* Harp [duet] arr. by Schlomovitz. Palo Alto, Calif.: Harpress of California, c1988. 2 parts. For 2 harps; originally an anonymous work for lute.

3339. Rice, Joyce, 1940–, arr. *Danny boy; The harp that once thro' Tara's halls.* Arr. Joyce Rice. S.l.: Joyce Rice, 1993. Score 15 pp. and parts. Ensembles in 2 to 5 parts.

3340. ———, arr. *Silent night; What child is this?* Arr. Joyce Rice. S.l.: Joyce Rice, 1993. Score 12 pp. and parts. Ensembles in 2 to 5 parts.

3341. Rossini, Gioacchino, 1792–1868. [Mosè in Egitto. Dal tuo stellato soglio; arr.] *Prayer: from Mosé in Egitto.* Arranged for two harps or harp & piano by John Thomas. London: Leonard, Gould & Bolttler, [19—?]. 2 scores.

3342. Salzedo, Carlos, 1885–1961, arr. *Pavane.* Transcribed for two harps by Carlos Salzedo. New York: Lyra Music Co., c1985. 2 parts (1 leaf each). By an unknown composer of the 16th century.

3343. ———. *Second harp parts for three famous compositions by Carlos Salzedo.* New York: G. Schirmer, 1958, c1955. 13 pp. Second harp parts only. CONTENTS: Chanson dans la nuit = Song in the night; Tango; Rumba.

3344. Satie, Erik, 1866–1925. [Gymnopédies. Selections; arr.] *Two gymno-pédies: for two harps.* Trans. Mimi Allen. [Santa Monica, Calif.]: Salvi, 1978. Score 8 pp. Originally for piano.

3345. Scarlatti, Domenico, 1685–1757. [Sonatas, harpsichord, K. 95, C major; arr.] *Sonata in do, n. 358.* Trascritta e diteggiata per due arpe da Irene Rossi. Milan: Edizioni Curci, 1981, c1972. Score 7 pp. For 2 harps.

3346. Schuëcker, Edmund, 1860–1911. *Remembrances of Worcester: fantasia for two harps, op. 40.* Leipzig: J. H. Zimmermann, c1902. 2 parts. Originally for harp solo.

3347. Schumann, Robert, 1810–1856. [Album für die Jugend. Wilder Reiter; arr.] *The wild horseman: from Album for the young (1848).* Transcribed for two harps by Hulda E. Kreiss. West Babylon, N.Y.: Harold Branch Publishing, c1967. Score 2 pp. Originally for piano solo.

3348. Soler, Antonio, 1729–1783. [Concertos, organs (2), no. 3, G major; arr.] *Concierto no. III: para dos instrumentos de tecla del Padre Soler.* Transcripcion para quinteto de arpas por Maria Rosa Calvo-Manzano. Madrid: Editorial de Musica Española Contemporanea, c1987. Score 83 pp. For 5 harps; originally for 2 organs.

3349. Strauss, Johann, 1825–1899. [An der schönen blauen Donau; arr.] *The blue Danube: duet for folk harp and pedal harp.* Arranged by Louise Trotter. Houston, Texas: Louise Trotter, [1980?]. 2 parts. Harp I for non-pedal harp; Harp II for pedal harp. Originally for orchestra. [NP]

3350. Thomé, Francis, 1850–1909. *En ramant: duet for harps.* Transc. Rosalie Pratt. Upper Montclair, N.J.: SARO Publishing Co., n.d. 2 parts. Originally for piano solo.

Thomson, Lucien, arr. [Christmas carols] *Ten Christmas carols.* See 3111.

3351. Tournier, Marcel, 1879–1951. [Preludes, harp, op. 16; arr.] *Quatre préludes: pour harpe: [arr.] pour deux harpes en deux suites par l'auteur.* Paris: Louis Rouhier, c1921. 2 v. For 2 harps; originally for harp solo.

3352. ———. [Preludes, harp, op. 16; arr.] *Quatre préludes: pour deux harpes, op. 16.* Paris: Alphonse Leduc, c1921. Score 2 v. For 2 harps; originally for harp solo.

Trotter, Louise, arr. *American heritage harp: solos and duets for all harps: folksongs.* See 3115.

3353. ———, arr. *American heritage harp: book two: nonpedal harp duets: folksongs.* Arranged by Louise Trotter. Houston, Tex.: Louise Trotter, c1987. 2 parts. [NP] CONTENTS: Aura Lee; Cielito lindo; Blue-tail fly; Shortnin' bread; Swing low, sweet chariot; Oh! Susanna.

3354. ———, arr. *Fun with two harps: duets for folk harps.* Arranged by Louise Trotter. Houston, Texas: Louise Trotter, n.d. Score 8 pp. [NP] CONTENTS: Cielito lindo; Londonderry air; Aura Lee (also known as Love me tender); Oh! Susanna; Happy birthday; Railroad boogie (also known as Eyes of Texas).

3355. ———, arr. *Popular hymns for two: duets for non-pedal harp in the key of C.* Arranged by Louise Trotter. [S.l.]: Louise Trotter, 1982. 2 parts (9 pp. each). [NP] CONTENTS: A mighty fortress is our God; Battle hymn of the republic; Swing low, sweet chariot; Morning has broken.

3356. Weidensaul, Jane B., 1935–, arr. *Songs and carols for two: a duet album for harpists.* Arranged and edited by Jane B. Weidensaul. Teaneck, N.J.: Willow Hall Press, c1971. 2 parts (8 pp. each). CONTENTS: Ye banks and braes; My dancing day; Patapan; Coventry carol; To Portsmouth; Greensleeves.

NAME AND TITLE INDEX

This index does not duplicate the entries in the main sections. Titles of works described in the numbered citations in the main sections are shown in italic. Personal names include arrangers and composers whose works are included in anthologies. (Citations for these anthologies are entered under the names of the compilers in the main sections.) As in the main sections, titles following personal names are constructed according to *Anglo-American Cataloguing Rules* (2nd ed., 1988 revision). Listed also are composers whose works served as a basis for another's composition (see, for example, the variations, potpourris, and fantasies under the entry Bellini, Vincenzo).

À Capri, 2093
A chuaichín bhinn dílis, 2367
A consolarmi affrettisi, 2461
À deux mains, 549
À doigts croisées, 549
À fresca, 3163
A hader, 1088
À la claire fontaine, 2560
À la française, 510
À la manière de Fauré, 1607
À la manière de Lully, 1607
À la pointe sèche, 412
À l'entree de l'este, 2889
À l'espagnole, 510
À l'estompe, 412
A nád jancsi csárdában, 2707
A revederla, 1893
A rúin, fan agam, 413
A te diro, 2465
ABC of harp playing, 49
Abendfrieden, 1627
Abendlied, 1904, 3069
Aber, Alice Lawson: 395, 513, 514, 515, 516, 555, 556, 557, 687, 1160, 1161, 1167, 1168, 1171, 2217, 2422, 2530, 2946, 3040, 3125
Abide with me, 1072, 1619, 2787, 2795, 2864, 2886, 3151
Abigail Judge, 2388
Abondante, Giulio, fl. 1546–1587: *Napolitana (arr.)*, 2611
About a quarter to nine, 2893

About strange lands and people, 2860
Abschied, 2207
Absidioles, 203
Acalèphes, 204
Acceleration waltz, 150
Accordeon, 625
Accords, 676
Ach neni tu neni, 2267
Achenwalder Harfenländler, 1855
Acker, Dieter, 1940–: *Caprice*, 1240
Acrospores, 205
Acrostic paraphrase, 665
Ad libitum, 1405
Adagietto, 676
Adagio, 235, 1276, 2094, 2324, 2325, 2326, 2327, 2898, 2949, 2952, 3126
Adagio patetico, 1345
Adam, Adolphe, 1803–1856: *Si j'étais roi. Overture*, 105
Adam, Louis, 1758–1848: 599; *Fileuse*, 2729
Adazhio, 1276
Addio a trachis, 1885
Adeste fideles, 1619, 2390, 2457, 2794
Adieu, 3044
Adieu, fair love, 2568
Adieux, 294, 713, 846, 1937
Adios, 2334
Adios mariquita linda, 2334
Adirondacks sketches, 1609, 1610, 1611
Adleisiau'r rhaeadr, 1995
Admired airs from Guillaume Tell, 2987

Benediction, 747
Béniowsky, 2346, 2347, 2348
Béon, Tiny: 2275, 2294, 2651, 2842,
    3034
Berceuse, 525, 764, 940, 941, 1044,
    1086, 1220, 1221, 1339, 1340,
    1582, 2036, 2100, 2177, 2564,
    2728, 2802, 3173
Berceuse and rondo, 197
Berceuse antique, 3230
Berceuse brève, 751
Berceuse de Dolly, 2494
Berceuse de noël, 1524, 1529
Berceuse du petit loir, 700
Berceuse du vent dans le cerisiers, 2046
Berceuse irlandaise, 2728
Berceuse nègre, 2048
Berceuse pour la poupée chinoise, 676
Berceuse russe, 2037
Berceuse triste, 527, 528
Berenice, 2626
Berg, Alban, 1885–1935: *Lulu.*
    Selections, 172; *Wozzeck,* 172
Bergers, 1204
Bergfee-Walzer, 1854
Bergmändle, 1241
Berlioz, Hector, 1803–1869: *Harold en*
    Italie, 118; *Nuits d'été,* 119; *Orchestra*
    music. Selections, 149; *Roméo et Juliette,*
    119; *Symphonie fantastique,* 118;
    Troyens. Marche troyenne, 118
Berman Harris, Ruth. *See* Harris, Ruth
    Berman
Bernard, Joëlle: 408
Bernart, de Ventadorn, 12th cent.: *Can*
    vei l'alauzeta (arr.), 2889
Bernauer Landler, 1855
Bertheaume, Pierre: 3297, 3299, 3307,
    3308
Bertie's mazurka, 575
Bertini, Henri, 1798–1876: *Petite*
    marche (arr.), 2728; *Prélude (arr.),*
    2244
Besard, Jean Baptiste, b. ca. 1567:
    Campanae parisienses (arr.), 2611
Beth yw'r haf i mi?, 886
Betsan, 1506
Betty O'Brien, 2369
Beverly's troubadour piece, 931
Beyond beeches, beyond woods, 1954
Bhreathnach, Siobhán: 2753
Bianchini, Domenico, ca. 1510–ca.
    1576: *Tant que vivrai (arr.),* 2611

Bianco fiore, 87
Bichromation, 2164
Bicycle built for two, 2334
Bicycle ride, 2394
Bicyclettes de Belsize, 2893
Bid me discourse, 338
Bidin' my time, 2541, 2542, 2601, 2893
Biehl: *Andante maestoso (arr.),* 2393
Big brown bear, 1525, 1526
Bilbro, Mathilde: *Woodcutters (arr.),*
    2785
Bill Bailey, 2334
Billy goat, 2887
Biondina, 1417
Biondina in gondoletta, 305
Bird, Chuck, 1925–: 3089
Bird waltz, 1517, 1518, 1519, 1520,
    1521, 1658
Birth of the blues, 2335
Bisbigli, 2237
Bishop, Henry R. (Henry Rowley),
    1786–1855: *Aladdin* (Pastorale by
    R.N.C. Bochsa), 376; *Guy Mannering.*
    Oh, rest thee, babe (Fantasia by R.N.C.
    Bochsa), 332; *Twelfth night. Bid me*
    discourse (Fantaisie by R.N.C.
    Bochsa), 338
Bist du bei mir, 2795
Bittendes Kind, 3069
Bittersweet, 1721
Bivens, Burke: 2693
Bizet, Georges, 1838–1875: *Arlésienne.*
    Selections, 106; *Carmen. Selections,*
    106; *Pêcheurs de perles. Je crois entendre*
    encore (arr.), 3113; *Spanish dance*
    (arr.), 1369
Bjorn, Frank: *Alley cat,* 2483; *Frankie*
    and Johnny, 2483
Black cat polka, 648
Black cats, 1226
Black is the color, 2383, 2759
Black is the color of my true love's hair,
    1311, 1659, 1660, 2483, 3116
Black mountains, 1954
Black nag, 1722, 2759
Black panther, 921
Black seabream or porgy, 293
Black Sir Harry, 3108
Black widow, 1580
Blackbird, 2887, 3108
Blacksmith's song, 1369
Blaenhafren, 1010
Blancland races, 3279

Pagode de l'harmonie céleste, 782
Paine, J. Russell: 24
Palace lake, 2083
Paléro, Francisco Fernandez, 16th
  cent.: *Mira, nero de Tarpeya (arr.),* 189
Palestinalied, 2889
Palestrina, Giovanni Pierluigi da,
  1525?-1594: *Strife is o'er (arr.),* 2959
Palestrina, 172
Palimpsest, 3247
Palmer, Lynne Wainwright, 1919-:
  2247, 2345, 2384, 2456, 2535,
  2601, 2693, 2895, 2975, 3266
Paloma, 1369
Paloma azúl, 1369
Panis angelicus, 2515
Pankow, James, 1947-: *Colour my world,*
  2483
Panorama of the Celtic harp, 419
Panormo, Francis, 1764-1844: *Bird
  waltz,* 1658
Pant Corlan yr Wyn, 1010
Pantalon, 359
Pantomime, 560, 1739, 3242
Papagallo, 1561, 1562
Papandopulo, Boris, 1906-: *Sonatas,
  harp,* 690
Paper moon, 2334
Papillon, 1484, 1922, 2029
Papillons gris, 1093
Parable, 1590
Parade, 859, 860
Paradies, Pietro Domenico, 1707-
  1791: *Sonatas, harpsichord, no. 4.
  Toccata (arr.),* 2950
Paradigm, 1104
Paradis, 1339, 1340
*Paraphrase auf Rheingold von Richard
  Wagner,* 1913
Paraphrase from Lucia di Lammermoor,
  2159
Paraphrase from Rigoletto, 2160
*Paraphrase on Angels we have heard on
  high,* 1785
Paraphrase on Greensleeves, 1785
*Paraphrase on It came upon a midnight
  clear,* 1785
*Paraphrase on Liszt's Second Hungarian
  rhapsody,* 1795, 1796
Paraphrase on O little town of Bethlehem,
  1785
Paraphrase on The sweetest story ever told,
  1615

Paraphrase on We three kings of orient are,
  1785
Paret, Betty: 2309; *Harp music.
  Selections,* 1527
Parish-Alvars, Elias, 1808-1849: 2810,
  2990; *Harp music. Selections (arr.),*
  2173
Parisian bells, 2349
Parkhurst, H. E. (Howard Elmore),
  1848-1916: *Melody (arr.),* 1725
Parodia, 2092
Parry, John, 1710-1782: *Sonata, D
  major (arr.),* 2173; *Sonata, harp,* 1570
Parsifal, 167
Parsifal prelude, 165
Partant pour la Syrie, 360, 361, 1485
Partenza, 2990
Particule, 2020
Parting, 2004
Parting glass, 2969, 3152
Parting hymn of praise, 2795
Parting of friends, 2512
Partita, 1129, 1152, 1264, 2244, 2304,
  3087, 3260
Partite, 1281
Partons tous deux, 2560
Parvis, 219, 3165
Pas galop, 2348
Paseos, 1129
Pasquali, Liana, 1915-: 733, 2304,
  2491
Passacaglia, 1311, 1344, 2244, 2653,
  3306
Passacaglia dans le style oriental, 1267
Passacaille, 2350, 2651, 2728, 2898
Passamezzo, 1155
Passamezzo antico, 2520
Passé et l'avenir, 1486
Passeggiata nel chiostro, 899
Passemezzo, 1587
Passepied, 211, 875, 2278, 2725, 2904
Passi difficili, 146
Passing by, 36, 881
Pässler, E.: *Rondo (arr.),* 2595
Passo a due, 2236
Pastels du vieux Japon, 2046
Pastheen Fionn, 2512
Pastoral i tants, 1135
Pastoral reverie, 1610
Pastorale, 519, 722, 764, 819, 874, 925,
  1508, 2956, 2984, 3015, 3087
Pastorella, 2933
Pastourelle, 2076, 2802

Soldier, soldier, 2502
Soldier's delight, 1481
Soldier's joy, 2458, 3152
Soldiers' march, 2457
Soldiers song, 2367
Soleil se lève, le calme regne sur la campagne, 2442
Soler, Antonio, 1729–1783: *Sonatas, harpsichord, A minor (arr.),* 2902
Solfège pratique, 89
Solfeggietto, 255, 2268, 2269, 2270, 2557, 2558
Soliloquy, 1229, 1310
Solitaire, 233
Solo, 191, 610
Solo pro Krale Davida, 1252
Solos, 796, 1221
Solos for Sonja, 1086
Solov'ev-Sedoi, V. P. (Vasilii Pavlovich), 1907–1979: *Moscow nights (arr.),* 1311
Som coïman, 2968
Some enchanted evening, 2974, 2977
Somebody loves me, 2893
Someday, 1085
Someone to watch over me, 2551, 2552, 2893
Somersault song, 1087
Somewhere in time, 2315, 2316, 2922
Sommeil de Juliette, 2578
Son of prophet bird, 1148
Sonantia, 3211
Sonata, 242, 243, 245, 246, 275, 276, 512, 513, 514, 515, 516, 530, 555, 556, 557, 605, 606, 607, 608, 609, 611, 690, 708, 748, 769, 819, 911, 912, 1004, 1023, 1025, 1057, 1150, 1153, 1162, 1163, 1164, 1171, 1178, 1232, 1245, 1275, 1361, 1399, 1458, 1504, 1661, 1763, 1899, 2023, 2024, 2173, 2230, 2257, 2258, 2260, 2274, 2415, 2531, 2535, 2559, 2606, 2663, 2818, 2879, 2880, 2881, 2900, 2902, 3017, 3021, 3174, 3264, 3265, 3328, 3345
Sonata en sol mayor, 1129
Sonata in classic style, 1658
Sonata in Ishartum, 931
Sonata lamento, 1136
Sonata para arpa, 1129
Sonata-pastorale, 686
Sonata quasi fantasia, 2325

Sonatas, 554, 1058, 1167, 1168, 1571, 1754, 3014, 3016, 3018, 3071, 3072
Sonatas españolas, 2371
Sonate, 241, 244, 248, 353, 395, 717, 1006, 1012, 1021, 1054, 1076, 1157, 1170, 1269, 1365, 1367, 1637, 1755, 1970, 2139, 2662, 2870, 2878, 3167
Sonate au clair de lune, 2949
Sonate avec variations, 2841
Sonate de concert, 1188
Sonate facile, 2950
Sonate luthée, 1366
Sonate pathétique, 2952
Sonate popularesche italiane, 1588
Sonates, 604, 623, 624, 1166, 1169, 1433, 1434, 3013, 3239
Sonates non difficilles, 1165
Sonates progressives, 1437, 1438
Sonatin, 710
Sonatina, 818, 1132, 1295, 1448, 1449, 1527, 1747, 1753, 1955, 1956, 2073, 2244, 2898, 2968
Sonatina in classic style, 1369
Sonatina in classical style, 1330
Sonatina in G, 1369
Sonatina prodigio, 1403
Sonatinas, 711, 1300
Sonatine, 86, 1502, 2055, 2056, 2082, 2169, 2181, 2244, 2730, 2731, 3193
Sonatines, 712, 3175
Sonaty, variatsii i fantazii, 689
Soneria, romanza e mazurca, 1342
Song, 36, 881, 2725
Song at night, 2018
Song for the lonely, 3081
Song in the night, 1792, 3243, 3343
Song of Alsace, 2862, 2863
Song of olden times, 1778, 1779
Song of the bells, 500
Song of the birds, 1071
Song of the boatmen of Volga, 2659
Song of the chanter, 413
Song of the coqui, 2718
Song of the evening bell, 1525, 1526
Song of the lark, 3092
Song of the river, 2458
Song of the Volga boatmen, 2458, 3005, 3009
Song of the watch, 2458
Song to the evening star, 2457
Song tune, 2689
Song with a sharp, 1087

WORKS PLAYABLE ON NON-PEDAL HARPS

Method Books

4, 18, 20, 30, 36, 38, 41, 42, 43, 45, 46, 51, 53, 60, 63, 68, 70, 76, 82, 86, 87, 90, 98, 99, 100, 101, 102

Original Works for Solo Harp

174, 183, 184, 197, 209, 210, 212, 214, 217, 218, 221, 230, 260, 261, 322, 411, 413, 417, 418, 419, 420, 434, 436, 437, 438, 439, 442, 443, 485, 486, 487, 488, 499, 502, 504, 506, 509, 519, 538, 541, 542, 546, 547, 548, 549, 550, 552, 567, 598, 625, 634, 635, 636, 642, 648, 693, 694, 713, 730, 731, 774, 779, 781, 782, 783, 797, 798, 806, 855, 871, 874, 881, 883, 888, 889, 895, 896, 904, 905, 906, 907, 910, 912, 924, 929, 1008, 1010, 1053, 1055, 1066, 1068, 1070, 1079, 1080, 1085, 1086, 1087, 1088, 1102, 1106, 1109, 1111, 1112, 1115, 1118, 1126, 1128, 1131, 1141, 1190, 1191, 1204, 1212, 1213, 1214, 1217, 1224, 1226, 1227, 1233, 1235, 1236, 1262, 1277, 1278, 1311, 1336, 1337, 1338, 1339, 1340, 1368, 1369, 1373, 1377, 1400, 1405, 1412, 1424, 1426, 1451, 1508, 1509, 1512, 1516, 1572, 1600, 1637, 1641, 1670, 1671, 1672, 1683, 1685, 1699, 1711, 1712, 1719, 1721, 1722, 1725, 1741, 1750, 1752, 1766, 1813, 1816, 1817, 1825, 1826, 1827, 1828, 1829, 1832, 1887, 1891, 1918, 1919, 1925, 1947, 1963, 2017, 2018, 2019, 2079, 2155, 2158, 2161, 2177, 2179, 2180, 2184, 2185, 2192, 2194, 2195

Arranged Works for Solo Harp

2246, 2249, 2251, 2283, 2284, 2285, 2286, 2314, 2315, 2319, 2334, 2343, 2351, 2352, 2353, 2362, 2363, 2364, 2367, 2368, 2369, 2375, 2376, 2380, 2381, 2385, 2386, 2389, 2391, 2395, 2420, 2423, 2460, 2496, 2498, 2499, 2502, 2503, 2517, 2519, 2520, 2521, 2522, 2560, 2568, 2595, 2612, 2616, 2617, 2633, 2635, 2636, 2643, 2646, 2660, 2671, 2672, 2680, 2683, 2684, 2688, 2689, 2691, 2702, 2704, 2715, 2720, 2723, 2724, 2725, 2727, 2728, 2729, 2730, 2731, 2750, 2753, 2755, 2758, 2759, 2762, 2763, 2764, 2765, 2777, 2780, 2802, 2803, 2812, 2828, 2837, 2863, 2868, 2887, 2888, 2889, 2915, 2926, 2933, 2937, 2938, 2939, 2941, 2942, 2943, 2944, 2967, 2968, 2969, 2974, 2981, 2992, 3025, 3028, 3046, 3064, 3068, 3075, 3080, 3084,

3085, 3090, 3101, 3111, 3113, 3114, 3115, 3116, 3119, 3149, 3150, 3151, 3152, 3158

Original Works for Harp Duet and/or Ensemble

3162, 3164, 3166, 3168, 3173, 3175, 3176, 3187, 3188, 3189, 3204, 3228, 3238, 3240, 3258, 3261

Arranged Works for Harp Duet and/or Ensemble

3265, 3272, 3275, 3276, 3280, 3281, 3282, 3283, 3284, 3285, 3295, 3303, 3311, 3312, 3313, 3315, 3320, 3325, 3326, 3349, 3353, 3354, 3355

Mark Palkovic is Record Librarian at the University of Cincinnati College-Conservatory of Music. He is the translator and editor of Hans Joachim Zingel's *Harp Music in the Nineteenth Century* and author of articles in *The American Harp Journal*, where he serves as Associate Editor.